Optimise

Teacher's Book Premium Pack

A2

macmillan education

Welcome

ABOUT *OPTIMISE*

- *Optimise* is a fantastic new secondary-level exam-preparation course for 21st century learners. The course is designed to prepare teenagers for international exams (Key (KET) for Schools, etc.) or local state exams.
- *Optimise*'s highly respected authors Malcolm Mann and Steve Taylore-Knowles brought their exam expertise and many years of experience of official exams as Course Consultants on this level of the course, ensuring your students achieve exam success.
- *Optimise* offers attractive images, stimulating, age-appropriate topics and carefully guided skills development, which prepare students for everyday life as well as exams.
- *Optimise*'s print and digital package gives you the flexibility to choose the approach that works best for your teaching situation: from print to blended to a fully interactive digital approach.

For students

Student's Book or Digital Student's Book

See pages 4–13 for details of the Student's Book content.

See page 14 for more on the Digital Student's Book.

Workbook with/without answer key or Online Workbook

See pages 17–20 for details of the Workbook content.

See page 21 for more on the Online Workbook.

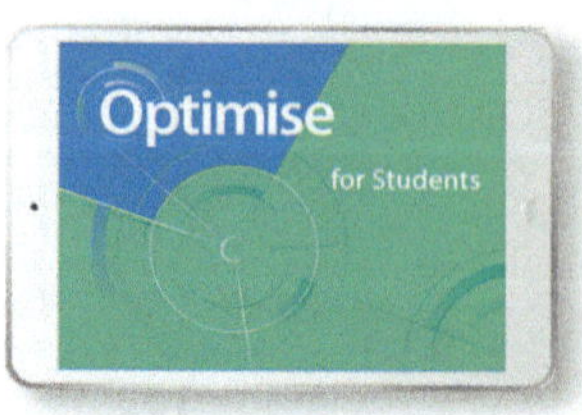

Student's Resource Centre

See page 22 for a full list of resources available on the Student's Resource Centre.

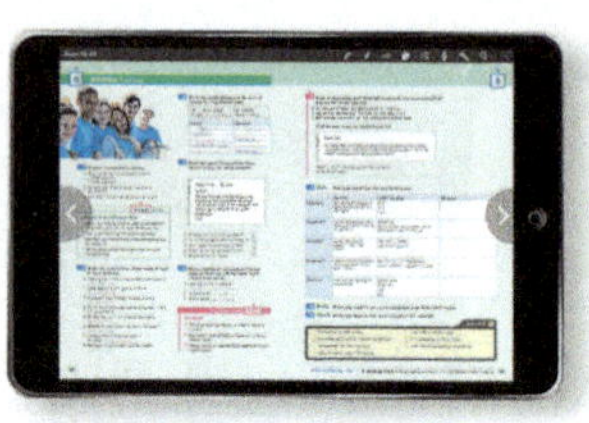

Student's eBook

An eBook version of the Student's Book is included.

For teachers

Teacher's Book

Your Teacher's Book Premium Pack includes:

- Presentation Kit
- Digital Student's Book
- Student's eBook
- Online Workbook
- Test Generator
- Teacher's Resource Centre
- *Talk2Me* videos
- Speaking test videos
- Class and Workbook audio

See pages 22–23 for details of the worksheets and tests available.

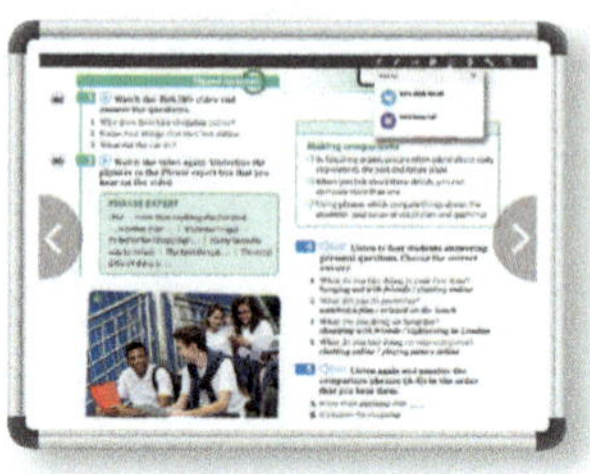

Presentation Kit

See page 15 for more information about the Presentation Kit.

Teacher's Resource Centre
Digital Student's Book
Online Workbook
Test Generator
Student's eBook

See page 22 for a full list of resources available on the Teacher's Resource Centre.

Class Audio CDs

Class audio on CDs. Also available on the Resource Centres.

ABOUT THE *OPTIMISE* COURSE DEVELOPERS

Malcolm Mann and Steve Taylore-Knowles have written a number of exam courses for teenagers, including the highly successful *Laser* series. They are also the series editors of Macmillan's *Improve your Skills for First (FCE)* and *Improve your Skills for Advanced (CAE)* series.

Malcolm

Malcolm lives and works in Athens, Greece. He's responsible for the production of the LAAS exam suite, and is a former Chairperson of TESOL Greece.

Steve

Steve lives and works in the UK. He is a former Cambridge oral examiner and also provides government-endorsed teacher training in many countries throughout Europe, Asia and South America.

A MESSAGE FROM THE *OPTIMISE* COURSE DEVELOPERS

Thank you for choosing to use *Optimise*.

Optimise is an exam course with a difference.

In *Optimise*, we effectively combine exam training, language development and 21st century skills to prepare students not only for language exams, but also for life beyond the classroom.

Below we have listed our principles and the key features which we believe make *Optimise* an outstanding exam-preparation course.

We very much hope you and your students enjoy using *Optimise A2* and benefit from its motivating content, syllabus and structure.

All the very best for the school year!

Malcolm and Steve

Principles

The following principles are at the heart of the *Optimise* series:

- **Motivation:** The more that 21st century teens can be motivated by engaging and interesting content (texts, topics, tasks, etc.), the more likely they are to improve their skills, and develop their linguistic competence.
- **Practice:** Exam practice is essential. In order for students to feel confident and perform at their optimum, they need to be familiar with exam tasks. Language and exam skills tested in the exam have to be practised and developed.
- **Guidance:** The most effective way to help students develop their language and exam skills is to deal with them in a systematic and guided way, through a carefully-planned course syllabus.
- **Coverage:** Vocabulary does not only consist of individual words; it also includes collocations, phrasal verbs, word formation and word patterns, as well as topic vocabulary, which all need to be covered comprehensively.
- **Support:** Students require expert guidance and support in order to produce exam-level pieces of writing. The process of writing involves different drafts, proofreading and feedback, and is essential in helping students develop their skills.
- **Consolidation:** Regular consolidation makes a vital contribution towards ensuring students understand and retain the information they need in order to prepare for exams.
- **Personalisation:** Personalisation is key in enabling students to relate the material in their Student's Book to their own lives, opinions and culture.

Key features

- An extensive range of print and digital materials, providing you with a variety of flexible options for your students.
- Strong focus on exam-skills development, with each lesson focusing on a specific skill and offering detailed advice on how to complete the task effectively.
- Resource Centres for both students and teachers, with a wide variety of worksheets including CLIL and Culture, Grammar and Vocabulary.
- Unit tests, Progress tests, End-of-year test, all set at two levels – Standard and Higher – are available as PDFs and also adaptable to suit your own requirements on the Test Generator.
- A Placement test to check your students' level and a Diagnostic test to highlight students' strengths and weaknesses.
- Key (KET) for Schools Practice tests: one at the back of the Workbook and another complete Practice test available on the Teacher's Resource Centre as a printable PDF.
- Systematic language and exam-preparation development throughout every lesson.
- Personalisation tasks to foster 21st century skills, such as critical analysis, collaboration and learning strategies, presented through the Think, Research, Culture, Learn and Me features.
- *Talk2Me* videos in every Speaking lesson feature teenagers using everyday functional language in a variety of situations that students will relate to. The Flipped classroom approach is suggested as an alternative approach for this video to encourage learner autonomy and create more time to focus on activating the target language.
- A Speaking test video with an examiner shows a pair of students completing a speaking test. This video is exploited in the *Optimise your speaking* section of the Student's Book *Optimise your exams* pages, along with an additional worksheet on the Resource Centre, which encourages students to analyse the video further.
- Systematic Writing lessons which include a writing model, a paragraph planner and a writing exam task, along with a post-writing Checklist for students to refer to.
- A Progress check, after every two units, reviews the grammar and vocabulary of the preceding two units and includes a self-assessment tool for students to chart their learning.

Course components

STUDENT'S BOOK | Reading lesson

Every unit starts with a 2-page Reading lesson.

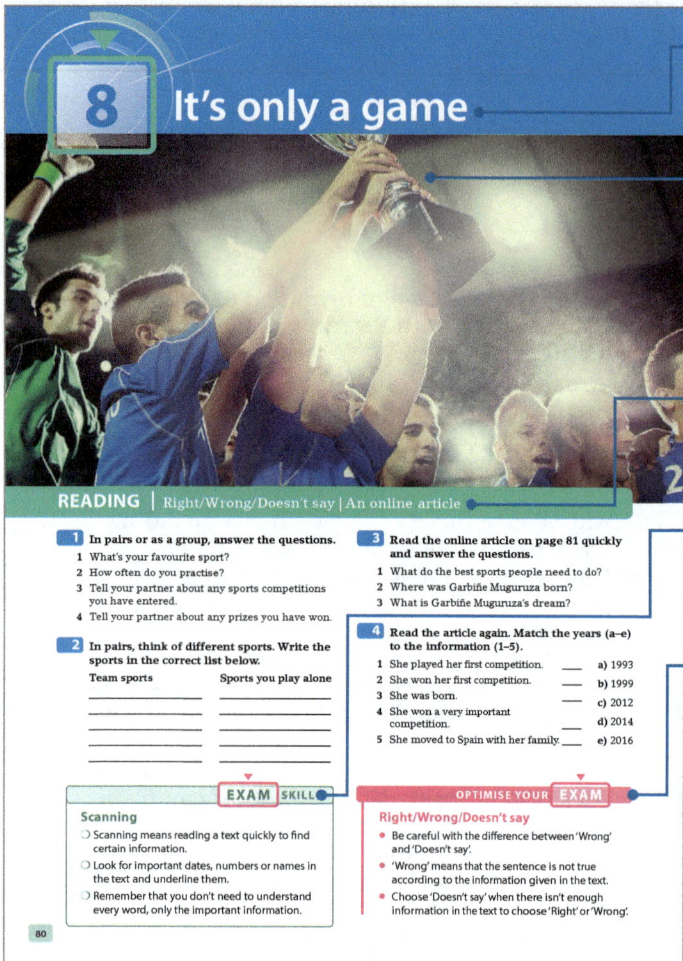

8 It's only a game

READING | Right/Wrong/Doesn't say | An online article

1 In pairs or as a group, answer the questions.

1 What's your favourite sport?
2 How often do you practise?
3 Tell your partner about any sports competitions you have entered.
4 Tell your partner about any prizes you have won.

2 In pairs, think of different sports. Write the sports in the correct list below.

Team sports	Sports you play alone
________	________
________	________
________	________
________	________
________	________

EXAM SKILL

Scanning

- Scanning means reading a text quickly to find certain information.
- Look for important dates, numbers or names in the text and underline them.
- Remember that you don't need to understand every word, only the important information.

3 Read the online article on page 81 quickly and answer the questions.

1 What do the best sports people need to do?
2 Where was Garbiñe Muguruza born?
3 What is Garbiñe Muguruza's dream?

4 Read the article again. Match the years (a–e) to the information (1–5).

1 She played her first competition. ___ a) 1993
2 She won her first competition. ___ b) 1999
3 She was born. ___ c) 2012
4 She won a very important competition. ___ d) 2014
5 She moved to Spain with her family. ___ e) 2016

OPTIMISE YOUR EXAM

Right/Wrong/Doesn't say

- Be careful with the difference between 'Wrong' and 'Doesn't say'.
- 'Wrong' means that the sentence is not true according to the information given in the text.
- Choose 'Doesn't say' when there isn't enough information in the text to choose 'Right' or 'Wrong'.

80

Unit topics and themes chosen to be interesting and engaging for teenage students.

The opening spread of each unit has a colourful and impactful images connected to the unit topic, which can be used at the start of the lesson to stimulate on-topic discussion.

Clear labelling of the exam task and text type in the lesson will help you and your learners.

All Reading lessons feature an *Exam skill* box, with targeted advice on how to approach different exam tasks and the specific sub-skills required.

All Reading lessons include an *Optimise your exam* feature, which gives students tips and strategies to help them prepare for the lesson exam task.

READING 8

THE WAY TO WIN

How long do you think it takes a sports person to become one of the best?

1 Can you do any sport really well? Would you like to do it professionally? It may seem easy to you to swim, run or throw a ball for a job. However, to compete at a high level, you must start young and you have to practise for many hours every day for years before you'll be ready to enter important competitions. If you fall over, get tired or injure yourself, you mustn't give up. This might be why only a few people become professional. Garbiñe Muguruza made it. In 2016, when she was 22 years old, she won the French Open, one of the sport's most important competitions.

2 Garbiñe was born in Venezuela in 1993. She could hold a racket when she was three, so she started playing tennis. When her family moved to Spain in 1999, she went to a special tennis school, and in 2012 she entered her first professional competition. Two years later, in 2014, she won a competition for the first time.

3 Garbiñe loves playing tennis, but she thinks that tennis players needn't spend all their time thinking about tennis. 'I like to listen to music, hang out with family and friends, dance, sing.' She is sometimes unhappy that she can't live a normal life. Recently, she couldn't go on holiday with her friends because she needed to play tennis. So why does she do it? Garbiñe says that she is just a normal girl with a dream. And that is to be number one!

5 2.23 **Read the article about a famous tennis player. Are sentences 1–7 'Right' (A) or 'Wrong' (B)? If there is not enough information to answer 'Right' (A) or 'Wrong' (B), choose 'Doesn't say' (C).**

Example: The writer says it takes a long time to become very good at a sport.
(A) Right B Wrong C Doesn't say

1 Sports people practise alone for many hours a day.
A Right B Wrong C Doesn't say
2 Garbiñe's family moved to Spain because there are a lot of tennis schools there.
A Right B Wrong C Doesn't say
3 She learnt to play tennis at school in Spain.
A Right B Wrong C Doesn't say
4 She won the first competition she entered.
A Right B Wrong C Doesn't say
5 She likes rock music.
A Right B Wrong C Doesn't say
6 She thinks it's a good idea for tennis players to spend time with other people.
A Right B Wrong C Doesn't say
7 She has never been on holiday with her friends.
A Right B Wrong C Doesn't say

6 Match the highlighted words in the article to a definition (1–8).

1 finished first in a competition ________
2 an object used to hit a ball in tennis, badminton, etc. ________
3 use your hand to send an object through the air ________
4 to have something in your hands ________
5 needing rest or sleep ________
6 to do an activity very often so you become good at it ________
7 to move through water by moving your arms and legs ________
8 feeling sad or upset ________

THINK | RESEARCH | CULTURE | LEARN | ME

Find out about a famous sports person in your country. Make a poster about him or her.

Workbook Unit 8: Reading, pages 60–61, exercises 1, 2, 3, 4, 5 81

Reading texts focus on stimulating, out-of-the-ordinary topics, which will be of interest to teenage students.

Every Reading lesson has an exam task. These tasks are level-appropriate and reflect the tasks students are likely to encounter in most official exams.

All lessons include references to the Workbook, and other relevant reference material.

Every unit has two separate Grammar lessons.

8 **GRAMMAR 1** | Modals (1): ability, necessity, obligation, possibility

Every Grammar lesson presents a different grammar point.

Grammar in context

Find these sentences in the text on page 81 then choose the correct words to complete sentences a to d.

1 *Can you do any sport really well?* (paragraph 1)
2 *It* ***may*** *seem easy to you to swim, run or throw a ball for a job.* (paragraph 1)
3 *... to compete at a high level, you* ***must*** *start young...* (paragraph 1)
4 *... you* ***have to*** *practise for many hours every day for years before you'll be ready to enter important competitions.* (paragraph 1)
5 *... tennis players* ***needn't*** *spend all their time thinking about tennis.* (paragraph 3)
6 *Recently, she* ***couldn't*** *go on holiday with her friends because she* ***needed*** *to play tennis.* (paragraph 3)

a) We use *can* to talk about **ability / necessity**.
b) We use *have* to talk about **possibility / obligation**.
c) We use *may* to talk about **possibility / ability**.
d) We use *must* to talk about **possibility / obligation**.
e) We use *need(n't)* to talk about **necessity / ability**.

The *Grammar in context* box introduces the grammar lesson by asking students to identify the target structures in a context they have already seen.

REMEMBER

- Modal verbs do not change their form and are followed by the bare infinitive (without *to*) of another verb.
- We use *can/can't (cannot)* to talk about ability in the present and *could/couldn't* to talk about ability in the past.
- We can use *must / have to* for rules made by other people or when the person doing the action believes it is necessary. There is no past form of *must*, we use *had to*. The negative form is *don't have to*.

▶ See Grammar reference, Unit 8, page 157

1 Choose the correct words.

1 When my dad was at school, he **can't / couldn't** understand maths.
2 All football players **may / must** follow the rules of the game.
3 The weather forecast says it's going to snow tomorrow so we **might / needn't** go snowboarding.
4 Sports people **could / have to** train every day.
5 We **couldn't / needn't** go for a run today if we don't want to.
6 You **can't / must** tell the sports teacher if you don't feel well.

2 Complete the conversation with the words in the box.

can	can't	don't have
have	might	needn't

Robert: (1) __________ you see who's got the ball?
Anna: No, I (2)__________. I think it's number 10.
Robert: Oh, that's Harry Kane. He's an amazing player. But dad says he (3) __________ move to a different team next year. I hope not.
Anna: Oh, you (4) __________ worry. He loves this team so I don't think he'll want to leave.
Robert: Look! He's scored a goal! That's 1-1.
Anna: That's great! There's only a few more minutes left, so shall we go now?
Robert: No way! We (5) __________ to stay until the end. There's still time for another goal.
Anna: OK, then. We (6) __________ to hurry, anyway. We've got lots of time until the next bus.
Robert: That's good. Now let's enjoy the end of the game!

3 Complete the text with the correct form of the modals ***can('t), could(n't), had (to), have (to), may/might, need(n't).***

Exercises are staged so as to be progressively more challenging as students work through the lesson.

Keep on running...!

At 15, Emil Zátopek was a young Czech who worked in a shoe factory. When he was younger he **(1)** __________ do any sports particularly well, so he **(2)** __________ never have become a runner. However, one day, the factory sports coach told him he **(3)** __________ to run in a race. Everyone was surprised when he came second. Zátopek then started to think that he **(4)** __________ work in the factory forever. He thought maybe he could be a runner instead!

Everyone knows that to be the best at any sport you **(5)** __________ to train hard, and he did. Zátopek ran in the 1952 Olympic Games, and he won the 5,000- and 10,000-metre races. He also ran in the marathon, the longest race in the Games. It was his first marathon, but he ran the 42-kilometre race and won! Today most people still **(6)** __________ believe he did this ... but he did! Zátopek showed that if you really want something, you **(7)** __________ worry about what other people **(8)** __________ think. Just believe in yourself.

82 ▶ **Workbook Unit 8:** Grammar 1, page 62, exercises 1, 2, 3

GRAMMAR 2 | Modals (2): advice, permission, polite requests, prohibition 8

Grammar in context

Look at these sentences from the audio in the listening lesson then match them to the descriptions (a–e).

1 *You* ***should*** *start playing again, Dad – it's good exercise ...*
2 *Camp rules say we* ***mustn't*** *swim if there's a strong wind ...*
3 *...* ***could*** *you take some photos of the boats, please?*
4 *You* ***shouldn't*** *be out all day in the sun if it's very hot.*
5 *The camp leader says we* ***can*** *go to the pool today instead.*

a) something is not allowed ____
b) we have permission ____
c) someone is making a request ____
d) something is a good idea ____
e) something isn't a good idea ____

REMEMBER

- We use modals to:
  - ask for / give advice: *should/shouldn't*
  - ask for / give permission: *can/could*
  - refuse permission: *can't/couldn't*
  - make a polite request: *could*
  - say something is prohibited: *mustn't*
- To make the negative form, you add 'not' after the modal verb and this is usually contracted, e.g. *need not = needn't*.
- Sometimes the negative form changes the modal's meaning: *In the UK, you* ***must*** *drive on the left.* (obligation) *In the UK, you* ***mustn't*** *drive on the right.* (prohibition)
- To make a question, the subject and modal swap position: ***Could you*** *pass me my racket, please?*

▶ See Grammar reference, Unit 8, page 158

Remember boxes on the grammar pages present additional information in a clear way for students to remember, and end with a signpost to the *Grammar reference* at the back of the Student's Book, where further explanations and examples are provided.

1 Choose the correct words.

1 We're very happy because the teacher says we **shouldn't / can** all watch a video for the last half hour this afternoon.
2 'Amber, come back and get your helmet! You **could / mustn't** ever go out on your bike without it.'
3 Ed, **should / could** you help me with my school project, please?
4 Please turn the computer off. You **shouldn't / can** play video games all evening. It's not a good thing to do!
5 You look very tired. You **mustn't / should** go to bed earlier.

2 Choose the correct words (a, b or c) to complete each sentence.

1 I'm not sure how to do this. ____ you help me, please?
a) Could b) Should c) Shouldn't
2 You ____ eat for 30 minutes before you go swimming.
a) could b) can c) shouldn't
3 I think you ____ try learning a new sport. It's fun!
a) mustn't b) couldn't c) should
4 The teacher says we ____ use her tennis rackets. That's kind of her.
a) can b) shouldn't c) couldn't
5 The boys ____ go to the match last night because their dad said no.
a) shouldn't b) couldn't c) mustn't
6 The rule here is that you ____ do any water sports if you ____ swim 500 metres.
a) should, can b) mustn't, can't c) could, mustn't

3 Complete the text about a summer camp with the phrases from the word box.

can use	can't do	could you ask
could you bring	mustn't leave	
should bring (×2)	should have	
shouldn't arrive		

Whenever possible, short texts are included on the grammar pages, to give your students the opportunity to see and practise grammar in realistic contexts.

A WELCOME from our Camp Manager

We're really excited about meeting everyone at Super Sports Summer Camp next month. Before you come, I want to give you some important information.

- **What to bring** First of all, everyone (1) __________ these things to camp: a pair of trainers, shorts or leggings and a T-shirt. You (2) __________ sports without them. Secondly, don't bring your best clothes, because we don't want them to get dirty. So (3) __________ some old clothes for art activities, please? People often ask us if they (4) __________ their own rackets, bats or balls. The answer is no. We have all the equipment here and you (5) __________ it whenever you want.
- **When to arrive** The camp starts at 11:30 am on Saturday 7th July. You (6) __________ too early, as the leaders won't all be here until 10, so please try and arrive at about 10:30 if possible.
- **And finally ...** When you arrive, (7) __________ your parents to park in the Rees Lane car park. There's plenty of room there for everyone. And, one last thing ... always remember the camp rule while you're here – you (8) __________ the camp at any time without permission. See you on Saturday!

▶ **Workbook Unit 8:** Grammar 2, page 63, exercises 1, 2, 3 85

The Vocabulary lesson in each unit has three separate word sets, one of which is always topic vocabulary.

Each lesson has three clearly-labelled vocabulary areas.

Topic vocabulary sections increase students' lexical knowledge in topics that commonly appear in exams.

Word formation tasks appear regularly to extend students' word knowledge as well as serving to prepare them for common exam tasks.

Collocations help students increase their vocabulary competence and prepare for a number of different exam tasks.

VOCABULARY | Topic vocabulary | Word formation | Collocations **8**

Words connected with *sport*

1 2.24 **Write a word from the box to match each definition. There are two extra words you do not need. Listen and check.**

badminton | cricket | kit | pool
skiing | stadium | table tennis | winner

1 You need a small plastic ball to play this game. ________
2 You can go swimming here. ________
3 You can do this sport on snow in the mountains. ________
4 You can watch a football game here. ________
5 This is the person who is first in a competition or race. ________
6 You need a racket to play this game. ________

2 2.25 **Choose the best word to complete each sentence. Listen and check.**

1 The ________ told us what exercises to do and helped us play better.
A team B coach C member
2 Can you ________ a horse?
A play B skate C ride
3 You need a ________ to go to the basketball game tonight.
A ticket B bat C club
4 I can't go swimming because I haven't got my ________ .
A swimsuit B beach C pool
5 Ed was the winner of the 800-metre ________ .
A race B bat C club
6 They played in a rugby ________ yesterday, and won 35-3!
A club B goal C match

Verbs/nouns

3 2.26 **Complete the table. Listen and check.**

verb	noun
win	winner
(1) ________	surfer
swim	(2) ________
(3) ________	runner
play	(4) ________

4 **Complete the sentences with the correct form of some of the words from Exercise 3.**

1 There are over 50 ________ in the pool today!
2 Novak Djokovic ________ the tennis match.
3 The eight best ________ waited in the stadium to start the 500-metre race.
4 Who do you think is the best football ________ in the world this year?
5 If you want to learn to ________ , it's important that you can swim.

Collocations with verbs

5 2.27 **Complete the sentences with the correct form of the verbs in the box. Listen and check.**

climb | enter | go | play | throw | win

1 Greg ________ the ball into the road.
2 My class ________ swimming at the city pool every Wednesday.
3 Everyone can ________ the competition but only one person can win.
4 In the summer, lots of people in England ________ cricket.
5 Do I need to practise a lot before I ________ a mountain?
6 Emil Zátopek was very happy when he ________ the 5,000-metre race at the Olympic Games.

▶ Vocabulary reference, page 166 ▶ **Workbook Unit 8:** Vocabulary, pages 62–63, exercises 1, 2, 3 83

Lessons include details of the *Vocabulary reference* at the back of the Student's Book. This provides reference materials to support students during vocabulary tasks and also acts as a revision tool.

TOPIC VOCABULARY | Words connected with *sport*

Word	Example sentence
badminton (n)	Badminton is the best sport I have ever played!
cricket (n)	My grandpa is very good at cricket and plays every weekend in the summer.
kit (n)	Mum, where's my kit? I'm going to play football.
pool (n)	The pool near my school is busy on Saturdays because lots of children go swimming at the weekend.
skiing (n)	She loves skiing, but it doesn't snow very often where she lives.
stadium (n)	We enjoyed going to the stadium to watch the rugby match.
table tennis (n)	Will you teach me to play table tennis?
winner (n)	And Will is the winner of the competition!

The Listening lesson in each unit focuses on a specific exam skill and always includes an exam task.

All class audio material is available on CDs as well as being provided on the Resource Centres.

Listening lessons always feature a specific exam skill and provide support and guidance to help students develop the skill further.

The initial task helps students to start thinking about the topic of the lesson in more depth.

The *Exam skill* boxes in Listening lessons focus on specific sub-skills needed to achieve success in listening.

The *Optimise your exam* box in the Listening lessons always gives students advice on how to approach this kind of task.

Every Listening lesson includes an exam task which allows students an opportunity to apply the advice given in the preceding *Optimise your exam* box.

Personalisation tasks at the end of the Listening lessons relate to the unit topic, giving students a chance to develop the topic further.

8 LISTENING | Multiple matching

1 Work in pairs. Look at the poster for a summer camp and answer the questions.

1 What sports are the young people doing?
2 Would you like to do the sports in the poster? Why / Why not?
3 What other sports would you like to do at a summer camp?

EXAM SKILL

Listening for important information

- You don't need to understand every word to answer the questions.
- The first time you listen, think about the important words.
- When you listen again, think carefully about what the speakers mean.

2 2.28 Listen to five people talking about sports. Match each speaker to a sport.

Speaker 1 ___	a) running
Speaker 2 ___	b) windsurfing
Speaker 3 ___	c) badminton
Speaker 4 ___	d) cycling
Speaker 5 ___	e) table tennis

3 2.28 Listen again and write the names of the other sports the people talk about in each conversation.

Conversation 1 ___football___
Conversation 2 ______
Conversation 3 ______
Conversation 4 ______
Conversation 5 ______

OPTIMISE YOUR EXAM

Multiple matching

- Read the question and all the possible answers carefully.
- Remember that there are three possible answers that you don't need.
- When you listen again, check the three possible answers you didn't choose, to make sure they aren't correct.

4 2.29 Listen to Bea talking to her dad about her summer camp. What sport did she do on each day? Write a letter A–H next to each day. There are some extra letters you do not need.

Example:
Monday morning _H_

1 Monday afternoon	___	A swimming
2 Tuesday	___	B badminton
3 Wednesday	___	C volleyball
4 Thursday	___	D tennis
5 Friday	___	E sailing
		F football
		G cricket
		~~H running~~

THINK | RESEARCH | CULTURE | LEARN | ME

Work in pairs and answer the questions.

- How popular are summer camps in your country?
- What sports and other activities can you do there?

84 ▶ Workbook Unit 8: Listening, page 64, exercises 1, 2, 3

There is a reference to the relevant Workbook pages at the end of each Listening lesson.

STUDENT'S BOOK | Speaking lesson

Talk2Me video in every Speaking lesson

Speaking lessons include a video which features target functional language.

Speaking lessons focus on one of two task types which students will need to develop in preparation for a speaking test.

All Speaking lessons suggest using an optional Flipped classroom approach, in which students watch the video and complete some exercises at home in order to prepare for the lesson.

The *Exam skill* box in the Speaking lesson highlights one of the sub-skills that are required for success in speaking tests.

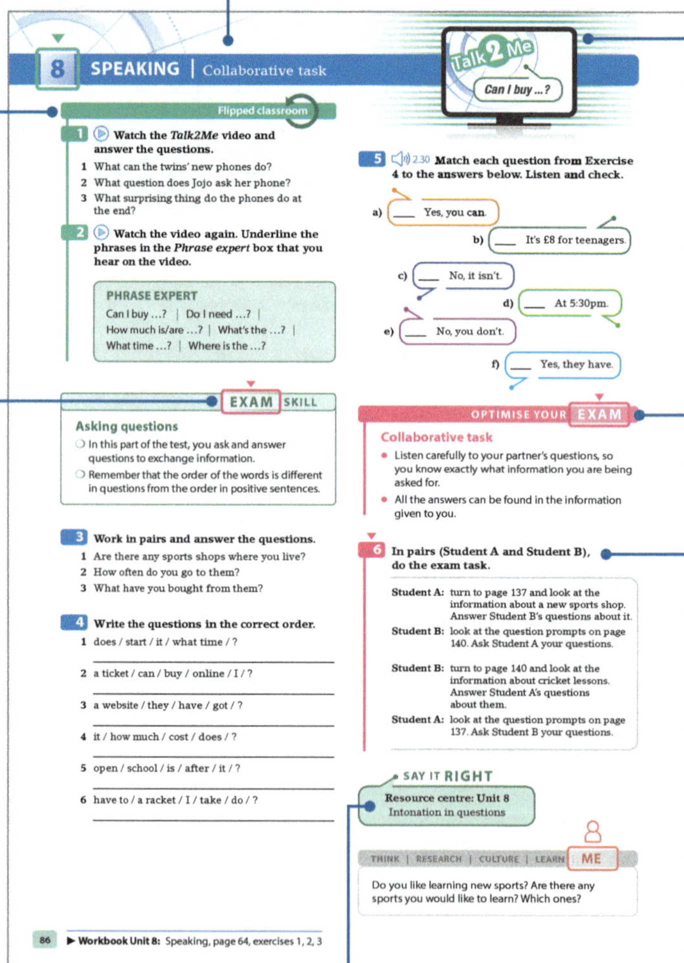

8 SPEAKING | Collaborative task

Talk2Me
Can I buy ...?

Flipped classroom

1 Watch the *Talk2Me* video and answer the questions.

1 What can the twins' new phones do?
2 What question does Jojo ask her phone?
3 What surprising thing do the phones do at the end?

2 Watch the video again. Underline the phrases in the *Phrase expert* box that you hear on the video.

PHRASE EXPERT
Can I buy ...? | Do I need ...? | How much is/are ...? | What's the ...? | What time ...? | Where is the ...?

EXAM SKILL
Asking questions
In this part of the test, you ask and answer questions to exchange information.
Remember that the order of the words is different in questions from the order in positive sentences.

3 Work in pairs and answer the questions.
1 Are there any sports shops where you live?
2 How often do you go to them?
3 What have you bought from them?

4 Write the questions in the correct order.
1 does / start / it / what time / ?
2 a ticket / can / buy / online / I / ?
3 a website / they / have / got / ?
4 it / how much / cost / does / ?
5 open / school / is / after / it / ?
6 have to / a racket / I / take / do / ?

5 2.30 Match each question from Exercise 4 to the answers below. Listen and check.
a) ___ Yes, you can.
b) ___ It's £8 for teenagers.
c) ___ No, it isn't.
d) ___ At 5:30pm.
e) ___ No, you don't.
f) ___ Yes, they have.

OPTIMISE YOUR EXAM
Collaborative task
- Listen carefully to your partner's questions, so you know exactly what information you are being asked for.
- All the answers can be found in the information given to you.

6 In pairs (Student A and Student B), do the exam task.
Student A: turn to page 137 and look at the information about a new sports shop. Answer Student B's questions about it.
Student B: look at the question prompts on page 140. Ask Student A your questions.
Student B: turn to page 140 and look at the information about cricket lessons. Answer Student A's questions about them.
Student A: look at the question prompts on page 137. Ask Student B your questions.

SAY IT RIGHT
Resource centre: Unit 8
Intonation in questions

THINK | RESEARCH | CULTURE | LEARN | ME
Do you like learning new sports? Are there any sports you would like to learn? Which ones?

86 ▶ Workbook Unit 8: Speaking, page 64, exercises 1, 2, 3

All Speaking lessons include a *Talk2Me* video, featuring native speakers. They discuss topics related to the unit, modelling target functional language, which students then practise and use in their final task.

The *Optimise your exam* box develops the lesson skill in order to prepare students for the exam task that follows.

The lesson ends in a speaking-test task consolidating the skill developed on this page.

Every unit contains a *Say it right* feature, which develops a specific aspect of pronunciation that appears in one of the lessons. The worksheet for this is available on the Resource Centre.

STUDENT'S BOOK | Language in Use

All Language in Use lessons provide comprehensive coverage of all aspects of grammar and vocabulary that students need in order to prepare for exams.

Every Language in Use lesson is based on a specific task type that students will be tested on in their English exams.

Language in Use exam skills are language-focused for exam preparation, but also for students' general language development.

The *Optimise your exam* box develops the lesson skill in order to prepare students for the exam task that follows.

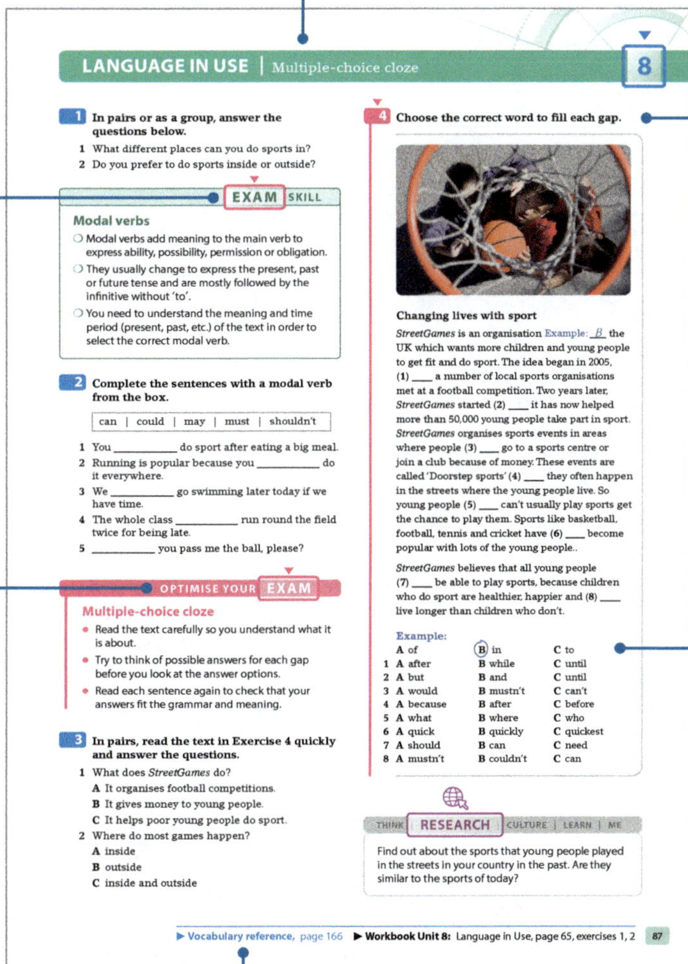

LANGUAGE IN USE | Multiple-choice cloze

8

1 **In pairs or as a group, answer the questions below.**

1 What different places can you do sports in?
2 Do you prefer to do sports inside or outside?

EXAM SKILL

Modal verbs

- Modal verbs add meaning to the main verb to express ability, possibility, permission or obligation.
- They usually change to express the present, past or future tense and are mostly followed by the infinitive without 'to'.
- You need to understand the meaning and time period (present, past, etc.) of the text in order to select the correct modal verb.

2 **Complete the sentences with a modal verb from the box.**

can | could | may | must | shouldn't

1 You __________ do sport after eating a big meal.
2 Running is popular because you __________ do it everywhere.
3 We __________ go swimming later today if we have time.
4 The whole class __________ run round the field twice for being late.
5 __________ you pass me the ball, please?

OPTIMISE YOUR EXAM

Multiple-choice cloze

- Read the text carefully so you understand what it is about.
- Try to think of possible answers for each gap before you look at the answer options.
- Read each sentence again to check that your answers fit the grammar and meaning.

3 **In pairs, read the text in Exercise 4 quickly and answer the questions.**

1 What does *StreetGames* do?
A It organises football competitions.
B It gives money to young people.
C It helps poor young people do sport.
2 Where do most games happen?
A inside
B outside
C inside and outside

4 **Choose the correct word to fill each gap.**

Changing lives with sport

StreetGames is an organisation Example: _B_ the UK which wants more children and young people to get fit and do sport. The idea began in 2005, (1) ___ a number of local sports organisations met at a football competition. Two years later, *StreetGames* started (2) ___ it has now helped more than 50,000 young people take part in sport. *StreetGames* organises sports events in areas where people (3) ___ go to a sports centre or join a club because of money. These events are called 'Doorstep sports' (4) ___ they often happen in the streets where the young people live. So young people (5) ___ can't usually play sports get the chance to play them. Sports like basketball, football, tennis and cricket have (6) ___ become popular with lots of the young people.

StreetGames believes that all young people (7) ___ be able to play sports, because children who do sport are healthier, happier and (8) ___ live longer than children who don't.

Example:

	A	B	C
	A of	(B) in	C to
1	A after	B while	C until
2	A but	B and	C until
3	A would	B mustn't	C can't
4	A because	B after	C before
5	A what	B where	C who
6	A quick	B quickly	C quickest
7	A should	B can	C need
8	A mustn't	B couldn't	C can

THINK | RESEARCH | CULTURE | LEARN | ME

Find out about the sports that young people played in the streets in your country in the past. Are they similar to the sports of today?

▶ Vocabulary reference, page 166 ▶ Workbook Unit 8: Language in Use, page 65, exercises 1, 2 87

Exercises build up throughout the lesson, preparing students for the final Key (KET) for Schools Reading and Writing exam task.

All the common Key (KET) for Schools Reading and Writing exam tasks are covered: open cloze, multiple-choice dialogue, multiple-choice cloze, multiple-matching dialogue, multiple-choice sentences and Right, Wrong or Doesn't say.

Any extra material in the *Vocabulary reference* which is relevant to the Language in Use lesson is signposted at the bottom of the page.

Every unit ends with a two-page Writing lesson.

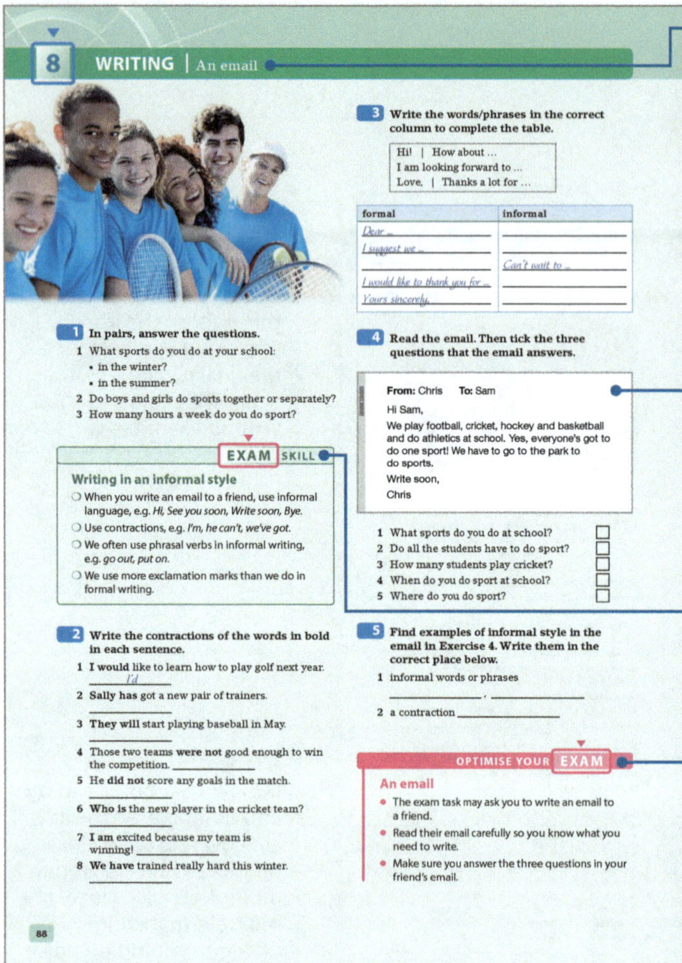

8 WRITING | An email

3 Write the words/phrases in the correct column to complete the table.

Hi! | How about …
I am looking forward to …
Love, | Thanks a lot for …

formal	informal
Dear …	
I suggest we …	
	Can't wait to …
I would like to thank you for …	
Yours sincerely,	

1 In pairs, answer the questions.
1 What sports do you do at your school:
• in the winter?
• in the summer?
2 Do boys and girls do sports together or separately?
3 How many hours a week do you do sport?

EXAM SKILL
Writing in an informal style
- When you write an email to a friend, use informal language, e.g. *Hi, See you soon, Write soon, Bye.*
- Use contractions, e.g. *I'm, he can't, we've got.*
- We often use phrasal verbs in informal writing, e.g. *go out, put on.*
- We use more exclamation marks than we do in formal writing.

4 Read the email. Then tick the three questions that the email answers.

From: Chris To: Sam
Hi Sam,
We play football, cricket, hockey and basketball and do athletics at school. Yes, everyone's got to do one sport! We have to go to the park to do sports.
Write soon,
Chris

1 What sports do you do at school?
2 Do all the students have to do sport?
3 How many students play cricket?
4 When do you do sport at school?
5 Where do you do sport?

2 Write the contractions of the words in bold in each sentence.
1 **I would** like to learn how to play golf next year. *I'd*
2 **Sally has** got a new pair of trainers.
3 **They will** start playing baseball in May.
4 Those two teams **were not** good enough to win the competition.
5 He **did not** score any goals in the match.
6 **Who is** the new player in the cricket team?
7 **I am** excited because my team is winning!
8 **We have** trained really hard this winter.

5 Find examples of informal style in the email in Exercise 4. Write them in the correct place below.
1 informal words or phrases
2 a contraction

OPTIMISE YOUR EXAM
An email
- The exam task may ask you to write an email to a friend.
- Read their email carefully so you know what you need to write.
- Make sure you answer the three questions in your friend's email.

88

Writing lessons focus on the different types of writing that students may be expected to produce in an exam situation.

Every Writing lesson includes a model, which students can use to inform and guide their own writing when they complete the exam task later in the lesson.

The *Exam skill* box develops key language functions that students will need to apply in writing tasks.

In Writing lessons, the *Optimise your exam* box provides guidance and advice to help students prepare for the lesson exam task.

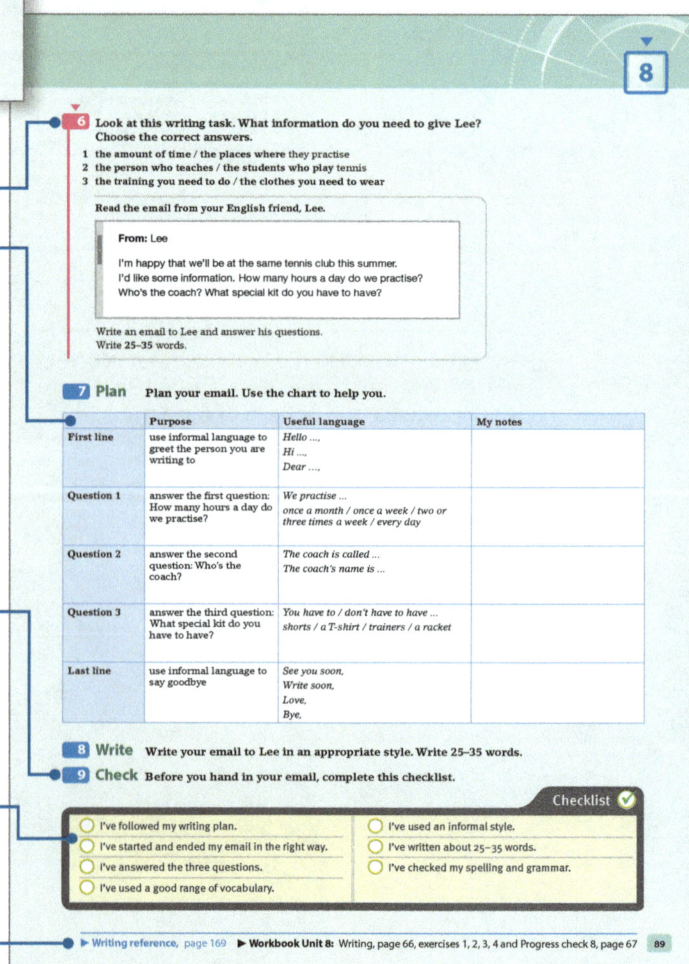

8

6 Look at this writing task. What information do you need to give Lee? Choose the correct answers.
1 the amount of time / the places where they practise
2 the person who teaches / the students who play tennis
3 the training you need to do / the clothes you need to wear

Read the email from your English friend, Lee.

From: Lee
I'm happy that we'll be at the same tennis club this summer.
I'd like some information. How many hours a day do we practise?
Who's the coach? What special kit do you have to have?

Write an email to Lee and answer his questions.
Write 25–35 words.

7 Plan Plan your email. Use the chart to help you.

	Purpose	Useful language	My notes
First line	use informal language to greet the person you are writing to	*Hello …, Hi …, Dear …,*	
Question 1	answer the first question: How many hours a day do we practise?	*We practise … once a month / once a week / two or three times a week / every day*	
Question 2	answer the second question: Who's the coach?	*The coach is called … The coach's name is …*	
Question 3	answer the third question: What special kit do you have to have?	*You have to / don't have to have … shorts / a T-shirt / trainers / a racket*	
Last line	use informal language to say goodbye	*See you soon, Write soon, Love, Bye,*	

8 Write Write your email to Lee in an appropriate style. Write 25–35 words.

9 Check Before you hand in your email, complete this checklist.

Checklist
- I've followed my writing plan.
- I've started and ended my email in the right way.
- I've answered the three questions.
- I've used a good range of vocabulary.
- I've used an informal style.
- I've written about 25–35 words.
- I've checked my spelling and grammar.

▶ Writing reference, page 169 ▶ Workbook Unit 8: Writing, page 66, exercises 1, 2, 3, 4 and Progress check 8, page 67

89

Students analyse the task and make notes to prepare for the writing in each unit.

After writing, students are encouraged to check their work carefully.

There is a Checklist at the end of every Writing lesson so that students take responsibility for reviewing and assessing their work.

In the *Writing reference*, there are longer writing tasks covering a range of different text types, to offer more extensive practice to students.

STUDENT'S BOOK | Progress check

There is a two-page Progress check after every two units.

PROGRESS CHECK UNITS 7–8

GRAMMAR AND VOCABULARY

The *Progress checks* cover grammar and vocabulary from the preceding two units.

1 Complete the conversation using the correct form of *will* or *going to*.

Simona: What (1) __________ you __________ do in the summer holidays?
Martin: I (2) __________ stay with my cousins in France for two weeks. After that, I (3) __________ visit my grandparents. (4) __________ you __________ go on holiday?
Simona: No, I'm not. I (5) __________ study English at a summer school in London. But I need to pass an exam first.
Martin: You're one of the best students in the class. I'm sure you (6) __________ pass.
Simona: I hope so. I have to go now. I (7) __________ do my history homework in the library.
Martin: I'm really bad at history. (8) __________ you help me?
Simona: OK. I (9) __________ help you find the information you need, but I (10) __________ tell you the answers.
Martin: That's great. Thanks a lot.

__/10

2 Choose the correct answers (A, B or C).

1 What do I need to play tennis?
A It's a good idea.
B A racket and some trainers.
C Don't forget your bat and ball.
2 I want to take an English course in September.
A You should speak to my teacher. He's great.
B I don't think so.
C Can you help me?
3 Have you seen my dictionary?
A I have to go.
B It's on the bookshelf.
C It's after lunch.
4 Who won the race?
A Not at the moment.
B It doesn't take long.
C I don't know. They're still running.
5 I'm going to enter this competition.
A I hope you win.
B You don't have to run.
C Wait until it finishes.

__/5

The *Progress checks* include a variety of task types, all designed to provide extra exam preparation as well as reviewing the Student's Book material.

3 Choose the correct modal verb to complete each sentence.

1 My sister **could** / **may** / **should** play tennis when she was five.
2 My cousin **can't** / **couldn't** / **shouldn't** read or write until he was eight.
3 I **can** / **have to** / **may** need your help with my homework, but I'm not sure yet.
4 You **can't** / **needn't** / **couldn't** use your mobile phone during the exam. Leave it in your bag.
5 You **don't have to** / **should** / **may** wear a coat to school because it might be cold later on.
6 In football, only the goalkeeper **doesn't have to** / **has to** / **can** touch the ball with his hands.
7 You **have to** / **shouldn't** / **couldn't** eat too much before you do sport.
8 The runners **don't have to** / **can** / **shouldn't** stop for water, but it is a good idea.
9 You **can** / **needn't** / **have to** use a dictionary during French lessons if you want to find a word.
10 Everyone **could** / **may** / **has to** wear a swimsuit in the pool.
11 You **can** / **may** / **don't have to** go to school in the holidays.
12 I **may** / **couldn't** / **can't** come to the match on Saturday, but at the moment I don't know. I'll tell you tomorrow.

__/12

90

4 Complete the blog post by a Spanish teenager with one word in each gap.

I'm Paz Nevado, I'm 14 years old, I'm from Spain (**1**) __________ I love sport. I (**2**) __________ tennis three times a week and I'm also in the school team. Every year, we enter a big competition (**3**) __________ May. This year, it's (**4**) __________ to be in Madrid. We have (**5**) __________ practise a lot (**6**) __________ we go to the competition. We've never won it, (**7**) __________ last year we came second. It's great fun and I always (**8**) __________ lots of new friends there. I also love swimming. I can't swim very often (**9**) __________ there isn't a pool in my town. Every summer, we (**10**) ________ to the beach and I swim in the sea. I love it!

__/10

5 Complete the sentences with the verbs in the box.

climb	do	go	make	ride	take	throw	win

1 When you're at school, you need to __________ homework every night.
2 It's really useful to __________ notes when the teacher is talking.
3 Cora wants to __________ a really high mountain when she is older.
4 Who do you think will __________ the 10,000-metre race at the Olympics?
5 Lots of young people __________ to university when they're 18.
6 Don't __________ the ball into the road. It's dangerous.
7 It's OK to __________ mistakes when you're learning something new.
8 I'd really like to learn how to __________ a horse next year.

__/8

The *Progress checks* include exam-type tasks.

6 Read the descriptions about sports. What is the word for each one? The first letter is already there.

1 Two or four people play this game with a ball and rackets. t_ _ _ _ _
2 You hit a ball with a bat in this English summer game. c_ _ _ _ _ _
3 Moving through water. s_ _ _ _ _ _ _
4 You hit a ball with your hands in this team game. v_ _ _ _ _ _ _ _ _
5 Riding a board on the sea. s_ _ _ _ _ _

__/5

There is a total of 50 marks for every *Progress check*.

Total score __/50

Every *Progress check* ends with an *Exam skills can-do* checklist. This gives students the opportunity to assess what they can now do, having completed two more units of their Student's Book, and also provides references of where to look if there are any areas students feel they need to review.

EXAM SKILLS

Tick the statements that are true for you. Review the skills in the unit if you need more help.

I can ...	Unit/page
☐ understand *this, that, these, it* and *them* in a text.	Unit 7 p70
☐ think about the missing information I need to listen for.	Unit 7 p74
☐ talk about the future and make predictions.	Unit 7 p76
☐ make collocations with *make, do, have* and *take*.	Unit 7 p77
☐ understand similar information.	Unit 7 p78
☐ scan a text to find certain information.	Unit 8 p80
☐ listen for important information.	Unit 8 p84
☐ ask and answer questions.	Unit 8 p86
☐ use modal verbs.	Unit 8 p87
☐ write emails using an informal style.	Unit 8 p88

91

The 8-page *Optimise your exams* section at the back of the Student's Book brings together exam strategies for each of the key skills, plus advice on how to perform well under exam conditions.

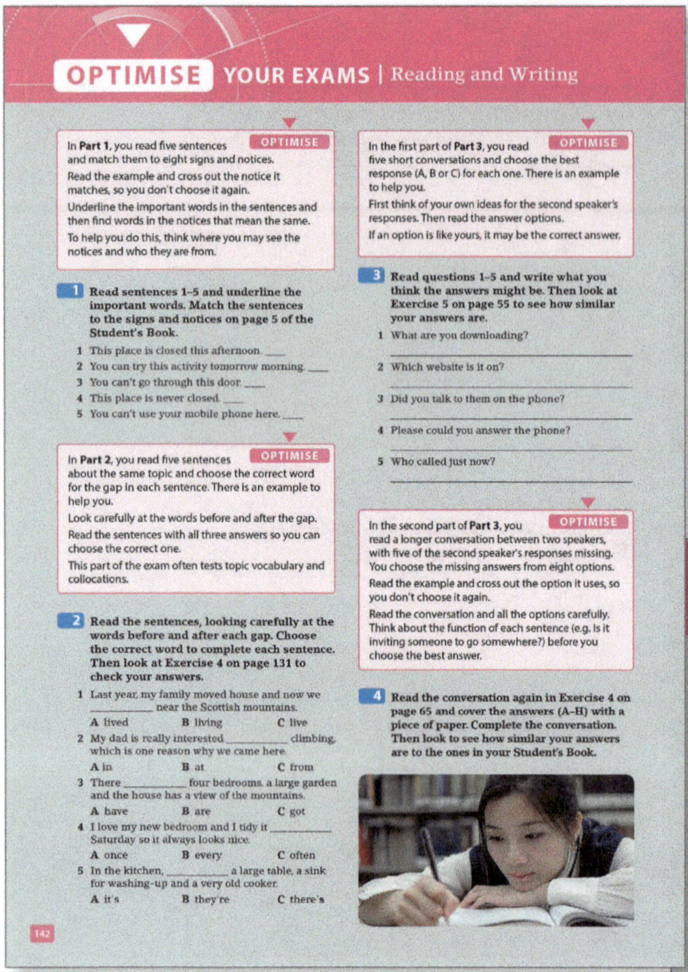

OPTIMISE YOUR EXAMS | Reading and Writing

OPTIMISE
In **Part 1**, you read five sentences and match them to eight signs and notices.
Read the example and cross out the notice it matches, so you don't choose it again.
Underline the important words in the sentences and then find words in the notices that mean the same.
To help you do this, think where you may see the notices and who they are from.

1 Read sentences 1–5 and underline the important words. Match the sentences to the signs and notices on page 5 of the Student's Book.

1 This place is closed this afternoon. ___
2 You can try this activity tomorrow morning. ___
3 You can't go through this door. ___
4 This place is never closed. ___
5 You can't use your mobile phone here. ___

OPTIMISE
In **Part 2**, you read five sentences about the same topic and choose the correct word for the gap in each sentence. There is an example to help you.
Look carefully at the words before and after the gap.
Read the sentences with all three answers so you can choose the correct one.
This part of the exam often tests topic vocabulary and collocations.

2 Read the sentences, looking carefully at the words before and after each gap. Choose the correct word to complete each sentence. Then look at Exercise 4 on page 131 to check your answers.

1 Last year, my family moved house and now we ________ near the Scottish mountains.
A lived B living C live
2 My dad is really interested ________ climbing, which is one reason why we came here.
A in B at C from
3 There ________ four bedrooms, a large garden and the house has a view of the mountains.
A have B are C got
4 I love my new bedroom and I tidy it ________ Saturday so it always looks nice.
A once B every C often
5 In the kitchen, ________ a large table, a sink for washing-up and a very old cooker.
A it's B they're C there's

OPTIMISE
In the first part of **Part 3**, you read five short conversations and choose the best response (A, B or C) for each one. There is an example to help you.
First think of your own ideas for the second speaker's responses. Then read the answer options.
If an option is like yours, it may be the correct answer.

3 Read questions 1–5 and write what you think the answers might be. Then look at Exercise 5 on page 55 to see how similar your answers are.

1 What are you downloading?
2 Which website is it on?
3 Did you talk to them on the phone?
4 Please could you answer the phone?
5 Who called just now?

OPTIMISE
In the second part of **Part 3**, you read a longer conversation between two speakers, with five of the second speaker's responses missing. You choose the missing answers from eight options.
Read the example and cross out the option it uses, so you don't choose it again.
Read the conversation and all the options carefully. Think about the function of each sentence (e.g. Is it inviting someone to go somewhere?) before you choose the best answer.

4 Read the conversation again in Exercise 4 on page 65 and cover the answers (A–H) with a piece of paper. Complete the conversation. Then look to see how similar your answers are to the ones in your Student's Book.

142

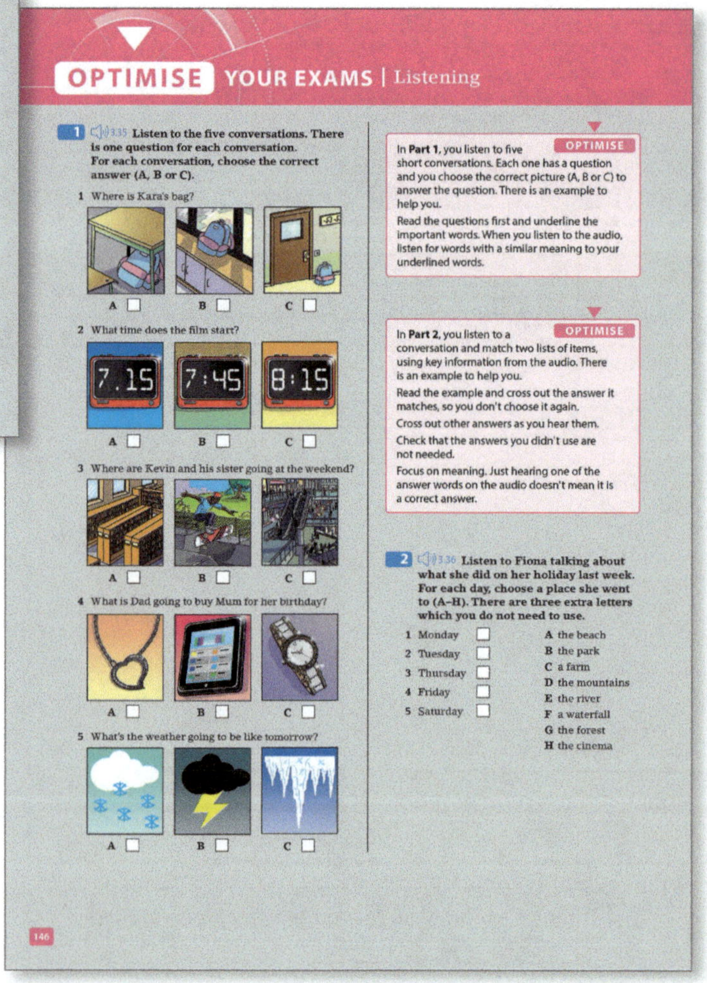

OPTIMISE YOUR EXAMS | Listening

1 3.35 Listen to the five conversations. There is one question for each conversation. For each conversation, choose the correct answer (A, B or C).

1 Where is Kara's bag?
A ☐ B ☐ C ☐
2 What time does the film start?
7.15 7:45 8:15
A ☐ B ☐ C ☐
3 Where are Kevin and his sister going at the weekend?
A ☐ B ☐ C ☐
4 What is Dad going to buy Mum for her birthday?
A ☐ B ☐ C ☐
5 What's the weather going to be like tomorrow?
A ☐ B ☐ C ☐

OPTIMISE
In **Part 1**, you listen to five short conversations. Each one has a question and you choose the correct picture (A, B or C) to answer the question. There is an example to help you.
Read the questions first and underline the important words. When you listen to the audio, listen for words with a similar meaning to your underlined words.

OPTIMISE
In **Part 2**, you listen to a conversation and match two lists of items, using key information from the audio. There is an example to help you.
Read the example and cross out the answer it matches, so you don't choose it again.
Cross out other answers as you hear them.
Check that the answers you didn't use are not needed.
Focus on meaning. Just hearing one of the answer words on the audio doesn't mean it is a correct answer.

2 3.36 Listen to Fiona talking about what she did on her holiday last week. For each day, choose a place she went to (A–H). There are three extra letters which you do not need to use.

1 Monday ☐
2 Tuesday ☐
3 Thursday ☐
4 Friday ☐
5 Saturday ☐

A the beach
B the park
C a farm
D the mountains
E the river
F a waterfall
G the forest
H the cinema

146

Optimise your exams features:

- Sections dedicated to each of the exam papers.
- Exercises to improve students' understanding of common exam tasks.
- Clear targeted advice on how to approach specific exam tasks.
- Exercises to encourage analysis of sample answers.
- A *Speaking test* video in which real candidates complete an authentic Speaking test, to watch and analyse.
- Sample writing plans to compare and critique.
- Advice on how much time to spend on different parts of the exams.

STUDENT'S BOOK | Reference material

There is a bank of reference material at the back of the Student's Book, designed to support students as they work through the lessons, and also intended to act as a revision tool when required.

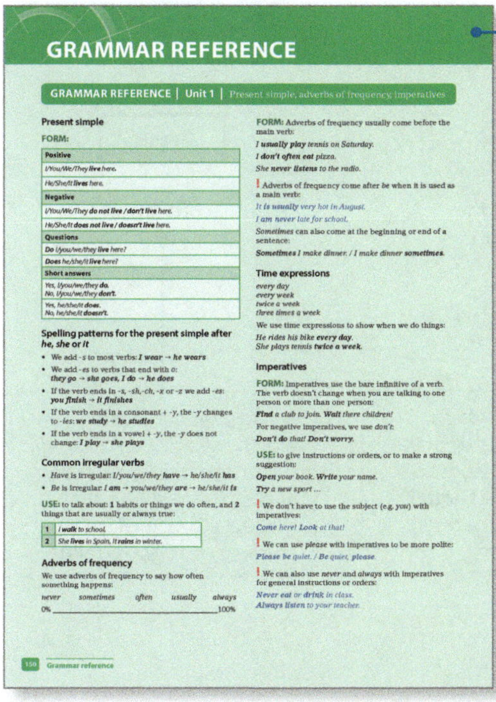

GRAMMAR REFERENCE

GRAMMAR REFERENCE | Unit 1 | Present simple, adverbs of frequency, imperatives

The *Grammar reference* pages provide more detailed explanations of the grammar points covered in every unit, along with example sentences showing how the structures can be used.

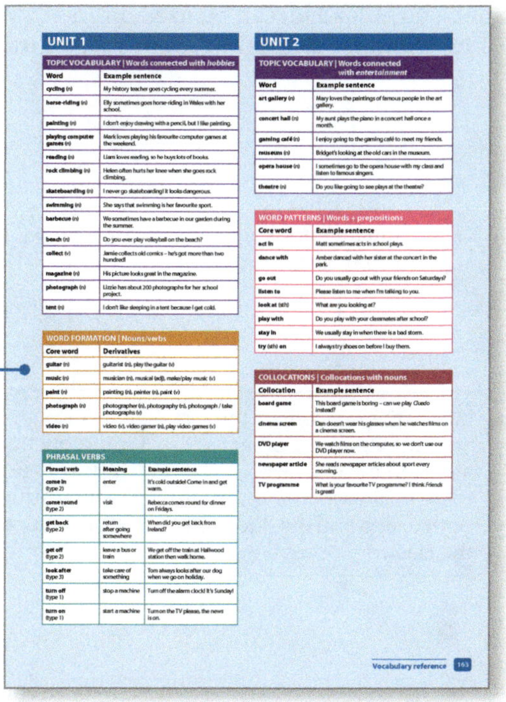

UNIT 1

UNIT 2

All three vocabulary sections from each unit are expanded upon in the *Vocabulary reference*. The sections on Topic vocabulary, Phrasal verbs, Collocations and Word patterns all include example sentences. The Word formation sections include a list of derivatives.

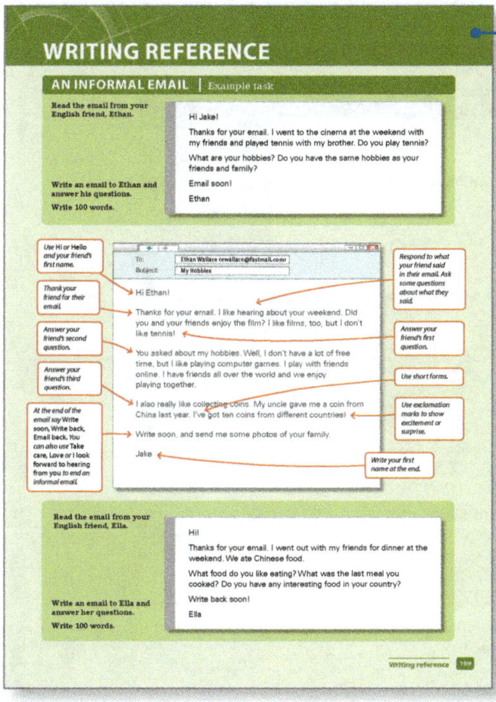

WRITING REFERENCE

AN INFORMAL EMAIL | Example task

There is a model text for each common writing genre, with annotations to highlight key points that students need to remember.

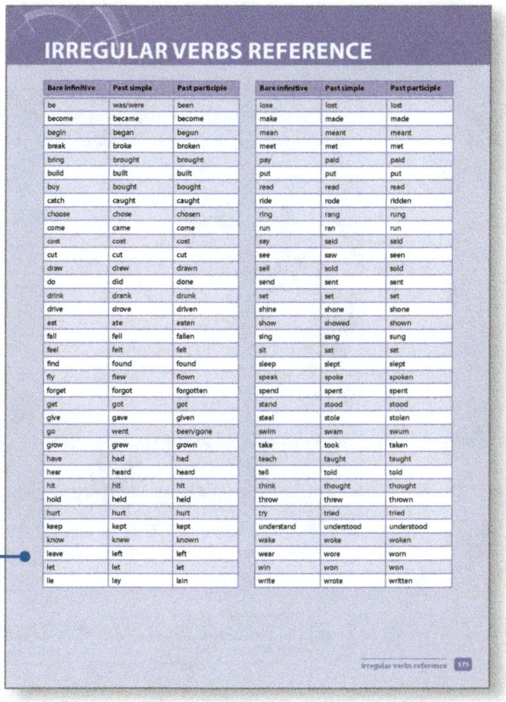

IRREGULAR VERBS REFERENCE

A list of irregular verbs used throughout the A2 Student's Book is provided at the end of the reference material.

DIGITAL STUDENT'S BOOK SB

Includes an access code for the Student's Resource Centre

The *Optimise* Digital Student's Book offers students the possibility of an interactive learning experience, which engages the class as a whole and enables lessons to be dynamic and motivating. The material is easily downloadable and, once downloaded, can be used offline.

The *Optimise* Digital Student's Book includes:

Interactive Student's Book Activities
Interactive versions of the Student's Book activities, allowing the option of more flexible learning both inside and outside the classroom situation.

Complete class audio / **Integrated video**
Easy-to-navigate digital reproduction of the Student's Book pages, which includes embedded audio and video material.

Note-taking function
A notes facility, which enables students to make their own notes about all aspects of the Digital Student's Book material.

Score report
A score report facility, which means exercises will be automatically marked and scores will be sent through to you when the student next goes online.

PRESENTATION KIT

Includes digital versions of the Student's Book and Workbook

You can use the *Optimise* Presentation Kit in the classroom to promote interactive, heads-up lessons, allowing for the option of collaborative learning. The Presentation Kit provides you with a versatile, digital presentation and teaching tool. Built-in functionality enables you to annotate and customise your presentation in advance, making the lesson more suited to the needs of your class. The Presentation Kit can be easily downloaded and, once downloaded, can be used offline.

The *Optimise* Presentation Kit includes:

Interactive Student's Book activities
Interactive versions of the Student's Book activities, giving you the opportunity to complete activities and check answers as a whole class.

Complete Class and Workbook audio / **Integrated video**
All class audio and video material, which can be played instantly by clicking on the hotspots throughout the Presentation Kit material.

Student's Book and Workbook Answer key feature
Answer keys for the Student's Book and Workbook are embedded within each activity, meaning you can show the next answer at the touch of a button. Additional answer key pop-ups are also provided, with suggested answers for open activities.

Note pad feature
A notes facility, enabling you to add your own comments on the material. This helps you deliver more effective and engaging lessons.

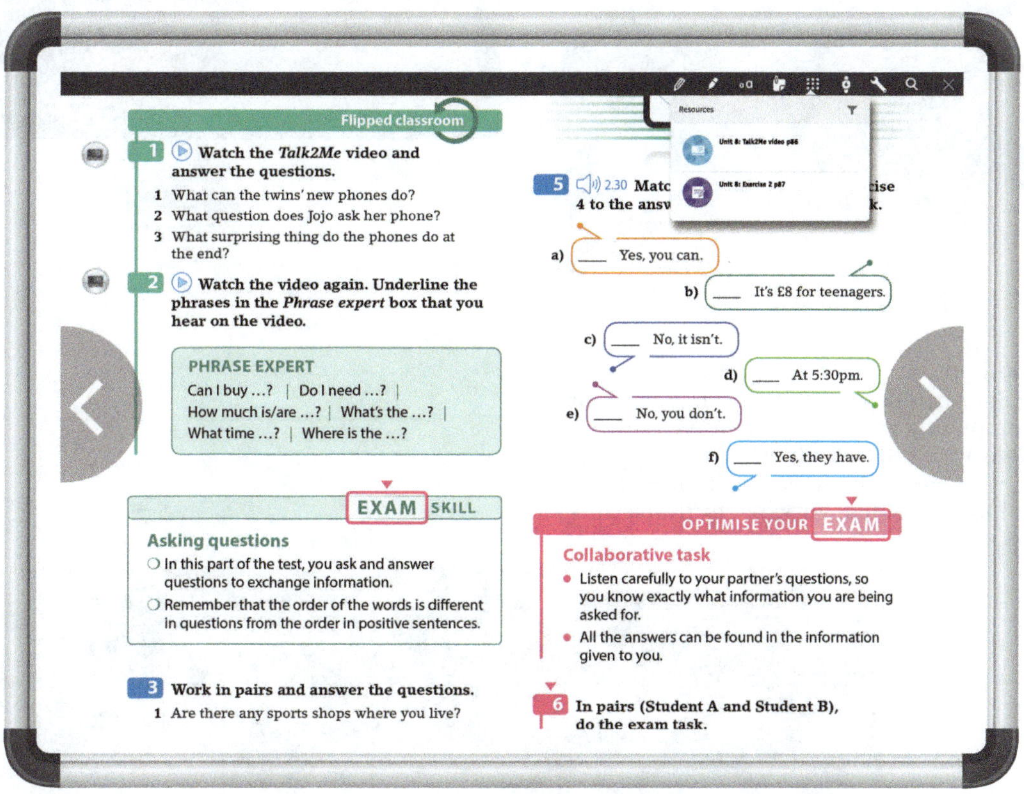

VIDEOS

Use in class or for self-study

Optimise videos provide comprehensive support for students to develop their speaking skills. The course features two different video strands, both of which are flexible and versatile resources that can be used in a number of different ways to support and extend listening and speaking skills.

Talk2Me

1 *Talk2Me* videos

Every Speaking lesson includes a *Talk2Me* video. These exciting videos feature three teenagers (twins Jojo and Max and their best friend, Evie) in a variety of everyday situations, where things sometimes don't go quite as planned!

The videos present key functional language in a natural and original context.

Flipped classroom

Flipped classroom option

You can choose to use the Flipped classroom approach for these videos and set them for homework. Students watch the videos and complete the exercises in the Student's Book at home to prepare for the Speaking lesson. This allows more class time to activate the functional language and develop fluency for the exam task.

Classroom option

Of course, the videos can be watched together as a class with students completing the exercises individually or sharing their ideas with other students.

The videos are available on the Resource Centre and are accompanied by additional worksheets, transcripts and answer keys.

2 Speaking test videos

Optimise includes Speaking test videos as part of the *Optimise your exams* section. The videos provide students with a chance to observe the performance of candidates doing complete Speaking tests under exam conditions.

Watching and discussing the video also enables students to have a greater understanding of the format and processes involved in speaking tests, giving them more confidence and helping them to feel better prepared for the exam.

WORKBOOK | Reading lesson

Complete *Optimise Practice test* at the back of the Workbook

Each Workbook unit has eight pages, with a section for each separate lesson in the Student's Book, and one page for an end-of-unit Progress check.

8 It's only a game

All exam skills match the corresponding Student's Book lesson.

READING | Right/Wrong/Doesn't say | An online article

→Student's Book, pages 80–81

Every unit includes a reference to the corresponding Student's Book lesson.

1 Read the article on page 61 quickly. Complete the sentences with the years in the box.

2014 | 2015 | 2016 (× 2)

1 Josh Bayliss started his last year at school in ________ .
2 Josh left school in ________ .
3 Josh played for the Bath Rugby Club under-18 team in ________ .
4 Josh played for the England under-18 team in South Africa in ________ .

2 Read these sentences about Josh Bayliss and underline the important words.

1 Josh Bayliss comes from a large city.
2 There were many pupils at Josh's school.

3 Read the first sentence in the article. Are the sentences in Exercise 2 'Right' (A) or 'Wrong' (B)? If there is not enough information to answer 'Right' (A) or 'Wrong' (B), choose 'Doesn't say' (C).

1 A Right B Wrong C Doesn't say
2 A Right B Wrong C Doesn't say

Exercises check students' comprehension of the reading text and are designed to develop students' reading skills.

4 Read the article about Josh Bayliss again. Are sentences 1–7 'Right' (A) or 'Wrong' (B)? If there is not enough information to answer 'Right' (A) or 'Wrong' (B), choose 'Doesn't say' (C).

1 Josh Bayliss' school was quite far from his house.
A Right B Wrong C Doesn't say
2 Josh started playing rugby before he was 12.
A Right B Wrong C Doesn't say
3 Josh studied hard at school and passed all his exams.
A Right B Wrong C Doesn't say
4 Josh can eat and drink anything he wants.
A Right B Wrong C Doesn't say
5 Josh left school and then played with the England under-18 team.
A Right B Wrong C Doesn't say
6 Josh's team won some of their matches in South Africa.
A Right B Wrong C Doesn't say
7 Josh is playing on the England team at the next Rugby World Cup.
A Right B Wrong C Doesn't say

New vocabulary from the Workbook reading text is highlighted.

60

It's only a game 8

5 Find these words and phrases in the article. Then match them to definitions (1–6).

bad luck | fitter | grew up | international | last | look after

1 got older, became an adult (paragraph 1) ________
2 including two or more countries (paragraph 1) ________
3 final (paragraph 2) ________
4 healthier (paragraph 2) ________
5 take care of someone (paragraph 2) ________
6 something bad that happens to someone and was not planned or wanted (paragraph 3) ________

www.JoshBa ...

Josh Bayliss

A young player with a bright future

Engaging images attract students' attention and interest in the text.

The Reading lessons feature a full-length reading text.

Josh Bayliss grew up in a town in south-west England and he went to school near there. When Josh was 10, he tried rugby at school and soon after he played for the school team. Then Bath Rugby Club invited him to join their schoolboy team and in 2014 he started playing for their under-18 team. Josh went to Millfield School, which is well known for its sports. Pupils can choose from over 30 different sports and there are around 100 coaches to help them. A large number of the pupils from the school enter international sports competitions every year.

In September 2015, Josh began his last year of school, so he had to study hard. He also wanted to play for the England under-18 rugby team, so he needed to find time to practise. Josh plays at the back of the team and during the match he has to run a lot. He needs to be stronger, faster and fitter than other players because he wants to play against the best teams in the world. He also needs to look after himself and he should be careful about what he eats.

Josh finished school in June 2016. Two months later he travelled to South Africa with the England under-18 rugby team. The team played well, but they lost all three of their matches. Their coach said that it was bad luck, but he thinks that they will be a very good team in the future. Josh is now playing for England's under-19 team and he may be on the England rugby team at the next Rugby World Cup. He certainly hopes so!

61

8 **GRAMMAR 1** | Modals (1): ability, necessity, obligation, possibility

→ Student's Book, page 82 → Grammar reference, Unit 8, Student's Book, page 157

> Grammar lessons throughout the Workbook reflect the material covered in the Student's Book and provide students with more opportunities to consolidate and practise the structures.

> The page number of the Student's Book *Grammar reference* is included in the Workbook so that students can refer back if they need to.

1 Complete the sentences with *can, can't, could* or *couldn't*.

1 All my friends __________ ride horses, but I can't.
2 My brother __________ go skiing last weekend because his leg hurt.
3 __________ you ride a bike when you were five?
4 When Laura was young, she __________ swim really well and she won prizes.
5 Can you speak more slowly, please? I __________ understand you.
6 I __________ play volleyball yesterday because I was ill in bed.
7 We __________ go swimming with you. We're studying for a test.
8 __________ you run faster than your friends or are they faster than you?

2 Complete the swimming club rules with the correct form of *have to* or *don't have to*.

Langton Swimming Club

1 If you are under 16, you __________ come with an adult or you can't use the club.
2 The club is free for members. They __________ pay.
3 Swimmers __________ wear a swimming cap in the pool. You can't swim without one.
4 Everyone __________ have a shower before going into the pool, or they can't go in.
5 You __________ bring your own towel or shampoo. We have everything you need here.
6 You __________ put your wet towels in the bins. Please do not leave them on the floor.

> Every grammar section contains two or three exercises, and where possible texts are included, giving students another chance to see the unit grammar in a realistic context.

3 Complete the sentences with the correct form of *may, must* or *need to* and the verbs in brackets.

1 I __________ (stay) at home today and watch the athletics on TV. I'm not sure.
2 We're playing at 11am, but you __________ (drive) us to the match. We're going by bus.
3 You __________ (run) near the swimming pool.
4 You can't leave now! You __________ (stay) and see the end of the match.
5 __________ I __________ (bring) my own tennis balls or can I borrow some?
6 My brother's won all his matches easily. I'm not sure, but I think he __________ (win) the final.

8 **VOCABULARY** | Topic vocabulary | Word formation | Collocations

→ Student's Book, page 83 → Vocabulary reference, Student's Book, page 166

> The corresponding page of the *Vocabulary reference* is included throughout the Workbook wherever relevant.

1 Read the descriptions of some words about sport. What is the word for each one? The first letter is there to help you. There is one space for each other letter in the word.

1 You hit a tennis ball with this. r _ _ _ _ _
2 Women wear this to swim. s _ _ _ _ _ _ _
3 You need to buy this to get into a match. t _ _ _ _ _
4 You sit on a horse and do this. r _ _ _
5 This person tells the team what to do in a match. c _ _ _ _
6 The clothes or things you need to play a sport. k _ _

2 Complete the sentences with the correct form of the words in the box.

play | run | surf | swim | win

1 Every morning, my mum __________ in the pool before she goes to work.
2 Our team were better, so we __________ the basketball match 45-32.
3 My brother loves to run. He is a fast __________. He won the 400-m race in the stadium yesterday.
4 I like tennis, but I'm a terrible __________.
5 I want to go to Hawaii with my surfboard and __________ in the sea there.

62

> Each of the three vocabulary sections is covered separately in the Workbook, giving your students another chance to reinforce their lexical knowledge.

It's only a game 8

3 Match to make sentences.

1 In basketball, you need to throw ___
2 You can't climb ___
3 My sister may enter ___
4 I've never played ___
5 In the summer, we often go ___
6 I hope I win ___

a) badminton, but I want to.
b) the race, but I can't run very fast.
c) swimming in the lake.
d) the skiing competition. She's very good.
e) the ball to someone in your team.
f) that mountain without good boots.

> A second grammar section in the Workbook corresponds to the second grammar lesson in the Student's Book.

8 **GRAMMAR 2** | Modals (2): advice, permission, polite requests, prohibition

→ Student's Book, page 85 → Grammar reference, Unit 8, Student's Book, page 158

1 Look at the table and complete the conversation with the correct form of *can*.

Ride a bike	Play tennis	Go swimming
?	✓	✗

Kim: (1) __________ I come with you to the sports centre this afternoon?
Sue: Yes, sure. Today we (2) __________ play tennis, but we (3) __________ go swimming.
Kim: That's a shame. Last week, we (4) __________ do both activities.
Sue: Yes, but the pool is closed today. (5) __________ you ride a bike? I'm going to cycle there.
Kim: I can, but I'm not sure if I'm allowed. I'll check with my parents. But (6) __________ you possibly lend me a bike? Mine is broken.

2 Complete the sentences with *should* or *shouldn't* and a verb from the box.

eat | get | play | talk | wear | worry

1 You __________ a big meal before you go swimming. It may make you feel ill.
2 Runners __________ comfortable shoes when they go running.
3 If we need to buy tickets, we __________ to the stadium early.
4 Shh! You __________ loudly at a tennis match.
5 Your sister __________ about the match. I'm sure she'll win!
6 If you think football is boring, you __________ basketball. I think it's more exciting.

3 Complete the second sentence so that it has a similar meaning to the first. Use the correct form of *have to, should* or *can* and any other words you need.

Example: It is prohibited to wear outdoor shoes in the sports hall.
You *mustn't wear* __________ outdoor shoes in the sports hall.

1 We weren't allowed to go into the gym because the teacher wasn't there.
We __________ into the gym because the teacher wasn't there.
2 Is it possible for you to open the window, please? It's hot in here.
__________ you __________ the window, please? It's hot in here.
3 It's a good idea to buy tickets for the match early.
We __________ tickets for the match early.
4 It is prohibited for students under 16 to use the gym.
You __________ the gym if you are under 16.

63

> Exercises in the Workbook are staged so as to be progressively more challenging.

WORKBOOK | Listening lesson | Speaking lesson | Language in Use lesson

The listening exam skill in the Student's Book is practised again in the Workbook.

The Workbook listening exercises have their own dedicated audio material, available on the Resource Centres and on the Online Workbook.

Workbook exercises give students more practice in exam-type tasks.

8 LISTENING | Multiple matching

→ Student's Book, page 84

1 Match the phrases a–e to the words 1–5 with a similar meaning.

1 running ___ a) walking to the top of a mountain
2 tennis ___ b) going out in a boat
3 climbing ___ c) riding a bike
4 sailing ___ d) moving very quickly on foot
5 cycling ___ e) playing a racket sport

2 🔊 10 Listen to five people talking about sport. As you listen, choose each person's favourite sport, a or b.

	a)	b)
Speaker 1 ___	a) sailing	b) swimming
Speaker 2 ___	a) tennis	b) table tennis
Speaker 3 ___	a) running	b) cycling
Speaker 4 ___	a) football	b) rugby
Speaker 5 ___	a) skiing	b) climbing

3 🔊 11 Listen to two people talking about their friends. For each friend, choose his or her favourite sport. There are three extra letters you do not need.

Friends	Sports
1 Ben ___	A table tennis
2 Harry ___	B swimming
3 Paula ___	C cricket
4 Lisa ___	D rugby
5 Steve ___	E surfing
	F sailing
	G basketball
	H skiing

8 SPEAKING | Collaborative task

→ Student's Book, page 86

As the Workbook is designed for independent use, the speaking lessons consist of written exercises specifically designed to provide essential preparation that will further improve students' speaking skills.

1 Look at the information opposite about a basketball competition. Then complete the questions about it.

1 Where ______________ competition?
2 When ______________ ?
3 What ______________ win?
4 ______________ for children?
5 ______________ telephone number?

2 Complete the answers to the questions in Exercise 1.

1 It's at the ______________.
2 It's from ______________ to ______________.
3 You can win ______________.
4 Yes, it is. It's for children aged ______________.
5 It's ______________.

3 Look at the information opposite about a tennis competition. Then write questions and answers like the ones in exercises 1 and 2.

____

64

It's only a game 8

8 LANGUAGE IN USE | Multiple-choice cloze

→ Student's Book, page 87

1 Complete the sentences with the correct modal verb in the positive or negative form.

can | could | may | must | should

Example: You *should* only go swimming in the sea when there are other people with you.

1 At school we ______________ walk in the corridors, not run.
2 ______________ you help me, please?
3 When I was three, I ______________ ride a bike. I learnt when I was five.
4 You ______________ go swimming straight after eating.
5 Ask Lauren, she ______________ be able to help you.

Workbook exercises give students the chance to examine and practise language in more detail.

2 Read the text below and choose the correct answer to fill each gap.

www.the world ...

Everyone has heard of the Olympic Games, (1) ___ you probably don't know about the World Alternative Games. These games started in Llanwrtyd Wells, Wales, (2) ___ 2012, which is the same year the Olympic Games were held in London. In fact, the idea for these games came (3) ___ they chose London for the Olympics. The people of this very small Welsh town decided that the town (4) ___ hold their own sporting event, and they started the World Alternative Games. In the first year, (5) ___ 2,000 people took part in 35 events, such as the Man versus Horse marathon. This race is 35 km, so it is shorter (6) ___ a marathon. It is for runners (7) ___ people riding horses. Perhaps the most important rule is that the horses (8) ___ to start 15 minutes after the runners.

	A	B	C
1	A before	B but	C because
2	A in	B on	C at
3	A until	B after	C but
4	A mustn't	B should	C have to
5	A over	B more	C most
6	A as	B from	C than
7	A but	B because	C and
8	A should	B can	C have

65

The Language in Use lessons in the Workbook include an exam-type task, so students get a further opportunity to apply the language skills they developed in the Student's Book lesson.

8 WRITING | An email

→ Student's Book, pages 88–89 → Writing reference, Student's Book, page 169

Details of the *Writing reference* in the Student's Book are included, so students can easily refer back to it.

1 Read the exam task. What information do you need to give Becca? Tick the correct answers (1–6).

Write an email to Becca and answer her questions.

From: Becca
To:

You haven't told me about your PE lessons at school. How often do you do PE at school? Who's your teacher? What clothes do you have to wear?

Write **25–35** words.

1 how often
2 the place
3 the person who teaches
4 the sports kit
5 the other students
6 the name of the school

Writing lessons begin by re-focusing students on the exam advice given in their Student's Book.

The Workbook includes a model answer in addition to the one found in the Student's Book.

2 Read the model emails below (A, B and C). Then complete the checklist. Which is the best email?

A
Dear Becca,
Thank you for your email. Im going to tell you about my PE lessons at school. My teacher is called Mr Hampton and he is very nice. Sometimes we can choose the sport and other times he tells us what we are going to do.
I would like to try badminton next.
Best wishes,
Jack

B
PE's three times on week. The teacher's name are Mrs Roberts. We don't have wear special clothes.

C
Hi Becca,
We've got PE twice a week. Our teachers called Mr Thomas. We have to wear a white T-shirt and blue shorts. We don't have to bring racket or balls!
Write soon,
Danny

Checklist

	A	B	C	ME
1 The email uses informal style.	○	○	○	○
2 It starts and ends in the right way.	○	○	○	○
3 It answers all of Becca's questions.	○	○	○	○
4 It's about 25–35 words.	○	○	○	○
5 The spelling and grammar is correct.	○	○	○	○

The best email is ___ .

3 Read these sentences from the emails in Exercise 2. Rewrite the underlined words correctly.

1 Im going to tell you about my PE lessons. ______________
2 Our teachers called Mr Thomas. ______________
3 PE's three times on week. ______________
4 The teacher's name are Mrs Roberts. ______________
5 We don't have wear special clothes. ______________

Exercises in the Workbook will help students to consolidate and develop their writing skills in general.

4 Write your own email to Becca. Then check your email using the checklist in Exercise 2.

Students usually do a complete writing task in the Workbook.

66

It's only a game 8

PROGRESS CHECK

Every Workbook lesson ends with a one-page *Progress check*.

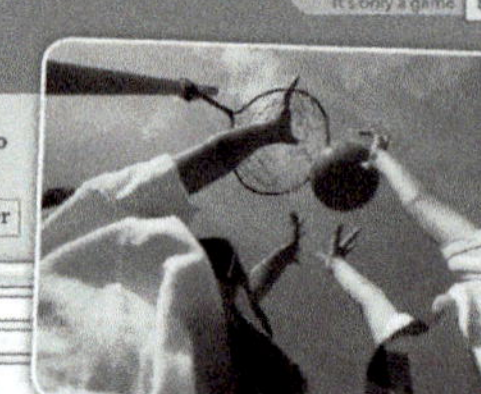

1 Complete the email with the words in the box. There are two extra words you do not need.

club | coach | go | kit | members | play | teams | throw | ticket | winner

From: Natalie
To: Emily

Hi Emily,

Thanks for your email. You asked me about my favourite sport. I've got two actually – tennis and netball. I know you **(1)** __________ tennis, so let me tell you about netball. There are two **(2)** __________ of seven players. It's like basketball, you get points by putting the ball, into a ring – the team with the most points is the **(3)** __________ . In basketball, you can move with the ball, but in netball you can't, you have to **(4)** __________ the ball to another player. The sports **(5)** __________ is similar to tennis – girls wear a T-shirt, a skirt and trainers, but the ball is much bigger and heavier than a tennis ball. I started playing on the school netball team about three years ago. Then our town's netball **(6)** __________ asked me to play in their under-16 team. Our **(7)** __________ is amazing; she never gets angry even when we lose. The next Netball World Cup is going to be near my home. I hope I can buy a **(8)** __________ to watch a match.

I hope this answers your question.

Write soon,

Natalie

2 Choose the correct answers.

1 A: Are you going to play tennis after school?
B: I **don't have to / can't / couldn't** play. I've hurt my hand.
2 A: I want to watch the match on TV.
B: You **should / don't have to / can't** tidy your room first. There are clothes everywhere!
3 A: When did you learn to climb trees?
B: I **can / could / should** climb them when I was six.
4 A: My brother would like to try a new exciting sport.
B: Well, he **shouldn't / couldn't / doesn't have to** play rugby. It's really dangerous.
5 A: **Can / Could / Should** your brother run as fast as you?
B: No, he isn't a fast runner. I'm much faster.
6 A: I need some new trainers.
B: You **should / can / don't have to** look online. They're much cheaper.
7 A: **Can I / Should I / Do I have to** go swimming with my friends?
B: Yes, but remember we're going to have dinner with Grandma later.
8 A: I'll never finish this homework and I've got a match this afternoon.
B: Don't worry, we **shouldn't / couldn't / don't have to** give it to the teacher until Monday.

The *Progress Check* always has one exercise based on the vocabulary from the unit, and one exercise based on the unit grammar.

Cumulative progress 1 2 3 4 5 6 7 8 9 10 11 12

3 Choose the best answer (A, B or C) to complete the conversations.

1 You should get a new racket from Sports World.
A Yes, of course it is. B That's a good idea. C I have to buy a new racket.
2 Have you ever been to a basketball match?
A We're going to be there soon. B I went to one last summer. C You've been to a match.
3 Are you going to enter the competition?
A I'm not sure. B I won't play. C I didn't.
4 Shall we go surfing later?
A I'm sorry. I can't swim. B You don't have to. C We couldn't go.
5 We couldn't play tennis because it was raining.
A Were you playing tennis? B Did you play tennis? C What did you do?

67

The final part of the *Progress check* is a *Cumulative progress* exercise, which includes vocabulary and grammar items from any of the preceding units.

ONLINE WORKBOOK OWB

The *Optimise* Online Workbook includes all the print Workbook content in a fully-interactive digital format, which students can use for independent self-study.

The *Optimise* Online Workbook includes:

- Interactive Workbook activities
- Complete Workbook audio
- Automated marking for instant feedback
- Gradebook

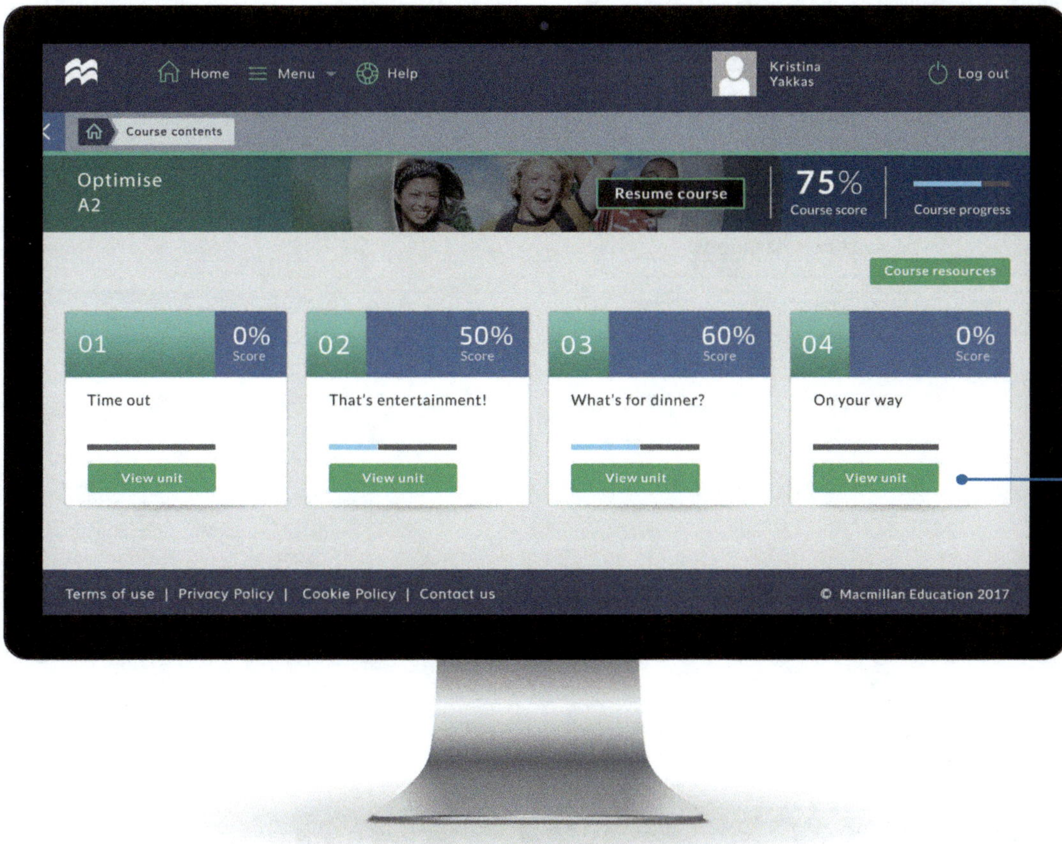

The automatic Gradebook facility will save you valuable marking time.

The Online Workbook enables you to manage multiple classes in a single location, and the content-locking facility gives you control over how you manage the tasks for your class.

Students have the chance to make multiple attempts at answering questions, enabling them to effectively consolidate their learning.

Scores are automatically collated and clearly displayed in the Gradebook, so it is easy to compare students and classes. Students' progress can be monitored at a glance, highlighting areas where they may require additional support.

The messaging and notification features allow you to correspond with your students, send homework reminders, and notify your classes when scores are available.

Detailed feedback on scores and progress creates a highly personalised self-study environment.

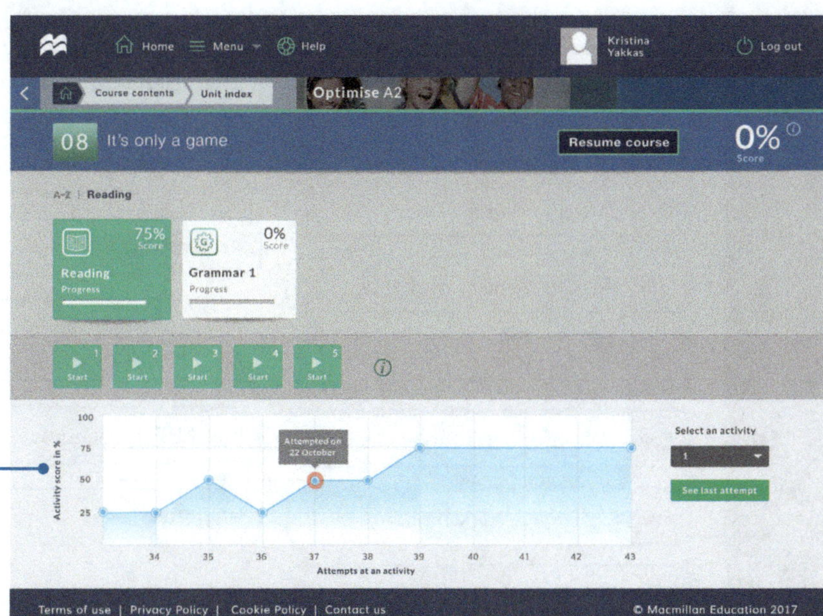

TEACHER'S AND STUDENT'S RESOURCE CENTRES

For teachers and students

The *Optimise* Resource Centres offer a huge bank of additional downloadable material and tests that have been designed to comprehensively support and enhance the core Student's Book and Workbook material.

For students, the Student's Resource Centre provides complementary materials to consolidate learning and encourage independent study.

STUDENT'S RESOURCE CENTRE

- *Optimise your grammar* worksheets (Standard and Higher)
- *Optimise your vocabulary* worksheets (Standard and Higher)
- *Talk2Me* videos and worksheets
- *Say it right* pronunciation worksheets
- Culture and CLIL worksheets
- Speaking test videos
- Class and Workbook audio

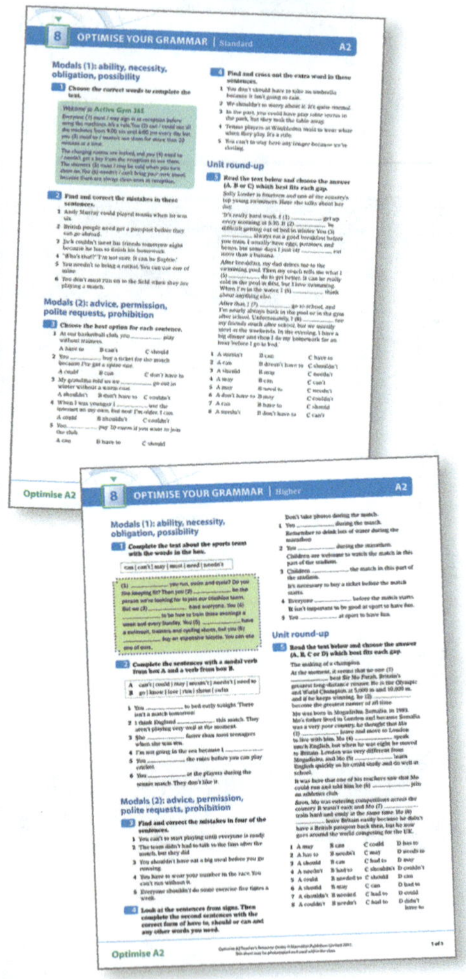

The Teacher's Resource Centre is your go-to place for resources to deliver dynamic lessons, assign for homework, and to support you in the classroom.

TEACHER'S RESOURCE CENTRE

- *Optimise your grammar* worksheets (Standard and Higher)
- *Optimise your vocabulary* worksheets (Standard and Higher)
- *Talk2Me* videos and worksheets
- Speaking test videos
- *Say it right* pronunciation worksheets
- *Everyday English* worksheets
- Grammar communication worksheets
- Culture and CLIL worksheets
- Class and Workbook audio
- Answer keys
- Placement and Diagnostic tests, Unit and Progress tests
- Key (KET) for Schools Practice test
- Wordlists

TESTING MATERIALS

Complete testing package

Optimise provides an extensive range of testing materials, which can be used throughout the school year to assess your students' progress and to prepare them for exams.

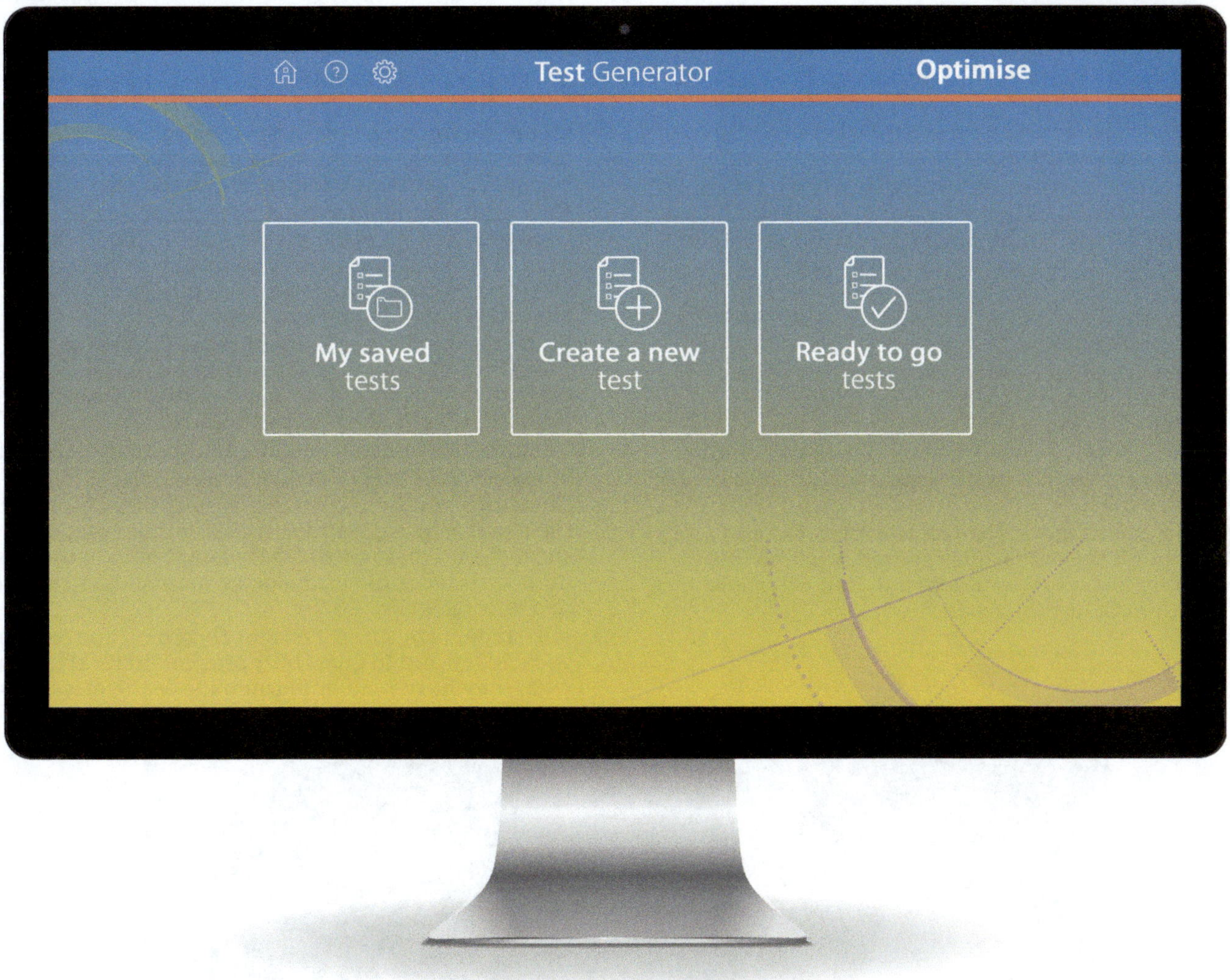

Printable tests

Optimise offers a comprehensive range of printable tests, available on the Teacher's Resource Centre in PDF format.
All the *Optimise* tests correspond to the course level.
Tests are aligned closely to the CEFR and to competency levels for international and state exams.

Tests include:

- *Diagnostic* and *Placement tests*
- *Unit tests*, *Progress tests* and *End-of-year tests* (Standard and Higher)
- *Key (KET) for Schools* practice tests:
  - an *Optimise Practice test* at the back of the Workbook
  - *Key (KET) for Schools Practice test* on the Teacher's Resource Centre, which can be taken under test conditions.

Complete answer keys, audio and audioscripts are provided for all tests.

Test Generator

The *Optimise* Test Generator allows you to create customised tests from the pre-prepared Unit and Progress tests.

- Tests are aligned to CEFR levels.
- The content reflects Reading and Writing, Listening and Speaking tasks from international and state exams.
- The Test Generator comes with the option to save tests in progress and to preview them before printing.
- With Standard and Higher levels available, it also allows for maximum flexibility in choosing the test content.

Teacher support

PREPARING STUDENTS FOR EXAMS

Knowing your exam

- It´s important that students become as familiar as possible with the different parts of the exam they are preparing for and understand what is required of them in each exam task.
- Carry out timed practice tests regularly with your students. As well as being excellent training, it's also an important way of highlighting specific areas for improvement.
- *Optimise* includes two Practice tests: one at the back of the Workbook and another on the Teacher's Resource Centre.
- After each test, draw up a class checklist of basic reminders or issues related to the exam.
- The *Optimise your exams* section at the back of the Student's Book provides detailed information about each of the different exam sections, so students know what to expect.
- Many students associate exams with stress and panic, but if they are well prepared, students will generally feel more confident and that will show through in their performance.

Reading preparation

- It´s important that students develop key strategies for dealing with a variety of question types. These include skimming, scanning, reading for detail and understanding the main idea of the text, as well as being able to identify lexical and structural words.
- Encourage students to refer to dictionaries or the *Grammar* and *Vocabulary references* at the back of the Student's Book. However, students also need to learn strategies for working independently, as reference material cannot be used in exams.
- Students should create an efficient system for recording all new vocabulary they learn. Encourage them to think about how they can record words and phrases in as much detail as possible.
- Remind students that spelling is important, especially in tasks such as *Word completion*.
- Encourage students to read a variety of texts outside the classroom, e.g. online articles, graded readers, short stories and novels. This should help to increase their knowledge of vocabulary, grammatical structures and writing styles.
- Ask students to share ideas for recording and learning vocabulary, and to give short presentations about what they have read or learnt outside the classroom.

PREPARING STUDENTS FOR EXAMS

Writing preparation

- Make sure students have regular opportunities throughout the year for writing. They can write things like short messages, invitations, plans for meeting, etc.
- Writing in another language can be challenging for most young students, so make sure they have plenty of practice, both in class and as homework, at writing the different types of Key Test tasks.
- Make sure students always read the question carefully and underline the key points. If they don't answer the question, respond to specific prompts or include all relevant information, they may lose marks.
- Remind students to think carefully about who they are writing for, and if the style required will be formal or informal.
- Encourage students to plan their work before writing. As well as planning their work, students should leave time at the end to check spelling and punctuation.
- Timing is important in a real exam and practice under timed conditions in class is the best way to prepare students for writing tasks.
- Students should try to write within the correct word limit. They won't lose marks for writing more words than the suggested amount (25–35), but will lose marks if they write fewer. Advise your students to try and write the required number of words.
- Encourage students to read each other's pieces of writing to give them ideas and develop their own writing further.

Listening preparation

- It's important that students develop key strategies for dealing with a variety of listening question types. These include answering multiple-choice questions on short conversations and on a longer conversation, matching two lists of items and completing gap fills based on a conversation and a monologue.
- Classroom discussions can help prior to doing a listening task. For example, ask students what they think the speakers will talk about, and if they will hear any specific information, such as times, names, dates and places.
- It can also be useful to vary the focus of a task in class before students attempt a set of exam questions. For example, students could listen once to give an overall summary of what was said on the audio, then listen again for specific information.
- When listening to short conversations, students need to look carefully at multiple-choice options in questions and underline key words. When the options are pictures, encourage students to think about what each of the three picture options have in common and what key words they might hear in the conversation.
- When listening to longer conversations or monologues, encourage students to listen for the overall idea(s) first before they focus on the actual words and phrases. Make sure students listen to stressed or key words that have an important message, rather than focusing on every individual word.
- Encourage students to listen to audio material outside class, for example on English-language digital radio or TV stations. They also need to hear a variety of accents, styles and age groups.
- When students listen to authentic material, encourage them to develop strategies such as picking out key information, or deducing meaning from context by focusing on key words and ignoring unimportant or unknown words.

Speaking preparation

- Some students may feel especially nervous about taking a speaking exam, so one way to reassure them is to make them familiar with the structure of the exam they are going to take.
- In some speaking exams, students are tested in pairs and there are two examiners: one interlocutor, who speaks to the candidates and directs the test as well as giving marks, and one assessor, who marks the students on specific criteria.
- It is important for students to understand the different types of interaction that will take place. For example, students need to know when they will speak with their partner or with the interlocutor.
- All classroom activities that encourage students to ask and answer questions, discuss issues in pairs or groups, or talk about themselves and their own experiences will give them practice in skills they will need in an exam, and will also help to build their confidence when speaking.
- When practising any activities for speaking, encourage students to speak clearly and to ask for clarification if they don't understand or aren't sure about something.
- Ask students to work in pairs or groups to do some simple role plays. They should use everyday language to ask and answer questions about things like their family, daily routines, hobbies and interests. It's helpful for them to also practice exchanging information about things like prices, dates, opening times, etc. of a local library or sports centre, for example.
- Encourage students to expand on their ideas and give examples or reasons when speaking.
- Give students as much practice as possible in talking with partners in class. Encouraging them to discuss different exercises as they work on them or their ideas for writing tasks all provide good speaking opportunities and, again, build confidence.

TEACHING MIXED-ABILITY CLASSES

Introduction

All classes have students of different abilities and with a range of different learning needs. The teacher's challenge is to engage the more advanced students at the same time as helping those who are finding lessons more difficult. Here are some practical tips to create a more inclusive classroom.

Group dynamics

Begin the whole class together with a lead-in activity to provide a sense of community and a foundation for the levelled tasks that will follow. Lead-in activities preview, present and practise language in a way that lends itself perfectly to whole-class, multi-level instruction. At the end of a lesson, always bring the class back together and assign a whole-class activity.

Group, pair and individual work

Vary the way students work in the class to address different levels and needs. Organise students to work in pairs, small groups and teams. It is less stressful for weaker students to work with other classmates because they have more time to think about tasks, and students can help and learn from each other.

In some schools, it may be possible to divide classes into two groups according to ability. The two groups can be given the same work to complete, or they can work on differentiated material.

Games and activities, such as brainstorming vocabulary, help to increase collaboration in the mixed-ability classroom. For example, ask students to work together to produce spidergrams as a way to help them remember topic vocabulary.

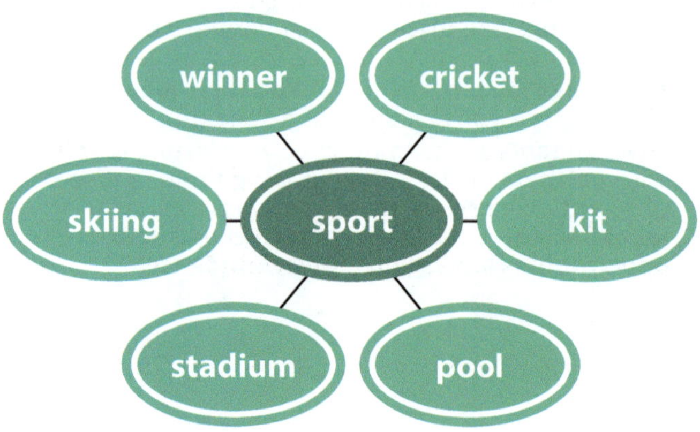

No matter what the level of the student, they all get better results through collaboration than they would have got by working on their own.

Pair work is usually successful in the mixed-ability classroom because it is easy to control and there is greater student participation. Depending on the task, decide how you organise your students into pairs: students with a similar level can work together at their own pace, or a stronger student can pair with a weaker student and help to support them. There are plenty of opportunities for pair work throughout *Optimise*.

Individual work allows for variations in speed and level. By giving a time limit rather than a quantity-of-work limit (e.g. *'Do as much as you can in three minutes.'* instead of, *'Do exercise 3.'*), students are able to work at their own pace.

Specific strategies for dealing with above-level students

- **Reading**

Set students more challenging work to keep the more advanced students motivated. For example, they could write their own comprehension questions to ask the class, select six new words from the reading text to write definitions for and learn, or create their own sentences using new vocabulary from the reading text.

- **Grammar and Vocabulary**

Ask stronger students to try to work out the meaning of new words from the context and to elicit grammar rules by looking at the language in context.

Encourage a higher level of fluency and accuracy from the stronger students.

Encourage students to support weaker classmates by explaining the grammar point to them or by clarifying the meaning of a new vocabulary item.

- **Listening**

Ask students to summarise what they heard after listening to it the first time (as a whole class or in pairs).

Encourage students to write their own comprehension questions to ask the class.

- **Speaking**

Demand a higher level of fluency and accuracy and ask stronger students to justify and defend their opinions.

Practise paraphrasing and brainstorm other phrases to use in the functional language (*Phrase expert*) boxes.

Encourage students to write their own conversations to act out in pairs.

- **Writing**

Indicate where something could be said in a more interesting or more complex way, and give creative tasks that students can do at their level.

Encourage peer correction by asking them to look at each other's work and suggest improvements. However, where more advanced students are reviewing work from below-level students, always make sure they are sensitive and constructive in their advice.

TEACHING MIXED-ABILITY CLASSES

Specific strategies for dealing with below-level students

- **General classroom organisation**

Make sure weaker students don't sit at the back, where it's more difficult for you to make eye contact with them.

Give clear instructions and check students have understood the task before they begin. For more complex tasks, ask stronger students to do an example of the task to check understanding.

- **Reading**

Ask weaker students easier questions, alternating with harder questions for stronger students.

Simplify multiple-choice tasks by reducing the number of options. Then gradually increase to exam level.

- **Grammar and Vocabulary**

Simplify gap-fill tasks by introducing optional answers, so students can identify the correct answer rather than having to produce it.

Be selective in your error correction and praise students for what they have managed to do, regardless of what others have produced.

Use homework to address weaknesses and consolidate classwork by using the mixed-ability Grammar and Vocabulary worksheets on the Teacher's Resource Centre.

- **Listening**

Pause the audio regularly to check understanding and explain if anything remains unclear. For more difficult texts, provide audioscripts after the first two listenings.

- **Speaking**

Provide useful phrases and model answers for less-able students to use as a basis for their answers.

- **Writing**

Additional model answers can assist students with their writing tasks. For students who need more support, provide a gapped or jumbled model answer for them to complete or put in order instead of asking them to write a text from scratch.

Mixed-ability features in *Optimise*

The **Mixed-ability** features in the *Optimise* Teacher's Book help to engage different groups of students using the same class material as the starting point, but with multi-level instruction. This way, you avoid increased preparation time, and the student group can still work together for most of the class.

As well as the **Mixed-ability** features in the *Optimise* Teacher's Book, the **Optional extension** and **Fast finishers** boxes also offer teachers a range of suggestions for ways to differentiate activities for stronger students.

Mixed ability

Ask stronger students to cover Exercise 5 and look at the highlighted words in the text and to try to work out what they mean purely from the context. Have less confident students complete the task as it appears in the Student's Book. Then pair stronger students with weaker students and have them share their ideas. Give students this model to follow: *I think* online *means* on the internet. *Do you agree?*

Optional extension

Have students play ***Preposition tennis*** in groups of three. Tell two students to work together with their books closed (Students A and B) and tell the third student (Student C) to act as the judge. Explain that Student A says a verb, e.g. *go*, and Student B has to say the corresponding preposition *out* and then a new verb, e.g. *stay*. Student A has to respond with the preposition *in* and so on. Student C monitors and checks they are using the correct prepositions and maintaining a regular rhythm. Monitor the groups in case Student C is unsure about the correct answer. If one student pauses for too long or repeats a verb, the other student wins a point. Have students change roles so they all take turns as judge.

Fast finishers

Ask students to explain what the incorrect alternatives mean and how they could be used, e.g. *a team* refers to a group of people who play a sport together, whereas *a member* is someone who belongs to a club or group: *Some members of the hockey team are friends of mine.*

The *Optimise* Teacher's Resource Centre provides additional Grammar and Vocabulary worksheets in addition to the Unit and Progress tests, all available at two levels (Standard and Higher).

The *Optimise* Test Generator also allows teachers to custom-build their own tests according to their students' needs.

Encourage students to use the Online Workbook. Students get immediate feedback on their work and they can do the tasks as many times as necessary in order to get them correct. It's perfect for students of all abilities.

TEACHING TIPS

Here are some useful teaching tips for you to refer to throughout the school year.

Encouraging language development

Optimise A2 provides your students with an excellent opportunity to consolidate and build on the language they have learnt up to this point. The material is rich with new vocabulary and presents comprehensive coverage of a full range of grammar structures. Lessons include a wide range of strategies that you can use to help your students develop their language. Exploiting all this material in as many ways as possible will help to consolidate the language and make students comfortable and confident about using it in other contexts.

Useful expressions

One important aspect of language development which you can help your students focus on at this level is learning expressions. Expressions are high-frequency, multi-word phrases that function as a unit. Very often, expressions are pronounced as if they were one word. Fixed expressions, such as expressions of opinion, perform specific functions and they can't always be defined by looking them up in a dictionary as individual words. Such expressions are important in helping students improve their fluency. If they can learn these fixed expressions, students can develop language competency by transferring them to a variety of different contexts.

It is often the case that students learn these expressions, use them in the class and then go back to using just one expression they were already familiar with. Point out to students they can gain more points in Speaking exams if they use a variety of expressions.

Developing accuracy and fluency in speaking

Accuracy is the ability to produce correct sentences with correct grammar and vocabulary. Fluency is the ability to read, speak or write easily, smoothly and with the correct intonation. The accuracy/fluency question depends on the purpose of the activity students are doing in the class. Controlled and semi-controlled speaking practice such as drills and information exchanges are working on accuracy. More open discussion should focus on fluency.

In general, try not to correct speaking too often in class as it interrupts the student's train of thought and can undermine their confidence. It's important to encourage students to talk and to keep talking. It's useful to note down errors while students are speaking then to take a few minutes at the end of class for a quick feedback session.

Memory and learning

Students are far more likely to remember words that they have analysed or focused on in some way than words they have learnt in isolation. If they have learnt the word in context and have fully understood it, rather than just learning it based upon a definition, it is much easier for students to remember the word in the long-term. Ask your students how they learn words best – do they need to hear them, see them written down or write them down themselves? Some students memorise vocabulary by associating new words with ideas or anecdotes. Help students to create mnemonic devices such as short phrases, tunes or poems to support their learning. In order to internalise vocabulary, students should also review vocabulary regularly. For strong lexical ability, students need to study vocabulary in context and that is best done by reading in English. Try to encourage your students to do this as much as possible. You could invite them to bring English books and magazines to class for group discussion or presentations. When your students come across a new word, encourage them to look at its place in the sentence, and to look at the words that appear either side of it. Remind them to think about the context and who the text is written for, and to look out for word patterns. They should always try to deduce meaning, but where they can't, point out that it's fine to use a dictionary as a tool for vocabulary building.

Teacher-talking time

As a teacher, you're always aware of how much time you spend speaking during the lesson. This is especially important in speaking lessons, where the key purpose is to encourage students to speak. That's not to say your speech isn't invaluable in providing models for pronunciation, functional language and appropriate discourse. But sometimes a large amount of teacher-talking time can slow the pace of a lesson and students can lose concentration and become bored or disinterested.

Some useful strategies to avoid this are:

- Wait for an answer when you ask a question. Students need 'thinking' time.
- Ask open-ended questions (e.g. *Wh-* questions) to encourage students to give longer answers, e.g. *What did you do last weekend?* instead of *Did you have a good weekend?*
- Vary the way students get feedback: they can check activities in pairs, for example.
- Encourage students to give explanations instead of giving them yourself.
- Present students with clear examples and guided questions so that they do not need to be 'told'. Guided discovery is a better and more rewarding way for students to learn.
- A useful guideline is to limit your talking to 30% of class time and no more than ten minutes at a time.

TEACHING TIPS

Pairwork

Pairwork is another opportunity for students to practise their speaking skills. Pairwork activities enable all students to have much more speaking time than if each student had an individual turn at speaking. When students are working in pairs, it also provides teachers with a chance to walk round and listen, and to give advice to students in a more discreet and personal way, rather than in front of the whole class.

If you ask students to work in pairs, they are likely to pair up with their friends or the person they sit nearest. It's a good idea to put students into 'new' pairs from time to time, so they can work with classmates of different abilities and with different approaches.

Certain speaking skills are necessary when working with another person, so it's useful to teach phrases that help students interrupt politely (*Yes, I agree, but … / May I … So you think …*, etc.).

Another idea to put students at their ease when they're speaking is to play some quiet music in the background. This helps students feel less self-conscious.

Personalisation

Students are more likely to want to speak when they are speaking about something they personally know about, are interested in or have experienced. Personalisation is important in learning a second language as it makes language more meaningful and therefore memorable to learners. There are plenty of personalisation opportunities throughout *Optimise*. Where possible, extend and adapt other activities to give students even more speaking opportunities.

Developing writing skills

Students are required to produce a short piece of writing (email, note or postcard). Whatever they write, the basic steps for all writing tasks are the same. This is reinforced by the approach used throughout *Optimise* – ***Plan, Write, Check***.

There are some extra points to keep in mind when helping students with writing tasks:

Before beginning to write, students need to consider the purpose of the text and who the text is for, as both things will affect the tone (*formal or informal*).

During the ***Plan*** phase, students should read the questions and any prompts carefully to make sure they know exactly what they have to include in their writing and/or what questions they have to answer. It is important to encourage students to spend time on this stage as it makes the writing task easier.

Next is the ***Write*** phrase. Students write a first draft as quickly as they can, including all the main points from the brainstorming phase. They should make sure they include all required information and that they fully answer the question.

The final stage is the ***Check*** phase, where students need to look closely at spelling, grammar, punctuation and word choice. They can use the *Optimise* **Checklist** for this.

Classroom management

It can be particularly challenging with larger class groups to keep all students engaged in the lesson.

Here are some ideas to consider:

- Move around and teach the class from different points in the classroom to give the students the feeling of being in the middle of the 'action' rather than an observer. Moving around the class makes the room feel smaller and encourages student involvement. It also means students who are furthest away from the front of the classroom can feel more involved.
- Check understanding regularly, and give students feedback to clarify points they haven't understood.
- Set up some class routines (weekly homework assignments of 20 minutes, class discussions every Friday, etc.). Where possible, involve students in deciding what these routines should be.
- Find ways to link what students have learnt to the exam, so they can clearly see their progress and the fact that they are achieving a common goal.
- Give regular short tests and dictations.
- Change the pace of the lesson from time to time and change delivery methods (speaking, using digital materials, playing video, etc.)
- Start lessons by writing a lesson outline on the board so students know what to expect.
- Give fast finishers something to do (see the unit teaching notes for suggestions) or direct them to the Workbook.

Games

As a useful change of pace, and sometimes to refocus students, games can be an excellent teaching tool. Students generally enjoy games and tend to remember more as a result. Vocabulary games are helpful for practising and reviewing language. Always make the 'rules' clear, and check understanding before playing the game. For example, after explaining what to do, ask the students to explain the game back to you. Or demonstrate the game by playing it yourself with a few students while the others watch.

When planning games you need to consider what your aims and objectives are. Games are particularly useful for reviewing work from the previous lesson, checking what students know before teaching a new language item, practising a new language item you have just presented, warming up at the beginning of the lesson or filling in at the end of a lesson. There are a variety of games suggested throughout the *Optimise* teaching notes.

LISTENING	SPEAKING	LANGUAGE IN USE	WRITING
Identifying factual information **Picture multiple choice**	Talking about yourself **Interview** Talk2Me	Focusing on the language **Multiple-matching dialogue**	Noting down key information **Information transfer**
Listening for words that mean the same **Multiple matching**	Talking about times **Collaborative task** Talk2Me	Thinking about context **Multiple-choice dialogue**	Using your own words **An email**
Predicting what the speaker will say **Multiple choice**	Explaining likes and dislikes **Interview** Talk2Me	Thinking about grammar (conjunctions, prepositions and pronouns) **Open cloze**	Using your vocabulary **A note**
Listening for important information **Gap fill**	Asking someone to repeat **Collaborative task** Talk2Me	Using linking words **Multiple choice**	Punctuation and spelling **A postcard**
Understanding when things happen **Picture multiple choice**	Making comparisons **Interview** Talk2Me	Pronouns **Multiple-choice dialogue**	Making notes: where and when **Information transfer**
Choosing the right answer **Multiple matching**	Giving details **Collaborative task** Talk2Me	Understanding functional language **Multiple-matching dialogue**	Giving your opinion **An online review**
Thinking about the missing information **Gap fill**	Talking about the future **Interview** Talk2Me	Learning word phrases **Multiple-choice cloze**	Understanding similar information **Information transfer**
Listening for important information **Multiple matching**	Asking questions **Collaborative task** Talk2Me	Modal verbs **Multiple-choice cloze**	Writing in an informal style **An email**
Understanding the speakers' questions **Picture multiple choice**	Talking about a topic **Interview** Talk2Me	Identifying key words **Multiple-choice dialogue**	Giving advice and instructions **A note**
Understanding when something happened **Multiple matching**	Giving yourself time to think **Collaborative task** Talk2Me	Giving short answers **Multiple-matching dialogue**	Giving advice **An online post**
Taking notes **Gap fill**	Talking about jobs **Interview** Talk2Me	Understanding the type of word that is missing **Open cloze**	Negative phrases and opposites **Information transfer**
Checking your answers **Multiple choice**	Talking about money **Collaborative task** Talk2Me	Learning vocabulary **Multiple-choice sentences**	Using adjectives **A postcard**

▶ **LISTENING** p 146–147 ▶ **SPEAKING** / ▶ **SPEAKING TEST VIDEO** p 148–149

Student's Resource Centre

- *Talk2Me* videos (flipped classroom)
- Speaking test videos
- *Optimise your grammar* worksheets
- *Optimise your vocabulary* worksheet
- *Say it right* pronunciation worksheets
- Culture and CLIL worksheets
- Class and Workbook audio

1 Time out

UNIT AIMS

Exam preparation in Unit 1:

- find words which mean the same in signs and notices
- identify factual information in a conversation
- talk about yourself in an interview
- focus on the language in a multiple-matching dialogue
- note down key information to transfer

TEACHER'S PRESENTATION KIT

- *Talk2Me* videos
- Speaking test videos
- Class and Workbook audio
- Workbook pages and answer key

UNIT OVERVIEW

Student's Book / Digital Student's Book SB		Workbook / Online Workbook OWB
LESSON / EXAM TASK	EXAM SKILLS / LANGUAGE FOCUS	CONSOLIDATION
Reading **Matching**	Finding words which mean the same Signs and notices	Workbook, pp 4–5, Exercises 1, 2, 3, 4 Unit 1, Reading, Exercises 1, 2, 3, 4
Grammar 1	Present simple, adverbs of frequency, imperatives	Workbook, p 6, Exercises 1, 2, 3 Unit 1, Grammar 1, Exercises 1, 2, 3
Vocabulary	Words connected with *hobbies* Nouns/verbs Phrasal verbs	Workbook, p 7, Exercises 1, 2, 3 Unit 1, Vocabulary, Exercises 1, 2, 3
Listening **Picture multiple choice (short conversations)**	Identifying factual information	Workbook, p 8, Exercises 1, 2 Unit 1, Listening, Exercises 1, 2
Grammar 2	Possessive *'s*, prepositions of time and place	Workbook, p 7, Exercises 1, 2 Unit 1, Grammar 2, Exercises 1, 2
Speaking **Interview**	Talking about yourself	Workbook, pp 8–9, Exercises 1, 2, 3 Unit 1, Speaking, Exercises 1, 2, 3
Language in Use **Multiple-matching dialogue**	Focusing on the language	Workbook, p 9, Exercises 1, 2 Unit 1, Language in Use, Exercises 1, 2
Writing **Information transfer**	Noting down key information	Workbook, p 10, Exercises 1, 2, 3, 4 Unit 1, Writing, Exercises 1, 2, 3, 4
		Workbook, p 11, Progress check and Cumulative progress Progress check and Cumulative progress

Additional material

PRESENTATION KIT	TEACHER'S/STUDENT'S RESOURCE CENTRE RC	TEST GENERATOR
Talk2Me video *My surname is …*	**Unit 1 worksheets:** *Optimise your grammar* (Standard and Higher), *Optimise your vocabulary* (Standard and Higher), *Talk2Me* video, *Say it right* **Units 1–2 worksheets:** CLIL, Culture, Everyday English (TRC only), Grammar communication (TRC only)	Unit Test 1 (Standard and Higher)

READING
Matching | Signs and notices

→ Student's Book, pages 4–5 SB

Lesson aims

- Focus on words which mean the same
- Practise a matching exam task
- Discuss which activity you would like to do

Lead-in

Ask students to look at the unit title ***Time out*** and the photos below it, and elicit what the phrase means (*a break from working or studying to do something else or rest).* Elicit what activities the teenagers in the photos are doing (*abseiling / rock climbing, dancing/gymnastics, mountain biking, tennis and painting*) and then ask students what they think the unit is will be about (*hobbies and free-time activities*).

1 Divide the class into pairs or groups to complete the task. Have students share their ideas with the class, giving reasons why they like or would like to do their chosen hobbies.

2 Explain to students that they need to scan the text and make a note of the hobbies. Have them work in pairs to check answers before checking answers as a class.

Answers
Nine: listening to music, playing games online / video games, reading comics, writing a blog, drawing, photography, skiing, skateboarding, climbing

3 1.01 **Note: The reading text is also available on the audio CD. You may want to have students listen as they read the text.** Have students complete the task individually. Ask them to rewrite any false sentences so that they are true. Then have volunteers share their answers with the class.

Answers
1 T **2** F (Kareem also writes a blog about new video games every month.) **3** T **4** F (Amaya never prints photos – she posts them online.) **5** T **6** F (It's fun trying out new things and meeting people.)

4 Go through the first definition as a class and elicit the correct answer. Then ask students to complete the exercise individually.

Answers
1 camera **2** simple **3** blog **4** comics **5** different **6** hobby
7 member **8** to discuss

EXAM SKILL

Finding words which mean the same

Ask students to read the tips.

- Point out that learning to identify synonyms can help students in all aspects of exams, not just in Reading tasks.
- Explain to students that it is very important to read the task carefully, look at all the material given and then reread the task to make sure that they understand it clearly.
- Point out that underlining important words is particularly useful when they have to match or find specific information (10 am–11 am & 2 pm–3 pm = twice a day; Remember = don't forget; water = drink).

5 Point out the underlined words in the example sentence in Exercise 6 and in the first notice. Have students work in pairs to complete the exercise. Then have pairs share their answers with the class. After the exercise, explain that the important words convey the main message of a sign or notice.

Suggested answers
1 opens again soon **2** open 24 hours **3** cannot do, in rain
4 twice a day, don't forget a drink **5** can't use, room this afternoon

B Turn off, phones, pool area **C** No tennis club, bad weather
D try climbing, open tomorrow 8 am **E** No entrance, photography studio, use other door **F** Art room closed, ten minutes
G Computer room closed today 3 pm–5 pm **H** Skateboarding park, always open

OPTIMISE YOUR EXAM

Matching

Ask students to read the tips.

- Explain to students that in order to get a general understanding of signs and notices they need to identify where each one would be displayed and who would read them.
- Then ask students to mention where they usually see signs and notices and what their purposes are.

▼ Exam task

6 Ask students to complete the exercise. Check in open class and ask students to justify their answers.

Answers
1 F **2** H **3** C **4** A **5** G

Optional extension

Ask students to work in pairs and think of all the signs and notices they can remember seeing in the last 24 hours. Remind them that they can use the signs and notices on page 5 as models, and may only need to change a few words, e.g. at the sports centre: *Sports centre. Open 9 am to 9 pm.* Have students share their partner's information with the class.

THINK | RESEARCH | CULTURE | LEARN | ME

In pairs or groups, students discuss the different activities. Invite them to share their ideas with the class.

Homework OWB

Assign students Reading exercises 1, 2, 3 and 4 on pages 4–5 of their Workbook.

GRAMMAR 1

Present simple, adverbs of frequency, imperatives

→ Student's Book, page 6 SB

Lesson aims

- Focus on the present simple, adverbs of frequency and imperatives
- Describe habits/regular actions and things that are usually/always true
- Express how often something happens
- Give instructions and orders

Lead-in

Write these notices on the board:
Only speak in English.
No mobile phones in class.
Put your hand up if you want to ask a question.

Ask students where they can see notices like these (*in a classroom*). Have students work in pairs to think of more notices they expect to see in a classroom. Then ask students to share the items they chose with the class.

Grammar in context

Ask students where the sentences come from (*the article on page 5*). Elicit what tense the two sentences are in by asking *Are the sentences about the present or the past?* (*present*). Have students complete the exercise and refer them to the *Remember* box if they aren't sure.

Remind students that they can find more information in the Grammar reference, Unit 1, page 150.

Answers
a 2 **b** 1 often

Language note

The present simple is used to talk about habits and routines (*He has his lunch at school.*) and things that are usually or always true (*Her name is Julie.*). Explain the general rule that adverbs of frequency go in the middle position within a sentence (*The park is always open.*), and time expressions go at the end of a sentence (*I ride my bike to school every day.*).

1 Go through the first sentence with the class and then have students complete the exercise individually. Check answers with the class.

Answers
2 goes **3** have **4** plays **5** play **6** go

2 Ask students to complete the exercise. Check answers with the class.

Answers
a do **b** do **c** does **d** have **e** gets **f** play

3 Ask students to match the questions and answers and then ask and answer the questions in pairs. Check answers with the class.

Answers
1 c **2** e **3** d **4** f **5** b **6** a

Optional extension

Write these questions on the board: ***1*** *Who is your best friend?* ***2*** *What do you like to do in the evenings?* ***3*** *What time does school start and finish?* ***4*** *How often do you walk to school?* ***5*** *What do you do at weekends?* In pairs, students ask and answer the questions. Walk round, monitoring students for good use of the present simple.

4 Elicit the rules for the position of adverbs of frequency within a sentence, encouraging students to refer to the *Remember* box if they are unsure. Then ask students to complete the exercise. Check answers in open class.

Answers
1 It's often very cold in the winter.
2 I usually watch TV with my sister.
3 He always goes to bed at 9 o'clock.
4 I never drink cola for breakfast.

Grammar in context

Explain to students that imperative forms are the bare infinitive of the verb and don't change in the third person. Tell students to refer to the information in the *Remember* box and then encourage them to give you more examples of giving instructions and orders.

Remind students that they can find more information in the Grammar reference, Unit 1, page 150.

Language note

- Use the infinitive without *to* for imperatives (*Take off your shoes.*). There is usually no subject.
- Make negatives by placing *don't* in front (*Don't talk in the library.*).

5 Ask students to complete the exercise. Check their answers in open class.

Answers
1 Remember **2** Don't **3** Please open

Mixed ability

Ask less confident students to think of three everyday situations and write an imperative sentence for each situation, e.g. *on a bus – Please give your seat to an older person.* Ask more confident students to write sentences to describe three situations in which people might need to use an imperative sentence, e.g. *Your mum works in a museum and someone is taking photos with flash.* Then, pair less confident students with more confident students. The less confident students read their imperative sentences and their partner has to guess the context. The more confident students read their sentences and their partner has to decide what to say.

6 Have students look at the title of the text and elicit what it refers to (*they go cycling and make films at the same time*). Then ask students to complete the exercise. Have students compare their answers in pairs before you check with the class.

Answers

1 lives **2** ride **3** put **4** Be **5** has **6** hits **7** watch **8** love

Cultural note

Videoing your surroundings and/or yourself while doing adventure sports is extremely popular these days. People use selfie sticks to see their reactions doing things or to get images of themselves and their friends in beautiful places. However, at times people prefer to film themselves hands-free, and in those cases they use small cameras which can be fitted to a helmet to capture the action when the person is doing an activity like climbing, surfing, cycling or running.

Homework

OWB

Assign students Grammar 1 exercises 1, 2 and 3 on page 6 of their Workbook.

VOCABULARY

Topic vocabulary | Word formation | Phrasal verbs

→ Student's Book, page 7 SB

Lesson aims

Understand the correct usage of:

- words connected with hobbies
- nouns and verbs from the same word family
- phrasal verbs

Lead-in

Draw a picture on the board to illustrate a hobby, e.g. a picture of a stick person with a camera and elicit the phrase (*taking photos*). Ask students to think of hobbies they know in English, then take turns to come up to the board and draw these for the other students to guess. For students who are not good at drawing, give them the option of miming doing the hobby instead.

Words connected with *hobbies*

1 1.02 Ask students what activities they recognise. Then play the audio for students to check their answers.

Answers/Audioscript

1 rock climbing **2** cycling **3** skateboarding **4** horse-riding **5** swimming **6** reading **7** playing computer games **8** painting

2 1.03 Ask students to complete the exercise. Play the audio for students to listen and check their answers.

Answers/Audioscript

1 You can take one of these with a camera. *photograph*
2 People who like swimming in the sea often go here. *beach*
3 A thin paper book with photographs, articles, stories, etc. *magazine*
4 When you buy and keep books or magazines, for example, you do this. *collect*
5 A meal when you cook and eat food outdoors. *barbecue*
6 You stay in this when you go camping. *tent*

Refer students to the Vocabulary reference, page 163, for more information on topic vocabulary.

Nouns/verbs

3 1.04 Complete the first two items as an example. Then ask students to complete the exercise. Play the audio for students to listen and check their answers. Check the spelling of all the missing words by writing them on the board.

Answers/Audioscript

object: painting, **person:** *painter*, **verb:** to paint
object: photograph, **person:** *photographer*, **verb:** to photograph / take photographs
object: music, **person:** *musician*, **verb:** to make or play music
object: guitar, **person:** guitarist, **verb:** to *play* the guitar
object: *video game*, **person:** video *gamer*, **verb:** to play video games

4 Ask students to complete the exercise individually. Check their answers in open class.

Answers

1 painting / to paint **2** music **3** plays (the guitar) **4** photographer **5** musician **6** (video) gamer

Extra support

Before students start Exercise 4, ask them to look at sentences 1–6 in pairs and decide if the words they need are objects, people or verbs. Check answers in open class before continuing.

Answers

1 object **2** object **3** verb **4** people **5** people **6** people

SAY IT RIGHT

Word stress

TRC

For the *Say it right* pronunciation activity and instructions, go to the Teacher's Resource Centre.

Refer students to the Vocabulary reference, page 163, for more information on word formation.

Phrasal verbs

5 1.05 Present the idea of the phrasal verb *come in* by leaving the classroom and coming in again. Elicit the meaning from the class (*to enter*). Then have students complete the exercise individually and check their answers in pairs. Play the audio for students to listen and check their answers.

Answers/Audioscript

1 (e) come in: to enter
2 (g) come round: to visit
3 (a) get back: to return after going somewhere
4 (d) get off: to leave a bus or train
5 (f) look after: to take care of someone or something
6 (c) turn off: to stop a machine
7 (b) turn on: to start a machine

Language note

These phrasal verbs belong to three different categories.

Come in, *come round* and *get back* are intransitive phrasal verbs (with no object). *Get off* (*the bus*) and *look after* (*this book*) are both non-separable phrasal verbs, and the object, whether it is a noun or pronoun, will always come after the particle.

Turn off/on could be problematic as the object can go between the verb and the particle (*turn the radio off*) or after the particle (*turn off the radio*) when it is a noun, but has to go between the verb and the particle when it is a pronoun (*turn it off*).

6 Ask students to complete the exercise individually. Have students compare their answers in pairs before you check them in open class.

Answers

1 off **2** in **3** on **4** off **5** round **6** after **7** back

Refer students to the Vocabulary reference, page 163, for more information on phrasal verbs.

Homework OWB

Assign students Vocabulary exercises 1, 2 and 3 on page 7 of their Workbook.

LISTENING

Picture multiple choice (short conversations)

→ Student's Book, page 8 SB

Lesson aims

- Listen to identify factual information
- Practise answering a picture multiple-choice exam task

Lead-in

Write these numbers, dates and times on the board:
£25 4:30 pm $15 Monday 7th 75 31st August €99 1:15 am

Divide the class into pairs or small groups to discuss how to say them. Have a feedback session with the whole class and point out any options students didn't think of. For example, *half past four* or *four thirty*.

1 Have students continue working with their partner or group to complete the exercise. Elicit answers from different students around the class. Ask them to give reasons for their answers and encourage the rest of the class to comment.

Answers

1 **1** all games **2** all are something to read **3** all are times **4** all are food **5** all are days of the week

2 **1** the games are different **2** the magazines and book are not the same **3** different times **4** different meals **5** different days of the week.

EXAM SKILL

Identifying factual information

Ask students to read the tips.

- Explain to students that it is important to answer questions (who, where, when, etc.) when making notes in order to create a good description of what they see.
- Tell students that picture multiple-choice exercises with short conversations can test a lot of different areas in a single exercise. In this particular exam task, students are being tested on prepositions of place, types of reading material, times, foods and days of the week. Remind them that, as each section is independent, they shouldn't panic if they don't understand one section well – they might have problems with the prepositions of place but understand the information about days of the week in the first recording.
- Encourage students to brainstorm all the prepositions they can think of so that they are aware of all the possibilities before they listen.

2 Have students look at the pictures and elicit the differences. Then have them complete the exercise. Check answers with the class.

Answers

1 C **2** B **3** A

3 1.06 Before students listen, have them predict possible words and phrases to complete the conversation. Then play the audio for students to check their predictions. Elicit which students' predictions were correct and incorrect. Ask the students to share their predictions with the class.

Answers

1 near **2** in the middle **3** under

OPTIMISE YOUR **EXAM**

Picture multiple choice

Ask students to read the tips.

- Remind students that, as well as underlining important words, they should also look carefully at the pictures and try to predict words/phrases they expect to hear in the recording.
- Explain to students that it is common to hear words that sound the same but have a different meaning. Therefore, it is important to listen specifically for words/phrases which mean the same as the words they predicted or underlined.

Extra support

Before students complete the exam task, split the class into five groups. Assign each group one of the questions in Exercise 4 and ask them to prepare a set of notes to match the pictures, using the notes in Exercise 2 as a model. Regroup students into new groups and have them share their notes and check if the others in their new groups can match them to the correct pictures.

▼ Exam task

4 1.07 Have students put their notes away before listening. Then play the track for students to complete the exercise.

5 1.07 Tell students to read through the questions one more time before you play the track again. Tell them to listen to any questions they were not sure about. After the second listening, elicit answers from students around the class.

Answers

1 A **2** C **3** B **4** C **5** A

Optional extension 1.07

Play the track again and ask students to call out *Stop!* when they hear the phrases that confirm the answers in Exercise 4. Repeat the specific phrases as a dictation for students to write them down and see exactly how the phrases in the recording relate to the questions.

Answers

1 The adventure game, please. **2** … my book! It's great. **3** It always begins at 9.30. **4** What about fish and chips? … OK. **5** I have art on Wednesday, yes.

Homework

Assign students Listening exercises 1 and 2 on page 8 of their Workbook.

OWB

GRAMMAR 2

Possessive 's, prepositions of time and place

→ Student's Book, page 9 SB

Lesson aims

- Distinguish possessive *'s* from the verb *to be*
- Identify the use of prepositions of time and place
- Practise using possessive *'s* and prepositions of time and place

Lead-in

Ask each student in the class to give you an item from their desk, bag or pocket, e.g. a pen or a notebook. Take each item, show it clearly to the class and say whose it is, e.g. *This is John's pen.* Place the items on your desk. Then test students' knowledge by holding up an item and asking *Whose is this?* Elicit a sentence, e.g. *That is John's pen.* before returning each item to its owner. Write the sentence on the board, without a contraction for *to be*, and circle the *'s* in the sentence. Tell students that the apostrophe plus *s* shows possession.

Grammar in context

Confusion with the use of *s* and *'s* at the end of words is common, even amongst native speakers (e.g. *it's* and *its*), so it is natural English language students will have problems too. Clarify that the possessive *'s* takes the place of the structure *the … of …* which is used in other languages. Write *the tent of your cousin* on the board and elicit from students how this phrase changes to include the possessive *'s* (*your cousin's tent*).

Also clarify that *'s* is also used as as a contraction to indicate missing letters for the third person singular forms of the verbs to be and *to have* (*got*), e.g. *He's my brother.* = *He is my brother. She has got a car.* = *She's got a car.*

Remind students that they can find more information in the Grammar reference, Unit 1, page 151.

Answer

statement b

1 Go through the first sentence with the class before asking students to complete the exercise. Have students compare their answers in pairs before you check answers with the whole class.

Answers

1 Anna's book **2** boys' bags **3** my parents' **4** children's desks

2 Ask students if the apostrophe in the first sentence represents a contraction or possession (*possession*). Have students complete the exercise in pairs. Then elicit answers with the class.

Answers

1 P **2** B **3** P **4** B

Optional extension

Revise family vocabulary by drawing a simple family tree on the board using stick figures and writing names under each person. Use the family tree to elicit different sentences about the family, e.g. *Francisco is Alicia's brother.* Check that students use the possessive *'s* correctly in the sentences.

Grammar in context

Ask students what the words in bold are (*prepositions*) and then have them complete the task. Refer them to the information in the *Remember* box if they aren't sure. Then check their answers.

Remind students that they can find more information in the Grammar reference, Unit 1, page 151.

Answers

a in, near, under **b** at, on

3 Ask students to complete the exercise. Have students check their answers with a partner before you check with the whole class.

Answers

1 last week **2** to, on **3** in **4** In **5** in, today **6** on

4 Ask students to complete the exercise. Have students compare answers in pairs before you check their answers in open class.

Answers

1 on **2** in **3** near **4** next **5** At **6** in front

Fast finishers

Have fast finishers extend the table in the *Remember* box with additional items to make the lists more complete, e.g. *at lunchtime, in winter,* etc. After you check the answers to Exercise 4, ask students to share the words/phrases they thought of.

Homework OWB

Assign students Grammar 2 exercises 1 and 2 on page 7 of their Workbook.

Assign students the Flipped classroom tasks on page 10 of their Student's Book if you'd like them to prepare for the next lesson. To complete this task, students need to watch the *Talk2Me* video which can be found on the Resource Centre.

SPEAKING
Interview

→ Student's Book, page 10 SB

Lesson aims

- Focus on talking about yourself
- Practise answering personal questions in an interview

The *Talk2Me* video in this unit focuses on free time, hobbies and activities. The people in the video talk about a dance competition. They discuss their timetables and when they can arrange to practise for the competition.

Students answer some comprehension questions and then listen for key phrases in the video.

The video can be used in one of two ways:

Flipped classroom

Flipped classroom option

Using this approach, students watch the video and complete the exercises for homework. This prepares students for the speaking lesson by introducing them to the topic and the key phrases to use in the exam task. Teachers who use this method will find they have more class time to spend on activating the target language and developing fluency for the final task.

***Talk2Me* worksheet**

Ask students to also complete the *Talk2Me* worksheet from the Resource Centre for more detailed comprehension exercises and more practice of the key phrases.

Classroom option

1 Ask students to spend a minute or two reading the questions. Play the *Talk2Me* video for students to complete the exercise. Play the video again, if necessary, before checking their answers.

2 Play the *Talk2Me* video again, so students underline the phrases in the *Phrase expert* box. Pause the video from time to time if necessary. Check answers in open class.

***Talk2Me* worksheet**

Ask students to complete the *Talk2Me* worksheet on the Resource Centre for more detailed comprehension exercises and more practice of the key phrases.

Answers

The transcript and answer key for the *Talk2Me* video exercises and Worksheet can be found on the Teacher's Resource Centre.

Lead-in

Show students a photo of you and your family. Describe when and where it was taken, who the people are and a little about them. Use the text in Exercise 4, on Student's Book page 9 as a model and use possessive *'s* and prepositions where appropriate.

3 1.08 Play the track for students to listen and repeat. Then write some letters at random on the board and elicit their names. In pairs, students ask and answer the three questions.

EXAM SKILL

Talking about yourself

Ask students to read the tips.

- Encourage students to practise spelling out their basic personal information such as their name, surname and address. Point out that regular practice with different words will help them to spell out fluently during a speaking exam.
- Remind students that it is really important to be proactive rather than reactive as language learners. Students should find out the vocabulary they need to talk about things in 'their world' if this is not covered in class.
- Elicit ways students can practise in their free time and encourage them to be autonomous.

4 1.09 Before you play the track, ask students what they are going to listen to. Remind them to identify factual information while they are listening. After students complete the exercise, ask them to compare their answers in pairs before you check with the whole class.

Answers

Surname: Santos
Hobbies: swimming and skateboarding
Evenings: do homework, have dinner / a meal with family, go to bed at 9 pm
Weekend: go to the beach, swim and play with friends
Holidays: visit grandparents (in countryside)

Extra support

Give students the first word of each question to guide them in Exercise 5 (*1 What, 2 How, 3 Do, 4 What, 5 What, 6 How).*

5 1.09 Ask students what questions the examiner asks before playing the track again. Have students write down the questions they remember. Then have them listen and check or complete their answers.

Answers

1 What's your name? **2** How do you spell your surname? **3** Do you have any hobbies? **4** What do you usually do in the evenings? **5** What do you like doing at the weekends? **6** How do you usually spend your holidays?

6 Ask students if they can remember the words or phrase the student used. If necessary, play the phrase again for students to check their ideas.

Answer

Sorry, can you say that again, please?

OPTIMISE YOUR EXAM

Interview

Ask students to read the tips.

- Remind students that it is extremely important that they ask the examiner to repeat the question if they haven't understood. Explain that no marks will be deducted as long as a candidate uses an appropriate phrase to do this. Also explain that if candidates answer a different question to the one they are asked, the examiners will assume they don't understand the language being used and they will lose marks accordingly.
- Remind students that Speaking exams are principally designed to test their ability to communicate, and adding some extra information, even if they make a few mistakes, gives a very positive impression.

Exam task

7 Divide the class into pairs to complete the exercise. Walk round the class, monitoring students for good use of language and errors to go over at the end of the activity.

Write any errors on the board and go through them with students, eliciting corrections from them where possible. After the class feedback, students could then repeat this activity with another partner, to try to improve their performance.

Optional extension

Have students work in pairs or groups to brainstorm other personal questions they could be asked in Speaking exams, e.g. *How old are you? Where do you live? Do you like studying English? Why? / Why not?* Have pairs practise asking and answering these questions.

Homework OWB

Assign students Speaking exercises 1, 2 and 3 on pages 8–9 of their Workbook.

LANGUAGE IN USE
Multiple-matching dialogue

→ Student's Book, page 11 SB

Lesson aims

- Focus on language in exam tasks
- Practise a multiple-matching dialogue exam task
- Discuss places for young people to do activities

Lead-in

Write this notice on the board:

The s_ _ _ _ _ _ _ _ _ _ _ club

1 *Come to the p_ _ _. Open all day, every day!*

2 *Be c_ _ _ _ _! Always wear a h_ _ _ _ _.*

3 *Don't forget your b_ _ _ _!*

Then have students work in pairs and decide what words complete the gaps. Invite volunteers to come to the board and complete the notice.

Answers
skateboarding **1** park **2** careful, helmet **3** board

1 Focus students' attention on the text and ask them where they would see a similar text. Then have them answer the questions in pairs.

Answers
1 Make new friends, try new activities, climb trees, ride your bike, build dens, join an art class, learn nature photography, cook wild food, go to barbecues and mini music festivals, go camping
2 No, only children aged 11 and over. **3** It's free but special classes cost £10. **4** Students' own answers

EXAM SKILL

Focusing on the language

Ask students to read the tips.

- Remind students that before doing Language in Use exam tasks, it is important to read the text carefully and check they have understood the language.
- Tell students that there will always be enough information to guide them to the correct answer if they read carefully.
- Stress the importance of using the grammar and vocabulary surrounding missing items to confirm that the answers they have chosen are correct.

2 Ask students to complete the exercise. Check answers as a class and then have volunteers practise the conversation in front of the class.

Answers
a 4 **b** 6 **c** 2 **d** 8 **e** 3 **f** 1 **g** 7 **h** 5

3 Ask students to complete the exercise. Students compare in pairs before you check in open class.

Suggested answers
Students should underline:
a) Between, close **b)** study, school **c)** tickets, music festival
e) first, camp **g)** student discount **h)** Right, student

OPTIMISE YOUR EXAM

Multiple-matching dialogue

Ask students to read the tips.

- Encourage students to read through the dialogue and the answer options quickly at first to get the general meaning.
- Point out that it is a good idea to cross out or make a mark next to each answer that they use, to make it clearer to see the remaining options.

Exam task

4 Ask students to complete the exercise. Check their answers.

Answers
1 G **2** A **3** H **4** C **5** D

Fast finishers

Have students underline the words that helped them complete the conversation in the same way they did in Exercise 3. As you check the answers to Exercise 4, ask individual students to explain the connections between sentences to the class.

Suggested answers
Students should underline:
A eleven **C** Really, go too **D** brother, lets, borrow his
E Oh, hi **H** When do they meet

THINK | RESEARCH | **CULTURE** | LEARN | ME

Divide the class into groups to discuss the question. Open out the discussion to a class debate if there is time.

Homework OWB
Assign students Language in Use exercises 1 and 2 on page 9 of their Workbook.

WRITING
Information transfer

→ Student's Book, pages 12–13 SB

Lesson aims

- Focus on identifying and noting down key information
- Complete a form
- Focus on transferring information

Lead-in

Have students practise giving each other personal information to register for an after-school club. Give them these prompts and elicit the questions they will need:

Activity booking form: *name? surname? spell? age? from? activity?*

Answers
What's your name? What's your surname? How do you spell that? How old are you? Where do you come from? What activity/ activities do you like?

Have students ask and answer the questions in pairs. Explain that they can can use their imagination.

1 Have students work in different pairs or groups to ask and answer the questions. Elicit answers from different students around the class.

Answers
Students' own answers

Mixed ability

Pair stronger students with less confident students for exercises 2–4. This will allow stronger students to help less confident students as necessary and ensures stronger students do not race ahead.

2 After students complete the exercise, ask them what they think the relationship between the three texts is (*they are part of the process of applying for a course*). Check their answers.

Answers
A poster **B** email **C** booking form

EXAM SKILL

Noting down key information

Ask students to read the tips.

- Tell students that for exams it is important to be able to identify key information quickly when reading. Also explain that they need to make sure they know what things refer to, e.g. if they see a number, is it an age, a time, a quantity or something else?
- Remind students that they should look for words that mean the same wherever possible. They practised this technique in the Reading lesson on pages 4–5.

3 Ask students to look at the poster and the email and complete the exercise.

Answers
Poster: Tuesday, Thursday, Wednesday, Monday; 3.30–4.30, 4.30–5.30 pm, 5.30–6.30 pm **Email:** Monday, Tuesday; 4 pm; 14

4 Draw students' attention to the example answer. Ask them to tell you which words in the email tell them his age (Paulo says *I'm almost 14 years old* in the email, so that means he is 13 at the moment). Have students complete the exercise in pairs. Check the answers as a class.

Answers
2 The activity is correct, but there is a spelling mistake. It should be *basketball.* **3** The level is wrong. He is a beginner because he wants to start a new hobby. **4** The day is wrong. The activity is on Tuesday. **5** The starting time is wrong. The course starts at 4.30 pm.

OPTIMISE YOUR EXAM

Information transfer

Ask students to read the tips.

- Explain to students that they should read the texts quickly first to get a general idea of the topic before starting to look at the details. Remind them that for some questions they may need to combine information from the two texts, as they saw in exercises 3 and 4.
- Tell students to mark the links between the texts to be sure of their answers. Remind them that it is only possible to complete this task type correctly if they really concentrate on the details and read very carefully.

Exam task

5 Ask students to complete the exercise in pairs or groups. Check their answers.

Answers
1 5 **2** the horse-riding course

6 Plan Have students work in pairs to complete the exercise. Encourage students to share what they ticked on the list and give reasons for their answers.

Answers
Students should tick:
1, 2, 3

7 Write Have students complete the information on the booking form individually. Remind them that spelling and correct use of capital letters are both important in writing exams. Check their answers as a class.

Answers
1 14 **2** Modern dance **3** Advanced **4** Wednesday **5** 3.30 pm

8 Check Have students complete the checklist. Explain that they should plan to leave a few minutes at the end of the exam for this. Tell them that they will be provided with a specific checklist in each writing lesson in the book in order to improve different writing skills.

Extra writing

9 Ask students to read the posters in Exercise 2 again and choose a course. Remind them to make a plan. Then tell students to answer the questions to help them plan their email.

Answers
1 After-school Activities Plus **2** Informal **3** Students' own answers **4** Students' own answers

Optional extension

For a slightly longer writing task, and for students to see other text types, refer them to one of the six tasks in the Writing reference (SB p169). Each one includes an annotated sample text and related writing task to challenge your students a little more.

Homework OWB

Assign students Writing exercises 1, 2, 3 and 4 on page 10 of their Workbook and Progress check 1 on page 11.

2 That's entertainment!

UNIT AIMS

Exam preparation in Unit 2:

- understand important words in a magazine article
- listen for words that mean the same in a conversation
- talk about times in a collaborative task
- think about context in a multiple-choice dialogue
- use your own words in an email

TEACHER'S PRESENTATION KIT

- *Talk2Me* videos
- Speaking test videos
- Class and Workbook audio
- Workbook pages and answer key

UNIT OVERVIEW

Student's Book / Digital Student's Book SB		Workbook / Online Workbook OWB
LESSON / EXAM TASK	EXAM SKILLS / LANGUAGE FOCUS	CONSOLIDATION
Reading **Right/Wrong/Doesn't say**	Understanding important words A magazine article	Workbook, pp 12–13, Exercises 1, 2, 3, 4 Unit 2, Reading, Exercises 1, 2, 3, 4
Grammar 1	Present simple and present continuous	Workbook, p 14, Exercises 1, 2 Unit 2, Grammar 1, Exercises 1, 2
Vocabulary	Words connected with *entertainment* Words + prepositions Collocations with nouns	Workbook, p 14, Exercises 1, 2, 3 Unit 2, Vocabulary, Exercises 1, 2, 3
Listening **Multiple matching**	Listening for words that mean the same	Workbook, p 16, Exercises 1, 2, 3 Unit 2, Listening, Exercises 1, 2, 3
Grammar 2	Present continuous for future use	Workbook, p 15, Exercises 1, 2 Unit 2, Grammar 2, Exercises 1, 2
Speaking **Collaborative task**	Talking about times	Workbook, pp 16–17, Exercises 1, 2 Unit 2, Speaking, Exercises 1, 2
Language in Use **Multiple-choice dialogue**	Thinking about context	Workbook, p 17, Exercises 1, 2, 3 Unit 2, Language in Use, Exercises 1, 2, 3
Writing **An email**	Using your own words	Workbook, p 18, Exercises 1, 2, 3, 4 Unit 2, Writing, Exercises 1, 2, 3, 4
Progress check	Check language progress for Units 1 and 2	Workbook, p 19, Progress check and Cumulative progress Progress check and Cumulative progress

Additional material

PRESENTATION KIT	TEACHER'S / STUDENT'S RESOURCE CENTRE RC	TEST GENERATOR
Talk2Me video *It starts at …*	**Unit 2 worksheets:** *Optimise your grammar* (Standard and Higher), *Optimise your vocabulary* (Standard and Higher), *Talk2Me* video, *Say it right* **Units 1–2 worksheets:** CLIL, Culture, Everyday English (TRC only), Grammar communication (TRC only)	Unit Test 2 (Standard and Higher)

READING
Right/Wrong/Doesn't say | A magazine article

→ Student's Book, pages 14–15

SB

Lesson aims

- Focus on understanding important words
- Practise a Right/Wrong/Doesn't say exam task
- Discuss the most popular forms of entertainment

Lead-in

Ask students to look at the unit title ***That's entertainment!*** and elicit what they think the theme of the unit will be (*different types of entertainment*). Ask students for a couple of examples of forms of entertainment, e.g. the cinema, the theatre, etc.

Draw students' attention to the photos in the article / on page 15 and elicit what form of entertainment they think the magazine article is about (*the world of video gaming*).

1 Divide the class into pairs or groups to discuss the questions. Then have students share their ideas with the class. Encourage them to give reasons for their answers.

2 Ask students to complete the exercise individually. Check the answer as a class and have students say what clues they used to find the correct answer.

Answers

Florian is a German teenager who helps Brandon with gaming products.

EXAM SKILL

Understanding important words

Ask students to read the tips.

- Tell students they are going to practise the technique of scanning to find key words in questions again. Students should remember the words they need to underline are verbs, nouns, adjectives or adverbs.
- Remind students not to get distracted if there are new words. If they think there is an important word that they don't understand, they should look at the word before and after it and try to work out the meaning from the context.

OPTIMISE YOUR EXAM

Right/Wrong/Doesn't say

Ask students to read the tips.

- Explain to students that they should do the following: (1) read the text quickly for gist, (2) read the sentences carefully and underline the important information, (3) then go back to the beginning of the text and read the relevant sections more carefully to decide if the answers are right or wrong.
- Clarify that if a topic is mentioned in a text but there is not enough evidence to say whether a sentence is *right* or *wrong*, then the answer is *doesn't say*.

3 Have students complete the exercise individually. Remind them to underline key words in the text as they read it. When checking answers, have students supply evidence for their answers.

Answers

1 right (*more young people are playing video games / The world of video gaming entertainment is growing quickly.*)
2 doesn't say (The text talks about some people earning money while they are playing, but it doesn't mention the price of video games.)
3 wrong (*Video gaming is … not quite as popular as listening to music and watching TV*)

▼ Exam task

4 1.10 **Note: The reading text is also available on the audio CD. You may want to have students listen and read the text before doing the exam task.**

Before students complete the exercise, go through the instructions and the example sentence as a class. Remind them to underline key words in the text as they read. After the students have finished the exercise, have them compare their answers in pairs before checking with the class. Encourage students to justify their answers with evidence from the text.

Answers

1 A (*There are places like the e-sports* Gfinity Arena *in London, where hundreds of people go to play online games with other fans around the world.*)
2 A (*Brandon earned £10,000 from his business before he was 16!*)
3 C (The text doesn't say where he lives.)
4 A (*Now Brandon works on his business for a few hours every night, when he isn't doing his homework.*)
5 B (*Brandon still designs attractive worlds, but now people buy them and use them in adverts.*)
6 C (The text says Brandon *lives with his parents so he doesn't need to spend money on an office*, but it doesn't say he gives all his money to his parents.)
7 B (*Brandon works with a German teenager called Florian …*)

Mixed ability

Ask stronger students to cover Exercise 5 and look at the highlighted words in the text and to try to work out what they mean purely from the context. Have less confident students complete the task as it appears in the Student's Book. Then pair stronger students with weaker students and have them share their ideas. Give students this model to follow: *I think* online *means* on the internet. *Do you agree?*

5 Remind students to use the skills they have learnt to guess the meaning of vocabulary through context before completing the exercise. Have students check their answers with a partner.

Answers

1 alone **2** few **3** popular **4** fan **5** attractive **6** ads **7** competitions **8** online

THINK | RESEARCH | **CULTURE** | LEARN | ME

Have students brainstorm all the types of entertainment they can think of then discuss them in pairs.

Cultural note

Brandon Relph lives with his family in Eastbourne, UK. Around the age of ten, he bought a copy of *Minecraft* and was inspired by the virtual worlds he was able to create. In 2014, he founded *goCreative*, which helps companies advertise their products through virtual worlds of *Minecraft*. He is now the CEO of his own rapidly-growing business. He has also been successful academically and hopes one day to study at either Oxford or Cambridge.

Minecraft is a hugely successful computer game in which players create worlds out of 3-D cubes. It has won numerous awards for innovation and was purchased by Microsoft in 2014 for £1.5 billion.

Homework

OWB

Assign students Reading exercises 1, 2, 3 and 4 on pages 12–13 of their Workbook.

GRAMMAR 1
Present simple and present continuous

→ Student's Book, page 16 SB

Lesson aims

- Understand the correct usage of the present simple and present continuous
- Practise talking about habits, routines, facts, permanent situations and actions in progress
- Discuss favourite types of entertainment

Lead-in

Describe a picture from the Student's Book using the present simple and present continuous, e.g. page 53: *This is a picture of three children working together, probably in school or in a class somewhere else. They are working on some kind of electronic equipment and they are all wearing goggles to protect their eyes. They look very interested in their activity.* Tell students to listen without taking notes. When you have finished the description, say *Go!* and encourage the students to look through the book and find the picture you were describing.

Grammar in context

Ask students to look back at the text to find the sentences and discuss the questions in pairs. Remind students to refer to the information in the *Remember* box if they aren't sure. Check their answers in open class.

Remind students that they can find more information in the Grammar reference, Unit 2, page 151.

Answers

a 2 **b** 3 **c** 1

Language note

Make a list of words and phrases we commonly use with the two tenses for students, e.g. present simple – *always, sometimes, every day/month, once a day/week*; present continuous – *at the moment, now, right now, this week, today.*

1 Ask students to complete the exercise. Check their answers.

Answers

1 'm learning **2** goes **3** plays **4** 're doing **5** usually spend **6** 's wearing **7** never read **8** doesn't like

2 Before students complete the exercise, revise some short forms if necessary (*I'm, you're, he's, she's, we're, they're, isn't, aren't*). Remind students to use them where possible. Then have students complete the exercise in pairs and check answers with the class.

Answers

1 Dad reads an online newspaper every week.
2 I'm playing a video game at the moment. / At the moment, I'm playing a video game.
3 Mum isn't working this week.
4 Chris comes from Slovenia and speaks three languages.
5 I usually like his books, but I'm not enjoying this one.
6 I like fruit, but I don't eat it every day.

Fast finishers

Have fast finishers look at the article on page 15 again and find more examples of the present simple and the present continuous. Have them classify each sentence according to its function: *habit, routine, fact, actions in progress*, etc.

SAY IT RIGHT

TRC

Pronunciation of *-ing*

For the *Say it right* pronunciation activity and instructions, go to the Teacher's Resource Centre.

3 Ask students to look at the photo and say what the people are doing (*They are watching a musical show.*) and where they are (*They are in a theatre.*) Ask students to complete the exercise. Then have students compare in pairs before checking their answers with the class.

Answers

1 loves **2** spends **3** plays **4** goes **5** 's dancing **6** prefers **7** 's enjoying **8** is doing **9** 's smiling **10** isn't watching **11** 's sleeping

THINK | RESEARCH | CULTURE | LEARN | **ME**

Ask students to talk about their favourite types of entertainment in pairs. Elicit interesting or unusual answers from students around the class.

Homework

OWB

Assign students Grammar 1 exercises 1 and 2 on page 14 of their Workbook.

VOCABULARY
Topic vocabulary | Word patterns | Collocations

→ Student's Book, page 17 SB

Lesson aims
Understand the correct usage of:
- words connected with entertainment
- verb + preposition word patterns
- noun + noun collocations

Lead-in

Play the game ***Stop*** with the class. Explain that you will start saying the alphabet and students have to say the word 'Stop'. Repeat the last letter and have students say a form of entertainment beginning with that letter. For example, *m – musicals*, *c – concerts*. Have the student who answers first say the alphabet next. Continue the same process so that other students can participate.

Words connected with *entertainment*

1 1.11 Have students describe what they see in the pictures. Then have them complete the exercise individually. Play the audio for students to listen and check their answers. Then elicit which of the activities students like to do.

Answers/Audioscript

1 (C) *see an exhibition of famous paintings – at an art gallery*
2 (D) *see a play – at a theatre* **3** (A) *learn about a period in history – at a museum* **4** (F) *listen to a famous classical singer – at an opera house*
5 (E) *download a game – at a gaming café* **6** (B) *see a well-known band – at a concert hall*

2 Have students complete the exercise individually. Then they compare their answers in pairs before you check them in open class.

Answers

1 art gallery **2** concert hall **3** opera house **4** gaming café
5 museum **6** theatre

Fast finishers

Ask fast finishers to write alternative sentences for the words in Exercise 1. Then encourage volunteers to read their sentences out loud after you check the answers to Exercise 2.

Refer students to the Vocabulary reference, page 163, for more information on topic vocabulary.

Words + prepositions

3 1.12 Ask students to complete the exercise. Play the audio for students to listen and check their answers.

Answers/Audioscript

1 On Friday nights I stay *in* and listen *to* music. Every Saturday evening I go *out* with my friends.

2 We like looking *at* the new fashions. Sometimes we try *on* different clothes.

3 I really like the theatre. I go to an after-school drama club. I want to act *in* a play.

4 I love street dancing. Most kids I know prefer to play video games, but they thought it was cool when I danced *with* my club in a competition. And we won!

Optional extension

Have students play ***Preposition tennis*** in groups of three. Tell two students to work together with their books closed (Students A and B) and tell the third student (Student C) to act as the judge. Explain that Student A says a verb, e.g. *go,* and Student B has to say the corresponding preposition *out* and then a new verb, e.g. *stay*. Student A has to respond with the preposition *in* and so on. Student C monitors and checks they are using the correct prepositions and maintaining a regular rhythm. Monitor the groups in case Student C is unsure about the correct answer. If one student pauses for too long or repeats a verb, the other student wins a point. Have students change roles so they all take turns as judge.

Refer students to the Vocabulary reference, page 163, for more information on word patterns.

Collocations with nouns

4 1.13 Ask students to complete the exercise. Play the audio for students to listen and check their answers.

Answers/Audioscript

1 Chess is a well-known board *game*. I love playing it.

2 Did you see the newspaper *article*? There are some good photographs in it.

3 I'm watching a great TV *programme* about the history of rock music.

4 I'm getting a new MP3 *player* soon – I want one I can record films on too.

5 I'm going to watch a film on the big new 3-D cinema *screen* in town.

Refer students to the Vocabulary reference, page 163, for more information on collocations.

Homework OWB

Assign students Vocabulary exercises 1, 2 and 3 on page 14 of their Workbook.

LISTENING
Multiple matching

→ Student's Book, page 18 SB

Lesson aims
- Listen for words with the same meaning
- Practise a multiple-matching exam task
- Discuss how the internet is changing entertainment

Lead-in

Ask students to brainstorm different types of TV programmes in pairs. Encourage them to give an example of a programme for each type, e.g. *reality show – Big Brother, cartoon – The Simpsons*. Then have students look at the photo on page 18 and see which types of TV programmes they can identify. Compare the programmes in the book with the ones students thought of.

1 Divide the class into pairs or groups to answer the questions. Elicit answers from different students around the class, encouraging them to give reasons for their answers.

EXAM SKILL

Listening for words that mean the same

Ask students to read the tips.

- Remind students of the work they did on finding words that mean the same in Unit 1 and tell them that they are going to continue to develop that technique here.
- Tell students that in Listening exams, they will always have time to read the questions before they hear the audio. Stress the importance of using this preparation time to read the questions carefully and think of vocabulary they would expect to hear in the recording.

2 After students complete the exercise, have volunteers come to the front of the class and write their ideas on the board. Go through students' answers and explain that more than one answer is possible.

3 Have students complete the exercise individually and then compare their answers with a partner.

Answers

1 c **2** a **3** b

4 Have students continue working in pairs to complete the exercise. Check answers with the class.

Answers

1 not very interesting = a bit boring, hard = difficult **2** nice = pleasant, a bit slow = not very fast **3** not excellent = terrible, unusual = strange

OPTIMISE YOUR EXAM

Multiple matching

Ask students to read the tips.

- Remind students that it is unlikely they will hear the exact words (A–H) given in the exam task and that if they do, they should be suspicious as the word may have been included to distract them. Stress the importance of understanding the speaker's general opinion or feeling about each item and that they should use words that mean the same to help them do this.
- After listening the first time, students should have an idea of which opinions/feelings match which TV watching habits. The second time they listen they should focus very carefully on the specific words or phrases that confirm their ideas.

5 Ask students to complete the exercise by taking notes. Encourage them to compare their ideas with a partner before checking ideas with the class.

Suggested answers

A clever – intelligent **B** excellent – great **C** exciting – fantastic **D** funny – crazy **E** terrible – awful **F** noisy – loud **G** unhappy – sad **H** interesting – original

Mixed ability

Ask stronger students to turn their backs to the board and complete the exercise. Write *awful, crazy, fantastic, great, intelligent, loud, sad, pretty* on the board for weaker students to match to the opinions/feelings. When both groups have finished, wipe the board and pair stronger students with weaker students. Ask the stronger students to guess the words their partner has. Have pairs report their answers back to the class.

Exam task

6 1.14 Before playing the audio, tell students that they are going to listen to a conversation between two friends. Play the track for students to complete the exercise. Don't check answers at this stage as students will check their answers in Exercise 7.

Extra support

If students are struggling, guide them to the words/phrases that mean the same. Write these extracts on the board and tell students to listen for them very carefully.

They're exciting.

a good … channel

They're really bad.

… that make me laugh

They make me feel sad.

7 1.14 Play the track again for students to check if their answers are correct or change them for new ones. Elicit answers from students around the class.

Answers

1 D **2** C **3** G **4** B **5** E

THINK | RESEARCH | CULTURE | LEARN | ME

Ask students how often they use the internet for entertainment purposes. Then divide the class into pairs or groups to discuss the questions. Extend to a class discussion and ask students to justify their ideas where possible.

Homework

OWB

Assign students Listening exercises 1, 2 and 3 on page 16 of their Workbook.

GRAMMAR 2
Present continuous for future use

→ Student's Book, page 19 SB

Lesson aims

- Understand how to use the present continuous to talk about the future
- Practise talking about future plans and arrangements

Lead-in

Tell students about your present and future actions using the present continuous, e.g. *I'm studying Spanish in my free time. Next weekend, a Spanish friend is coming to stay.* Some actions should be actions happening now or temporary/changing situations and some should use the present continuous for future plans/arrangements. Then elicit which actions refer to the present and which refer to the future.

Grammar in context

Ask students to read the sentences and complete the task individually. Remind students to refer to the information in the *Remember* box if they aren't sure. Check answers with the class. Elicit more examples of future time expressions, e.g. *next week, tomorrow night,* etc.

Remind students that they can find more information in the Grammar reference, Unit 2, page 152.

Answers
a 1 **b** 2

Language note

Explain that the present continuous is used for the future when we have made firm plans or arrangements, often involving other people, so we are very confident that they are going to happen.

Check the present continuous *yes/no* question form and short answer. Write *Is he visiting his grandparents on Saturday?* and ask students to identify the verbs. Then elicit the short answer: *Yes, he is. / No, he isn't.*

1 Go through the first set of questions with the class. Ask students to complete the exercise. Check their answers in open class.

Answers
2 Are, cooking, are you cooking **3** Are, doing, are you doing
4 Are, meeting, are you meeting **5** Are, studying, are you studying
6 are you playing, are you playing

2 Have students practise asking and answering the questions in pairs or groups. Walk round, monitoring students for good use of language and errors to go over at the end of the activity. Invite volunteers to practise the dialogues in front of the class.

3 Have students complete the exercise individually. Then have them compare their answers in pairs before checking answers with the class.

Answers
A 1 follow **2** 'm/am learning **3** 'm/am starting **4** have **5** 're/are going **6** leaves
B 1 'm/am listening **2** 'm/am making **3** are starting **4** 're/are going **5** 'm/am spending **6** 'm/am getting
C 1 are playing **2** live **3** build **4** play **5** 're/are meeting **6** are designing

Cultural note

Carcassonne is a medieval French town near Toulouse, famous for its city walls and fortifications. It was listed as a World Heritage Site in 1997. It is also famous for inspiring the successful board game.

Homework OWB

Assign students Grammar 2 exercises 1 and 2 on page 15 of their Workbook.

Assign students the Flipped classroom tasks on page 20 of their Student's Book if you'd like them to prepare for the next lesson. To complete this task, students need to watch the *Talk2Me* video which can be found on the Resource Centre.

SPEAKING
Collaborative task

→ Student's Book, page 20 SB

Lesson aims

- Focus on talking about times
- Practise using useful phrases in a collaborative exam task

The *Talk2Me* video in this unit focuses on entertainment. The people in the video talk about entertainment. They discuss going to the cinema, the times of the films, and which films they would like to see and why.

Students answer some comprehension questions and then listen for key phrases in the video.

The video can be used in one of two ways:

Flipped classroom

Flipped classroom option

Using this approach, students watch the video and complete the exercises for homework. This prepares students for the speaking lesson by introducing them to the topic and the key phrases to use in the exam task. Teachers who use this method will find they have more class time to spend on activating the target language and developing fluency for the final task.

***Talk2Me* worksheet**

Ask students to complete the *Talk2Me* worksheet on the Resource Centre for more detailed comprehension exercises and more practice of the key phrases.

Classroom option

1 Ask students to spend a minute or two reading the questions. Play the *Talk2Me* video for students to complete the exercise. Play the video again, if necessary, before checking their answers.

2 Play the *Talk2Me* video again, so students underline the phrases in the *Phrase expert* box. Pause the video from time to time if necessary. Check answers in open class.

Talk2Me worksheet

Ask students to complete the *Talk2Me* worksheet on the Resource Centre for more detailed comprehension exercises and more practice of the key phrases.

Answers
The transcript and answer key for the *Talk2Me* video exercises and Worksheet can be found on the Teacher's Resource Centre.

Lead-in

Draw a horizontal line on the board and draw a stick figure of a girl at one end and a boy at the other. Give students a form of entertainment, e.g. *video gaming* and ask students where on the line they would put it. Aim to challenge the stereotypes, so if students want to put it on the scale near the boy, ask them questions like *Do you know any girls who play video games?* or if you have a mixed class, ask the girls, *What do you think about that?* Aim to provoke discussion wherever possible. Continue with different activities, e.g. *dancing, going to the cinema, playing board games,* etc.

3 Focus students' attention on the poster and elicit what they can see. Then have students work in pairs or groups to discuss the questions. Elicit answers from different students around the class.

Answers
1 a school concert **2** at 1 pm **3** one hour

EXAM SKILL

Talking about times

Ask students to read the tips.

- Remind students that in speaking exams, the reason candidates often do tasks in pairs is because the examiners want to see how candidates interact.
- Using appropriate phrases to talk about time and the correct prepositions to use with time phrases can improve a candidate's mark in an exam.
- Remind students that it is extremely important that they use appropriate phrases/questions to ask their partner (or the examiner) to repeat something, if they have not understood something correctly.

4 1.15 Tell students that this exercise will help them to practise formulating questions to ask about an event. After they've finished the exercise, play the track for students to listen and check.

Answers/Audioscript
1 What time does the concert start? It starts at 8 pm **2** What are the opening hours of the museum? The opening hours are 10 am until 5 pm. **3** How long does the film last? It lasts 90 minutes. **4** When is football training? It's on Saturdays from 9 am until 11 am. **5** What time does the concert finish? It finishes at 10 pm.

OPTIMISE YOUR EXAM

Collaborative task

Ask students to read the tip.

- Candidates are not usually given time to prepare what they are going to say in speaking exams, so learning useful phrases to stall for time is essential.
- Give students some additional phrases, e.g. *Just give me a moment, Well, …, That's a good question*, and elicit more ideas from the class.

Exam task

Extra support

Do Exercise 5 in two stages. First, group students together to prepare the questions they will need. Have half the pairs prepare the questions on page 136 while the other half prepare the questions on page 139. Do not allow them to write anything down. Monitor and correct students' errors discretely. Regroup students so that in each pair there is a Student A and a Student B. Students then complete the tasks in Exercise 5.

5 Assign each student a letter, A or B, and put them into A/B pairs. Give them a moment to look at their information / question topics on page 136/139. Time students (two minutes) and give them an update, e.g. *One minute to go …* Remind students to use phrases to allow themselves more time to answer, if necessary, and to check anything their partner says that they don't understand. Walk round, monitoring students for good use of language and errors to go over at the end of the activity.

Write any errors on the board and go through them with students, eliciting corrections from them where possible. After the class feedback, students could then repeat this activity with another partner, to try to improve their performance.

Suggested answers
Student B's questions
What (type of) music can I/you listen to at the disco?
What time does it start?
Is the disco / it on Saturdays?
Can I/you buy / Is there a student ticket? How much is it?
Has it got / Is there wi-fi?
Student A's questions
What can I/you see at the film festival?
Is/Does it open on Mondays?
Can I/you buy a student ticket? How much is it?
Can I/you buy a drink there?
What is the telephone number of the film festival?

Homework

OWB

Assign students Speaking exercises 1 and 2 on pages 16–17 of their Workbook.

LANGUAGE IN USE

Multiple-choice dialogue

→ Student's Book, page 21 SB

Lesson aims

- Think about the context of a dialogue
- Practise a multiple-choice dialogue exam task
- Discuss things people talk about when they meet

Lead-in

Write *The news* on the board. Ask students to brainstorm all the different sections of the news they can think of, e.g. *local, national, international, culture, business*, and all the places people can access the news from, e.g. *TV, podcasts, newspapers, Facebook, Twitter, internet, news apps*.

1 Before students read the text, have them predict what they think the text will be about (*how people access the news*). After students complete the exercise, encourage them to share their ideas with the class.

Answers

Students' own answers

EXAM SKILL

Thinking about context

Ask students to read the tips.

- For students to complete this task type successfully, they need to form a clear idea of who is speaking, what the situation is and who the speaker might be before choosing their answers. Tell students they will need to use their imagination and common sense to do this.
- Explain to students that this task type deals with everyday situations, and that they would almost certainly be able to do tasks like this in their own language without thinking. Tell them that the objective is to transfer that same skill into English and remind them that when communicating in English, there is the possibility of confusion due to unfamiliar grammar and vocabulary.

2 Ask students what type of things they might hear people say at a ticket office, e.g. *Can I have two tickets, please?* and at the other places in the word box. Then have them complete the exercise. Check answers in open class.

Answers

1 on the phone **2** in school **3** at home **4** on the street
5 in a shop **6** at a ticket office

Mixed ability

Have stronger students close their books while weaker students keep their books open. Read out the questions in Exercise 2 one at a time with natural stress and intonation. Encourage stronger students to try to imagine possible contexts for each question while weaker students match the words in the box to the questions.

3 Have students write possible answers individually. In pairs, students discuss their ideas before you check answers with the class.

Possible answers

1 Hello, I'd like some information about train times, please.
2 We're on page 21.
3 OK, let's see if there are some cartoons on.
4 It's at the end of this road, next to the park.
5 They are in the corner over there.
6 Adults are £10 and children are £7, so it will be £17 in total.

OPTIMISE YOUR EXAM

Multiple-choice dialogue

Ask students to read the tips.

- Tell students that they should use the same technique they used in exercises 2 and 3 to complete the exam task: (1) look at the questions, (2) think about the context, and (3) imagine possible answers.
- Remind students to cover the A–C options for all the questions before they start. Look at the example as a class and discuss who might be speaking (e.g. *a friend, classmate or family member*) and what the situation could be (e.g. *the speaker wants to know if the other person is busy or not, possibly on the phone*).
- Tell students to note down their ideas before comparing them with the options.

▼ Exam task

4 Remind students to look at the example before they complete the exercise individually if they have not already done so. Then have students compare their answers in pairs before eliciting answers from the class.

Answers

1 C **2** A **3** C **4** A **5** C

Extra support

Discuss why the incorrect options are not valid answers to the questions with students.

Answers

1 A The question refers to the future, but this answer refers to the present. B The tense is the same, but this answer refers to the present and we don't know what *it* refers to.

2 B The question asks *Where ...?*, it's not asking for an opinion about the music. C The person isn't asking for a ticket for the concert.

3 A The question refers to a permanent situation, but this answer refers to an action happening now. It also is the standard question to ask about someone's job. B This answer refers to the future and we don't know what *there* refers to.

4 B We expect a *yes/no* answer to questions with *Did you …?* The pronoun is also wrong – we could perhaps say '*It isn't interesting*', but it is an unlikely answer. C The question is not about preferences, and the fact that the verb *read* is used in both the question and answer is irrelevant.

5 A It's not logical to answer a *What …?* question with *'why'*. B The verb in the question, *playing*, doesn't match with the noun in the answer, *the news*. This answer would match the question '*What are you watching?*'

THINK | RESEARCH | **CULTURE** | LEARN | ME

In groups, students discuss the question.

Homework

OWB

Assign students Language in Use exercises 1, 2 and 3 on page 17 of their Workbook.

WRITING
An email

→ Student's Book, pages 22–23 SB

Lesson aims

- Focus on using your own words
- Plan and write an email

Lead-in

Play ***Hangman*** with some of the words from the unit. Invite students to come to the front of the class to lead the game, if appropriate. Students may still struggle with the alphabet at this level, so correct them and clarify how we say problem letters if necessary.

1 Encourage students to share email-writing habits in pairs or groups. Elicit answers from the class.

EXAM SKILL

Using your own words

Ask students to read the tips.

- Remind students that they have done a lot of work on words that have the same meaning in Units 1 and 2. Tell them that it is also important to think about this area when writing too, as it will mean they can avoid repeating exact words from the exam text. Repeating, or 'lifting', words/phrases from exam texts lowers candidates' marks.
- Tell students to use part of their planning time to brainstorm alternative words and phrases, which they can use in their answers to demonstrate how much English they know.

2 After students complete the exercise, elicit why this type of exercise may be important (*to find out what the sender wants*).

Answer

What are you doing this afternoon? Can you come to the art gallery? Are you free?

3 In pairs, students compare the two emails. Check their answers in open class.

Answers

Email B is the best answer because it answers all three questions, and gives extra information.

Email A is OK, but it is too short and the information is not very clear.

Optional extension

Point out that in English it is rude to reply to an invitation simply by saying 'No'. People usually expect a reason. Have students write an invitation individually, e.g. *I'm meeting a friend at the cinema on Friday night. Do you want to come with me?* Elicit some ways to refuse invitations, e.g. *I'm sorry, I can't … because … / I'd love to, but I'm …* Then have students stand up and invite each other to do something or go somewhere. Everybody should refuse at least four invitations, giving a reason why, e.g. *Friday night? Oh, what a pity! I'm going to a party with my friend Claire.*

4 Elicit another way to say *really like* from students. Then have them complete the exercise with a partner. Check students' answers in open class.

Suggested answers

really like = love
later today = later on
See you later = Meet you later
I'm busy = I'm not free
go to = visit
Have fun! = Enjoy yourself!

OPTIMISE YOUR EXAM

An email

Ask students to read the tips.

- Tell students that planning is an essential part of successful task completion. Advise them to take the time to think carefully about the context, check exactly what information they need to include and brainstorm useful language to show how much English they know before they start writing.
- Inform students that they will be given enough time to plan and write their text when in an exam.

5 While students are completing the exercise, walk round the class helping students by suggesting alternative words/phrases they can use. Remind students not to repeat words from the exam task.

Exam task

6 Ask students to complete the exercise and remind them of the importance of answering the questions. Check answers in open class.

Answers

1 What are you doing tonight? Do you want to see it? Do you want to come?

2 She's going for a pizza with her friend Holly.

7 Students compare their ideas from Exercise 6 with the two plans to complete the exercise. Then have students share their ideas with the class, giving reasons.

Answers

Plan B is better because it gives an apology, direct answers and a suggestion.

8 **Plan** Ask students to complete the writing plan. You may want to look at students' plans to check them and give advice and suggestions for improvement before they take the next step.

9 **Write** After students write their email, remind them to proofread their work. If there is not enough time, set this and the subsequent checklist exercise for homework.

10 **Check** Students complete the checklist before handing in their email.

Optional extension

For a slightly longer writing task, and for students to see other text types, refer them to one of the six tasks in the Writing reference (SB p169). Each one includes an annotated sample text and related writing task to challenge your students a little more.

Homework

OWB

Assign students Writing exercises 1, 2, 3 and 4 on page 18 of their Workbook and Progress check 2 on page 19.

Answers PROGRESS CHECK Units 1–2

Exercise 1
1 tent **2** painting **3** article **4** swimming **5** out **6** musician **7** game **8** a classical **9** gamer **10** café

Exercise 2
1 plays **2** 'm/am looking **3** starts **4** 're/are practising **5** 's/is watching **6** 're/are doing **7** live **8** tries

Exercise 3
1 A **2** B **3** C **4** C **5** A **6** C **7** B **8** A

Exercise 4
1 get **2** come **3** go **4** look **5** turn **6** stay

Exercise 5
1 in **2** have **3** them **4** We **5** to **6** go **7** the **8** don't **9** 'm/am **10** It

Exercise 6
1 camping **2** competition **3** camera **4** guitarist **5** attractive **6** member **7** advert **8** popular

3 What's for dinner?

UNIT AIMS

Exam preparation in Unit 3:

- identify *'when'* and *'who'* in a magazine article
- predict what the speaker will say in a conversation
- explain likes and dislikes in an interview
- think about grammar in an open-cloze exercise
- use your vocabulary in a note

TEACHER'S PRESENTATION KIT

- *Talk2Me* videos
- Speaking test videos
- Class and Workbook audio
- Workbook pages and answer key

UNIT OVERVIEW

Student's Book / Digital Student's Book SB		Workbook / Online Workbook OWB
LESSON / EXAM TASK	EXAM SKILLS / LANGUAGE FOCUS	CONSOLIDATION
Reading **Multiple-choice cloze**	Identifying *'when'* and *'who'* A magazine article	Workbook, pp 20–21, Exercises 1, 2, 3, 4 Unit 3, Reading, Exercises 1, 2, 3, 4
Grammar 1	Past simple: regular verbs, *Wh-* words	Workbook, p 22, Exercises 1, 2, 3 Unit 3, Grammar 1, Exercises 1, 2, 3
Vocabulary	Words connected with *food* Verbs/adjectives Collocations with verbs	Workbook, pp 22–23, Exercises 1, 2, 3 Unit 3, Vocabulary, Exercises 1, 2, 3
Listening **Multiple choice**	Predicting what the speaker will say	Workbook, p 24, Exercises 1, 2, 3, 4 Unit 3, Listening, Exercises 1, 2, 3, 4
Grammar 2	Past simple: irregular verbs	Workbook, p 23, Exercises 1, 2, 3 Unit 3, Grammar 2, Exercises 1, 2, 3
Speaking **Interview**	Explaining likes and dislikes	Workbook, p 24, Exercises 1, 2, 3 Unit 3, Speaking, Exercises 1, 2, 3
Language in Use **Open cloze**	Thinking about grammar (conjunctions, prepositions and pronouns)	Workbook, p 25, Exercises 1, 2, 3 Unit 3, Language in Use, Exercises 1, 2, 3
Writing **A note**	Using your vocabulary	Workbook, p 26, Exercises 1, 2, 3, 4 Unit 3, Writing, Exercises 1, 2, 3, 4
		Workbook, p 27, Progress check and Cumulative progress Progress check and Cumulative progress

Additional material

PRESENTATION KIT	TEACHER'S/STUDENT'S RESOURCE CENTRE RC	TEST GENERATOR
Talk2Me video *It's my favourite because …*	**Unit 3 worksheets:** *Optimise your grammar* (Standard and Higher), *Optimise your vocabulary* (Standard and Higher), *Talk2Me* video, *Say it right* **Units 3–4 worksheets:** CLIL, Culture, Everyday English (TRC only), Grammar communication (TRC only)	Unit Test 3 (Standard and Higher)

READING
Multiple-choice cloze | A magazine article

→ Student's Book, pages 26–27 SB

Lesson aims

- Identify when actions take place and who does them
- Practise a multiple-choice cloze exam task
- Write a recipe and compare work with peers

Lead-in

Ask students to look at the unit title ***What's for dinner?*** and say what they think the unit is going to be about (*food, cooking, places to eat*). In pairs, ask students to brainstorm 'international' foods, e.g. *pizza, paella, tacos, curry, sushi*. Encourage students to share their ideas with the rest of the class.

1 Divide the class into pairs or groups to discuss the questions. Elicit some answers in open class to develop a class discussion.

EXAM SKILL

Identifying *'when'* and *'who'*

Ask students to read the tips.

- Elicit examples of verbs referring to the present and the future, which students revised in Units 1 and 2. Then elicit or give students examples of past tense verbs (e.g. *eat – ate, cook – cooked, think – thought*), which they will be revising in this unit.
- Remind students that pronouns are often important to help work out who is doing an action. Pronouns like *he, she* and *they* may refer to someone already mentioned, or we may need to use common sense and world knowledge to work out who the pronouns refer to. Students will look at this area in Exercise 4.

2 Before students complete the exercise, go through the first sentence as a class. Then check answers in open class.

Answers
1 present **2** past **3** future

3 Ask students to complete the exercise in pairs. Check answers in open class, eliciting justification for answers.

Suggested answers
1 prefer **2** worked, 10 years ago **3** is planning, one day

4 Tell students that they need to work out who the words in bold refer to. Ask students to complete the exercise. Check their answers in open class.

Answers
1 everybody **2** busy people **3** people who don't eat fish
4 the person reading the article

5 Have students discuss the question in pairs. Have a feedback session in open class and find out how many students know how to cook and how old they were when they started learning.

Answer
B

OPTIMISE YOUR EXAM

Multiple-choice cloze

Ask students to read the tips.

- Remind students that in this exam task type, they should try covering the options under the text when they read it for the first time, so they are not distracted by the possible answers.
- Tell students that they should focus on the words before and after each gap and make initial predictions about what words they might need before they look at the options given.
- If they don't know the answers, students should always eliminate any options they know don't fit in terms of grammar and/or meaning and then make a guess which could be correct.

▼ Exam task

6 1.16 **Note: The reading text is also available on the audio CD <u>but contains the missing words</u>. You may want to have students listen and read the text <u>after</u> doing the exam task to check their answers.**

Before students complete the exam task, remind them to use all the tips they remember from this and previous units. Tell them to read the instructions carefully and follow the example. Check each answer in open class or have students listen to the audio to check their own answers.

Answers
1 C (*The* defines or identifies a particular person or object.)
2 C (*was* refers to the past in singular.)
3 B (*cooks* refers to third person.)
4 B (*can* is followed by a main verb.)
5 B (*at* is a preposition of place.)
6 A (*one* refers to a singular example.)
7 C (*it* refers to a specific thing already mentioned.)
8 C (*some* refers to multiple unspecified things.)

Fast finishers

Have students write down why the answers are correct, e.g. *1 is* The *because it identifies the object programme.* As you check the answers to Exercise 6, ask fast finishers to explain the reasons behind the correct answers.

7 Ask students to complete the exercise. Students compare in pairs before you check in open class.

Answers
1 chef **2** prepare **3** famous **4** idea **5** study **6** meals **7** recipes
8 show

THINK | RESEARCH | **CULTURE** | LEARN | ME

If you have access to the internet, students can research their recipes themselves. If not, be prepared to provide vocabulary and language students need to explain their recipes clearly.

Cultural note

MasterChef was first broadcast in 1990 by the BBC. A new version of the programme was created in Australia in 2009 and this is the version which many countries around the world have adopted. The spin-off *Junior MasterChef* was first seen in 1994 and *Celebrity MasterChef* in 2006.

The 'ADHD Cooking School' (ADHD – Attention Deficit Hyperactivity Disorder) was set up in August 2015 by Goma with rapper Loyle Carner (Ben Coyle-Larner). Goma works on a range of social projects and wanted to create a cookery school for teenagers with ADHD. Loyle Carner has suffered from the disorder since childhood and finds he can channel it through his music and cooking, hence his involvement in the project.

Homework OWB

Assign students Reading exercises 1, 2, 3 and 4 on pages 20–21 of their Workbook.

GRAMMAR 1
Past simple: regular verbs, *Wh-* words

→ Student's Book, page 28 SB

Lesson aims

- Understand the correct usage of past simple, regular verbs and *Wh-* question words
- Practise talking about the past and asking questions

Lead-in

Write these unusual food items on the board:

bat soup, alligator chilli, kangaroo steak, chicken feet, mosquito eggs

Have students work in pairs and discuss which of the foods they would eat and which they wouldn't. Have a feedback session in open class.

Grammar in context

Ask students to complete the task. Check their answers and ask them to read more about past simple, regular verbs in the *Remember* box.

Remind students that they can find more information in the Grammar reference, Unit 3, page 152.

Answers

1 started **2** helped **3** opened

1 Focus students' attention on the text and ask them where they might find it (*in a magazine*). Then have them complete the exercise. Check their answers and spelling in open class.

Answers

1 started **2** watched **3** practised **4** preferred **5** used **6** baked **7** asked **8** wanted

Mixed ability

Give weaker students the verbs in the order they appear in the text (*start, watch, practise, prefer, use, bake, ask, want*) so that they can focus purely on the correct spelling. Have fast finishers circle all the words in the text related to food and cooking, e.g. *baking (n), cook (v), bake (v).*

SAY IT RIGHT

Pronunciation of *-ed* TRC

For the *Say it right* pronunciation activity and instructions, go to the Teacher's Resource Centre.

Cultural note

Amy's Baking Year was first published in 2014 when Amy-Beth Ellice was just 14 years old. The book contains numerous recipes organised according to the seasons and special occasions through the year.

Grammar in context

Students at A2 level are expected to be able to use the basic *Wh-* question words correctly to refer to the present, past and future. Ask students to complete the task. Remind them to refer to the information in the *Remember* box if they aren't sure. Then check their answers.

Remind students that they can find more information in the Grammar reference, Unit 3, page 152.

Answers

a past **b** a time

2 Go through the example. Then have students complete the exercise. Check their answers.

Answers

2 c **3** d **4** a **5** e **6** b

3 Read the title of the text and elicit what it means (*A start-up is a small business that has just started up.*). Ask students to complete the exercise. Elicit answers from different students around the class.

Answers

1 talking **2** When **3** travelled **4** decided **5** Who **6** talked **7** Where **8** What **9** Which **10** What

Homework OWB

Assign students Grammar 1 exercises 1, 2 and 3 on page 22 of their Workbook.

VOCABULARY

Topic vocabulary | Word formation | Collocations

→ Student's Book, page 29 SB

Lesson aims

Understand the correct usage of:

- words connected with food
- verbs and adjectives from the same word family
- verb + noun collocations

Lead-in

Write these jumbled questions on the board and ask students to put them in the correct order and complete the *Wh-* question word.

1 house / in / wh_ / your / the cooking / does / usually
2 to Friday / wh_ / have / do / you / lunch / from Monday
3 was / the last time / a meal / for / wh_ / you / went out

Answers

1 Who usually does the cooking in your house?
2 Where do you have lunch with from Monday to Friday?
3 When was the last time you went out for a meal?

Words connected with *food*

1 1.17 Before students complete the exercise, elicit which food they like/dislike or which food is healthy/unhealthy. Play the audio for students to listen and check their answers. (Potatoes as carbohydrates and tomatoes as fruit are also acceptable answers.)

Answers/Audioscript

Vegetables: beans, *carrots, lettuce, onions, potatoes* (could also go in the 'carbohydrates' list), *tomatoes*
Fruit: apple, *banana, oranges, strawberries*
Carbohydrates: bread, *cereal, pasta, rice*
Meat: beef, *chicken, steak*
Dairy: cheese, *milk, yoghurt*
Other: honey, *oil, salt, vinegar*

2 Ask students what snacks they like. Then have them complete the exercise individually. Have students compare answers in pairs before checking answers in open class.

Answers

1 cereal **2** yoghurt **3** bread **4** honey **5** beef/steak **6** oil/salt **7** cheese **8** onions **9** lettuce **10** strawberries

Refer students to the Vocabulary reference, page 164, for more information on topic vocabulary.

Verbs/adjectives

3 1.18 Ask students to complete the exercise. Play the audio for students to listen and check their answers. Then have students close their books. Call out the verbs and have volunteers say the correct adjectives to check their pronunciation.

Answers/Audioscript

verb: bake, **adjective:** *baked*
verb: boil, **adjective:** *boiled*
verb: *fry*, **adjective:** fried
verb: grill, **adjective:** *grilled*
verb: roast, **adjective:** *roasted*

Language note

Both *bake/baked* and *roast/roasted* refer to preparing food in an oven. The difference is that foods that are baked are cooked 'dry', e.g. cakes and bread, while those that are roasted are baked in oil or fat, e.g. potatoes, beef.

4 1.19 Ask students to complete the exercise individually. Then play the audio for students to listen and check their answers.

Answers/Audioscript

1 I ate some delicious *fried* fish at the new Thai restaurant.
2 He *boiled* the pasta for a long time. It tasted terrible.
3 We need to *grill* this chicken for 20 minutes.
4 I like *baked* potatoes with cheese and beans.

5 Ask students to complete the exercise. Check their answers.

Answers

I ate some <u>delicious</u> <u>fried</u> fish at the <u>new</u> <u>Thai</u> restaurant. Then I had some <u>cold</u> <u>coconut</u> ice cream with <u>fresh</u> <u>green</u> grapes.

6 Have students complete the exercise. Remind students to refer to the information in the *Remember* box if they aren't sure. Check answers in open class.

Answers

1 A **2** A **3** B

Extra support

Read the following items and ask students to decide if the adjectives are in the correct order. Ask students to correct the ones that sound strange.

1 *some baked horrible pasta*
2 *a young Japanese chef*
3 *a green small apple*
4 *some fantastic new recipes*
5 *an Indian old cookbook*

Answers

1 horrible baked **3** small green **5** old Indian

Refer students to the Vocabulary reference, page 164, for more information on word formation.

Collocations with verbs

7 1.20 Remind students that collocations are word combinations that go together. Have students complete the exercise. Then play the audio for them to listen and check their answers.

Answers/Audioscript

1 *have* lunch / *have* a drink / *have* a good time
2 *take* an exam / *take* a train / *take* a photo
3 *do* homework / *do* the washing-up / *do* sports
4 *make* breakfast / *make* a picnic / *make* a mistake
5 *bake* bread / *bake* a cake / *bake* a potato

8 Ask students to complete the exercise. Check answers in open class.

Answers

2 bake, make/have **3** ✓ **4** ✓ **5** do, make

Refer students to the Vocabulary reference, page 164, for more information on collocations.

Homework OWB

Assign students Vocabulary exercises 1, 2 and 3 on pages 22–23 of their Workbook.

LISTENING
Multiple choice

→ Student's Book, page 30 SB

Lesson aims

- Listen for detail after predicting content
- Practise a multiple-choice exam task
- Research places to eat

Lead-in

Divide the class into teams. Call out one of the verbs for preparing food from the previous lesson, e.g. *bake*. Set teams a time limit of 30 seconds to think of phrases with the verb, e.g. *biscuits, cakes, bread*. Repeat the process with *boil, fry, grill* and *roast*. Check answers, giving one point for each correct answer. The team with the most points wins.

1 Have students ask and answer the questions in pairs or groups. Elicit answers from around the class to see which restaurant is the most popular.

EXAM SKILL

Predicting what the speaker will say

Ask students to read the tips.

- Remind students of the work they have already done on predicting. In Unit 1 they practised predicting content for a picture multiple-choice listening exam task. Here they will be practising the same techniques, but with words rather than pictures.
- Remind students that they should prepare to listen for words that have the same meaning. Taking notes can be a valuable part of the predicting process and help organise a candidate's ideas, and students will be looking at this in detail in exercises 3 and 4.

2 Ask students to look at the exam question and tell you what it will be about (*a new café*). Then have them complete the exercise. Check their answers in open class.

Suggested answers

reason, likes, café, cheap cake, good coffee, friendly staff

3 Have students complete the exercise in pairs. Then discuss the two sets of notes as a class and make sure students understand why B is much better.

Answers

B are the better notes. They use the information from the questions to predict what the speaker might say.

4 1.21 Remind students how important it is to listen very carefully and not just choose the first word they hear. Play the track for students to listen and answer the question. Check in open class.

Answer

1 B

OPTIMISE YOUR EXAM

Multiple choice

Ask students to read the tips.

- Point out that in this type of exam task it is common to focus more on one of the speakers. However, tell students they should also pay attention to the other speaker because he or she will give important information, or ask specific questions to guide the conversation.
- Candidates can normally predict who the focus of the conversation will be by reading the instructions. In this case it is the woman, Clare.
- Tell students that Simon will be using questions to guide the conversation and that it is possible to predict many of these questions before they listen. This will provide students with more focus.

5 Before the exercise, remind students that this is a pre-listening task. After students complete the exercise, elicit answers from different students around the class and accept all sensible suggestions.

▾ Exam task

6 1.22 Ask students who they will listen to (*two friends talking: Clare and Simon*). Play the track for students to listen and complete the exercise. Don't check answers at this stage, as students will do this in Exercise 7.

7 1.22 Play the track again for students to check their answers. Remind them to always choose an answer, even if they are not totally sure. Check their answers in open class.

Answers

1 B **2** C **3** C **4** B **5** A

Optional extension 1.22

Play the track again, pausing where necessary, for students to listen and note down words from the answer options that were mentioned in the recording but were not the correct answers.

Answers

1 Simon asked if they went to the café on *Friday evening* (A), but Clare says they went on Saturday afternoon (B).

2 Clare says there were only five tables (C), but she also says there were *three* people in her group (A).

3 Clare says they *enjoyed* looking at the old records (A), but that the food wasn't good (C).

4 Clare says she thought about having an *omelette* (A), but in the end she had grilled fish (B).

5 Clare says she chose a glass of cold lemonade (A), but that the lemonade had *fruit* in it (B) and was more like *a dessert* (C).

Homework

OWB

Assign students Listening exercises 1, 2, 3 and 4 on page 24 of their Workbook.

GRAMMAR 2
Past simple: irregular verbs

→ Student's Book, page 31 SB

Lesson aims

- Focus on past simple irregular verbs
- Understand the use of the auxiliary *did* for negative statements and questions in the past
- Practise using irregular verbs to talk about the past
- Discuss interesting restaurants

Lead-in

Play the memory game: *Yesterday, I went to the shops and bought …* with the class. Start by saying a food with an adjective, e.g. *Yesterday, I went to the shops and bought some fresh fish.* Nominate a strong student to repeat the sentence and add an item, e.g. … *some fresh fish and some small tomatoes.* Continue with more students. Have students who cannot repeat all the food sit down. The last student standing wins. With a large class, divide students into groups.

Grammar in context

Ask students what they remember about Clare and Simon's conversation in the previous lesson. Then have them complete the task. Check their answers and ask students to read the information in the *Remember* box. Remind them that they need to learn irregular verbs off by heart. Encourage them to study the Irregular verbs reference on page 175.

Remind students that they can find more information in the Grammar reference, Unit 3, page 153.

Answers

1 thought **2** eat **3** had **4** chose **5** pay

Language note

Some irregular verbs can be organised into groups that behave in a similar way, e.g.

- verbs where /ɪ/ changes to /æ/, e.g. *begin* > *began*, *drink* > *drank*, *swim* > *swam*
- verbs where the past form ends in /ɔːt/, e.g. *buy* > *bought*, *teach* > *taught*, *think* > *thought*
- verbs where /iː/ changes to /e/, e.g. *keep* > *kept*, *meet* > *met*, *sleep* > *slept*

Highlighting similarities between irregular verbs can help students remember them.

Mixed ability

Pair stronger students with less confident students. Ask the less confident students to test their partners' knowledge of irregular verbs. Less confident students refer to the Irregular verbs reference on page 175 and ask questions, e.g. *What's the past of 'bring'? How do you spell it?* This activity will help both groups reinforce their knowledge of the verbs. In Exercise 1, allow less confident students to refer to the Irregular verbs reference.

1 Go through the example sentence as a class and then ask students to complete the exercise. Check answers in open class, eliciting both the spelling and pronunciation of the irregular verbs.

Answers

2 Helen didn't go to the restaurant last week.
3 Paul got up early this morning.
4 He saw his friends after school last night.
5 Rob couldn't come for dinner last Monday.
6 She bought a sandwich at the local shop this morning.
7 We met in the park in 2014.
8 I had a lot of comics as a child.

2 Have students complete the exercise individually. Walk round the class, helping if necessary. Have students compare their sentences in pairs. Invite volunteers to share their answers in open class.

Answers

Students' own answers with:
2 … taught me English last year.
3 The best programme I saw on TV yesterday was … / … was the best programme I saw on TV yesterday.
4 I went to … with my friends at the weekend.
5 I … before bed last night.
6 The best meal I had last week was … / … was the best meal I had last week.

3 Ask a strong student: *What did you eat for breakfast this morning?* Then divide the class into pairs to practise speaking. After the exercise, ask students to share any interesting answers they heard.

Mixed ability

Pair stronger students with weaker students and have the stronger students ask the questions first. This way the weaker students have a chance to hear the questions before having to formulate them. Alternatively, elicit the questions from the class before students start to ask and answer.

4 Ask students to complete the exercise. Have students compare in pairs before you check their answers in open class.

Answers

1 went **2** saw **3** got **4** didn't have **5** heard **6** thought **7** said **8** understood **9** ate **10** didn't leave

THINK | RESEARCH | CULTURE | LEARN | **ME**

In pairs, students tell each other about their experience.

Cultural note

The Little Yellow Door café is in Notting Hill Gate in London. In summer 2016, they launched a special Emoji Menu where customers can order using text messages from their phones.

Homework

OWB

Assign students Grammar 2 exercises 1, 2 and 3 on page 23 of their Workbook.

Assign students the Flipped classroom tasks on page 32 of their Student's Book if you'd like them to prepare for the next lesson. To complete this task, students need to watch the *Talk2Me* video which can be found on the Resource Centre.

SPEAKING
Interview

→ Student's Book, page 32 SB

Lesson aims

- Talk about your likes, dislikes and daily life
- Practise answering personal questions in an interview task

The *Talk2Me* video in this unit focuses on food and drink. The people in the video talk about preparing food for Mother's Day, their favourite cakes and cleaning the house.

Students answer some comprehension questions and then listen for key phrases in the video.

The video can be used in one of two ways:

Flipped classroom

Flipped classroom option

Using this approach, students watch the video and complete the exercises for homework. This prepares students for the speaking lesson by introducing them to the topic and the key phrases to use in the exam task. Teachers who use this method will find they have more class time to spend on activating the target language and developing fluency for the final task.

***Talk2Me* worksheet**

Ask students to also complete the *Talk2Me* worksheet on the Resource Centre for more detailed comprehension exercises and more practice of the key phrases.

Classroom option

1 Ask students to spend a minute or two reading the questions. Play the *Talk2Me* video for students to complete the exercise. Play the video again, if necessary, before checking their answers.

2 Play the *Talk2Me* video again, so students underline the phrases in the *Phrase expert* box. Pause the video from time to time if necessary. Check answers in open class.

Talk2Me worksheet

Ask students to also complete the *Talk2Me* worksheet on the Resource Centre for more detailed comprehension exercises and more practice of the key phrases.

Answers

The transcript and answer key for the *Talk2Me* video exercises and Worksheet can be found on the Teacher's Resource Centre.

Lead-in

Make sure students have their books closed. Answer the two questions in Exercise 3 with examples. Ask students to listen carefully to your answers and work out what they think the questions are. Have students make notes and compare their ideas in pairs. Then have students check their questions with the ones on Student's Book page 32.

EXAM SKILL

Explaining likes and dislikes

Ask students to read the tips.

- Remind students that it is extremely important to ask the examiner to repeat questions they don't understand. Explain that reformulating (repeating what you think the examiner is asking for) is a good technique, as it shows that the candidate was paying attention and wants to confirm before answering, e.g. *So, you want me to talk about the meal I like most?* (in response to *What is your favourite meal of the day?*).
- Remind students that adding some extra information in the form of examples or opinions, even if it has a few mistakes in it, makes a very positive impression on examiners.

3 Divide the class into pairs or groups to ask and answer the questions. Elicit answers from different pairs or groups around the class.

4 1.23 Tell students that they will hear an extract from an oral exam, and have them read the questions. Play the track for students to listen and answer. Have them compare their answers in pairs before checking answers with the class.

Answer

1 pasta **2** pears **3** chocolate cake

5 1.23 Play the track again, pausing where necessary, for students to listen and note down the reasons the student gives.

Answers

1 It's tasty and easy to eat.
2 She has to eat so many of them.
3 She loves both chocolate and cake.

OPTIMISE YOUR EXAM

Interview

Ask students to read the tips.

- Remind students to find the vocabulary they need to talk about their personal likes and dislikes. They can use dictionaries or ask the teacher and should try to use this vocabulary whenever they get an opportunity.
- Explain that students need to be prepared for all sorts of questions. Remind them that they should also think about asking and answering relevant questions in their head.

6 Elicit or point out that the categories in the mind map relate to the questions from the oral exam in Exercise 4. Give students time to complete the mind map with their own answers and a reason for each one. Monitor students and help where necessary.

▾ Exam task

7 Divide the class into pairs to ask and answer the questions in Exercise 4. Ask students to use their notes from Exercise 6 and the words and phrases in the *Phrase expert* box to help them give extra information in their answers. Walk round and monitor students, noting down errors and good use of language to go over at the end of the activity.

Write any errors you hear on the board and go through them with students, eliciting corrections from them where possible. If there is time, have students repeat the task with another partner to help improve their performance.

Fast finishers

Ask students to brainstorm other topics connected to food, which they think might come up in the exam, e.g. *Special food in your country, Special food for special times of the year, The worst meal ever.* When everyone has finished, have students share their ideas in open class.

Homework OWB

Assign students Speaking exercises 1, 2 and 3 on page 24 of their Workbook.

LANGUAGE IN USE
Open cloze

→ Student's Book, page 33 SB

Lesson aims

- Focus on thinking about grammar
- Practise an open-cloze exam task
- Describe food

Lead-in

Tell students about a place where you like to eat. Use the sentences in Exercise 1 to guide you and try to cover all the areas mentioned there. Explain that they can take notes if they wish. Afterwards, put students in pairs to look at the sentences in Exercise 1 and, based on what you told them, they should try to agree on what the most important thing is for you. Then give them feedback on their ideas.

1 Have students complete the exercise individually. If necessary, encourage them to think about the example you gave when they are deciding the order.

2 Divide the class into pairs or groups of students who don't usually work together to promote a little diversity in the class. Ask them to discuss and explain their opinions.

3 In the same pairs or groups, have students come to a consensus on a final order. Then have them present their ideas to the class with reasons for their decision.

Optional extension

Give students the name of a local restaurant they all know. Have a brainstorming session for students to describe it, e.g. *Nino's – delicious (pasta), cheap (menu), top quality (ingredients), tasty (pizzas).* Repeat the process with two or three different local restaurants to elicit as much vocabulary as possible.

EXAM SKILL

Thinking about grammar (conjunctions, prepositions and pronouns)

Ask students to read the tips.

- Explain that different tasks in exams focus on different areas, and open-cloze tasks like the one on this page focus particularly on grammar.
- Write the following sentence on the board. Elicit the part of speech of each word and write them underneath.
  Joe likes chocolate, but he doesn't like ice cream.
  noun (subject) – verb (third person) – noun (object) – conjunction – subject pronoun – auxiliary verb (third person) – verb (infinitive) – noun (object)

Tell students that knowing how sentences are formed can help them figure out what the missing words are in an open-cloze task.

4 Focus students' attention on the words in the box and elicit the part of speech of each one (*conjunction: and, because, but; preposition: from, in; pronoun: we*). Then ask students to complete the exercise. Check their answers and elicit the reasons for each one.

Answers

1 from (follows a verb)
2 and (in the middle of two parts of a sentence, showing added information)
3 We (subject of the sentence – matches *brother and I*)
4 in (comes before a noun – shows where something is)
5 because (in the middle of two parts of a sentence, showing reason)
6 but (in the middle of two parts of a sentence, showing contrast)

OPTIMISE YOUR EXAM

Open cloze

Ask students to read the tips.

- Point out that open-cloze exam tasks look similar to multiple-choice cloze tasks. Explain that the only obvious difference is that students are not given options beneath the text in open-cloze tasks. However, multiple-choice cloze places more emphasis on vocabulary, and open-cloze more focus on grammar.
- Tell students to think only about the type of words they could use in each space the first time they read and not to get distracted by exact words. It's important that they get a general understanding of the whole text before completing the task.

Exam task

5 Ask students what the text is (*a post from a food blog*). Go through the example and then have them complete the exam task. Elicit answers and ask students to identify the types of words for each gap.

Answers

1 on (preposition) **2** We (pronoun) **3** went (irregular past simple form of *go*) **4** and (conjunction) **5** but (conjunction) **6** the (definite article) **7** for (preposition) **8** in/at (preposition) **9** a (indefinite article) **10** for (preposition)

THINK | RESEARCH | CULTURE | LEARN | ME

Monitor the task and help students with vocabulary. Have groups share their sentences and try to guess each other's food.

Homework OWB

Assign students Language in Use exercises 1, 2 and 3 on page 25 of their Workbook.

WRITING
A note

→ Student's Book, pages 34–35 SB

Lesson aims

- Focus on using your own vocabulary
- Plan and write a note

Lead-in

Play a spelling game with the class. Ask all students to stand up. Choose a strong student and ask *What's the past of* teach? *How do you spell it?* If the student does not answer both questions correctly, he or she sits down. Repeat the process, nominating students at random. Have students who hesitate also sit down. Include both regular and irregular verbs and continue until only one student is left standing.

1 As students answer the questions, make a list of their ideas on the board.

2 Ask students who the note is from (*Tom*). Then have them complete the exercise.

Answer

Tom asks three questions; Students should underline: What, you, buy, What, we, eating, Can, friend, come

EXAM SKILL

Using your vocabulary

Ask students to read the tips.

- Tell students that they need to answer the three questions within the word limit they have been given. Explain that if they exceed the word limit and the answer to a question is at the end of the text, it may not be counted.
- Remind students to use their preparation time effectively. Also remind them that planning is an essential part of successful task completion.

3 After students read both texts, have them highlight the main differences between the two. Check the answers in open class and ask students to justify their answers.

Answers

A completes the task.

B does not answer all of the questions in Tom's note.

4 Ask students what they have to do before they complete the exercise. Then check their answers in open class.

Answer

1 bought **2** preparing **3** told **4** invited

OPTIMISE YOUR EXAM

A note

Ask students to read the tips.

- Remind students they have worked with words that have the same meaning and have used their own words rather than repeating or lifting words/phrases from the exam texts.
- Tell students that writing is an opportunity for candidates to show examiners how much English they know, so taking time to think of interesting vocabulary can make a real difference. Explain that the more they can show their knowledge of vocabulary, the more marks they will get.

Exam task

5 Invite different volunteers to read the instructions and the note. Monitor students and help where necessary. Then have students share their answers in pairs.

Answers

1 Ella
2 25–35
3 three
4 What you made in cookery class today, what you are making next week and what to bring to next week's class
5 past simple to answer the first question and present continuous and simple to answer the second and third questions
6 words and phrases for food and cooking

6 Plan Tell students to use all the tips they have seen so far to complete the plan. You may want to look at students' plans to check them and give advice and suggestions for improvement before they take the next step.

Extra support

Look at the plan with students. Elicit suggestions for how to complete the *Detail* column from the class and prompt them to write the questions that they need to answer. Give them a couple of minutes to write down some ideas in the *My notes* column. Then have students brainstorm ideas in pairs or small groups for the *Useful language* column. Collate these on the board so all students have plenty of ideas to choose from before they start writing.

7 Write Make sure students understand what is meant by the appropriate style (*informal language that is used for writing notes*). Offer help where needed. If there is not enough time, set this and the subsequent checklist exercise for homework.

8 Check Students complete the checklist before they hand in their note. Tell students that this is an important part of every task they do.

Optional extension

For a slightly longer writing task, and for students to see other text types, refer them to one of the six tasks in the Writing reference (SB p169). Each one includes an annotated sample text and related writing task to challenge your students a little more.

Homework OWB

Assign students Writing exercises 1, 2, 3 and 4 on page 26 of their Workbook and Progress check 3 on page 27.

4 On your way

UNIT AIMS

Exam preparation in Unit 4:

- decide on the general message in signs and notices
- listen for important information in conversations
- ask someone to repeat in a collaborative task
- use linking words in a gap fill exercise
- punctuation and spelling in a postcard

TEACHER'S PRESENTATION KIT

- *Talk2Me* videos
- Speaking test videos
- Class and Workbook audio
- Workbook pages and answer key

UNIT OVERVIEW

Student's Book / Digital Student's Book SB		Workbook / Online Workbook OWB
LESSON / EXAM TASK	**EXAM SKILLS / LANGUAGE FOCUS**	**CONSOLIDATION**
Reading **Matching**	Deciding the general message Signs and notices	Workbook, pp 28–29, Exercises 1, 2, 3, 4, 5 Unit 4, Reading, Exercises 1, 2, 3, 4, 5
Grammar 1	Past continuous, linking words	Workbook, p 30, Exercises 1, 2 Unit 4, Grammar 1, Exercises 1, 2
Vocabulary	Words connected with *travel* Compound nouns Phrasal verbs	Workbook, pp 30–31, Exercises 1, 2, 3 Unit 4, Vocabulary, Exercises 1, 2, 3
Listening **Gap fill**	Listening for important information	Workbook, p 32, Exercises 1, 2, 3 Unit 4, Listening, Exercises 1, 2, 3
Grammar 2	Past simple and past continuous	Workbook, p 31, Exercise 1 Unit 4, Grammar 2, Exercise 1
Speaking **Collaborative task**	Asking someone to repeat	Workbook, pp 32–33, Exercises 1, 2 Unit 4, Speaking, Exercises 1, 2
Language in Use **Multiple choice**	Using linking words	Workbook, p 33, Exercises 1, 2 Unit 4, Language in Use, Exercises 1, 2
Writing **A postcard**	Punctuation and spelling	Workbook, p 34, Exercises 1, 2, 3, 4 Unit 4, Writing, Exercises 1, 2, 3, 4
Progress check	Check language progress for Units 3 and 4	Workbook, p 35, Progress check and Cumulative progress Progress check and Cumulative progress

Additional material

PRESENTATION KIT	TEACHER'S/STUDENT'S RESOURCE CENTRE RC	TEST GENERATOR
Talk2Me video *Did you say ...?*	**Unit 4 worksheets:** *Optimise your grammar* (Standard and Higher), *Optimise your vocabulary* (Standard and Higher), *Talk2Me* video, *Say it right* **Units 3–4 worksheets:** CLIL, Culture, Everyday English (TRC only), Grammar communication (TRC only)	Unit Test 4 (Standard and Higher) Progress Test (Standard and Higher)

READING

Matching | Signs and notices

→ Student's Book, pages 36–37 SB

Lesson aims

- Focus on understanding the general message in signs
- Practise a matching exam task

Lead-in

Ask students to look at the unit title ***On your way*** and the photo and say what they think the unit will be about (*transport, travel*). Ask them if they like to travel and, if so, where and how they like to travel. Also ask them about their favourite places, when they last visited and why they liked them. Encourage students to give reasons and examples with their answers if possible.

1 Before students complete the task, make sure they understand all the vocabulary. Then elicit answers from different students around the class.

2 1.24 **Note: The reading text is also available on the audio CD. You may want to have students listen and read the text after doing the scanning task.**

Ask students to look at the photos on page 37 and describe what they see. Then have them complete the exercise. Check answers in open class.

Answers

1 C **2** A **3** B

3 Invite a volunteer to read out the first definition. Elicit the correct word from the text. Then have students complete the exercise individually. Check answers in open class.

Answers

1 sightseeing **2** pack **3** trip **4** journeys **5** storm **6** wet **7** flight **8** festival

EXAM SKILL

Deciding the general message

Ask students to read the tips.

- Tell students that to help understand a text fully, it is important to think about the context it is written in. Explain that figuring out where texts are from and who is likely to read them can make exam tasks much easier.
- Remind students that they studied imperatives in Unit 1. Imperatives are often used in signs and notices because they give people instructions.

4 Go through the instructions with the class and ask them what symbol you should use if a sign or notice tells you not to do something (✗). Point out the example answer and then have students complete the exercise and check answers in open class.

Answers

B ✗ **C** ✗ **D** ✓ **E** *i* **F** *i* **G** *i* **H** ✓

OPTIMISE YOUR EXAM

Matching

Ask students to read the tips.

- Remind students that thinking about the topic vocabulary before completing an exercise will help them complete the exam task more successfully.
- Remind them that there are always some additional items they do not need to use in multiple-matching tasks. Tell them to be careful as some of the items may look like the correct answer even though they are not.

▼ Exam task

5 Go through the example answer. Then ask students to complete the exercise individually. Check answers in open class and elicit the key words which helped them to match the sentences and the signs and notices.

Answers

1 F **2** D **3** A **4** B **5** H

and students' own answers

Optional extension

Split the class into six groups. Assign each group one of the following places: *airport, bus station, campsite, park, petrol station, train station* and ask them to brainstorm topic vocabulary for that place. Regroup students so that everyone is in a different group and have students share their vocabulary with each other. Encourage them to explain the meaning of any unfamiliar words to their new groups if necessary.

Cultural note

Note that American English has different names for some of these places: *petrol station = gas station; train station = railroad station; bus station = bus terminal; campsite = campground.*

Homework

OWB

Assign students Reading exercises 1, 2, 3, 4 and 5 on pages 28–29 of their Workbook.

GRAMMAR 1

Past continuous, linking words

→ Student's Book, page 38 SB

Lesson aims

- Understand the correct usage of the past continuous and linking words
- Practise talking about actions that were happening over a specific period of time in the past
- Practise using linking words to connect ideas

Lead-in

Tell the class that you want each student to stand up and simultaneously mime an action to you, e.g. play the piano, kick a football. Ask one student to time 30 seconds and then call out 'Stop'. Students immediately stop miming their actions. Try to remember what each student was doing and formulate it as a past continuous sentence, e.g. *Ahmed was playing the piano*. The student then sits down. You win if you are able to remember what everyone was doing, but the class wins if any students are left standing. Write the last sentence you said on the board, circle the past continuous verb form and elicit the name for the tense before continuing. Students can play this game again in small groups after Exercise 2.

Grammar in context

Have students complete the task and check their answers. Ask them if they got their answers correct and, if not, encourage them to read more about the past continuous in the *Remember* box.

Remind students that they can find more information in the Grammar reference, Unit 4, page 153.

Answers

1 was reading **2** wasn't studying **3** were my friends doing

1 Ask students who's speaking in the conversation and what they are talking about (*Joe and Ben, a trip to France*). Check their answers and have students practise the conversation in pairs.

Answers

1 was walking **2** were you going **3** was driving **4** was taking **5** was doing **6** were both cycling **7** were being **8** wasn't looking

2 Go through the example as a class and then have students complete the exercise individually. Have students compare in pairs before you check answers in open class.

Answers

2 She was playing music last night.

3 James was studying in London last year.

4 No, I was sightseeing.

Grammar in context

Ask students to complete the task. Refer them to information in the *Remember* box if they aren't sure. Check their answers.

Remind students that they can find more information in the Grammar reference, Unit 4, page 153.

Answers

1 because **2** when **3** but

3 Before students complete the exercise, ask them why they think the web page is called *Around the world in 80 ways (the posts are always about unusual ways to travel and the title also makes reference to the famous novel,* Around the world in 80 days, *by Jules Verne*). Check answers in open class.

Answers

1 was feeling **2** but **3** were travelling **4** when **5** was speaking **6** was working **7** because **8** were leaving

Fast finishers

Have fast finishers read the text again and underline all the words for people (*travellers, parents, Dad, Mum, driver, mechanic, son, football fan*).

SAY IT RIGHT

/ə/ TRC

For the *Say it right* pronunciation activity and instructions, go to the Teacher's Resource Centre.

Homework

OWB

Assign students Grammar 1 exercises 1 and 2 on page 30 of their Workbook.

VOCABULARY

Topic vocabulary | Word patterns | Phrasal verbs

→ Student's Book, page 39 SB

Lesson aims

Understand the correct usage of:

- words connected with travel
- noun + noun word patterns (compound nouns)
- phrasal verbs

Lead-in

Write *Places in town* on the board and put students into small groups to brainstorm ideas, e.g. *chemist, bus station, supermarket, car park*, etc. Then encourage the class to write them on the board. Ask students questions about some of the items, e.g. *Where can you get a stamp and post a letter?* (*the post office*), *Where do you go if you want a magazine?* (*the newsagent*).

Words connected with *travel*

1 1.25 Ask students who they think Amelie is (*a new pupil*). Then have students complete the exercise individually. Play the audio for students to listen and check their answers.

Answers/Audioscript

Hi Amelie,

Here is the information about getting to school tomorrow. We can catch the bus at the *bus stop* outside my house at 7:40 am. We arrive at school at about 8:15, unless the bus is *delayed* or we *miss* it. :-(We don't need tickets because we have student ID cards. We cross the *bridge* over the river, then Kelly gets on the bus in town. We go through three *traffic lights*, then arrive at Jamie's stop. Then we go past the *railway station*, where we pick up passengers from the train – so, Yasmin and Leo get on the bus there. Next, the bus goes round a *roundabout* and then after a few more stops we arrive at school. Sometimes there's a lot of *traffic* and the journey's slow – but then we get more time to chat! ☺

2 Ask students to complete the exercise. Have them compare their answers in pairs before checking them in open class.

Answers

1 roundabout **2** traffic **3** bridge **4** bus stop **5** traffic lights

Refer students to the Vocabulary reference, page 164, for more information on topic vocabulary.

Compound nouns

3 1.26 Elicit what compound nouns are (*two words that go together to form one noun*). Give a few examples, e.g. *railway station, bus stop*. Then ask students to complete the exercise. Play the audio for students to listen and check their answers.

Answers/Audioscript

1 (d) car park **2** (e) driving licence **3** (a) helicopter ride
4 (c) petrol station **5** (b) sailing boat **6** (g) ticket machine
7 (f) tour guide **8** (h) traffic news

4 Ask students to complete the exercise. Check their answers.

Answers

1 traffic news **2** tour guide **3** helicopter ride **4** driving licence
5 ticket machine **6** car park **7** petrol station **8** sailing boat

Refer students to the Vocabulary reference, page 164, for more information on word patterns.

Phrasal verbs

5 1.27 Have a volunteer go outside the classroom and knock on the door. Say *come in*, and elicit the meaning of *come in*. Then have students complete the exercise. Play the audio for students to listen and check their answers.

Answers/Audioscript

1 to enter a place: *go in*
2 to leave the ground and go into the sky: *take off*
3 to start a journey: *set off*
4 what somebody says to invite you into a place: *come in*
5 to collect something or somebody, often in a car: *pick up*
6 to leave a main road: *turn off*

Language note

These phrasal verbs belong to three different categories.

Come in, *go in* and *set off* are intransitive phrasal verbs (with no object). Note that when these verbs are followed by a place, this is introduced with *to*. *Turn off (the road)* is a non-separable phrasal verb, and the object, whether it is a noun or pronoun, will always come after the particle.

Pick up is taught with two meanings and in both cases the object can go between the verb and the particle (*pick the children up*) or after the particle (*pick up the children*) when it is a noun, but a pronoun has to go between the verb and the particle (*pick them up*).

Take off could be problematic when it means 'how a plane leaves' as it works in the same way as *come in*, *go in* and *set off*. However, when it means 'to remove something' it works in the same way as *pick up*.

6 Ask students what the message is about (*a school trip update*). Then have them complete the exercise. Check their answers.

Answers

1 take off **2** pick up **3** set off **4** come in **5** turn off

Refer students to the Vocabulary reference, page 164, for more information on phrasal verbs.

Homework OWB

Assign students Vocabulary exercises 1, 2 and 3 on pages 30–31 of their Workbook.

LISTENING
Gap fill

→ Student's Book, page 40 SB

Lesson aims

- Listen for important information
- Practise a gap-fill exam task
- Discuss ways to check spelling

Lead-in

Books closed. Explain to students that you are going to describe a photo and that they have to listen to your description and try to draw what you describe. Use the photo at the top of Student's Book page 40, e.g. *In the top half of the photo there's an open suitcase with clothes in it. In front of …* Have students compare their drawings in pairs or small groups before looking at the Student's Book.

1 Ask students what tourists usually do when they visit a new place. Brainstorm ideas on the board. Then have students complete the exercise in pairs or as a group.

Answers
Students' own answers

EXAM SKILL

Listening for important information

Ask students to read the tips.

- Remind students that it is important to predict the possible format(s) of the numbers they are going to hear. For example, the way we say numbers in a time (1:15 could be *one fifteen* or *quarter past one*) is very different to the way we say numbers in a date (15/01 could be *the fifteenth of January* or *January the fifteenth*) and students should try to prepare for this.
- Tell students that if they are unsure about a number they heard, they should listen very carefully to that number in the second listening.

Extra support

Play ***Bingo*** with the class. Write the following pool of numbers on the board and ask students to draw a grid, (three columns by two rows) and choose six items to complete it.

32 £2.50 16th 4:30 pm 30 October 3.8 230.5 44 £9.99 17 15 60th 14 70

Read out numbers at random, making a note of the order to check the winner's answers at the end. Before you call out the numbers, explain that the number *44* can also be said as 'double four' and the number zero as 'oh'. The first student to call 'bingo' wins.

2 1.28 Tell students they are going to listen to five short conversations. Then play the audio for them to complete the exercise. Play the track again for students to check their answers.

Answers
1 32a **2** 4 **3** 786 934 **4** 16th **5** 12:14

OPTIMISE YOUR EXAM

Gap fill

Ask students to read the tips.

- Point out that if the speaker spells a word out in listening exam tasks, that means students are expected to spell the word correctly. However, if they hear a word that is not spelt out, they should write it how they think it is spelt.
- When speaking, point out that a useful technique is to say a word that begins with the letter causing problems, e.g. *No, not 'z' for 'zoo', it's 'c' for 'Canada'.*

3 1.29 Explain that students will hear eight short conversations and have to write down the words that are spelt out. Play the audio and then have them compare their answers in pairs before checking them in open class.

Answers
2 5 Solomon Street **3** Cambourne school **4** Alisha Pieters **5** Leicester **6** Clapham Junction **7** Borough Road **8** Tom Maltravers

4 1.30 Tell students they will hear a phone conversation between a customer and an agent in a travel company. Have them look at the information and predict the type of numbers they will hear (*2 a list of numbers, 4 a date, 5 a price*). Play the audio. Have students review their answers before they listen again. Play the track again and elicit answers from students around the class.

Answers
1 Johnstone **2** A79916 **3** Australia **4** 30th November **5** (no cost / free)

Exam task

5 1.31 Have students read the information before they listen. Play the audio. Don't check answers at this stage, as students will listen again to check in Exercise 6.

6 1.31 Have students review their answers. Play the track again. Elicit answers from students around the class.

Answers
1 Nunthorpe **2** 8:15 / quarter past eight **3** 4:30 / half past four **4** Activity Centre **5** (drinking) water

THINK | RESEARCH | CULTURE | **LEARN** | ME

Point out that many web search engines and some online dictionaries / dictionary apps now have 'fuzzy searches', so even if you don't spell the word correctly, it will still offer suggestions of what it thinks the word you are looking for might be.

Homework OWB

Assign students Listening exercises 1, 2 and 3 on page 32 of their Workbook.

GRAMMAR 2
Past simple and past continuous

→ Student's Book, page 41

Lesson aims

- Understand the differences between the past simple and past continuous
- Practise using the past simple and past continuous
- Discuss things different people were doing in the past

Lead-in

Write this sentence starter on the board:

I was doing my homework last night when …

Tell students you want to hear the most ridiculous excuse possible for why they haven't done their homework, e.g. *I was doing my homework last night when a spaceship landed and aliens took my school bag.* Have students think of ways to complete the sentence in pairs. Elicit the best ideas from different pairs around the class.

Grammar in context

Ask students to complete the task. Refer them to the information in the *Remember* box if they aren't sure. Check their answers.

Remind students that they can find more information in the Grammar reference, Unit 4, page 154.

Answers

1 were sailing, fell **2** were sailing **3** fell (into the water)

1 Go through the first sentence as a class. Elicit the continuous activity that was interrupted (*everyone was having a good time*). Have students complete the exercise individually. Then check answers as a class.

Answers

1 arrived, was having **2** was listening, called **3** did you break, Were you running **4** was riding, fell **5** stopped, was driving **6** was shopping, lost

2 Ask students to complete the exercise. Check answers in open class.

Answers

1 said, were looking **2** were walking, saw, was shopping **3** didn't want, was raining **4** were driving, stopped **5** changed, were chatting

Mixed ability

Give weaker students the tenses they need for each item (e.g. ***1*** *past simple, past continuous;* ***2*** *past continuous, past simple*) and ask them to focus on choosing the correct form of the verb *to be* in the past continuous, and on spelling the *-ing* and past simple forms correctly. Ask stronger students to write additional sentences using different combinations of the verbs in item 2, e.g. *drive + begin – We were driving home yesterday when it began to snow.*

3 Tell students to look at the travel blog and describe what they see in the picture (*a person looking at the sky*). After students complete the exercise, have them compare their answers in pairs. Then check answers in open class.

Answers

1 didn't post **2** were staying **3** didn't stream **4** weren't camping **5** took **6** was beginning **7** was looking **8** flew **9** were taking **10** started **11** kept **12** was standing

Cultural note

The Uyuni Salt Flats (Salar de Uyuni in Spanish) are in the north-east of Bolivia, high in the Andes. They cover over 10,000 km^2 and are at an altitude of just over 3,500 m. They were formed from a giant prehistoric lake tens of thousands of years ago and contain large quantities of lithium, which is extracted for use in batteries. Tourism is becoming more popular in the area and hotels are often built from blocks of salt.

THINK | RESEARCH | CULTURE | LEARN | ME

In pairs, students discuss what they are doing.

Homework

Assign students Grammar 2 exercise 1 on page 31 of their Workbook.

Assign students the Flipped classroom tasks on page 42 of their Student's Book if you'd like them to prepare for the next lesson. To complete this task, students need to watch the *Talk2Me* video which can be found on the Resource Centre.

SPEAKING
Collaborative task

→ Student's Book, page 42

Lesson aims

- Focus on asking someone to repeat
- Practise asking for repetition
- Practise responding to questions in a collaborative exam task

The *Talk2Me* video in this unit focuses on exercise. The people in the video talk about the best type of exercise and the benefits of cycling, then arrange to buy some bikes.

Students answer some comprehension questions and then listen for key phrases in the video.

The video can be used in one of two ways:

Flipped classroom

Flipped classroom option

Using this approach, students watch the video and complete the exercises for homework. This prepares students for the speaking lesson by introducing them to the topic and the key phrases to use in the exam task. Teachers who use this method will find they have more class time to spend on activating the target language and developing fluency for the final task.

Talk2Me worksheet

Ask students to also complete the *Talk2Me* worksheet on the Resource Centre for more detailed comprehension exercises and more practice of the key phrases.

Classroom option

1 Ask students to spend a minute or two reading the questions. Play the *Talk2Me* video for students to complete the exercise. Play the video again, if necessary, before checking their answers.

2 Play the *Talk2Me* video again, so students underline the phrases in the *Phrase expert* box. Pause the video from time to time if necessary. Check answers in open class.

Talk2Me worksheet

Ask students to also complete the *Talk2Me* worksheet on the Resource Centre for more detailed comprehension exercises and more practice of the key phrases.

Answers

The transcript and answer key for the *Talk2Me* video exercises and Worksheet can be found on the Teacher's Resource Centre.

Lead-in

Ask students to work in teams to brainstorm as many words as possible related to travel and transport in one minute.

3 Divide the class into pairs or groups to ask and answer the questions. Elicit answers from different pairs or groups around the class.

4 Have students describe the flyer before completing the exercise in pairs. Don't check answers at this stage as students check their answers in Exercise 5.

Extra support

Write these prompts on the board:

be / car park?
How much / be / student ticket?
What / see / museum?
buy / anything?
be / open / weekends?

Have students use the prompts to write the five questions and match them to the information in Exercise 4. Tell them that some are *yes/no* questions and some are *Wh-* questions.

5 1.32 Have students review the questions they wrote before listening and make any changes. Play the track. Elicit answers from students around the class and have students say how their questions were similar or different to the audio.

Answers/Audioscript

1 What can I see at the museum?
2 Is it open at the weekends?
3 Can I buy anything?
4 Is there a car park?
5 How much is a student ticket?

6 1.32 Play the track for students to compare the answers on the recording with the information on the flyer. Have them compare their answers in pairs before you check with the class.

Answers

1 There are more than 50 classic cars in the museum, not 15.
4 The parking is free, not £12.

EXAM SKILL

Asking someone to repeat

Ask students to read the tips.

- Point out that, in the same way as it is very important to understand what the examiner says, students also need to understand what their partner says in order to successfully complete the collaborative task.
- Remind them that they can ask for general clarification with questions like *Could you say that again, please?* or they can ask about a specific piece of information again, e.g. *How much did you say?*

7 1.33 Read the instructions out loud and have students prepare to write notes. Play the track. Elicit answers from students around the class.

Answers

1 Sorry, can you say that again, please?
2 Did you say 'How much is the car park?'?
3 I'm sorry, could you repeat that?

OPTIMISE YOUR EXAM

Collaborative task

Ask students to read the tips.

- Remind students that in many speaking exams there is a part where students work together on a collaborative task.
- One of the marking criteria in many speaking exams is interactive communication. This refers to the students' ability to participate actively in a two-way conversation at an appropriate level without intervention from the examiner.
- Tell students that in this exam task type, both candidates are being assessed all the time. Examiners will be listening both for the candidates' ability to form questions correctly, and their ability to answer questions in full sentences with the correct information.

▾ Exam task

8 Assign each student a letter, A or B, and put them into A/B pairs. Give them a moment to look at their information / question topics on page 136/139. Time students (two minutes) and give them an update, e.g. *One minute to go …* Remind students to use phrases from the *Phrase expert* box for asking someone to repeat something. Walk round, monitoring students for good use of language and errors to go over at the end of the activity.

Write any errors on the board and go through them with students, eliciting corrections from them where possible. After the class feedback, students could then repeat this activity with another partner, to try to improve their performance.

Suggested answers

Student A's questions

What can I/you see at the motor show?
Is it open at the weekend?
Can I/you get a student ticket? How much is it?
Can people buy cars at the show?
Can I/you buy food there?

Student B's questions

What can I/you see at the photography exhibition?
What's the address?
Is it open on Wednesdays?
Do I need a ticket? / Where can I get a ticket?
How much are the tickets?
Where can I/you get more information?

Homework OWB

Assign students Speaking exercises 1 and 2 on pages 32–33 of their Workbook.

LANGUAGE IN USE
Multiple choice

→ Student's Book, page 43 SB

Lesson aims

- Focus on linking words
- Practise a multiple-choice exam task

Lead-in

Write *Down Under* on the board and ask students if they know what it means. If they don't, draw a globe on the board with the United Kingdom at the top and Australia at the bottom. Draw an arrow to the UK and another to the bottom of the globe and ask students what country it is. Explain that 'down under', refers to Australia. Ask students to tell you everything they can think of about Australia, e.g. *koala bears, kangaroos, Sydney Opera House, barbecues, surfing, Uluru (Ayer's Rock).*

1 Ask students what the difference between a tour and a journey is and elicit the correct option for the first sentence. Have students complete the exercise and compare their answers in pairs. Then check the answers in open class and make sure that students are clear about the meaning of all the words.

Answers

1 A **2** B **3** A **4** C **5** C **6** A **7** C **8** A

Language note

Some commonly confused words

A *tour* is the act of travelling round a place to see interesting things; a *journey* is the act of travelling from one place to another.

A *chair* is a piece of furniture you sit on. You sit on a *seat* on a form of transport.

Luggage means all the bags you take on holiday. A *suitcase* is one piece of luggage; it has flat sides and a handle.

EXAM SKILL

Using linking words

Ask students to read the tips.

- Remind students that it is important to link ideas smoothly when writing or speaking. Naturally sounding language with appropriate linking words, rather than short disjointed sentences will always get better marks.
- Point out that linking words are often tested in exams and students should learn and practise different words and phrases for each linking function. This will not only prepare them better for multiple-choice and cloze tasks, but will allow them to produce greater variety in their written work.

2 Have students complete the exercise and then compare their answers in pairs before you check them in open class.

Answers

1 before **2** until **3** but **4** when **5** because

OPTIMISE YOUR EXAM

Multiple choice

Ask students to read the tips.

- Make sure students understand they need to read all the sentences or text before they start answering, as the context may help them to choose the correct answers.
- Remind students that multiple-choice tasks often test their knowledge of linking words, articles, prepositions and pronouns, as well as other grammatical points. Point out that they need to look at the whole sentence and remember that the clues could be before or after each gap and that there may be other words in between.

Exam task

3 Ask students what they know about Australia before completing the exercise. Go through the example question with the class. Tell students to use all the tips they need to complete the exam task the best way possible. Check answers in open class.

Answers
1 C **2** B **3** B **4** A **5** C **6** C **7** B **8** A

Fast finishers

Have fast finishers write the reasons why their answers are correct, e.g. *1 is 'Her' because it refer to Réka.* As you check the answers to Exercise 3, ask the students who wrote reasons to share them with the class.

Homework
Assign students Language in Use exercises 1 and 2 on page 33 of their Workbook.

OWB

WRITING
A postcard

→ Student's Book, pages 44–45

SB

Lesson aims

- Focus on punctuation and spelling
- Plan and write a postcard

Lead-in

Write these sentences on the board and ask students to tell you which country each one is about:

1 We saw the Eiffel Tower yesterday and we're visiting Versailles tomorrow.

2 I'm looking at the Christ the Redeemer Statue at the moment – the cruise is fantastic!

3 We went to the Taj Mahal yesterday. It's great here, but the food is very hot!

Ask students where they might read sentences like these. Elicit that they are all sentences that might appear on postcards.

Answers
1 France **2** Brazil **3** India

1 Ask students if they like to buy, send or receive postcards. Have students discuss the questions, and then elicit answers from different students around the class.

2 Draw students' attention to postcard and elicit information about the place, e.g. *it's near the sea and mountains.* Then have them read the task and answer the questions. Check the answers in open class.

Answers
A postcard of your town; Why do people visit your town? How do people get to your town? What's the best way to get around it?

EXAM SKILL

Punctuation and spelling

Ask students to read the tips.

- Explain that an error in punctuation or spelling could have an effect on the message they want to send. Students should make sure they read their work after they have finished.
- Remind students to look back at the spelling rules for regular verbs and tell them to revise the Irregular verbs reference so that they don't confuse regular and irregular verbs.

3 Tell students to think about the possible mistakes they can find. Check answers in open class.

Answers
Dear Agnes,

My town is near the sea. <u>Most</u> visitors come by ship. <u>There</u> are lots of ships <u>arriving</u> every day. A taxi can take you to the hotel, <u>but</u> you can walk. <u>It's</u> not far.

Maria

4 Have two volunteers read the answers out loud before students complete the exercise. Elicit ideas from students around the class.

Suggested answer
B is the better answer. Jordi answers all three questions clearly, although he also gives information about the airport, which isn't relevant. It is easy to understand what he means, and he uses a better range of vocabulary.

Julia uses more informal language and it is easy to understand what she means, but she doesn't answer the second question.

OPTIMISE YOUR EXAM

A postcard

Ask students to read the tips.

- Remind students of the importance of replying to specific questions. Tell them that it is possible to answer two questions with one answer.
- Tell students that while it is good to experiment with new language in class (trying out new words and finding new ways to say things), an exam is not the place to do this. Explain that it should be written using informal language.

▾ Exam task

5 Invite different volunteers to read the instructions and the postcard. Monitor students and help where necessary. Then have students share their answers in pairs.

Answers

1 Felix
2 25–35
3 three
4 where you last travelled to, what you saw and how you travelled
5 past simple, past continuous
6 words related to holidays and travel

6 Plan Ask students to complete the plan individually. You may want to look at students' plans to check them and give advice and suggestions for improvement before they take the next step.

Extra support

Look at the plan with students. Elicit suggestions for how to complete the *Detail* column from the class and prompt them to write the questions that they need to answer. Give them a couple of minutes to write down some ideas in the *My notes* column. Then have students brainstorm ideas in pairs or small groups for the *Useful language* column. Collate these on the board so all students have plenty of ideas to choose from before they start writing.

7 Write Tell students that they can use their plan as a starting point, but it is OK to change this while they are writing. If there is not enough time, set this and the subsequent checklist exercise for homework.

8 Check Students complete the checklist before they hand in their postcard.

Optional extension

Put the postcards up around the classroom and invite students to read them all. Then ask which place they'd like to visit, which is the most interesting place, etc.

Optional extension

For a slightly longer writing task, and for students to see other text types, refer them to one of the six tasks in the Writing reference (SB p169). Each one includes an annotated sample text and related writing task to challenge your students a little more.

Homework

OWB

Assign students Writing exercises 1, 2, 3 and 4 on page 34 of their Workbook and Progress check 4 on page 35.

Answers PROGRESS CHECK Units 3–4

Exercise 1
1 stop **2** near **3** in **4** on **5** outside **6** ride **7** off **8** there

Exercise 2
1 up **2** in **3** off **4** in **5** off **6** bake **7** take **8** have

Exercise 3
1 C **2** B **3** A **4** B **5** A **6** C **7** B **8** B

Exercise 4
1 asked, was shouting **2** was travelling, ate **3** decided, was shining **4** bought, were cooking

Exercise 5
1 What **2** Did **3** who **4** whose **5** was **6** why **7** Where **8** weren't **9** which **10** when

Exercise 6
1 recipes **2** fried **3** prepare **4** journey **5** traffic light **6** petrol station **7** railway station **8** tour guide

5 Technology talks

UNIT AIMS

Exam preparation in Unit 5:

- understand how often something happens in an online article
- understand when things happen in different situations
- make comparisons in an interview
- understand pronouns and use them in a multiple-choice exercise
- make notes about when and where for an information transfer exercise

TEACHER'S PRESENTATION KIT

- *Talk2Me* videos
- Speaking test videos
- Class and Workbook audio
- Workbook pages and answer key

UNIT OVERVIEW

Student's Book / Digital Student's Book SB		Workbook / Online Workbook OWB
LESSON / EXAM TASK	**EXAM SKILLS / LANGUAGE FOCUS**	**CONSOLIDATION**
Reading **Right/Wrong/Doesn't say**	Understanding how often An online article	Workbook, pp 36–37, Exercises 1, 2, 3, 4 Unit 5, Reading, Exercises 1, 2, 3, 4
Grammar 1	Quantifiers with countable and uncountable nouns	Workbook, p 38, Exercises 1, 2 Unit 5, Grammar 1, Exercises 1, 2
Vocabulary	Words connected with *communication and technology* Compound nouns Collocations with verbs	Workbook, pp 38–39, Exercises 1, 2, 3 Unit 5, Vocabulary, Exercises 1, 2, 3
Listening **Picture multiple choice**	Understanding when things happen	Workbook, p 40, Exercises 1, 2 Unit 5, Listening, Exercises 1, 2
Grammar 2	Comparatives and superlatives	Workbook, p 39, Exercises 1, 2 Unit 5, Grammar 2, Exercises 1, 2
Speaking **Interview**	Making comparisons	Workbook, pp 40–41, Exercises 1, 2, 3 Unit 5, Speaking, Exercises 1, 2, 3
Language in Use **Multiple-choice dialogue**	Pronouns	Workbook, p 41, Exercises 1, 2, 3 Unit 5, Language in Use, Exercises 1, 2, 3
Writing **Information transfer**	Making notes: where and when	Workbook, p 42, Exercises 1, 2, 3, 4 Unit 5, Writing, Exercises 1, 2, 3, 4
		Workbook, p 43, Progress check and Cumulative progress Progress check and Cumulative progress

Additional material

PRESENTATION KIT	TEACHER'S/STUDENT'S RESOURCE CENTRE RC	TEST GENERATOR
Talk2Me video *It's better to …*	**Unit 5 worksheets:** *Optimise your grammar* (Standard and Higher), *Optimise your vocabulary* (Standard and Higher), *Talk2Me* video, *Say it right* **Units 5–6 worksheets:** CLIL, Culture, Everyday English (TRC only), Grammar communication (TRC only)	Unit Test 5 (Standard and Higher)

READING
Right/Wrong/Doesn't say | An online article

→ Student's Book, pages 48–49 SB

Lesson aims

- Focus on how often something happens
- Practise a Right/Wrong/Doesn't say exam task
- Discuss owning a mobile phone

Lead-in

Ask students to look at the unit title ***Technology talks*** and the photo and ask them what they think the unit will be about (*communications and technology*). Elicit what functions and icons they recognise in the photo , e.g. *mail, cloud*. Then ask students approximately how much time they spend communicating using technology every day.

1 Hold up your phone and elicit all the things people can use a mobile phone for. Write students' ideas on the board. After students discuss the questions, elicit answers from the class. Open out the final question to a class debate.

EXAM SKILL

Understanding how often

Ask students to read the tips.

- Remind students that we usually use the present simple to talk about routines and this is often combined with adverbs of frequency, which students practised in Unit 1.
- Explain that there are other types of expressions that can help students understand how often things happen, too. Tell students that some of these words are in the text and you will focus on them later in the unit.

2 Read out the first sentence and the two possible answers to the class. Elicit the correct answer. Then have students complete the exercise. Check answers in open class.

Answers

1 B **2** A **3** B

3 Students complete the exercise. Don't check answers at this stage as students will compare their answers in Exercise 4.

Fast finishers

Fast finishers make a note of the meaning of the other numbers in the text.

Answers

52% The percentage of people who regularly do their shopping online in China. **88%** The percentage of Venezuelans who use their mobiles to take photos. **90%** The percentage of Nigerians who have a mobile phone. **50%** The percentage of Filipinos who chat online about sport. **15%** The percentage of the British population who live in a 'mobile-only' home.

4 After students compare their answers, ask fast finishers to share the information they found out with the class.

Answers

1 The number of hours a week people in the Philippines spend on social networking sites.

2 The number of hours a week people in the USA spend on social networking sites.

3 The percentage of Nigerians with a landline phone in their home.

SAY IT RIGHT

Missing vowel sounds in questions

For the *Say it right* pronunciation activity and instructions, go to the Teacher's Resource Centre. TRC

OPTIMISE YOUR EXAM

Right/Wrong/Doesn't say

Ask students to read the tips.

- Explain to students that in *right/wrong/doesn't say* exam tasks, the questions are always in the same order as the text.
- Remind students that they should always check their answers carefully and underline the part of the text which gives them the answer. Tell students that if they are underlining sections in a different order, they are almost certainly looking at the wrong part of the text.

Exam task

5 2.01 **Note: The reading text is also available on the audio CD. You may want to have students listen and read the text before doing the exam task.**

Go through the example with the class. Then ask students to complete the exercise. Have students compare in pairs before you check in open class. Elicit the evidence for their answers from the text as you check answers.

Answers

1 A (*Does your family shop online? Many people around the world do.*)

2 C (The text says, *There are now some important online stores in China, such as Alibaba …*, but it doesn't say people from the UK shop at Alibaba.)

3 B (*In fact, 60% of Chileans, Argentinians and Brazilians regularly take photos with their phones.*)

4 B (*In the Philippines, people spend about 37 hours a week using social networking sites. That's more hours than in the USA …*)

5 C (The text says, *… 70% of Filipinos talk about music and films, and over 50% chat about sport*, but it doesn't say whether or not they talk about video games.)

6 A (*In Nigeria, a lot of people own a mobile phone – nearly 90% of the population.*)

7 C (The text says, *Only 15% of the British population live in a 'mobile-only' home*, not that this percentage of people in Britain have a landline phone.)

Optional extension

Ask students to write a brief summary of how much time people in each country spend on social networking sites.

6 Have students scan the text for the answer to the first definition. Then have them complete the exercise. Check students' answers in open class.

Answers

1 shopping online **2** population **3** stores **4** spend **5** facts **6** selfies **7** chat **8** sites

Optional extension

Ask students to write personal sentences using the words in Exercise 6 saying how often they do each action, e.g. *I never shop online. I spend four hours a day online. I always chat with my friends on my mobile.* Have students compare their sentences in pairs and see how similar or different they are.

THINK | RESEARCH | CULTURE | LEARN | ME

Tell students to brainstorm all of their ideas. Then have pairs or groups present their ideas to the class, giving reasons for their answers.

Homework

OWB

Assign students Reading exercises 1, 2, 3 and 4 on pages 36–37 of their Workbook.

GRAMMAR 1

Quantifiers with countable and uncountable nouns

→ Student's Book, page 50 SB

Lesson aims

- Focus on quantifiers with countable and uncountable nouns
- Practise talking about the quantities of things

Lead-in

Divide the board in half down the centre and write *a/an* at the top of the left side and *some* at the top of the right side. Have students copy this in their notebooks. Read out the following items for students to decide which group they belong to:

singer steak bridge computer game honey beach traffic musician exhibition cereal oil bus stop

Have students compare their answers in pairs before you check answers in open class and collate the items on the board. Ask students what the difference is between the words on the left and the words on the right, and explain that the words on the left can also be used with *some* if these are made plural.

Answers

a/an (+ countable noun): singer, steak, bridge, computer game, beach, musician, exhibition, bus stop

some (+ uncountable noun): honey, traffic, cereal, oil

Grammar in context

Ask students to complete the task and look at the text to check their answers. Tell students to read the information in the *Remember* box if their answers are incorrect.

Remind students that they can find more information in the Grammar reference, Unit 5, page 154.

Answers

1 much **2** many **3** a few **4** some **5** a little **6** lot

Language note

Countable nouns are items we can count using numbers. We cannot count uncountable nouns, but we can measure them, for example, in weight: *100 grams of sugar*; or with containers *a bag of potatoes, a box of cereal*, etc. Uncountable nouns don't take *-s* or other plural forms; they take the singular form of verbs.

1 Ask students to complete the exercise individually. Remind them to refer to the information in the *Remember* box if they aren't sure. Ask students to compare their answers with a partner before checking in open class.

Answers

1 a little **2** a lot of **3** A few **4** any **5** a lot of **6** much

2 Focus students' attention on the photo and have them describe what they see before they complete the exercise. Then check answers in open class.

Answers

1 B **2** A **3** B **4** B **5** C **6** C **7** B **8** C **9** A

Fast finishers

Ask students to look again at the gaps and see if any other quantifiers could be used in each space. Elicit ideas while going through the answers.

Suggested answers

1 a lot **2** many / lots of / a lot of **3** Lots **4** any **5** lots of / some **6** some **7** a few **8** some **9** lots of

3 Ask students what they can write about emails. Elicit ideas and then have students complete the exercise individually. Walk round the class, helping students and monitoring for good use of the quantifiers. Elicit some answers from different students around the class.

Homework

OWB

Assign students Grammar 1 exercises 1 and 2 on page 38 of their Workbook.

VOCABULARY
Topic vocabulary | Word patterns | Collocations

→ Student's Book, page 51

Lesson aims

Understand the correct usage of:

- words connected with communication and technology
- noun + noun word formation (compound nouns)
- verb + noun collocations

Lead-in

Play the memory game *In my room at home I have ...* with the class. Start by providing a model sentence, e.g. *In my room at home I have a lot of papers.* Nominate a strong student to repeat the sentence and add an item, e.g. ... *a lot of papers and some books*, and then another student, e.g. ... *a lot of papers, some books and a computer.* Highlight that every item should use a suitable quantifier. When students have understood the activity, put them in small groups to play. Walk round the class, monitoring students' use of language. Make a note of any errors you hear.

Words connected with *communication and technology*

1 2.02 Ask students what parts of a computer they can name. Then have them complete the exercise individually. Play the audio for students to check their answers.

Answers/Audioscript

1 screen **2** keyboard **3** laptop **4** printer **5** camera **6** mouse

2 2.03 Ask students what the text type is (*a blog*) and have them complete the exercise individually. Play the audio for students to check their answers. Ask students if they regularly read blogs and, if so, what they are about.

Answers/Audioscript

Hi everyone! Sorry I've been quiet! I've just moved house. It's good to get *online* again – I missed *blogging*! I have a lovely big desk for my *laptop* in the new house. So, I can use that when I'm at home. It's got a really big *screen*, which is perfect for watching videos. I decided to get a *printer* as well, so I can print the photos I like. The laptop is good for gaming too. The *graphics* in the games look much better. The *keyboard* is a bit different from my last one, so sorry if I make any spelling mistakes! The wireless *mouse* is great and isn't noisy when you click it. I still need to *download* my files from the old computer. And I need some new *software* so that I can *stream* music faster.

Tomorrow, I'll use the *camera* and upload some new photos of me at my new desk!

Refer students to the Vocabulary reference, page 165, for more information on topic vocabulary.

Compound nouns

3 2.04 Ask students to complete the exercise. Play the audio for students to listen and check their answers.

Point out that *website* is written as one word, but that all the other words are written as two. Highlight that for most of these items the main stress is on the first word, except for *mobile phone, laptop computer* and *personal computer* where the main stress is on the second word.

Answers/Audioscript

1 *player*: CD player, DVD player, MP3 player

2 *phone*: camera phone, cell phone, mobile phone

3 *web*: web address, web page, website

4 *computer*: laptop computer, personal computer, computer file, computer software

Language note

A 'mobile phone' and a 'cell phone' are the same thing – the term *mobile phone* is British English whereas *cell phone* is used mainly in American English.

4 Write the sentences *His mobile / camera phone is really old. You can't even take pictures with it.* on the board and elicit the correct option to complete it (*mobile*). Then ask students to complete the exercise. Elicit answers from different students around the class.

Answers

1 MP3 **2** website **3** page **4** software

Refer students to the Vocabulary reference, page 165, for more information on word patterns.

Collocations with verbs

5 2.05 Ask students to cover items 1–6 and to suggest words which might come after each of the verbs in the box. Have students complete the exercise individually. Play the audio for students to check their answers.

Answers/Audioscript

1 *make* a phone call / *take* a phone call **2** download a piece of software **3** *download* a file / *open* a file **4** *download* a photograph / *take* a photograph **5** *send* a text message **6** *start* a conversation

6 Remind students to use the skills they learnt in previous lessons when completing multiple-choice activities. Have them compare ideas in pairs before checking answers in open class.

Answers

1 started a conversation **2** making a phone call **3** open/download a file **4** download a piece of software **5** take a photograph **6** send a text message

Mixed ability

To check the answers to Exercise 6, pair strong students with weak students and have stronger students close their books. Ask weaker students to read the first part of the sentence, up to the verb in the correct form, e.g. *1 I met her on the train and she …* Tell their partner to say the rest of the sentence from memory. Have weaker students help their partners by giving them some of the key words from the second part of the sentence if they get stuck, e.g. *1 social networking sites, 2 brother, Canada, talk*, etc.

Refer students to the Vocabulary reference, page 165, for more information on collocations.

Homework

OWB

Assign students Vocabulary exercises 1, 2 and 3 on pages 38–39 of their Workbook.

LISTENING

Picture multiple choice

→ Student's Book, page 52 SB

Lesson aims

- Listen and understand when things happen
- Practise a picture multiple-choice exam task

Lead-in

Write the number *3* on the board. Put students into pairs and tell them to write down:

three words you can use before 'player'

three things you can do with a file

three words you can use after 'web'

three things you can download

three words you can use before 'phone'

Check their answers.

Suggested answers

CD/DVD/MP3 player; open/save/close a file; web page / website / web address; download music/films/apps; cell/ mobile/camera phone

1 Ask students if they are creative and, if so, what they like to create. Then have them look at the photo and discuss the questions. Elicit answers from different students around the class.

EXAM SKILL

Understanding when things happen

Ask students to read the tips.

- Remind students that they have used language to talk about the past (with the past simple and past continuous), the present (with the present simple and present continuous), and the future (with the present simple and present continuous). Elicit an example of each and remind students that they are now prepared to identify these tenses when listening.
- Explain that, as well as the tenses, there are usually other clues to help students understand when things happen and the exact order of events. Tell students not to panic if they don't hear the tense clearly, and to simply focus on the rest of the sentence for specific words in these cases.

2 Invite two volunteers to read out the conversation. Then ask students to complete the exercise individually. Check their answers in open class.

Answers

1 I looked **2** I'm writing **3** It says

3 Tell students to refer back to the conversation in Exercise 2. In pairs, students put the events in order. Check answers in open class.

Answers

a 3 **b** 4 **c** 2 **d** 1

OPTIMISE YOUR EXAM

Picture multiple choice

Ask students to read the tips.

- Opinions are an expression of a person's feelings and are based on facts or emotions but can't be proven to be true or false. Opinions can be preceded with terms such as *I think* (which students will see on the *Speaking* page in this unit), or with adjectives, comparatives and superlatives (which students will see on the next *Grammar* page).
- Point out that the word *like* is a commonly used word in English, but it does not always mean 'something we enjoy'. Highlight that in questions such as *What's X like?* we use it to ask for descriptions. Also explain that students might hear the word *like* within a negative sentence, in which case the meaning is the opposite, or could even be as extreme as *hate*, depending on the exact words chosen.

Exam task

4 2.06 Before students listen, tell them that they will hear five situations and need to identify the correct image for each one. Go through the example and then play the audio for students to complete the exercise. Ask them to compare their choices in pairs. Then, play the track again for students to check their answers and discuss as a class.

Answers
1 C **2** A **3** B **4** C **5** A

Homework OWB
Assign students Listening exercises 1 and 2 on page 40 of their Workbook.

GRAMMAR 2
Comparatives and superlatives

→ Student's Book, page 53 SB

Lesson aims

- Understand the correct usage of comparatives and superlatives
- Practise comparing two or more things
- Discuss useful pieces of technology

Lead-in

In pairs, students race to make a list of adjectives for every letter of the alphabet in a three-minute time limit. Do a feedback session in open class and ask students to share the items they chose for each letter. Check that they have spelt them correctly. Write the adjectives on the board, if possible using one colour for adjectives which form the comparative/superlative with *-er/-est* and a different colour for adjectives which take *more / the most*. At the end, ask students to tell you why you have used the two colours.

Possible answers
High-level items in brackets
angry, **b**ad, **c**omfortable, **d**irty, **e**arly, **f**ast, **g**ood, **h**igh, **i**mportant, (**j**ealous), **k**ind, **l**oud, **m**odern, **n**ew, **o**ld, **p**retty, **q**uiet, (**r**ude), **s**mall, **t**hin, **u**nusual, (**v**ictorious), **w**orried, (**x**enophobic), **y**oung, (**z**ealous)

Grammar in context

Tell students that the sentences are extracts from the listening they heard in the previous lesson. Ask students to complete the task and refer them to the information in the *Remember* box if they aren't sure. Then check their answers.

Remind students that they can find more information in the Grammar reference, Unit 5, page 155.

Answers
1 best **2** better **3** more

Language note

Students are tested on comparative and superlative forms in all parts of official exams at this level. Remind students that this language point is also useful in oral exams, e.g. when giving full answers to personal questions and for discussing things with a partner in collaborative tasks.

1 If students aren't confident doing this type of 'sentence transformation', as this is their first appearance in the book, consider doing the second item together as a class. Ask students to complete the exercise individually. Have students compare answers in pairs before checking in open class.

Answers
2 The PC is more expensive than the laptop.
3 Rap is more popular than rock music.
4 Her blog is more interesting than yours / your blog.
5 The video of the surfer is stranger than the video of the skateboarder.
6 My computing class is bigger than the photography class.
7 His email was longer than hers / her email.
8 The design of the laptop is more modern than the PC.

2 Ask students to complete the exercise. Check answers in open class.

Answers
1 newer than **2** bigger than **3** more expensive **4** the best
5 more **6** heavier than **7** the most popular

3 Before students complete the exercise, remind them to think carefully about whether the adjectives form the comparative/superlative with *-er/-est* or with *more / the most* and to be very careful with spelling. Have students compare their answers in pairs before you check answers with the class.

Answers
1 more exciting **2** the most interesting **3** better **4** more careful
5 more difficult **6** the best **7** busier **8** the most unusual

THINK | RESEARCH | CULTURE | LEARN | **ME**

Tell students to think about what inventions have had the biggest impact on the world and what they think it would be difficult to live without. Have students discuss their ideas with a partner. Then elicit answers from different students in the class and try to develop a class discussion.

Homework OWB
Assign students Grammar 2 exercises 1 and 2 on page 39 of their Workbook.
Assign students the Flipped classroom tasks on page 54 of their Student's Book if you'd like them to prepare for the next lesson. To complete this task, students need to watch the *Talk2Me* video which can be found on the Resource Centre.

SPEAKING
Interview

→ Student's Book, page 54

Lesson aims

- Focus on making comparisons
- Practise answering personal questions in an interview task

The *Talk2Me* video in this unit focuses on communications and technology. People talk in the video talk about the advantages of online shopping and they order some food items online.

Students answer some comprehension questions and then listen for key phrases in the video.

The video can be used in one of two ways:

Flipped classroom

Flipped classroom option

Using this approach, students watch the video and complete the exercises for homework. This prepares students for the speaking lesson by introducing them to the topic and the key phrases to use in the exam task. Teachers who use this method will find they have more class time to spend on activating the target language and developing fluency for the final task.

***Talk2Me* worksheet**

Ask students to also complete the *Talk2Me* worksheet on the Resource Centre for more detailed comprehension exercises and more practice of the key phrases.

Classroom option

1 Ask students to spend a minute or two reading the questions. Play the *Talk2Me* video for students to complete the exercise. Play the video again, if necessary, before checking their answers.

2 Play the *Talk2Me* video again, so students underline the phrases in the *Phrase expert* box. Pause the video from time to time if necessary. Check answers in open class.

***Talk2Me* worksheet**

Ask students to also complete the *Talk2Me* worksheet on the Resource Centre for more detailed comprehension exercises and more practice of the key phrases.

Answers

The transcript and answer key for the *Talk2Me* video exercises and Worksheet can be found on the Teacher's Resource Centre.

Lead-in

Write some commonly used text-messaging abbreviations on the board and put students into pairs to discuss what they think they mean (answers in brackets).

2moro (tomorrow)* *2nte* (tonight)* *BFF* (Best friends forever!) *BTW* (by the way) *CTN* (Can't talk now.) *CU* (See you!)* *GR8* (Great!)* *IDK* (I don't know.) *TMI* (Too much information!) *L8R* (later)* *LOL* (laughing out loud) *P911* (Parent alert!)* *THX* (thanks) *TTYL* (Talk to you later.) W8 (wait)*

Explain that not all text-messaging abbreviations are simply the first letters of the words. In some cases (marked with *), they are a play on the sounds (e.g. 'two'morrow), or rely on common knowledge (e.g. *P911*, 911 is the emergency number in a variety of countries). Have students share the abbreviations they know with the class and elicit their favourite one.

3 Have students look at the photos and say where the people are (*The people in photo A are possibly at school and the people in photo B are at home*). Then have them complete the exercise in pairs or groups. Elicit answers from the class.

EXAM SKILL

Making comparisons

Ask students to read the tips.

- Tell students they should now be able to understand people talking about the past, present and future, and should also be able to use these tenses themselves.
- Explain that in a Speaking exam, they will get better marks if they try to compare more than one thing, as this will allow them to use a wider range of grammatical structures. Using appropriate phrases, like the ones in the *Phrase expert* box, to introduce their ideas can also make a difference to their marks.

4 2.07 Have students read through the questions and options before you play the track. Check answers in open class.

Answers

1 chatting online **2** watched a film **3** shopping with friends **4** playing games online

5 2.07 Tell students they are going to listen to the audio in more detail. Play the track for them to listen and number the phrases in order. Elicit answers from different students around the class, encouraging them to repeat the information they heard.

Answers

1 D **2** C **3** B **4** A

OPTIMISE YOUR EXAM

Interview

Ask students to read the tips.

- Remind students that when they are revising, they should look back through the topics in the book, check they feel confident talking about each of the areas and make sure they have personal examples for each topic to talk about.
- Encourage them to think about the type of questions that they may be asked – they can do this by looking through the Speaking lessons in their Student's Book and making a few notes about each topic. They should include past experiences, present situations and future plans.
- Remind them that they need to listen carefully to the question they are asked so that they can answer in the correct tense. However, point out that the examiner will be impressed if they can introduce some comparisons with other periods in their life. For example, if they are asked *What is your favourite type of film?* They could answer *I love watching action and adventure films now, although when I was younger, I used to enjoy cartoons, especially Disney films.* Help with names of film genres if needed.

Exam task

6 Divide the class into pairs and have them complete the exercise. Remind students to use phrases for making comparisons from the *Phrase expert* box. Walk round the class, monitoring students for good use of language and errors to go over at the end of the exercise.

Write any errors you hear on the board and go through them with students, eliciting corrections from them. After the class feedback, you could have students repeat this activity with another partner, to try to improve their performance.

Extra support

Answer one of the questions in Exercise 4 yourself as a model for students. Ask students to listen to you carefully and identify the question you are answering and make a note of the main areas you talk about and the comparisons you make between different things. Make sure your answers are not overcomplicated, so that students can see how they might be able to answer the questions themselves and not feel your model is intimidating.

Mixed ability

With a weaker class, give students the verb tense they need to form each *Wh-* question and give them time to work in pairs formulating each question together. Check the questions and drill them for correct pronunciation and intonation before continuing. Ask stronger classes to think of two additional items to 'surprise' their partner with; one *Wh-* question and one item with *Tell me …*

Homework

OWB

Assign students Speaking exercises 1, 2 and 3 on pages 40–41 of their Workbook.

LANGUAGE IN USE

Multiple-choice dialogue

→ Student's Book, page 55 SB

Lesson aims

- Focus on pronouns and people
- Practise a multiple-choice dialogue exam task
- Discuss communication

Lead-in

Ask students *How many different forms of communication did you use yesterday?* Have students make a list of all the different ways they remember communicating individually and then compare lists with their partner. Find out which student used the most forms of communication and ask him or her to share them with the class. Have the other students listen and add to their lists.

1 2.08 Before students listen, tell them what the teenagers will be talking about (*communication*). Play the track. Check answers in open class.

Answers

1 C **2** A **3** B

2 Divide the class into pairs or groups to answer the questions. Elicit some ideas and have a discussion in open class.

EXAM SKILL

Pronouns

Ask students to read the tips.

- Remind students that pronouns are particularly important in tasks like multiple-choice cloze and open cloze, but that they are also important in other parts of the exam as they make it clear who or what we are talking about.
- If your students speak a language that has both a singular and plural and/or a formal and informal way of saying *you*, remind them that in English there is only one form.

3 Remind students that we use pronouns to replace the nouns we have already used. Ask students to complete the exercise and then compare their answers in pairs. Elicit answers from the class.

Answers

1 It's **2** I **3** he **4** we **5** them **6** them

OPTIMISE YOUR EXAM

Multiple-choice dialogue

Ask students to read the tips.

- Remind students that this type of exam task focuses on the candidate's understanding of functional language, i.e. what to say (and what not to say) in specific situations. Tell students that although some of the options might be correct grammatically, they may be incorrect in the context because it would not be the right thing to say.
- Remind them that they should always decide who is speaking and what the situation is when they are working on a multiple-choice dialogue exam task.

4 Ask students to complete the exercise. Have them compare their answers in pairs before checking them in open class.

Answers
1 I **2** They **3** I **4** us

Exam task

5 Go through the example conversation as a class. Then ask students to complete the exercise individually. Elicit some of their ideas about who the speakers are and what the situation is as you check answers with the class.

Answers
1 B **2** A **3** B **4** C **5** B

Fast finishers

Ask students to look for relationships between nouns and pronouns in the questions and answers in Exercise 5.

Answers
1 What – It **2** website – one **3** you – I **4** you – you **5** –

THINK | RESEARCH | CULTURE | LEARN | ME

Students work in small groups to discuss the questions. Remind students that questions like these, asking for opinions, are often part of an oral examination. Remind them of the importance of giving examples to support their ideas.

Homework

OWB

Assign students Language in Use exercises 1, 2 and 3 on page 41 of their Workbook.

WRITING

Information transfer

→ Student's Book, pages 56–57 SB

Lesson aims

- Focus on making notes about when and where to meet people
- Plan and write a message

Lead-in

Draw a selection of clock faces and calendar dates on the board showing a variety of times and dates. Make some of these traditional clocks with hands, and some digital clocks (some am/pm and some 24-hour clocks) and a phone/computer calendar. Give each one a letter: *a*, *b*, *c*, etc. for students to refer to. Elicit the questions used to ask about the date and time, i.e. *What's the date/time? What day/time is it?* and put students into pairs to take turns to ask and answer questions about the clocks.

1 Give students an example of a form of technology you use at home and how you use it differently at school. Then have students discuss the questions in pairs or groups. Elicit answers from students around the class.

EXAM SKILL

Making notes: when and where

Ask students to read the tips.

- Remind students that, in exams, it is important to be able to understand the time of an activity and where it takes place. It is also important to be able to give this information correctly in writing and speaking exams.
- There is almost always more than one way of giving the same information, so students should think about this when reading texts or listening to recordings. They should also bear this in mind when writing and speaking, as it will allow them to use a greater variety of language, rather than repeating themselves unnecessarily.

2 Focus students' attention on the two texts and elicit what they are (*A is an advert, B is a text message*). Individually, students complete the exercise. Ask students to compare in pairs before you elicit answers in open class.

Answers
Students should underline:
2.30, 4.30pm, 10.00am, 12.00pm
Matching: 4.30pm = half past four, 12.00pm = twelve

3 Tell students to look for patterns the same way as they did in the previous exercise. Ask students to complete the exercise individually. Check their answers.

Answers
1 d **2** c **3** e **4** a **5** f **6** b

4 Tell students that the information they need to complete the exercise is in the advert and the message in Exercise 2. Don't check the answers at this stage as students will check them in Exercise 5.

Answers
1 Room 11a **2** 4 **3** 3:30 pm **4** 10 am **5** 12

5 Tell students to follow the example and provide evidence of their correct answers. Check answers in open class.

Suggested answers
1 (2) Text A says *chat online with students from four other countries.*
(3) Text B says *I'm busy until half past three on Wednesday, but I could go for the last hour.*
(4) Text A says *Saturday morning 10:00 am–12:00 pm* and Text B says *Saturday morning looks OK.*
(5) Text A says *Saturday morning 10:00 am–12:00 pm.*
2 Students' own answers

OPTIMISE YOUR **EXAM**

Information transfer

Ask students to read the tips.

- Tell students that they should always read the two texts carefully before they complete information transfer exam tasks.
- Remind students that the next step is to read the notes. They should pay close attention to the words around the gaps, as these can give clues as to what to write.
- Finally, tell students to look at the texts again and look for the information they need to complete the notes. Point out that some things may appear in both texts, e.g. a phone number, so they need to be careful to pick the right piece of information in each case.

▼ Exam task

6 **Plan** Ask students to cover the table of notes at the bottom of the exercise and look just at the advert and the message. Tell students to read both texts and match the words or phrases that say the same thing. Then ask them to complete the exercise.

Answers
2 Students should underline:
on, at

7 **Write** Go through the table with students to check they are clear about what they probably need to write in each gap, e.g. *1 a day or date, 2 a time (in the morning), 3 a number, 4 an object or objects (special clothes? food? drink?), 5 a phone number for 'OGC'.* Then ask them to complete the exercise and check their answers in pairs.

Answers
1 26 October **2** 9:00 **3** eight **4** own food/snacks **5** 931844

8 **Check** Students complete the checklist before they hand in their answers.

Extra writing

9 Read out the instructions and have students complete the exercise individually. Monitor the task and then elicit ideas from different students around the class. Students write their message. If there is not enough time, set this for homework.

Suggested answers
1 informal
2 What's yours? (mobile number) Is that OK? (for you to bring the snacks) Can you meet me outside main door at 9 am?
3 Words and phrases connected with communication and technology, comparative and superlative adjectives and students' own answers

Optional extension

For a slightly longer writing task, and for students to see other text types, refer them to one of the six tasks in the Writing reference (SB p169). Each one includes an annotated sample text and related writing task to challenge your students a little more.

Homework OWB

Assign students Writing exercises 1, 2, 3 and 4 on page 42 of their Workbook and Progress check 5 on page 43.

6 Teen fashion

UNIT AIMS

Exam preparation in Unit 6:

- choose between similar answers in an online article
- choose the right answer in a multiple-matching exercise
- give details in a collaborative task
- understand functional language and apply it in a multiple-matching dialogue
- give your opinion in an online review

TEACHER'S PRESENTATION KIT

- *Talk2Me* videos
- Speaking test videos
- Class and Workbook audio
- Workbook pages and answer key

UNIT OVERVIEW

Student's Book / Digital Student's Book SB		Workbook / Online Workbook OWB
LESSON / EXAM TASK	EXAM SKILLS / LANGUAGE FOCUS	CONSOLIDATION
Reading **Multiple-choice cloze**	Choosing between similar answers An online article	Workbook, pp 44–45, Exercises 1, 2, 3 Unit 6, Reading, Exercises 1, 2, 3
Grammar 1	Present perfect simple with *ever* and *never*	Workbook, p 46, Exercises 1, 2, 3 Unit 6, Grammar 1, Exercises 1, 2, 3
Vocabulary	Words connected with *fashion, clothes and shopping* Verbs + prepositions Collocations with verbs	Workbook, p 47, Exercises 1, 2, 3 Unit 6, Vocabulary, Exercises 1, 2, 3
Listening **Multiple matching**	Choosing the right answer	Workbook, p 48, Exercises 1, 2, 3 Unit 6, Listening, Exercises 1, 2, 3
Grammar 2	Present perfect simple and past simple	Workbook, p 47, Exercises 1, 2 Unit 6, Grammar 2, Exercises 1, 2
Speaking **Collaborative task**	Giving details	Workbook, p 48, Exercises 1, 2 Unit 6, Speaking, Exercises 1, 2
Language in Use **Multiple-matching dialogue**	Understanding functional language	Workbook, p 49, Exercises 1, 2, 3 Unit 6, Language in Use, Exercises 1, 2, 3
Writing **An online review**	Giving your opinion	Workbook, p 50, Exercises 1, 2, 3, 4 Unit 6, Writing, Exercises 1, 2, 3, 4
Progress check	Check language progress for Units 5 and 6	Workbook, p 51, Progress check and Cumulative progress Progress check and Cumulative progress

Additional material

PRESENTATION KIT	TEACHER'S / STUDENT'S RESOURCE CENTRE RC	TEST GENERATOR
Talk2Me video *The address is …*	**Unit 6 worksheets:** *Optimise your grammar* (Standard and Higher), *Optimise your vocabulary* (Standard and Higher), *Talk2Me* video, *Say it right* **Units 5–6 worksheets:** CLIL, Culture, Everyday English (TRC only), Grammar communication (TRC only)	Unit Test 6 (Standard and Higher)

READING

Multiple-choice cloze | An online article

→ Student's Book, pages 58–59 SB

Lesson aims

- Choose between similar answers
- Practise a multiple-choice cloze exam task
- Discuss change in fashion

Lead-in

Write the unit title ***Teen fashion*** on the board and elicit what the title refers to (*clothes, accessories, shopping, trends, fashion magazines, fashion vloggers/bloggers*).

1 Focus students' attention on the photos and elicit which of the styles of clothes they like. Encourage them to give reasons for their answers. Then have students discuss the questions. Elicit some answers from the class and try to develop a class discussion.

EXAM SKILL

Choosing between similar answers

Ask students to read the tips.

- Tell students that they need to look past the words immediately before or after the gap or possible options to help them choose the correct answer.
- Stress that students should read the complete sentence or text after they complete an exercise to check that their answers make sense.

2 Ask students what they have to do to complete the exercise (*choose the correct options*). Then have them complete the exercise and check their answer in pairs.

Answers

1 at **2** from **3** on **4** in

3 Ask students to complete the exercise. Check their answers.

Answers

1 is **2** Do **3** are **4** was **5** Did **6** Does

OPTIMISE YOUR EXAM

Multiple-choice cloze

Ask students to read the tips.

- Remind students that for all text-based exam tasks, they should read the text first quickly and ask themselves questions like the examples to establish what the text is about, where it might be from, who the author is expecting to read it, etc.
- Many students overlook titles and pictures, but these can often give context. Look at the title together and elicit what they can see in the photos and how this relates to the title. Elicit or explain the meaning of trend (*a fashion that apppears quite quickly and usually disappears just as quickly*).

4 Remind students that scanning helps to read a text quickly in order to find specific information. Then have students complete the exercise in pairs. You could set a time limit of three minutes. Check answers in open class.

Answers

plastic bottles, bamboo, coconut, banana, tyres, coffee

Exam task

5 2.09 **Note: The reading text is also available on the audio CD but contains the missing words. You may want to have students listen and read the text after doing the exam task to check their answers.**

Tell students to read the instructions and the possible answers before completing the exercise. Check answers in open class and ask students to justify their choices.

Answers

1 B (*lot* is part of the quantity expression *a lot of*)

2 A (we use the infinitive form of the verb with *to* to show purpose)

3 C (here we need the auxiliary to show the verb's tense and form a negative in third person plural)

4 B (here we need the auxiliary to form the negative – *it doesn't matter* is a common phrase)

5 C (we use *a* here because the writer is not referring to a specific T-shirt)

6 A (*in* is part of the adjective + preposition word combination, *interested in*)

7 C (the text is referring to a specific time)

8 B (*their* is the possessive adjective that refers to 'people')

6 Tell students to read through the definitions and try to guess the correct words before looking for them in the text. After the exercise, check answers in open class.

Answers

1 hungry **2** normal **3** prices **4** follow **5** busy **6** shop assistant **7** unusual **8** companies

Mixed ability

Ask stronger students to cover the text and look at the definitions and try to work out what the words are. Have less confident students complete the task as it appears in the Student's Book. Pair stronger students with less confident students and ask less confident students to check their ideas by saying, for example, *I think the word that means 'feeling that you want food' is 'hungry'. Do you agree?*

THINK | RESEARCH | **CULTURE** | LEARN | ME

Check students know the meaning of *vlogger* (= *video blogger, i.e. someone who, rather than writing a blog, posts a series of video posts talking to the camera*). Tell students to start by brainstorming ideas. Then tell them to come to a consensus with their partner / in their groups. Have students present their ideas and opinions to the class, giving reasons for their answers.

Cultural note

Vlogging has become more and more popular over the last decade. Numerous sites, including YouTube, actively encourage vloggers to upload their content and offer them support to help them make money from their work. The most popular vloggers can accumulate millions of followers and be paid large sums of money to promote products and services to their subscribers.

Homework

OWB

Assign students Reading exercises 1, 2 and 3 on pages 44–45 of their Workbook.

GRAMMAR 1

Present perfect simple with *ever* and *never*

→ Student's Book, page 60 SB

Lesson aims

- Understand the correct usage of the present perfect simple with *ever* and *never*
- Practise describing life experiences

Lead-in

Have a class discussion about fashion trends amongst young people. Ask students to tell you which fashion brands are popular at the moment, classify them and then ask them to organise them in order of preference.

Grammar in context

Tell students that the sentences are extracts from the article they read in the previous lesson. If students need extra support, remind them to refer to the information in the *Remember* box. Check answers in open class.

Remind students that they can find more information in the Grammar reference, Unit 6, page 155.

Answers

1 has **2** changed **3** Have **4** never

1 Go through the example sentence as a class before students complete the exercise. Check answers by having volunteers read out their answers.

Answers

2 Have you ever travelled by train alone? **3** Have you ever seen the Eiffel Tower? **4** Have you ever worn socks in bed? **5** Have you and your friends ever eaten together in a restaurant? **6** Have you and your family ever moved house?

2 Read the example question from Exercise 1 out loud and encourage students to give you the correct answer (***d*** *Yes, I have. I've made pizza and salad for my mum a few times.*). Students complete the exercise. Check answers in open class.

Answers

1 d **2** e **3** f **4** c **5** b **6** a

3 Draw students' attention to the example question and answer. Ask students to complete the exercise in pairs. Walk round the class, monitoring students' use of the present perfect and *ever/never*. Invite volunteers to ask and answer one of the questions in front of the class.

4 Focus students' attention on the dialogue and ask them what word they think they'll need to use to complete most of the gaps (*different forms of the auxiliary* have *and* ever *and* never). After completing the exercise, have students practise reading it in pairs.

Answers

1 been **2** haven't **3** has **4** ever **5** hasn't **6** Have **7** never **8** have

5 Check that students know what the UAE stands for (*the United Arab Emirates*) and ask them what they know about the country. After students complete the exercise, have volunteers read the text to check answers.

Answers

1 've/have had **2** Have you ever heard **3** 've/have never seen **4** 've/have eaten **5** 've/have ridden **6** 've/have never tried **7** haven't / have not written **8** haven't / have not forgotten

SAY IT RIGHT

TRC

Pronunciation of *have*

For the *Say it right* pronunciation activity and instructions, go to the Teacher's Resource Centre.

Homework

OWB

Assign students Grammar 1 exercises 1, 2 and 3 on page 46 of their Workbook.

VOCABULARY
Topic vocabulary | Word patterns | Collocations

→ Student's Book, page 61 SB

Lesson aims

Understand the correct usage of:

- words connected with fashion, clothes and shopping
- verb + preposition word patterns
- verb + noun collocations

Lead-in

Draw two human figures on the board, one male and one female. Divide the class in half and assign one half to the male figure and one half to the female figure. Have students work in pairs or small groups to brainstorm all the clothes worn by that gender and what clothes can be worn by both. Elicit vocabulary from the class. Write the words students suggest on the board with arrows pointing to the part of the body where the clothes are worn.

Words connected with *fashion, clothes and shopping*

1 2.10 Ask students to look at the words in the box and check that they know the meaning of each one before completing the exercise. Play the audio for students to listen and check their answers.

Answers/Audioscript

people: customer, *shop assistant, shopper*
places: *department store, market, shopping centre, supermarket*
money (verbs): *buy, change, cost, spend*
money (nouns): *bill, cash, change, cheque, credit card, receipt*

2 Ask students to complete the exercise. Then have them compare their answers in pairs before checking them in open class.

Answers

1 cash, credit card(s) **2** buy, spend **3** department stores, shopping centres **4** shoppers, customers **5** bill, change **6** receipt, cost

Optional extension

Ask students to work in pairs and write a short vox pop (a short idea or opinion about a topic collected by people who make radio and television programmes) about fashion, clothes and shopping using the words from Exercise 1 that weren't used in Exercise 2 (*shop assistant, market, supermarket, cheque* and *change* as a verb). Ask pairs to read their vox pops to the class.

Refer students to the Vocabulary reference, page 165, for more information on topic vocabulary.

Verbs + prepositions

3 2.11 Remind students that word patterns are groups of words that frequently appear together. Ask students to complete the exercise. Play the audio for students to check their answers. Then have students say which answer they got correct and incorrect in order to check the similarities/ differences in students' understanding.

Answers/Audioscript

1 When I go shopping, I always pay *in* cash.
2 Write *down* what you want and I'll go to the supermarket for you.
3 Please take *off* your wet boots before you go into the house.
4 It's raining so put *on* your raincoat before you go out.
5 Did you pay *for* the online shopping by credit card?
6 Most shops give you 30 days to take *back* anything you don't want.

Language note

Note that all the word patterns in this section include phrasal verbs, and that these belong to three different categories.

Pay for (something) and *pay in* (e.g. *cash*) are non-separable phrasal verbs so the object will always come after the particle. However, with *take back, put on, take off* and *write down*, the object can go between the verb and the particle (*put your coat on*) or after the particle (*put on your coat*) when it is a noun, but has to go between the verb and the particle when it is a pronoun (*put it on*).

4 Ask students to complete the exercise. Then have them compare their answers in pairs before checking them in open class. Ask students what they found easy or difficult about the exercise.

Answers

1 pay for **2** take off **3** pay in **4** write down

Refer students to the Vocabulary reference, page 165, for more information on word patterns.

Collocations with verbs

5 2.12 Ask students to complete the exercise. Play the audio for students to listen and check their answers.

Answers/Audioscript

1 Do you prefer to *go* shopping with your friends or with your mum?
2 You can *save* money for a new computer game if you stop buying chocolate and cakes!
3 We usually *catch* the bus when we want to go to the shopping centre.
4 The bill was nine pounds and twenty pence, so Dad gave the waiter £10 and told him to *keep* the change.
5 'Mum, there's no milk left.' 'It's OK - I'm going to *do* the shopping later.'
6 There are some lovely clothes *for* sale in that shop.

Refer students to the Vocabulary reference, page 165, for more information on collocations.

Homework

Assign students Vocabulary exercises 1, 2 and 3 on page 47 of their Workbook. OWB

LISTENING
Multiple matching

→ Student's Book, page 62

Lesson aims
- Listen to identify the right answers from various options
- Practise a multiple-matching exam task
- Discuss changes in buying habits

Lead-in

Play a game to recycle the word patterns from the previous lesson (*pay for …, take off …, pay in …, take back …, write down, put on …*). Split the class into two teams. Call out a word pattern and ask teams to think of a grammatically correct sentence using the word pattern. The first team to write a sentence and hold it up gets a point. After you have used all the word patterns, the team with the most points is the winner.

1 Ask students to look at the photo and say which of the things they enjoy buying and which they are not interested in at all. After students discuss the questions, elicit some answers from different students around the class.

EXAM SKILL

Choosing the right answer

Ask students to read the tips.

- Explain to students that in multiple-matching exam tasks there are usually distractors. In Exercise 2, for example, students will hear both the items, A and B, in all the recordings. Make clear that the correct answer is not necessarily the one that students hear first.
- Remind students they need to identify which of the options didn't happen. Explain that it could be something the person thought about doing but didn't do, or something he or she did in the past but doesn't do now, etc.

2 2.13 Tell students to read the instructions and possible answers before they listen. Play the audio for students to listen and answer. Then check their answers in open class.

Answers

1 B **2** A **3** A **4** A

OPTIMISE YOUR EXAM

Multiple matching

Ask students to read the tips.

- Students often miss correct answers because they are busy writing down incorrect answers and stop listening for a moment. Tell students not to stop listening even if they think they have heard an answer. As in Exercise 2, students may hear an incorrect answer first and then hear the correct answer in the next phrase.
- Explain that it is common practice to put a line through answers. Remind students they should only do this when they are totally sure. If not, they should leave the items and consider them for later gaps.

Exam task

3 2.14 Tell students they will hear two friends talking. Play the audio. Don't check answers at this stage, as students check their answers in Exercise 4.

Mixed ability

Have stronger students complete the task as it appears in the Student's Book. Tell weaker students to choose from B, D, F, G and H only.

4 2.14 Tell students to read through their answers before you play the track again for them to check.

Answers

1 D **2** G **3** H **4** B **5** F

THINK | RESEARCH | CULTURE | LEARN | ME

Encourage students to think of things like credit cards and how they have made an impact on people's spending. Invite some students to share their ideas with the class.

Homework OWB

Assign students Listening exercises 1, 2 and 3 on page 48 of their Workbook.

GRAMMAR 2
Present perfect simple and past simple

→ Student's Book, page 63

Lesson aims
- Understand the correct usage of the present perfect simple and past simple
- Practise talking about things that happened at specific and unspecified times in the past
- Share some recent news with a partner

Lead-in

Write *Have you ever …?* in large letters on the board. Ask a question, e.g. *Have you ever given me your homework late?* Ask several students to reply to elicit the responses, e.g. *Yes, I have. / No, I haven't.* Now ask students to come up with three of their own questions beginning with *Have you ever …?* Monitor students' work, making any necessary corrections. Students then ask other students in the class their questions and make a note of their answers. Once completed, ask for some feedback about what information students have gathered about their classmates.

Grammar in context

Ask students to complete the task individually before checking their answers with a partner. Then ask pairs to give reasons for their answers. Tell them to use the information in the *Remember* box to help them explain.

Remind students that they can find more information in the Grammar reference, Unit 6, page 156.

Answers

a 1 **b** 2 and students' own answers

Language note

The present perfect is often used as a 'conversation starter' as it allows us to ask about life experiences, or introduce a new topic, as students saw in Grammar 1. We usually switch to the past simple to ask for more details and discuss the topic further.

In this section, students will see how the present perfect can be used to give a sense of immediacy to actions. This is usually because we want to emphasise the results of something and we consider these more important than exactly when the action happened, e.g. *I've opened the window. I've moved house.* In cases like this, we use the present perfect without *ever/never.*

1 Ask students to complete the exercise individually. Check students' answers.

Answers

1 've done **2** bought **3** 've lost **4** started **5** Did you sell **6** 've had

2 Go through the example with the class and remind students that the normal structure is to introduce a situation with the present perfect and then give details or explanations in the past simple. After students complete the exercise, have them compare their answers in pairs.

Answers

2 The boys have walked into town. They left at 2 o'clock.

3 I've/have got Mum a present for her birthday. I paid 10 euros for it.

4 He didn't like his old flat. He's lived in three different flats this year.

5 She's/has lost an earring. She dropped it in the street.

6 I haven't / have not worn these boots before. My old ones were very comfortable.

3 Ask students to complete the exercise individually. Have them compare their answers in pairs before you check them with the class. Check the spelling of all the past simple verbs and past participles.

Answers

1 Have you ever made **2** started **3** looked **4** decided **5** told **6** wanted **7** thought **8** 've/have helped **9** began **10** 've/have learnt **11** met **12** 've/have shared

THINK | RESEARCH | CULTURE | LEARN | **ME**

Ask students to tell their partner about real things that have happened to them recently. If necessary, remind students not to bring up or ask about sensitive areas.

Homework

OWB

Assign students Grammar 2 exercises 1 and 2 on page 47 of their Workbook.

Assign students the Flipped classroom tasks on page 64 of their Student's Book if you'd like them to prepare for the next lesson. To complete this task, students need to watch the *Talk2Me* video which can be found on the Resource Centre.

SPEAKING

Collaborative task

→ Student's Book, page 64 SB

Lesson aims

- Focus on giving details in a conversation
- Practise showing you are interested in the speaker and the topic in a collaborative task
- Research interesting places to shop

The *Talk2Me* video in this unit focuses on clothes and a clothes sale. The people in the video talk about what style of clothes they like and what they would like to buy and sell at a clothes sale.

Students answer some comprehension questions and then listen for key phrases in the video.

The video can be used in one of two ways:

Flipped classroom

Flipped classroom option

Using this approach, students watch the video and complete the exercises for homework. This prepares students for the speaking lesson by introducing them to the topic and the key phrases to use in the exam task. Teachers who use this method will find they have more class time to spend on activating the target language and developing fluency for the final task.

***Talk2Me* worksheet**

Ask students to also complete the *Talk2Me* worksheet on the Resource Centre for more detailed comprehension exercises and more practice of the key phrases.

Classroom option

1 Ask students to spend a minute or two reading the questions. Play the *Talk2Me* video for students to complete the exercise. Play the video again, if necessary, before checking their answers.

2 Play the *Talk2Me* video again, so students underline the phrases in the *Phrase expert* box. Pause the video from time to time if necessary. Check answers in open class.

Talk2Me worksheet

Ask students to complete the *Talk2Me* worksheet on the Resource Centre for more detailed comprehension exercises and more practice of the key phrases.

Answers

The transcript and answer key for the *Talk2Me* video exercises and Worksheet can be found on the Teacher's Resource Centre.

Lead-in

Ask each student to write an interesting statement about him or herself, using the present perfect (and *never* if appropriate), e.g. *I've entered lots of competitions, but I've never won anything.* Have students take turns reading their statements to you. For some of the statements, give a very bored, uninspired response (*Oh. Aha.*), or keep silent with an unimpressed look (without being rude) and nominate the next student. To the other statements, sound as interested as you can. At the end, ask students if they noticed the difference in your responses. Point out how important body language is when deciding if the listener is interested or not.

3 In pairs, students ask and answer the questions. Encourage students to show that they are interested in their partner's information by responding to their comments as well as using suitable body language. Elicit answers from different students around the class and invite other students to respond appropriately.

EXAM SKILL

Giving details

Ask students to read the tips.

- Point out that students will need to be able to both give and understand specific information in order to do well in Speaking and in Listening tests. Practising this information exchange regularly with a partner is very useful.
- Ask students to find an advert that includes information like addresses, phone numbers, opening times, web pages, etc. and have them read the information to the class or group who should make a note of the most important details.
- Remind students that the spoken style for dates is usually longer than the written style, e.g. *24 June* becomes *the twenty-fourth of June*. The years of the noughties, 2001–2009, are usually expressed as, e.g. *two thousand and eight*, but from 2010 onwards, we usually say *twenty ten*, etc.

4 2.15 Before students listen, explain that they will hear some short extracts of information, e.g. phone numbers, that they need to write down. Play the track a second time for students to check their answers. Have them compare their answers in pairs before you check them in open class.

Answers / Audioscript

1 07785 926553 **2** the tenth/10th of April **3** the thirty-first/31st of October **4** w-w-w dot / www. **5** 07882 554433 **6** dot com / .com

5 2.16 Ask students to read through the advert before you play the audio. Then play the track and elicit answers from different students around the class.

Answers

1 25th **2** at 9 am **3** 173 **4** Road **5** 5896

OPTIMISE YOUR EXAM

Collaborative task

Ask students to read the tips.

- In oral exams, examiners will be looking to see how candidates interact with each other, and speakers need to show they are interested in the speaker and the topic (even if they aren't interested).
- Point out how important it is to use appropriate phrases in collaborative tasks to ask for repetition (*Sorry, I missed that.*), to ask for time to think (*Let me see, …*) and to self-correct (*No, sorry, what I mean is …*). To get the best possible marks in an exam, students also need to use phrases to show interest.

Optional extension 2.16

Play the track again, pausing after each question for students to copy the sentence stress and intonation. Repeat each question as necessary until students can pronounce it naturally.

6 Assign each student a letter, A or B, and put them into A/B pairs. Give them a moment to look at their information / question topics on page 137/140. Time students (two minutes) and give them an update, e.g. *One minute to go …* Remind students to use phrases from the *Phrase expert* box as well as phrases to show interest. Walk round, monitoring students for good use of language and errors to go over at the end of the activity.

Write any errors on the board and go through them with students, eliciting corrections from them where possible. After the class feedback, students could then repeat this activity with another partner, to try to improve their performance.

Suggested answers

Student A's questions
What can I/you buy at the fashion store?
What's the address of the store?
Is it closed on Mondays?
Is it cheap or expensive?
What's the telephone number of the store?

Student B's questions
What's the address of the book shop?
Does it sell music books?
Is it closed on Sundays?
What's the telephone number of the shop?
Has it got a car park?

THINK | **RESEARCH** | CULTURE | LEARN | ME

If you have access to the internet, students can research information in class. Alternatively, they could prepare this for homework and present their information at the start of the next lesson.

Homework

OWB

Assign students Speaking exercises 1 and 2 on page 48 of their Workbook.

LANGUAGE IN USE
Multiple-matching dialogue

→ Student's Book, page 65 SB

Lesson aims

- Focus on understanding functional language
- Practise a multiple-matching dialogue exam task
- Discuss people you speak to daily

Lead-in

Write the following statements on the board:
Buying the latest fashionable clothes is a total waste of money – it's better to buy clothes in a supermarket.
Buying cheap, ugly clothes is stupid – it's better to spend more and get something fashionable.

Divide the class into two groups and allocate a statement to each group. Have a class discussion – students can only make points that reflect the statement of their group. Encourage the class to come to a consensus at the end of the discussion.

1 In pairs, students discuss and complete the exercise. Check answers in open class.

Suggested answers
1 a shop assistant in a shop / supermarket / department store
2 a student after a lesson in school
3 a customer in a clothes shop / department store
4 a son or daughter at home

EXAM SKILL

Understanding functional language

Ask students to read the tips.

- Remind students that the Language in Use exam tasks in Unit 5 focused on the candidate's understanding of functional language. Explain that it is not only important to think about what people say in specific situations, but also necessary to understand why people say things.
- Tell students that they will work out what people are trying to say in Exercise 2. Tell them to make sure they always think about this when working on a lettered multiple-matching dialogue exam task.

2 Go through the first question with the class. Then tell students to read through the remaining sentences before matching them. Check answers by asking different students around the class.

Answers
1 an opinion **2** a greeting **3** an explanation **4** inviting
5 a description **6** future plans

3 Ask students to complete the exercise and then compare their answers in pairs. Elicit answers from volunteers in the class.

Answers
2 a **3** e **4** f **5** c **6** b

OPTIMISE YOUR EXAM

Multiple-matching dialogue

Ask students to read the tips.

- Remind students to cover the A–H options when they read the conversation for the first time and make initial predictions about what the other person might be saying. Then tell them to read the example and the options. Also remind students to cross out the example sentence before they start.
- Remind students to think about what speakers are trying to say as well as the words they use. For example, if they are making plans, they will undoubtedly talk about where and when they will meet.

▼ Exam task

4 Read out the instructions and ask students to complete the exercise individually. Check answers as a class. Answer any doubts students may have about incorrect answers.

Answers
1 H **2** G **3** A **4** D **5** F

Fast finishers

Have students who finish quickly underline the words that helped them complete the conversation. As you check the answers to Exercise 4, ask individual students to explain the connections between sentences to the class, e.g. when Robbie says that he's changed his mind about staying at home, Fiona is surprised and asks *'Really? Where would you like to go?'*

THINK | RESEARCH | CULTURE | LEARN | ME

After students make their lists individually, they share their information in pairs. Encourage them to look at the functions in Exercise 2 for ideas, if necessary. Then elicit some ideas from different students.

Homework

OWB

Assign students Language in Use exercises 1, 2 and 3 on page 49 of their Workbook.

WRITING
An online review

→ Student's Book, pages 66–67 SB

Lesson aims

- Focus on using personal experiences and giving opinions
- Plan and write an online review

Lead-in

Divide the students into two teams. Ask teams to make a list of as many words as possible connected to clothes and personal possessions. Set a time limit and then go through students' lists as a class. Award a point for every word both teams have. Award two points for unique words. Then have teams add up their scores. The team with the most points wins.

1 After students discuss the questions in pairs or groups, have them share their ideas with the class.

OPTIMISE YOUR EXAM

An online review

Ask students to read the tips.

- Stress the importance of answering all parts of the question within the word limit and tell students to make sure they know exactly what information they need to give.
- Tell students to use appropriate language for specific functions the task asks for. Explain that otherwise, they are unlikely to get top marks on the exam.

2 Ask students to complete the exercise individually. Don't check answers at this stage as students will compare their answers in Exercise 3 and then look at sample examiners' comments in Exercise 4.

3 Tell students to revise both texts while they are comparing answers. Have pairs report any major disagreements they have to the class.

Answer

B is the better answer because it gives more information and answers two questions. A only answers one question.

4 After matching the comments and texts, ask students to compare their own answers to Exercise 2 with the examiner's comments. Then elicit how their own comments were similar or different.

Answers

1 B **2** A

EXAM SKILL

Giving your opinion

Ask students to read the tips.

- Remind students that the present perfect can be used to introduce experiences and the past simple can be used for giving more details.
- Tell students to think about good and bad reviews they have read in their own language and encourage them to use them as a reference when giving their own opinions.

5 After students complete the exercise, ask them what they thought of the answer. Elicit students' opinions while you check answers with the class.

Answers

1 A week ago, **2** because **3** However, **4** In my opinion **5** believe

Extra support

Point out that the model answer in Exercise 5 contains some key features that would help a student get a very good mark in the exam. Write the following items on the board and ask students to match them to items 1–5 in Exercise 5.

a) conjunction to connect sentences

b) verb to express an opinion, other than 'think'

c) time phrase to introduce the situation

d) phrase to introduce a point of view

e) conjunction to contrast with previous sentence

Tell students to try and use a similar range of features in their own writing.

Answers

1 c **2** a **3** e **4** d **5** b

Exam task

6 Encourage students to base their answers on a real experience if possible. As students complete the exercise, walk round the class, helping them answer the questions if necessary.

Answers

1 Students' own answers **2** three **3** Students' own answers **4** present perfect and past simple **5** words for fashion, clothes and shops **5** 25–35

7 Plan Ask students to use the example as an idea to complete the plan. You may want to look at the students' plans to check them and give advice and suggestions for improvement before students take the next step.

8 Write Remind students to keep all the exam tips in mind while writing. Students write their review. If there is not enough time, set this and the subsequent checklist exercise for homework.

9 Check Students complete the checklist before they hand in their reviews.

Optional extension

For a slightly longer writing task, and for students to see other text types, refer them to one of the six tasks in the Writing reference (SB p169). Each one includes an annotated sample text and related writing task to challenge your students a little more.

Homework

OWB

Assign students Writing exercises 1, 2, 3 and 4 on page 50 of their Workbook and Progress check 6 on page 51.

Answers PROGRESS CHECK Units 5–6

Exercise 1
1 walked **2** Have, worked **3** bought **4** Did, wear **5** 've/have lost **6** 've/have never shopped **7** haven't seen **8** didn't like

Exercise 2
1 start **2** software **3** on **4** open **5** for **6** send **7** cash **8** screen

Exercise 3
1 A **2** B **3** C **4** A **5** A **6** A **7** A **8** C

Exercise 4
1 has **2** in **3** ever **4** much **5** lots **6** than **7** biggest **8** older **9** never **10** some

Exercise 5
1 a few **2** many **3** lots **4** many **5** Some **6** little **7** much **8** any

Exercise 6
1 supermarket **2** software **3** online **4** customers **5** credit card **6** graphics **7** keyboard **8** download

7 The future of learning

UNIT AIMS

Exam preparation in Unit 7:

- understand *this, that, these, it, them* in a news article
- think about missing information in a gap fill exercise
- talk about the future in an interview
- learn word phrases and apply them in a multiple-choice cloze exercise
- understand similar information in an information transfer exercise

TEACHER'S PRESENTATION KIT

- *Talk2Me* videos
- Speaking test videos
- Class and Workbook audio
- Workbook pages and answer key

UNIT OVERVIEW

Student's Book / Digital Student's Book SB		Workbook / Online Workbook OWB
LESSON / EXAM TASK	**EXAM SKILLS / LANGUAGE FOCUS**	**CONSOLIDATION**
Reading **Multiple-choice cloze**	Understanding *this, that, these, it, them* A news article	Workbook, pp 52–53, Exercises 1, 2, 3, 4 Unit 7, Reading, Exercises 1, 2, 3, 4
Grammar 1	*going to*	Workbook, p 54, Exercises 1, 2 Unit 7, Grammar 1, Exercises 1, 2
Vocabulary	Words connected with *school and studying* Words + prepositions Collocations with verbs	Workbook, pp 54–55, Exercises 1, 2, 3 Unit 7, Vocabulary, Exercises 1, 2, 3
Listening **Gap fill**	Thinking about the missing information	Workbook, p 56, Exercises 1, 2 Unit 7, Listening, Exercises 1, 2
Grammar 2	*will* and *going to*	Workbook, p 55, Exercise 1 Unit 7, Grammar 2, Exercise 1
Speaking **Interview**	Talking about the future	Workbook, p 56, Exercises 1, 2, 3 Unit 7, Speaking, Exercises 1, 2, 3
Language in Use **Multiple-choice cloze**	Learning word phrases	Workbook, p 57, Exercises 1, 2, 3 Unit 7, Language in Use, Exercises 1, 2, 3
Writing **Information transfer**	Understanding similar information	Workbook, p 58, Exercises 1, 2, 3, 4 Unit 7, Writing, Exercises 1, 2, 3, 4
		Workbook, p 59, Progress check and Cumulative progress Progress check and Cumulative progress

Additional material

PRESENTATION KIT	TEACHER'S / STUDENT'S RESOURCE CENTRE RC	TEST GENERATOR
Talk2Me video *In one year's time …*	**Unit 7 worksheets:** *Optimise your grammar* (Standard and Higher), *Optimise your vocabulary* (Standard and Higher), *Talk2Me* video, *Say it right* **Units 7–8 worksheets:** CLIL, Culture, Everyday English (TRC only), Grammar communication (TRC only)	Unit Test 7 (Standard and Higher)

READING

Multiple-choice cloze | A news article

→ Student's Book, pages 70–71 SB

Lesson aims

- Focus on understanding *this, that, these, it* and *them*
- Practise a multiple-choice cloze exam task
- Think about ways computers can help you learn

Lead-in

Ask students to look at the unit title ***The future of learning*** and the picture and say what they think the unit will be about (*how education may change in the future*). Ask students to talk about the possible advantages and disadvantages of learning with technology. Ask students how they have used technology for education in, or outside, school.

1 After students discuss the questions, elicit the advantages and disadvantages of having technology in the classroom. Encourage different students in the class to participate.

2 Ask students to complete the exercise. Then check answers in open class.

Answers

1 them **2** it **3** That **4** these **5** this

EXAM SKILL

Understanding *this, that, these, it, them*

Ask students to read the tips.

- Point out that students are already familiar with the pronouns *I*, *you*, *he*, *she* and *we*, and that *this*, *that*, *these*, *it* and *them* work in the same way. Make sure students understand that *this*, *that*, *these* and *it* can be both subject or object pronouns (*I like this*. (= object); *This is really nice.* (= subject), but *them* is an object pronoun only (the corresponding subject pronoun is *they*).
- Show students how these pronouns can refer to larger pieces of text, not only one word, by writing the following on the board: *Studying with tablets in class is a great idea. I'd like to try it.* Elicit that *it* refers to 'Studying with tablets in class'.

3 Focus students' attention on the title of the article and the accompanying photo, and elicit what it is about (*using technology in classrooms around the world / Uganda*). After they complete the exercise, have students compare their answers in pairs before checking in open class.

Answers

1 two **2** more than 200 **3** 55

OPTIMISE YOUR EXAM

Multiple-choice cloze

Ask students to read the tips.

- Remind students that in this exam task type, they should cover the options under the text when they read it for the first time. Explain that they should try to understand the main ideas and make initial predictions about what words they might need before looking at the options.
- After students have chosen their answers, remind them to check the specific words and phrases before or after the gaps, which confirm their answers.
- Remind students to answer all questions, even if they don't know the correct answer.

Exam task

4 2.17 **Note: The reading text is also available on the audio CD but contains the missing words. You may want to have students listen and read the text after doing the exam task to check their answers.**

Tell students to read the instructions before completing the task. Check answers in open class.

Answers

1 A (*on* describes the position of the computers; *over* implies they are floating in the air, and if the computers were *inside* students' desks they would not be able to learn from them.)

2 C (*them* is the object pronoun referring to 'young people' in; *their* is a possessive adjective and *they* is a subject pronoun, therefore these are not possible answers.)

3 B (Context tells us that this must be a negative, not a positive verb. The structure is *there is/are* and must be in the plural form as it refers to 'computers'.

4 A (The phrase *since 2007* indicates present perfect here. The subject is *the Mobile Solar Computer Classroom*, so the verb must be third person singular.)

5 B (This sentence explains why something is happening, so the verb form needs to be an infinitive of purpose, i.e. *to* + bare infinitive.)

6 C (*In* describes the location of the equipment; *On* would imply all the equipment is on the roof of the car, and *To* is used to indicate movement, not position.)

7 A (*because* is a conjunction that introduces a reason, in this case, the reason for the battery; *but* implies a contrast and *so* introduces a reason, therefore these are not appropriate here.)

8 B (*these* relates to 'classrooms'; the other two options are singular.)

5 Ask a strong student to scan the text and find the word for the first definition. Then have students complete the exercise and compare their answers in pairs before checking in open class.

Answers

1 adults **2** battery **3** tablets **4** job **5** libraries **6** lucky **7** drivers **8** countryside

Mixed ability

Pair weak and strong students together. Have stronger students cover Exercise 5 and weaker students read each definition to their partner for him/her to guess. Then have students look for the words their partner couldn't guess together. Check answers in open class.

THINK | RESEARCH | CULTURE | LEARN | ME

After students make their lists, encourage them to share their ideas with the class, and write students' ideas on the board. Have students make a note of the ideas they didn't think of, and encourage them to make comments.

Homework

OWB

Assign students Reading exercises 1, 2, 3 and 4 on pages 52–53 of their Workbook.

GRAMMAR 1

going to

→ Student's Book, page 72 SB

Lesson aims

- Understand the correct usage of *going to*
- Practise making future plans and predictions

Lead-in

Tell the class about three things that you have arranged to do at the weekend, e.g. *At 10 o'clock on Saturday, I'm playing badminton with some friends. On Saturday evening, I'm having dinner in a new Japanese restaurant near my house. On Sunday, my cousins from Madrid are coming to visit.* Tell students to guess which two of the sentences are true and which one is false. Then ask students to write their own sentences using the present continuous to describe arrangements they have made for the weekend. Two should be true and the other should be false. In pairs, students read them to their partner who guesses which are true/false.

Grammar in context

Ask students to complete the task. Check their answers and ask students to read more about *going to* in the *Remember* box. Remind students that in Unit 2 they saw the present continuous to talk about the future; elicit that the present continuous is usually used for arrangements that we see as definite.

Remind students that they can find more information in the Grammar reference, Unit 7, page 156.

Answers

c) the future

Language note

Going to is used for the future. We use *going to* when we have made a personal plan or when we make a prediction based on evidence. Therefore, an action using *going to* is less likely to happen than an action using present continuous, which usually implies firm plans or arrangements. For example, you could say *I'm going to see a film with Sue on Friday.*, which means you want to go but haven't bought the tickets yet. Or you could say *I'm seeing a film with Sue on Friday.* In this case you have tickets.

1 Before students complete the exercise, elicit what type of text it is (*a conversation*). Have students complete it individually and then check answers by practising in groups of three. Have one group practise in front of the class.

Answers

2 's/is going to **3** are going to **4** isn't / is not going to **5** 's/is going to **6** 're/are going to **7** 's/is going to **8** Are you going to **9** 'm/am not going to **10** 's/is going to

2 Ask students to complete the exercise individually. Then ask different volunteers to read out a sentence to check answers.

Answers

1 's/is going to study **2** aren't / are not going to win **3** is, going to do **4** 'm/am not going **5** 's/is going to be **6** 's/is going to snow

Fast finishers

Have students rewrite the sentences using their own ideas. For example, *Guilio is going to study French in Paris.*

3 Ask students where the largest school in the world is (*India*). Then have them complete the exercise individually. Have students compare answers in pairs before checking in open class.

Answers

1 are going to be **2** aren't / are not going to use **3** 're/are going to have **4** 'm/am going to study **5** 's/is going to be **6** 'm/am not going to go **7** 're/are going to meet **8** 's/is going to be

SAY IT RIGHT

Pronunciation of *going to*

TRC

For the *Say it right* pronunciation activity and instructions, go to the Teacher's Resource Centre.

Cultural note

The City Montessori School in Lucknow, India, opened in 1959. It currently has over 50,000 students and, in 2010, broke the Guinness World Record for the largest school in the world. It uses the educational philosophy of the Italian specialist Maria Montessori who believed that great emphasis should be placed on play at school and on encouraging students' natural abilities. She opened her first school, the Casa dei Bambini, in Rome in 1907. Her ideas quickly spread to the USA and there are now Montessori schools all around the world.

Homework
OWB

Assign students Grammar 1 exercises 1 and 2 on page 54 of their Workbook.

VOCABULARY
Topic vocabulary | Word patterns | Collocations

→ Student's Book, page 73 SB

Lesson aims
Understand the correct usage of:
- words connected with school and studying
- verb + preposition word patterns
- verb + noun collocations
- Discuss school and homework

Lead-in
Tell students they are going to play a guessing game. Tell them to write down a word related to the school and two clues/descriptions of it: one that's obvious and one not so obvious. Tell students your not-so-obvious clue first: *This is a place in the school.*, and encourage the students to guess. Then say your more obvious clue: *You spend your break time there.* Have the student who guesses correctly (*playground*) continue, and keep going so that more students can participate.

Words connected with *school and studying*

1 2.18 Focus students' attention on the words in the box. Tell them to read them and check that they know the meaning of each one before completing the exercise. Then play the audio for students to listen and check their answers.

Answers/Audioscript
things in the classroom: board, bookshelf, desk, dictionary, eraser
school subjects: biology, geography, history, maths, music, physics
verbs for things people do at school: learn, practise, remember, study, teach

2 Ask students what their favourite school subjects are and why. Ask students to complete the exercise. Then have them compare their answers in pairs before you check them in open class.

Answers
1 history **2** geography **3** biology **4** maths **5** physics **6** music

Refer students to the Vocabulary reference, page 166, for more information on topic vocabulary.

Words + prepositions

3 2.19 Elicit from students what word patterns are (*two or more words that go together to form a 'chunk' of language*). As an example, ask students what word or phrase comes after *revise for* (*an exam/test*). After the exercise, play the audio for students to check their answers.

Answers/Audioscript
1 (C) You can learn a lot *from* books.
2 (A) You need to use technology when you study or are *at* work.
3 (C) Today we're going to learn *about* how the stomach works.
4 (B) Do you need any help *with* your homework?
5 (C) I usually arrive *at* school just before 9 am.
6 (A) You can borrow three books *from* the library at one time.

Refer students to the Vocabulary reference, page 166, for more information on word patterns.

Collocations with verbs

4 2.20 Go through the example as a class. Ask students to complete the exercise individually. Before you play the audio, ask students which options were difficult to match. Have them focus on those while they listen.

Answers/Audioscript
1 (d) do homework **2** (f) draw a picture **3** (a) take a course **4** (c) leave school **5** (b) go to university **6** (e) learn a foreign language

5 Ask students to complete the exercise individually. Then have them check their answers in pairs.

Answers
1 draw a picture **2** learn a foreign language **3** take a course **4** go to university **5** do homework **6** leave school

Extra support
Give stronger students one minute to memorise the collocations in Exercise 4 and then tell them to cover it and complete the sentences in Exercise 5 from memory. Give less confident students the verbs in the order they appear in Exercise 5 (*draw, learn, take, go, do, leave*) and tell them that they need to change the form of one of the verbs and one of the nouns. Check answers by reading each sentence up to and including the verb and then eliciting the missing noun from the class.

Refer students to the Vocabulary reference, page 166, for more information on collocations.

THINK | RESEARCH | CULTURE | LEARN | **ME**

Tell students to make a list of the things they like most about school and number them in order of preference. Then have them discuss the other questions.

Homework
OWB

Assign students Vocabulary exercises 1, 2 and 3 on pages 54–55 of their Workbook.

LISTENING
Gap fill

→ Student's Book, page 74 SB

Lesson aims

- Listen to missing information in gap-fill exam tasks
- Practise a gap-fill exam task
- Think about questions to ask someone in India

Lead-in

Ask students, *How do you communicate?* and write the words *friends*, *family* and *teachers* on the board. Encourage students to say why they use different ways of communicating with different groups and what they think the best ways of communicating are. Have them give reasons for their answers.

1 Have students discuss the questions in pairs. Then elicit some answers from different students around the class.

EXAM SKILL

Thinking about the missing information

Ask students to read the tips.

- Remind students that predicting the kind of information they are listening for – and the different formats that information could be given in – is a very important skill for listening exams.
- Tell students that they will need to find words that fit in the phrases they are given. Remind them of the work they did on the previous page with word patterns. For example, if they had to complete the phrase *learn from*, it could be completed with a thing or a person.

2 Write the word *in* on the board followed by *January, London, the morning* and have students brainstorm other words that follow *in*. After students finish the exercise, go through answers in open class.

Answers

in: March, 2018; Amsterdam, Paris; afternoon
on: Wednesday
at: 3:20, night; Halloween

3 Before students complete the exercise, tell them that in two sentences the words are not possible because they don't fit with the prepositions, and in three sentences the words are not possible because they are illogical. Check their answers and ask students to identify which is which.

Answers

1 a computer (illogical – no-one lives in a *computer*) **2** evenings (not possible after *on*) **3** Monday (not possible after *in*) **4** study (illogical – *study* is not a subject) **5** online (illogical – you can't take photos of *online*)

Optional extension

Ask students to add other possible words to each group, e.g. *1 a house/flat*, *2 summer courses*, etc. Have them share their ideas with the rest of the class after you check the answers.

OPTIMISE YOUR EXAM

Gap fill

Ask students to read the tips.

- Remind students to use their preparation time sensibly and think about what type of information to expect for each answer. Point out that, although they did some work on this in exercises 2 and 3, the answers may not be what they saw there.
- Remind students that it is very common in listening exams for the recording to include words that sound like they could be correct answers but are not.

Exam task

4 2.21 Ask students to read the instructions and the information in the box. Play the track and then check students' answers. Have students share their thoughts on how easy or difficult the task was.

Answers

1 granny **2** Wednesdays **3** April **4** history **5** garden

THINK | RESEARCH | CULTURE | LEARN | ME

Before students write their questions, brainstorm different topics they could ask about. Then have students share their questions with the class and number them in order of importance.

Homework OWB

Assign students Listening exercises 1 and 2 on page 56 of their Workbook.

GRAMMAR 2
will and *going to*

→ Student's Book, page 75 SB

Lesson aims

- Understand the correct usage of *will* and *going to*
- Practise using *will* for spontaneous decisions, offers/ requests and for predictions based on opinion
- Practise using *going to* for future plans and for predictions based on evidence

Lead-in

Draw a weekly planner on the board with the days of the week listed on the left and the heading *Things to do* on the right. Tell students about some of your arrangements and plans for the week, using the present continuous and *going to*. For example, *On Monday evening I'm going to relax at home with my family. On Tuesday it's my son's birthday so we're having dinner in a restaurant.*, etc. Then tell students to create their own planner in their notebooks. Give them a time limit and then have them share their lists with the class.

Grammar in context

Remind students that *I'm* is a contraction for *I am*. Elicit that *I'll* is the contraction for (*I will*). Then ask students to complete the task, and refer them to the information in the *Remember* box if they aren't sure.

Remind students that they can find more information in the Grammar reference, Unit 7, page 156.

Answers

1 b **2** c **3** d **4** e **5** a

Language note

Students have already seen how *going to* is used for personal plans and to make predictions based on evidence. Students will now see how *will* is used for spontaneous reactions, to make offers or requests and predictions based on opinions.

1 Ask students to complete the exercise individually. Then have them check their answers with a partner.

Answers

1 'm going to **2** 'll **3** Will you **4** aren't going to go **5** 'll **6** aren't going to

Mixed ability

Give weaker students the function that corresponds to each item (*1 a plan, 2 an instant decision, 3 a request, 4 a plan, 5 an offer/instant decision, 6 a plan*). When stronger students have finished, ask them to make a list of the function for each item. Check the functions as you go through the answers in open class.

2 Ask students to look at the conversation and tell you what the friends are talking about (*planning an end-of-term party*). Have students complete the exercise individually. Check answers in open class and then put students into groups to practise the conversation. Walk round the class, monitoring students for pronunciation and helping them where necessary.

Answers

1 're/are going to make **2** 'm/am going to sell **3** Will, choose **4** 'll buy **5** 's/is going to prepare **6** are going to come **7** will, check **8** 's/is going to be

3 Before students complete the exercise, ask them how they get to school. Have students check in pairs before you check their answers in open class. Then have the class compare their own journey with that of the students in Atuler.

Answers

1 going **2** going **3** are **4** will **5** will **6** to **7** will **8** will

Homework OWB

Assign students Grammar 2 exercise 1 on page 55 of their Workbook.

Assign students the Flipped classroom tasks on page 76 of their Student's Book if you'd like them to prepare for the next lesson. To complete this task, students need to watch the *Talk2Me* video which can be found on the Resource Centre.

SPEAKING

Interview

→ Student's Book, page 76 SB

Lesson aims

- Focus on talking about the future and making predictions
- Practise answering personal questions in an interview
- Research what students plan to do when they finish school

The *Talk2Me* video in this unit focuses on jobs and job interviews. The people in the video talk about getting a part-time job, preparing for a job interview and their plans for when they leave school.

Students answer some comprehension questions and then listen for key phrases in the video.

The video can be used in one of two ways:

Flipped classroom

Flipped classroom option

Using this approach, students watch the video and complete the exercises for homework. This prepares students for the speaking lesson by introducing them to the topic and the key phrases to use in the exam task. Teachers who use this method will find they have more class time to spend on activating the target language and developing fluency for the final task.

***Talk2Me* worksheet**

Ask students to also complete the *Talk2Me* worksheet on the Resource Centre for more detailed comprehension exercises and more practice of the key phrases.

Classroom option

1 Ask students to spend a minute or two reading the questions. Play the *Talk2Me* video for students to complete the exercise. Play the video again, if necessary, before checking their answers.

2 Play the *Talk2Me* video again, so students underline the phrases in the *Phrase expert* box. Pause the video from time to time if necessary. Check answers in open class.

Talk2Me worksheet

Ask students to also complete the *Talk2Me* worksheet on the Resource Centre for more detailed comprehension exercises and more practice of the key phrases.

Answers

The transcript and answer key for the *Talk2Me* video exercises and Worksheet can be found on the Teacher's Resource Centre.

Lead-in

Revise some of the personal questions students have already seen on the course. Write the following groups of question prompts around the unit numbers on the board:

Unit 1 – *How much / free time / you / have / ?*

Unit 3 – *What / be / favourite type of food / ?*

Unit 5 –*What / you / do / next weekend / ?*

Have students use the prompts to ask and answer the questions in pairs. Tell them to ask other personal questions they can remember. Walk round the class, monitoring students' use of English and helping them to form questions if necessary.

Answers

Unit 1 – How much free time do you have?

Unit 3 – What's your favourite type of food?

Unit 5 – What are you doing next weekend?

3 In pairs, students ask and answer the questions. Elicit answers from different students around the class and encourage a class discussion.

EXAM SKILL

Talking about the future

Ask students to read the tips.

- Explain to students that personal questions in speaking exams are usually chosen so candidates can use a variety of different verb tenses in their answers. On this page, for example, they are given opportunities to use both *going to* and *will* to talk about the future.
- Tell students that examiners are listening for candidates' correct use of grammar, but remind them that they can increase their marks by using appropriate phrases like those in the *Phrase expert* boxes.

4 2.22 Rearrange the first question as a class and elicit tips on how to do this from the class. For example, *The question should start with 'Are'.* Have students complete the rest of the exercise. Then play the audio for students to listen and check.

Answers

1 Are you going to take exams this term? **2** Will your classmates pass the test? **3** What languages will you study next year? **4** Are you going to study in the summer holidays?

Fast finishers

Ask students to cover Exercise 5 and brainstorm possible answers to the questions in Exercise 4. After matching the questions and answers in the next exercise, they can compare their ideas with the model answers.

5 2.22 After students complete the exercise, have them practise asking and answering the questions in Exercise 4 in pairs.

Answers

1 next term **2** 're/are going to **3** perhaps **4** 'm/am going to

OPTIMISE YOUR EXAM

Interview

Ask students to read the tips.

- Stress the importance of candidates answering the question they are asked and not something completely different. Remind students that if they are unsure about the question, they should use an appropriate phrase to confirm their understanding, e.g. *Sorry, could you repeat the question, please?*
- Remind students to listen for the tense used in the questions, as this will give them an idea of what the examiner is expecting. In many cases students will need to use the same tense in their answer as the examiner used in the question.
- Remind students to give extra information in their answers. Answering with short answers, even if these are grammatically correct, will not be enough to get top marks. It is much better to expand their answer to show their knowledge of the language even if the answer they give isn't true.

Exam task

6 Remind students to use time expressions from the *Phrase expert* box in their answers and to give appropriate additional information or reasons for their answers. Walk round the class, monitoring students for good use of language, making notes of any errors you hear. Write any errors on the board and go through them with students, eliciting corrections from them. After the class feedback, students could repeat this activity with another partner, to try to improve their performance.

Suggested answers

1 My favourite subjects at school are history and geography.
2 I'm going to study economics and biology (in the future).
3 I'm going to do 7 hours of homework this week.
4 I'm going to relax and watch TV at home.
5 When I leave school, I think I'll get a job at a bank.

Optional extension

Divide the class into small groups. Have students pick three or four personal questions to ask you that they think they could be asked in the speaking exam. Allow students to take turns asking you their questions. Make sure your model answers are the type of answers that you would expect students at this level to be able to produce themselves.

THINK | **RESEARCH** | CULTURE | LEARN | ME

Ask students to interview students from a different class and present their information to the class in the next lesson.

Homework

OWB

Students use their notes from Exercise 6 to write a summary of what they found out about their partner. Remind them to be particularly careful with the use of future tenses.

Assign students Speaking exercises 1, 2 and 3 on page 56 of their Workbook.

LANGUAGE IN USE

Multiple-choice cloze

→ Student's Book, page 77

SB

Lesson aims

- Focus on word phrases
- Practise a multiple-choice cloze exam task
- Discuss ideas for playing *Classcraft*

Lead-in

Revise some of the collocations students have already seen in the course. Write the following words in random order in two circles on the board:

Circle 1 – *board, cinema, do, DVD, make, newspaper, send, start, take, TV*

Circle 2 – *a conversation, a mistake, a text message, a train, article, game, player, programme, screen, the washing-up*

Tell students to look at the words in both circles. Then read a word out from Circle 1 and elicit the word it goes with from Circle 2. Continue with more students from around the class.

Answers

verb + noun: do the washing-up, make a mistake, send a text message, start a conversation, take a train

noun + noun: board game, cinema screen, DVD player, newspaper article, TV programme

1 After students discuss the questions, have them share their ideas with the rest of the class.

EXAM SKILL

Learning word phrases

Ask students to read the tips.

- Remind students how important it is to learn language in chunks, i.e. studying groups of words that go together, rather than lists of isolated words.
- Explain that multiple-choice cloze tasks often test collocations and other word phrases, such as verb + preposition phrases. Tell students to think about the meaning of the word they need to complete the gap and its correct form.
- Remind students to include some example phrases or sentences when they record new vocabulary.

2 After students complete the exercise, make a note of any common errors to focus on straight away or at a later date.

Answers

1 at **2** have **3** to **4** do **5** make **6** a

3 Ask students to complete the exercise. Have them compare their answers in pairs after they finish.

Answers

1 at **2** on **3** did **4** had **5** take

Optional extension

Split the class into four groups. Assign each group one of the verbs *make*, *do*, *have* and *take*. Set a strict time limit of two minutes. In their groups, students brainstorm all the collocations they can think of with the verb. Regroup students into groups of four so there is one student who has prepared each verb in each group. Students share their collocations and take notes if they wish.

OPTIMISE YOUR EXAM

Multiple-choice cloze

Ask students to read the tips.

- Remind students that they need to think carefully about 'chunks' of language as these are commonly tested.
- Remind students of the process they practised earlier in the course: read the text first for general understanding; complete the gaps and leave difficult options until the end; check the words before or after the gaps to confirm answers; guess the best answer for all the gaps, even the ones they are not sure of.
- Point out that as they become more familiar with the language, they will develop their intuition and will recognise whether or not their chosen option 'sounds right' / makes sense when they read through the text for the final time.

4 After students answer the question, ask them to predict what the text is about (*the game* Classcraft *and how it works*).

Answer
a) a term

Exam task

5 Tell students to implement the tips they have learnt to complete this task type. Ask students to complete the exercise individually and then compare their answers in pairs. Check answers in open class.

Answers
1 A **2** A **3** C **4** B **5** C **6** B **7** A **8** A

Mixed ability

Tell weaker students one incorrect option for each question so that they only have two options to choose from. Have stronger students complete the task as it appears in the Student's Book.

THINK | RESEARCH | CULTURE | LEARN | ME

After groups complete the exercise, have them present their ideas to the rest of the class. Have the groups evaluate each other and then vote for the best idea.

Cultural note

Classcraft was created by Canadian physics teacher Shawn Young in 2013. He decided to harness his students' love of video games to help with classroom management. In the game, students create virtual characters who can gain experience and skills, just like the characters do in the games they play. These characters inhabit an impressive virtual world, but the key difference is that students gain points to improve their learning in the real world of the classroom. This outcome has dramatic implications on students' motivation and interaction with their classmates. The platform has more than 1 million users and it is in more than 20,000 schools in more than 75 countries around the world.

Homework

OWB

Assign students Language in Use exercises 1, 2 and 3 on page 57 of their Workbook.

WRITING
Information transfer

→ Student's Book, pages 78–79 SB

Lesson aims

- Focus on understanding similar information
- Practise an information transfer exam task

Lead-in

Write the words *school trip* on the board and encourage the class to brainstorm all the places they can think of. Tell them to think of places they have been with the school and places they would like the school to take them.

1 After students complete the exercise, have them share their experiences with the class.

2 Give students a minute to read the notice and the email. Then have students discuss whether they would like to go on the school trip as a class. Ask students what they could do to improve the notice.

EXAM SKILL

Understanding similar information

Ask students to read the tips.

- Tell students that they have done this type of task before. Remind them that the key is to find connections between specific questions in the task and specific pieces of information in the two texts.

3 Remind students to find words that have the same meaning. After they complete the exercise, have students compare their ideas in pairs. Then check answers in open class.

Answers
a 2 (my parents) **b** 5 (after lunch) **c** 4 (water) **d** 3 (tell my teacher) **e** 1 (am)

Exam task

4 **Plan** Students read and tick the points in the plan. Elicit the steps they need to take and give any necessary advice or suggestions.

Answers
Students should tick:
1, 2, 3

OPTIMISE YOUR EXAM

Information transfer

Ask students to read the tips.

- Remind students that it's always important to read both texts first to get a general understanding of the situation and context before completing the task.
- Remind students that in some cases they may need to combine information from both texts in order to complete the exam task.
- Highlight the importance of spelling words correctly.

5 Write Ask students to complete the notes individually. Check their answers and discuss any problems they had. For example, *Item 1 is '10', not '10 am' – 'am' is not correct because it says 'in the morning'.*

Answers

1 10 **2** Thursday and Friday **3** eraser **4** bags and mobile phones **5** 6

Fast finishers

Ask students to underline the words in Alex's notes and the words in the exam texts that mean the same, e.g. *begin* = *start*, *don't take* = *leave*. Check these words while going through the answers.

6 Check Students complete the checklist before they hand in their notes.

Extra writing

7 Ask students what the appropriate style of an email is (*informal*). Students answer the questions. Check answers in open class. The students write their emails. If there is not enough time, set this for homework.

Answers

1 Rosie **2** informal

3 How do you feel about the exams next week?
Do you want to study together this weekend?
Would you like to come for dinner too?

Optional extension

For a slightly longer writing task, and for students to see other text types, refer them to one of the six tasks in the Writing reference (SB p169). Each one includes an annotated sample text and related writing task to challenge your students a little more.

Homework OWB

Assign students Writing exercises 1, 2, 3 and 4 on page 58 of their Workbook and Progress check 7 on page 59.

8 It's only a game

UNIT AIMS

Exam preparation in Unit 8:

- scan the text in an online article
- listen for important information in a conversation
- ask questions in a collaborative task
- use modal verbs in a multiple-choice cloze exercise
- write an email in an informal style

TEACHER'S PRESENTATION KIT

- *Talk2Me* videos
- Speaking test videos
- Class and Workbook audio
- Workbook pages and answer key

UNIT OVERVIEW

Student's Book / Digital Student's Book SB		Workbook / Online Workbook OWB
LESSON / EXAM TASK	EXAM SKILLS / LANGUAGE FOCUS	CONSOLIDATION
Reading **Right/Wrong/Doesn't say**	Scanning An online article	Workbook, pp 60–61, Exercises 1, 2, 3, 4, 5 Unit 8, Reading, Exercises 1, 2, 3, 4, 5
Grammar 1	Modals (1): ability, necessity, obligation, possibility	Workbook, p 62, Exercises 1, 2, 3 Unit 8, Grammar 1, Exercises 1, 2, 3
Vocabulary	Words connected with *sport* Verbs/nouns Collocations with verbs	Workbook, pp 62–63, Exercises 1, 2, 3 Unit 8, Vocabulary, Exercises 1, 2, 3
Listening **Multiple matching**	Listening for important information	Workbook, p 64, Exercises 1, 2, 3 Unit 8, Listening, Exercises 1, 2, 3
Grammar 2	Modals (2): advice, permission, polite requests, prohibition	Workbook, p 63, Exercises 1, 2, 3 Unit 8, Grammar 2, Exercises 1, 2, 3
Speaking **Collaborative task**	Asking questions	Workbook, p 64, Exercises 1, 2, 3 Unit 8, Speaking, Exercises 1, 2, 3
Language in Use **Multiple-choice cloze**	Modal verbs	Workbook, p 65, Exercises 1, 2 Unit 8, Language in Use, Exercises 1, 2
Writing **An email**	Writing in an informal style	Workbook, p 66, Exercises 1, 2, 3, 4 Unit 8, Writing, Exercises 1, 2, 3, 4
Progress check	Check language progress for Units 7 and 8	Workbook, p 67, Progress check and Cumulative progress Progress check and Cumulative progress

Additional material

PRESENTATION KIT	TEACHER'S / STUDENT'S RESOURCE CENTRE RC	TEST GENERATOR
Talk2Me video *Can I buy …?*	**Unit 8 worksheets:** *Optimise your grammar* (Standard and Higher), *Optimise your vocabulary* (Standard and Higher), *Talk2Me* video, *Say it right* **Units 7–8 worksheets:** CLIL, Culture, Everyday English (TRC only), Grammar communication (TRC only)	Unit Test 8 (Standard and Higher) Progress Test (Standard and Higher)

READING

Right/Wrong/Doesn't say | An online article

→ Student's Book, pages 80–81 SB

Lesson aims

- Focus on scanning
- Practise a Right/Wrong/Doesn't say exam task
- Research famous sports people

Lead-in

In pairs, ask students to look at the unit title ***It's only a game*** and brainstorm what the *it* in the question could refer to, e.g. *football, tennis, volleyball, cricket*. Explain that we sometimes say *It's only a game* when people get really excited about something, more than necessary – perhaps like the people in the photo celebrating their victory.

1 In pairs, students ask and answer the questions. Elicit answers from different students around the class and open out to a class debate about whether it's more important to enter sports competitions or to win them.

2 Ask students to think of different sports and to write them in the correct list.

Possible answers

Team sports: basketball, cricket, football, rugby, volleyball

Sports you do alone: athletics, badminton, skiing, surfing, tennis

EXAM SKILL

Scanning

Ask students to read the tips.

- Elicit situations where students need to find a particular piece of information quickly within a large amount of text (*looking up words in a dictionary, a sports score in a newspaper, a train/bus timetable*, etc.).
- Remind students that scanning is a strategy for speed reading to find specific information in the text.
- Highlight key techniques, such as looking for numbers rather than words (*in 1989*) and then reading the sentence in which they appear.

3 Ask students to complete the exercise in a two-minute time limit. Students compare in pairs before you check in open class.

Answers

1 They need to practise for many years. **2** She was born in Venezuela. **3** Her dream is to be number one.

4 Ask students to complete the exercise. Check answers in open class.

Answers

1 c **2** d **3** a **4** e **5** b

Cultural note

Garbiñe Muguruza Blanco is one the world's leading women's tennis players and is known for her aggressive style of play. She has won three WTA singles titles so far in her career, with the most important being the 2016 French Open when she beat Serena Williams in the final. She is also an accomplished doubles player and has already won four doubles titles on the WTA tour.

OPTIMISE YOUR EXAM

Right/Wrong/Doesn't say

Ask students to read the tips.

- For this type of exam question, students need to read the questions carefully and underline the important information, then read the text quickly for gist to get the main idea of the text. Next, they should go back to the beginning of the text and read the relevant sections more carefully to answer the questions.
- Remind students that the questions always follow the order of the text, and a good exam technique is to stop after the first question and decide if the answer is *Right*, *Wrong* or *Doesn't say* and to continue like this until they have answered all the questions.
- Check students understand that marks are not deducted for incorrect answers, so they should not leave any questions unanswered.

Extra support

In a less confident class, prepare students before the exercise by reading through the sentences with them and helping them to identify the important information. If you wish, tell them that the answer to 1 is in paragraph 1, the answers to 2, 3 and 4 are in in paragraph 2 and the answers to 5, 6 and 7 are in in paragraph 3.

Exam task

5 2.23 **Note: The reading text is also available on the audio CD. You may want to have students listen and read the text before doing the exam task.**

Ask students to complete the exercise. Have students compare in pairs before you check in open class. Elicit evidence for the answers.

Answers

1 C (The text says that sport stars *need to practise for many hours …*, but it doesn't say if they practise alone.)

2 C (The text says that Garbiñe's family moved to Spain and that she went to a special tennis school there, but it doesn't say this is the reason why the family moved.)

3 B (The text says that *She could hold a racket when she was three, so she started playing tennis.*, therefore she learnt before she arrived in Spain.)

4 B (*… in 2012 she entered her first professional competition. Two years later, in 2014, she won a competition for the first time.*)

5 C (Garbiñe says *I like to listen to music* but she doesn't say what kind of music she likes.)

6 A (*… tennis players needn't spend all their time thinking about tennis. 'I like to … hang out with family and friends …'*)

7 C (The text say says *Recently, she couldn't go on holiday with her friends*, but it doesn't say whether or not she has ever been on holiday with them.)

Fast finishers

Ask students to write an additional *Right/Wrong/Doesn't say* sentence for the text. They can try out their sentences with the class after you check the answers to Exercise 5.

6 Ask students to complete the exercise. Students compare in pairs before you check in open class.

Answers
1 won **2** racket **3** throw **4** hold **5** tired **6** practise **7** swim **8** unhappy

THINK | **RESEARCH** | CULTURE | LEARN | ME

If you have access to the internet, students can research this information in class. It could be a collaborative project with students working in pairs or groups. To avoid repetition, you may prefer to brainstorm famous sports people and then assign these yourself.

Homework OWB
Assign students Reading exercises 1, 2, 3, 4 and 5 on pages 60–61 of their Workbook.

GRAMMAR 1
Modals (1): ability, necessity, obligation, possibility

→ Student's Book, page 82 SB

Lesson aims

- Understand the correct usage of modals of ability, necessity, obligation and possibility
- Practise using modal verbs to talk about ability, necessity, obligation and possibility

Lead-in

Write these jumbled questions on the board and ask students to reorder them:

1 well / you / sports / what / do / can / ?

2 sports / what / do / at all / can't / you / ?

In pairs, students ask and answer the questions. Circle the words *can* and *can't* and elicit what kind of words they are and what they mean (*modal verbs; they are used to talk about abilities you have or don't have*).

Answers
1 What sports can you do well? **2** What sports can't you do at all?

Grammar in context

Ask students to complete the task and refer them to information in the *Remember* box if they aren't sure. Check their answers.

Remind students that they can find more information in the Grammar reference, Unit 8, page 157.

Answers
a ability **b** obligation **c** possibility **d** obligation **e** necessity

Language note

Modal verbs, also called modals, 'help' other verbs to express a meaning. Point out that modal verbs have no meaning by themselves.

1 Ask students to complete the exercise. Check answers in open class.

Answers
1 couldn't **2** must **3** might **4** have to **5** needn't **6** must

Extra support

Write *Present or past?* and *Ability? Possibility? Necessity? Obligation? No obligation or necessity?* on the board. Look at the sentences in Exercise 1 with the students and analyse each one, answering the questions. Check students understand the type of modal verbs: Ability: *can, could*; Possibility: *may, might, could*; Necessity: *need to*; Obligation: *must, have to*; No obligation or necessity: *not have to, needn't*

2 Ask students to complete the exercise. Students compare in pairs before you check in open class.

Answers
1 Can **2** can't **3** might **4** needn't **5** have **6** don't have

3 Ask students to look at the photo and say what sport they can see (*athletics/running*). Ask them to complete the exercise. Have students compare in pairs before you check their answers in open class.

Answers
1 couldn't **2** may/might **3** had **4** needn't/mightn't **5** have/need **6** can't **7** needn't **8** might/may

Fast finishers

Write these numbers on the board for students to find out what they refer to in the text: *15, 2nd, 1952, 5,000, 10,000, 42*

Answers
15 the age Zátopek was when the factory sports coach told him to run in a race
2nd the position he came in that first race
1952 the year he participated in the Olympic Games
5,000/10,000 the distances in metres of the races he ran and won at the Olympics
42 the length of a marathon, in kilometres

Homework OWB
Assign students Grammar 1 exercises 1, 2 and 3 on page 62 of their Workbook.

VOCABULARY

Topic vocabulary | Word formation | Collocations

→ Student's Book, page 83 SB

Lesson aims

Understand the correct usage of:

- words connected with sport
- verbs and nouns from the same word family
- verb collocations

Lead-in

In small groups, students take turns to mime sports for the other students in their group to guess.

Words connected with *sport*

1 2.24 Ask students to complete the exercise. Play the audio for students to listen and check.

Answers/Audioscript

1 You need a small white ball to play this game. *table tennis*
2 You can go swimming here. *pool*
3 You can do this sport on snow in the mountains. *skiing*
4 You can watch a football game here. *stadium*
5 This is the person who is first in a competition or race. *winner*
6 You need a racket to play this game. *badminton*

2 2.25 Read the first sentence with students and establish that all three answer options refer to people. The correct answer is the one that best fits the context. Encourage students to look for clues in the rest of the sentences to help them choose the correct word.

Ask students to complete the exercise individually. Play the audio for students to listen and check their answers.

Answers/Audioscript

1 (B) The *coach* told us what exercises to do and helped us play better.
2 (C) Can you *ride* a horse?
3 (A) You need a *ticket* to go to the basketball game tonight.
4 (A) I can't go swimming because I haven't got my *swimsuit*.
5 (A) Ed was the winner of the 800-metre *race*.
6 (C) They played in a rugby *match* yesterday, and won 35-3!

Fast finishers

Ask students to explain what the incorrect alternatives mean and how they could be used, e.g. a *team* refers to a group of people who play a sport together, whereas a *member* is someone who belongs to a club or group: *Some members of the hockey team are friends of mine.*

Refer students to the Vocabulary reference, page 166, for more information on topic vocabulary.

Verbs/nouns

3 2.26 Look at the first line of the table with students as an example. Ask them to complete the exercise. Play the audio for students to listen and check their answers.

Answers/Audioscript

verb: win, **noun:** winner
verb: *surf*, **noun:** surfer
verb: swim, **noun:** *swimmer*
verb: *run*, **noun:** runner
verb: play, **noun:** *player*

4 Ask students to complete the exercise. Check students have spelt the words correctly.

Answers

1 swimmers **2** won **3** runners **4** player **5** surf

Mixed ability

Give less confident students the words in the correct form and ask them to put them into the correct sentences. Ask stronger students to complete the exercise as given and then brainstorm additional verbs/nouns for people which they already know, e.g. *act/actor, teach/teacher, write/writer.*

Refer students to the Vocabulary reference, page 166, for more information on word formation.

Collocations with verbs

5 2.27 Write *run* in the centre of the board. And ask students to tell you what might come after *run*, e.g. *a race, a marathon, 5,000 metres*. Remind students that learning combinations of words which are often used together (collocations) is a very effective way of learning vocabulary.

Ask students to complete the exercise. Play the audio for students to listen and check their answers.

Answers/Audioscript

1 Greg *threw* the ball into the road.
2 My class *goes* swimming at the city pool every Wednesday.
3 Everyone can *enter* the competition but only one person can win.
4 In the summer, lots of people in England *play* cricket.
5 Do I need to practise a lot before I *climb* a mountain?
6 Emil Zátopek was very happy when he *won* the 5,000-metre race at the Olympic Games.

Refer students to the Vocabulary reference, page 166, for more information on collocations.

Homework

OWB

Assign students Vocabulary exercises 1, 2 and 3 on pages 62–63 of their Workbook.

LISTENING
Multiple matching

→ Student's Book, page 84 SB

Lesson aims

- Listen for important information
- Practise a multiple-matching exam task
- Discuss summer camps

Lead-in

Recycle the collocations from the previous lesson.

Call out a verb (*climb, enter, go, play, throw, win*) and ask students to work in pairs or small groups to think of a grammatically correct sentence using the verb and an appropriate collocation. Repeat with other verbs.

1 In pairs, students ask and answer the questions. Elicit answers from different students around the class. Ask students which verb usually collocates with each of the sports they mention.

Answers

1 table tennis, volleyball, trampolining
2 and 3 Students' own answers

EXAM SKILL

Listening for important information

Ask students to read the tips.

- Remind students that in listening exams it is not necessary to understand everything to be able to complete the task. If students prepare before listening by reading the questions carefully, they will then have an idea of what the recording is going to be about and can relax and will understand a lot more.
- In listening exams, students usually have 30 seconds before the first listening to prepare – in tasks like the one in Exercise 2, it can be useful to think of vocabulary which they expect to hear in connection with the topic, e.g. *running – athletics, a race, a stadium, winner; windsurfing – water, sea, (bad/good) weather*, etc.

2 2.28 Play the track for students to listen and complete the exercise. Elicit answers from students around the class.

Answers

1 e **2** d **3** b **4** a **5** c

3 2.28 Play the track again for students to identify the other sports the people talk about in the conversations.

Answers

1 football, rugby **2** volleyball **3** fishing **4** swimming **5** tennis

Optional extension 2.28

Write these questions on the board. Play the track again for students to answer them.

1 *What sort of sports does Dan enjoy?*
2 *Where did Lorna go cycling?*
3 *Does Chris often go windsurfing?*
4 *Why didn't Lily enjoy going running?*
5 *Was Pete good at playing badminton before?*

Answers

1 Sports where you run around. **2** in the mountains **3** No, it was his first time. **4** Because it was cold. **5** Probably not, because someone taught him how to play.

OPTIMISE YOUR EXAM

Multiple matching

Ask students to read the tips.

- Explain that in this type of task there are often distractors, i.e. items which look like they could be correct answers but in fact are not needed. In Exercise 4, for example, there are five days of the week but there are eight sports. Some or all of the distractors may be included in the recording, so students need to remember that they might hear a word that they don't actually need to use in an answer.
- Remind students that they will usually hear the recording twice, so they shouldn't panic if they aren't sure of some of the answers after the first listening. They should check carefully in the second listening that the answer they have chosen is correct and that they haven't been tricked by a distractor.

Exam task

4 2.29 Play the track for students to listen and complete the exercise. Ask students to compare their choices. Then, play the track again, pausing after each section. Check answers in open class.

Answers

1 C **2** B **3** E **4** G **5** A

Extra support

Give students a copy of the audioscript. Play the track again and ask students to identify the distractor, e.g. *I wanted to play tennis on Tuesday, but it was raining so I couldn't.*

THINK | RESEARCH | **CULTURE** | LEARN | ME

Ask students to discuss the questions. Point out that there are no right or wrong answers. Open out to a class discussion, if there is time, and find out if any students in the class have been on a summer camp.

Homework

OWB

Assign students Listening exercises 1, 2 and 3 on page 64 of their Workbook.

GRAMMAR 2

Modals (2): advice, permission, polite requests, prohibition

→ Student's Book, page 85 SB

Lesson aims

- Understand the correct usage of modals of advice, permission, polite requests and prohibition
- Practise using modal verbs to talk about advice, permission, polite requests and prohibition

Lead-in

Write these sentences on the board:
If you feel ill, you should …, If you work hard this morning, you can …, Can I go …?, In school, you mustn't …
Model a possible completion for the first sentence, e.g. *If you feel ill, you should go to see the nurse.* In pairs or small groups, students try to complete the sentences in as many different ways as possible. Elicit answers around the class.

Circle the modal verbs in the sentences and elicit the function of each (***should*** *= to give advice;* ***can*** *= to talk about permission, or to make a request;* ***mustn't*** *= to talk about prohibition).* Explain that in this lesson students will be learning about more modal verbs and their functions.

Grammar in context

Ask students to complete the task. Refer them to the information in the *Remember* box if they aren't sure. Then check their answers. Ask students to think of personalised sentences of their own, using the modals in the box. Elicit a few examples around the class.

Remind students that they can find more information in the Grammar reference, Unit 8, page 158.

Answers

a 2 **b** 5 **c** 3 **d** 1 **e** 4

Language note

Students have to be able to use a limited range of modal and semi-modal verbs for exams at this level.

On page 82 of their Student's Book, students saw how *can/can't* and *could/couldn't* are used to talk about ability. In this lesson, they will see that these same modals are also used to say that something *is/isn't* or *was/wasn't allowed*. Be prepared to give students further explanations and examples to help them distinguish *ability* (something that you are able to do because you have a natural talent, or that you have taught yourself to do) from *permission* (something that is allowed because another person or the rules say that this is acceptable).

The verb *have to*, like *need to* is a semi-modal verb and can be problematic.

- In terms of form, negatives and questions are formed with the auxiliary verbs *do/does* or *did/didn't*, not with the addition of *n't* to the end of the verb.
- Students may mistakenly use the negative *don't have to* to talk about things that are not allowed, so you need to clarify that in these cases the opposite of *have to* is *can't* (*In football, you can't touch the ball with your hands.*)
- The negative *don't have to* is used to talk about things which it is not necessary to do, but which you can do if you choose.

1 Ask students to complete the exercise. Check in open class.

Answers

1 can **2** mustn't **3** could **4** shouldn't **5** should

Mixed ability

Tell students five things you *have to* and *don't have to* do as a teacher, e.g. *I have to correct my students' homework. I don't have to work at weekends.* Ask weaker students to work in pairs and write sentences about what they *have to* and *don't have to* do as students. Ask stronger students to work in small groups and take turns to think of a job and make five sentences about it with *have to* and *don't have to*. The other students in their group have to guess the job. In both cases, walk round monitoring students for good use of language and errors to go over at the end of the activity.

2 Ask students to complete the exercise. Have students check in pairs before you check their answers in open class.

Answers

1 a **2** c **3** c **4** a **5** b **6** b

3 Ask students to complete the exercise. Students compare in pairs before you check in open class.

Answers

1 should bring **2** can't do **3** could you bring **4** should bring **5** can use **6** shouldn't arrive **7** could you ask **8** mustn't leave

Fast finishers

Ask students to expand the first paragraph of the text in Exercise 3 with additional ideas of things they should or shouldn't take to the camp, e.g. *You can bring a mobile phone, but you should leave it in your locker during the day.*

Homework

OWB

Assign students Grammar 2 exercises 1, 2 and 3 on page 63 of their Workbook.

Assign students the Flipped classroom tasks on page 86 of their Student's Book if you'd like them to prepare for the next lesson. To complete this task, students need to watch the *Talk2Me* video which can be found on the Resource Centre.

SPEAKING
Collaborative task

→ Student's Book, page 86

SB

Lesson aims

- Focus on asking and answering questions to exchange information
- Practise an information exchange exam task
- Discuss learning new sports

The *Talk2Me* video in this unit focuses on mobile phones and communication problems. The people in the video ask their phones questions using the voice recognition function, but the phones misunderstand.

Students answer some comprehension questions and then listen for key phrases in the video.

The video can be used in one of two ways:

Flipped classroom

Flipped classroom option

Using this approach, students watch the video and complete the exercises for homework. This prepares students for the speaking lesson by introducing them to the topic and the key phrases to use in the exam task. Teachers who use this method will find they have more class time to spend on activating the target language and developing fluency for the final task.

***Talk2Me* worksheet**

Ask students to also complete the *Talk2Me* worksheet from the Resource Centre for more detailed comprehension exercises and more practice of the key phrases.

Classroom option

1 Ask students to spend a minute or two reading the questions. Play the *Talk2Me* video for students to complete the exercise. Play the video again, if necessary, before checking their answers.

2 Play the *Talk2Me* video again, so students underline the phrases in the *Phrase expert* box. Pause the video from time to time if necessary. Check answers in open class.

***Talk2Me* worksheet**

Ask students to also complete the *Talk2Me* worksheet on the Resource Centre for more detailed comprehension exercises and more practice of the key phrases.

Answers

The transcript and answer key for the *Talk2Me* video exercises and Worksheet can be found on the Teacher's Resource Centre.

Lead-in

Create a word web to revise and extend the unit vocabulary. Write *SPORT* in the middle. To the right, draw a circle with *VERBS* in it, and to the left draw a circle with *EQUIPMENT* in it. Invite students to come up and add words.

EXAM SKILL

Asking questions

Ask students to read the tips.

- Point out that in this lesson, they will practise forming the kinds of questions they will need to use in an information exchange task.
- In this part of the test, candidates can show their ability both to formulate *Wh-* and *yes/no* questions correctly and to answer these appropriately. They may also receive extra credit for good sentence stress and pronunciation.
- Students are expected to ask and answer questions with a relatively high level of grammatical accuracy. Examiners will be checking that students use appropriate word order and auxiliary verbs where necessary in their questions. In their replies, students will need to answer *yes/no* questions with complete short answers, not just 'yes' or 'no'.

3 In pairs, students ask and answer the questions. Elicit answers in open class.

Language note

All the questions students are required to formulate in exercises 4 and 6 follow standard word order. Remind students of the standard word order pattern, QASI, by writing the following table on the board and talking them through some of the questions from the *Talk2Me* video:

Question word	Auxiliary verb	Subject	Infinitive
How often	*do*	*you*	*do* sports at school?
What sports	*would*	*you*	*like* to do at school?
–	*Do*	*you*	*like* sport?

4 Ask students to complete the exercise. Check their answers in open class.

Answers

1 What time does it start? **2** Can I buy a ticket online? **3** Have they got a website? **4** How much does it cost? **5** Is it open after school? **6** Do I have to take a racket?

5 2.30 Ask students to complete the exercise. Play the audio for students to listen and check their answers.

Answers

a 2 **b** 4 **c** 5 **d** 1 **e** 6 **f** 3

Extra support

Review the relationship between *yes/no* questions and short answers by looking at questions 2, 3, 5 and 6 in Exercise 4 and their corresponding answers in Exercise 5. Highlight how the auxiliary and the subject in each question relates to the short answer.

OPTIMISE YOUR EXAM

Collaborative task

Ask students to read the tips.

- Using preparation time effectively is a key part of this task. Students should look at the prompts and read through the information given. Point out that they will not have enough time to write out everything they are going to say, and that it is better to read through everything and anticipate what they have to say, than to write the first two questions and then run out of time.
- Being able to deal with minor problems of understanding is also expected in exams at this level. Students should not be afraid to use appropriate expressions (*I don't understand, I'm sorry. Can you say that again?*) to ask for repetition and clarification, both between themselves and with the examiner.

Exam task

6 Assign each student a letter, A or B, and put them into A/B pairs. Give them a moment to look at their information / question topics on page 137/140. Time students (two minutes) and give them an update, e.g. *One minute to go* … Remind students to use phrases from the *Phrase expert* box and to ask for any necessary clarification. Walk round, monitoring students for good use of language and errors to go over at the end of the activity.

Write any errors on the board and go through them with students, eliciting corrections from them where possible. After the class feedback, students could then repeat this activity with another partner, to try to improve their performance.

Suggested answers

Student A's questions
When are they?
Are there classes for children?
What's the price? / How much are they?
Do I need a bat?
What's the telephone number?

Student B's questions
What's its name? / What's it called?
Where is it?
Is it open on Sunday evening?
Does it sell tennis rackets?
Can I/you buy things online?

SAY IT RIGHT

Rising intonation in questions

TRC

For the *Say it right* pronunciation activity and instructions, go to the Teacher's Resource Centre.

THINK | RESEARCH | CULTURE | LEARN | ME

Ask students to discuss the questions in pairs or small groups. If there is time, ask students to share their views in open class.

Homework

OWB

Assign students Speaking exercises 1, 2 and 3 on page 64 of their Workbook.

LANGUAGE IN USE
Multiple-choice cloze

→ Student's Book, page 87 SB

Lesson aims

- Focus on modal verbs in a gap-fill exercise
- Practise a multiple-choice cloze exam task
- Research street games

Lead-in

Put students in pairs. Have them take turns to imagine they are a popular sports personality. Their partner asks them a series of questions to find out which sports personality they are. Make sure the students asking the questions use the modal verbs they have learnt so far in this unit (*can, could, need to, have to*, etc.).

1 In pairs or as a group, students ask and answer the questions. Elicit ideas from different students around the class.

EXAM SKILL

Modal verbs

Ask students to read the tips.

- Stress that learning to understand and use modal verbs is important for exams, where they are often tested in open-cloze and multiple-choice cloze exam tasks.
- Remind students that modal verbs convey a lot of important information which students need to understand in order to get a complete picture of a situation. These include how certain something is, any degree of obligation involved and, sometimes, a person's attitude.

2 Students complete the exercise individually. Check answers in open class.

Answers

1 shouldn't **2** can **3** may **4** must **5** Could

OPTIMISE YOUR EXAM

Multiple-choice cloze

Ask students to read the tips.

- In the exam, students should always read the text for general understanding first. They will do this in Exercise 3. Remind them that when they have finished the task, they should read the text again and make sure it makes sense with all the answers in place.
- This type of exam task is a test of vocabulary, and modal verbs and linking words are frequently tested. Students will need to look carefully before and after each gap to help them decide on the correct answer.
- Remind students that marks are not deducted for incorrect answers so they should not leave the answer sheet blank for any questions. If they don't know the answers, they should eliminate any options they know are not correct and make a guess.

3 Ask students to complete the exercise. Check their answers.

Answer

1 C (*… organises sports events in areas where people can't go to a sports centre or join a club because of money*) **2** B (*These events … often happen in the streets …*)

Extra support

Before reading the text in Exercise 4, have students cover the options under the text, and demonstrate the second bullet point from the *Optimise your exam* box. Point to the first gap and elicit from the class possible words to complete the sentence. Write all the possibilities on the board and repeat the process for all items.

Students then look at the options in their books and see which of them are also on the board. Tell them that even if the words are different, the technique is very useful because they have already thought carefully about the meaning of the words needed in each gap without being distracted by the three options.

Exam task

4 Ask students to complete the exercise. Students compare in pairs before you elicit answers in open class.

Answers

1 A **2** B **3** C **4** A **5** C **6** B **7** A **8** C

THINK | **RESEARCH** | CULTURE | LEARN | ME

If you have access to the internet, students can research this information in class. Alternatively, they could prepare this for homework, asking parents, grandparents, etc. what they played when they were younger. They can then present their findings at the start of the next lesson.

Cultural note

StreetGames started life in England in 2005 when a group of workers in local community regeneration programmes decided to found a charity to encourage young people to do more sport and physical activity, particularly in disadvantaged inner city areas. In 2009, it expanded into Wales and in 2011 a new programme called *Us Girls* was added to target young women and encourage them to participate in sport.

Homework OWB

Assign students Language in Use exercises 1 and 2 on page 65 of their Workbook.

WRITING
An email

→ Student's Book, pages 88–89 SB

Lesson aims

- Focus on writing in an informal style
- Plan and write an informal email

Lead-in

Play ***Hangman*** with some of the vocabulary from the unit. Suggested words: *competition, racket, badminton, winner, because, cricket, skiing, table tennis, surfer.*

1 In pairs, students ask and answer the questions. Elicit answers from different students around the class.

EXAM SKILL

Writing in an informal style

Ask students to read the tips.

- In writing exams, students need to demonstrate a basic understanding of the concept of 'register', i.e. using formal or informal language depending on what they are writing and who is to read it.
- Point out that informal style does not mean incorrect English. Although emails tend to be less formal in style than paper-based communication, students should still avoid the use of 'text-speak', e.g. acronyms such as 'LOL' or smileys.

2 Ask students to complete the exercise. Check the answers in open class and write the contractions on the board to make sure students have written them correctly.

Answers

2 Sally's **3** They'll **4** weren't **5** didn't **6** Who's **7** I'm **8** We've

Fast finishers

Ask students to think of all the other contractions they know. Students then share the additional contractions with the rest of the class when everyone has finished.

3 Ask students to complete the exercise. Have students compare in pairs before you check their answers in open class.

Answers

formal: I am looking forward to …

informal: Hi!, How about …, Thanks a lot for …, Love,

4 Ask students to complete the exercise.

Answers
Students should tick:
1, 2, 5

5 Students complete the exercise and then compare their answers in pairs. Check in open class.

Answers
1 Hi, Write soon **2** everyone's

Mixed ability

Ask more confident students to turn their backs to the board and complete the exercise. Write the answers on the board in jumbled order for less confident students to match to the categories. When both groups have finished, pair stronger students with weaker ones to compare their answers.

OPTIMISE YOUR EXAM

An email

Ask students to read the tips.

- In writing exams, students are sometimes asked to write a short email to a friend, including pieces of specific information. In Exercise 6, for example, they are required to answer three questions their friend has asked. If they only answer two, they will lose marks.
- Top marks will be given to candidates who include all the information they were asked to, and use an appropriate style. In Exercise 6, students need to make sure they use informal language, if possible including examples of contractions and phrasal verbs, and start and finish their email appropriately.

Exam task

6 Ask students to complete the exercise. Check answers in open class.

Answers
1 the amount of time **2** the person who teaches
3 the clothes you need to wear

7 **Plan** Ask students to complete the writing plan. You may want to look at students' plans to check them and give advice and suggestions for improvement before they take the next step.

8 **Write** Students write their email. If there is not enough time, set this and the subsequent checklist exercise for homework.

9 **Check** Students complete the checklist before they hand in their email.

Optional extension

For a slightly longer writing task, and for students to see other text types, refer them to one of the six tasks in the Writing reference (SB p169). Each one includes an annotated sample text and related writing task to challenge your students a little more.

Homework

OWB

Assign students Writing exercises 1, 2, 3 and 4 on page 66 of their Workbook and Progress check 8 on page 67.

Answers PROGRESS CHECK Units 7–8

Exercise 1

1 are, going to **2** 'm/am going to **3** 'm/am going to
4 Are, going to **5** 'm/am going to **6** 'll **7** 'm/am going to
8 Will **9** 'll **10** 'm/am not going to

Exercise 2

1 B **2** A **3** B **4** C **5** A

Exercise 3

1 could **2** couldn't **3** may **4** can't **5** should **6** can **7** shouldn't
8 don't have to **9** can **10** has to **11** don't have to **12** may

Exercise 4

1 and **2** play **3** in **4** going **5** to **6** before **7** but **8** make
9 because **10** go

Exercise 5

1 do **2** take **3** climb **4** win **5** go **6** throw **7** make **8** ride

Exercise 6

1 tennis **2** cricket **3** swimming **4** volleyball **5** surfing

9 Whatever the weather

UNIT AIMS

Exam preparation in Unit 9:

- skim the text in a magazine article
- understand the speakers' questions in different situations
- talk about a topic in an interview
- identify key words and use them in a multiple-choice dialogue exercise
- give advice and instructions in a note

TEACHER'S PRESENTATION KIT

- *Talk2Me* videos
- Speaking test videos
- Class and Workbook audio
- Workbook pages and answer key

UNIT OVERVIEW

Student's Book / Digital Student's Book SB		Workbook / Online Workbook OWB
LESSON / EXAM TASK	EXAM SKILLS / LANGUAGE FOCUS	CONSOLIDATION
Reading **Multiple-choice cloze**	Skimming A magazine article	Workbook, pp 68–69, Exercises 1, 2, 3, 4 Unit 9, Reading, Exercises 1, 2, 3, 4
Grammar 1	Zero conditional, first conditional	Workbook, p 70, Exercises 1, 2, 3 Unit 9, Grammar 1, Exercises 1, 2, 3
Vocabulary	Words connected with *weather and nature* Words + prepositions Nouns/adjectives	Workbook, pp 70–71, Exercises 1, 2, 3 Unit 9, Vocabulary, Exercises 1, 2, 3
Listening **Picture multiple choice**	Understanding the speakers' questions	Workbook, p 72, Exercises 1, 2, 3 Unit 9, Listening, Exercises 1, 2, 3
Grammar 2	Second conditional	Workbook, p 71, Exercises 1, 2 Unit 9, Grammar 2, Exercises 1, 2
Speaking **Interview**	Talking about a topic	Workbook, pp 72–73, Exercises 1, 2 Unit 9, Speaking, Exercises 1, 2
Language in Use **Multiple-choice dialogue**	Identifying key words	Workbook, p 73, Exercises 1, 2, 3 Unit 9, Language in Use, Exercises 1, 2, 3
Writing **A note**	Giving advice and instructions	Workbook, p 74, Exercises 1, 2, 3, 4 Unit 9, Writing, Exercises 1, 2, 3, 4
		Workbook, p 75, Progress check and Cumulative progress Progress check and Cumulative progress

Additional material

PRESENTATION KIT	TEACHER'S / STUDENT'S RESOURCE CENTRE RC	TEST GENERATOR
Talk2Me video *It's a fun place to live.*	**Unit 9 worksheets:** *Optimise your grammar* (Standard and Higher), *Optimise your vocabulary* (Standard and Higher), *Talk2Me* video, *Say it right* **Units 9–10 worksheets:** CLIL, Culture, Everyday English (TRC only), Grammar communication (TRC only)	Unit Test 9 (Standard and Higher)

READING

Multiple-choice cloze | A magazine article

→ Student's Book, pages 92–93 SB

Lesson aims

- Focus on skimming
- Practise a multiple-choice cloze exam task
- Research unusual weather

Lead-in

Ask students to look at the unit title ***Whatever the weather*** and the photo and say what they think the unit will be about (*the weather, the seasons, what people do at different times of the year*). Explain to students that *Whatever the weather* is a phrase which gives the idea that we won't let bad weather stop us from doing what we want to do. For example if I plan to meet you on Friday, I could say something like *Don't worry. I'll be there to meet you on Friday, whatever the weather!* Encourage some discussion about what students can see in the photo.

1 Have students stand up and look out of the window or door to see what the weather is like before completing the exercise. Elicit answers from different students around the class and encourage a class debate about what the best season is and why.

EXAM SKILL

Skimming

Ask students to read the tips.

- Explain to students that when we skim a text, we read it much faster than normal and do not stop to read every word. When skimming, it is best to focus on the first/topic sentence of each paragraph and on the content words (nouns, verbs and adjectives) rather than the grammatical words (*it*, *the*, *on*, etc.).
- Point out that it is also important to identify the type of publication the text is taken from and who is expected to read it. This is useful when doing research, e.g. on the internet, or when deciding what to read, e.g. in a newspaper.

2 Set a time limit of one minute and ask students to complete the exercise. Check answers in open class.

Answers

1 B **2** B (England, Sri Lanka, India, USA) **3** C

3 Give students another minute to complete this exercise. After checking answers with the class, highlight that the information they needed was at the beginning of each paragraph. Point out to students that they didn't need to read the entire text in order to get a clear idea of what it is about.

Answers

Students should tick:
2, 5, 6

OPTIMISE YOUR EXAM

Multiple-choice cloze

Ask students to read the tips.

- Point out that students should choose the correct options when they know where a text is from, what it is about, who it is for and the main topics mentioned within it.
- Remind students to pay close attention to the words before and after the gaps, as these will help them choose the correct answers.
- Tell students to try and justify their answers by reading complete sentences or paragraphs to confirm why they are correct.
- Stress the importance of making an educated guess. Explain that they won't lose marks if they are wrong. Tell them to eliminate the options they know are incorrect before guessing.

▼ Exam task

4 3.01 **Note: The reading text is also available on the audio CD but contains the missing words. You may want to have students listen and read the text after doing the exam task to check their answers.**

Tell students to read the instruction carefully before completing the exercise. After checking students' answers, elicit which tips they used to complete the task.

Answers

1 C (*to* and *on* both imply movement in the direction of something, but the direction is away from the sky.)

2 C (*this* refers to the situation just described and therefore needs to be singular. Both *they* and *these* are plural.)

3 A (The previous verb in the sentence is *liked* (past simple), so this verb needs to take the same form.)

4 B (*how* is the correct option here because the question *How often ...?* asks about frequency.)

5 C (The required meaning here is 'is possible'. *Must* is used for obligations and *need* is used for necessities.)

6 B (*For* expresses the duration of time something took place and in this case it happened for *a long time*.)

7 C (*in* is the preposition used for seasons.)

8 A (The required meaning here is 'was possible'. *Should* is used for advice and *have to* is used to express obligation and is not in the correct form.)

Fast finishers

Have students explain why the answers are correct, e.g. *The example is* say *because it follows the word 'people', which is third person plural.* As you check the answers to Exercise 4, ask individual students to explain the reasons behind the correct answers. Alternatively, you could have students give reasons for their answers before sharing the correct answers. (Details given in brackets in the key above.)

5 Ask students to complete the exercise. Check answers in open class.

Answers
1 c **2** e **3** b **4** d **5** h **6** f **7** a **8** g

THINK | **RESEARCH** | CULTURE | LEARN | ME

Have students work in groups to create a poster. Tell them to prepare their posters to share what they have learnt with the class in the next lesson. If you have access to the internet, have students research information in class. Alternatively, you could have students prepare this for homework.

Cultural note

The expression *raining cats and dogs* often intrigues students. No one is clear about its origin. The most common belief is that hundreds of years ago, people kept their animals outside. Often small animals would live in the thatched roofs of houses and when the rain was very heavy, they would either be washed off or jump off in order to hide from the rain. Others suggest that it may be because primitive sewage systems overflowed in heavy rain and dead animals floated out amongst other rubbish. Some believe it may be because the god Odin (responsible for storms in Norse mythology) had two pet dogs, or because witches fly with their cats on brooms.

Homework OWB
Assign students Reading exercises 1, 2, 3 and 4 on pages 68–69 of their Workbook.

GRAMMAR 1
Zero conditional, first conditional

→ Student's Book, page 94 SB

Lesson aims
- Understand the correct usage of zero and first conditionals
- Practise talking about things that are usually true and possible in the future
- Discuss future plans

Lead-in

Ask students to present their posters about the weather from the last lesson to the class. Encourage them to give detailed information about the poster and, if time, what parts of the creation process they found easy or difficult. Have the other groups ask questions and then have the class vote for the best poster.

Grammar in context

After students complete the task, test their understanding by asking them what we use each conditional for. Ask students to read the information in the *Remember* box to help them.

Remind students that they can find more information in the Grammar reference, Unit 9, page 158.

Answers
a 1 **b** 2

Language note

Explain that conditional sentences are divided into two clauses: a condition/cause and a result/effect. Tell students that we need both of these clauses to form conditional sentences and they can refer to different times. Point out that the clauses in both the zero and first conditional can be reversed, but that when the conditional (*if*) clause comes second, you don't use a comma, i.e. *If you heat water, it boils. Water boils if you heat it.*

1 After students complete the exercise, have them share their answers in pairs. Then check answers in open class.

Answers
1 is, changes **2** is, fall **3** feel, shines **4** don't, don't **5** Do, snows **6** have, don't

Mixed ability

Pair weaker and stronger students together and ask them to share answers. The stronger students should explain their answers using the examples on the board if necessary to reinforce which tense is used in which clause.

2 Before students complete the exercise, point out that the clauses in sentences 3, 4 and 6 are reversed. Make sure students are aware that when clauses are reversed, the grammar moves with the clauses. This is an important issue with the first conditional where the two clauses use different tenses. Highlight the fact that sentences 3, 4 and 6 do not have a comma separating the two clauses. Have students compare answers in pairs before checking in open class.

Answers
1 rains, won't **2** gets, will die **3** won't be, snows **4** Will, go **5** go, will need **6** won't, is

Optional extension

Give students a starter sentence, e.g. *If I fail my exam next week, my parents will get really angry.* Elicit a second sentence, connected to the first and starting with *If my parents get really angry, …* e.g. … *they won't give me any pocket money.* Then elicit another sentence, e.g. *If my parents don't give me any pocket money, …* When students have understood the idea, put them into pairs or small groups to see how long a 'conditional chain' they can make.

3 Ask students to complete the exercise. Have them compare in pairs before you check their answers in open class.

Answers
1 go **2** keep **3** is **4** feel **5** isn't **6** sleep **7** think **8** are **9** will grow **10** stops

Cultural note

The experiment described in the text in Exercise 3 was carried out in December 2013 by a group of 14- and 15-year-old schoolgirls from Hjallerup school in Denmark. They used twelve trays of cress plants and despite having the same conditions, the six trays near the two wi-fi routers didn't grow while those in another room did. Scientists are now looking into the potential negative effects of the radio waves in the air around us. However, is also thought that the heat from the two routers might have killed the cress.

THINK | RESEARCH | CULTURE | LEARN | **ME**

After students discuss the questions, encourage them to report their answers to the class using full first conditional sentences in order to consolidate the structure. Give feedback on students' use of language at the end of the task if necessary.

Homework OWB

Assign students Grammar 1 exercises 1, 2 and 3 on page 70 of their Workbook.

VOCABULARY

Topic vocabulary | Word patterns | Word formation

→ Student's Book, page 95 SB

Lesson aims

Understand the correct usage of:

- words connected with weather and nature
- word patterns with infinitives (*to*) and *-ing* form
- nouns and adjectives from the same word family

Lead-in

Draw a giant thermometer on the board and mark *0° C* at the bottom and *100° C* at the top. Write the words *boiling, cold, cool, freezing, hot, warm* under it. Have students copy the thermometer in their notebooks and, in pairs, write the words in order next to the thermometer. Check answers in open class. Use gestures to show the differences in meaning from the coldest (shivering, blowing on hands) to the hottest (fanning yourself, wiping your forehead) if necessary.

Answers

From top to bottom: boiling, hot, warm, cool, cold, freezing

Words connected with *weather and nature*

1 3.02 Focus students' attention on the illustration and elicit what the image is (*a weather map*). After students complete the exercise, play the audio for them to check their answers.

Mixed ability

Ask stronger students to cover the sentences in Exercise 1. They look at the pictures for the eight cities and write a sentence about the weather in each of them before checking their ideas against the items in Exercise 1.

Answers/Audioscript

1 It is warm and *sunny* in Madrid. **2** There is *snow* in Stockholm. **3** It is *rainy* in Dublin. **4** It is *sunny and windy* in Lisbon. **5** There is *fog* in Berlin. **6** There *are thunderstorms* in Prague. **7** It's *cloudy* in London.

2 3.03 After the exercise, ask students to write their own descriptions of the words in the box. Have volunteers share their descriptions and have the rest of the class guess the word.

Answers/Audioscript

1 A large area of trees and other plants. *forest*
2 It is very tall and sometimes there is snow on the top. *mountain*
3 It takes water from the mountains to the sea. *river*
4 It's by the sea and people go there in the summer. *beach*
5 The space above you that you see when you look up into the air. *sky*
6 It is smaller than a mountain. *hill*

Refer students to the Vocabulary reference, page 167, for more information on topic vocabulary.

Words + prepositions

3 3.04 After students complete the exercise and listen to check their answers, ask them to write new alternatives for the second parts of the sentences. Have students share what they wrote with the class.

Answers/Audioscript

1 (c) The students did experiments to see if wi-fi was dangerous.
2 (b) It is important to protect our forests and rivers.
3 (e) The students were good at thinking of new science experiments.
4 (f) Scientists want to find out why things happen.
5 (a) Summer is the best time to visit the beach, because it's sunny.
6 (d) They learnt about animals by visiting the zoo.

Refer students to the Vocabulary reference, page 167, for more information on word patterns.

Nouns/adjectives

4 3.05 Ask students to follow the example to complete the exercise. Play the audio for students to check their answers. Elicit the relevant spelling rules, i.e. *for most nouns, add -y; for nouns which end consonant + vowel + consonant, double the second consonant and add -y; for nouns which end in -e, change the -e to -y.*

Answers/Audioscript

noun: cloud, **adjective:** cloudy
noun: fog, **adjective:** *foggy*
noun: *ice*, **adjective:** icy
noun: rain, **adjective:** *rainy*
noun: *snow*, **adjective:** snowy
noun: sun, **adjective:** *sunny*

5 Remind students that one of the forms is a noun and the other is an adjective before they complete the exercise. Check answers in open class.

Answers

1 clouds **2** icy **3** sunny **4** fog **5** snow **6** rainy

Fast finishers

Ask students to write their own sentences using the nouns and adjectives in Exercise 4.

Refer students to the Vocabulary reference, page 167, for more information on word formation.

SAY IT RIGHT

/əʊ/ and /aʊ/ TRC

For the *Say it right* pronunciation activity and instructions, go to the Teacher's Resource Centre.

Homework OWB

Assign students Vocabulary exercises 1, 2 and 3 on pages 70–71 of their Workbook.

LISTENING

Picture multiple choice

→ Student's Book, page 96 SB

Lesson aims

- Listen to understand speakers' questions
- Practise a picture multiple-choice exam task
- Discuss winter free-time activities

Lead-in

Divide the board in half and write *Summer holidays* on one side and *Winter holidays* on the other side. Read out the following items and ask students to classify them into the two groups in their notebooks.

beaches blue skies grey clouds ice creams mountains rainy skiing snow sunny swimming

Check answers as a class and complete them on the board. Ask students if any of the words can be classified into both groups and elicit why (e.g. *mountains: people can go skiing on a winter holiday and camping on a summer holiday*).

Suggested answers

Summer holidays: beaches, blue skies, ice creams, mountains, sunny, swimming

Winter holidays: grey clouds, mountains, rainy, skiing, snow

1 After students discuss the questions, elicit some answers from different students around the class. Encourage students to say what they usually do and how next summer will be similar or different.

EXAM SKILL

Understanding the speakers' questions

Ask students to read the tips.

- Questions in listening exam tasks can test the candidates' ability to understand what the speaker says and how they say it. Students should listen out for the speaker's intonation and word choice for clues about the speaker's feelings.
- Speakers may avoid answering 'No' or 'I don't agree' in order to be polite, but their intonation can still make it clear what their real feelings are.

2 3.06 Before students listen, remind them to listen to the complete conversations before they choose their answer. Play the track and then check answers in open class.

Answers

1 yes **2** don't know **3** no **4** yes **5** don't know

3 After students complete the exercise, have them check their answers in pairs and then practise the conversations.

Answers

1 idea **2** sure **3** really **4** Maybe

Optional extension 3.06

Write the five expressions (*I'm not sure. Maybe. Good idea! Great. Not really.*) from Exercise 2 on the board in random order. Play the first conversation and ask students to focus on the intonation of the answer. Repeat the conversation, pausing for the class to repeat the answer with the appropriate intonation. Repeat the process with the other four conversations.

OPTIMISE YOUR EXAM

Picture multiple choice

Ask students to read the tips.

- Remind students to use the preparation time productively. Encourage them to use this time to read the questions carefully, underline the important words and check exactly what they will listen for. Tell them to also look at the pictures carefully and try to predict what words or phrases they expect to hear about each one in the recording.
- Remind students to listen to the complete conversation before selecting an answer. Explain that speakers may say more than one possible answer, but only one will be correct. Remind students that they will have a second opportunity to listen to the recording to make sure they have chosen the right answers.

▾ Exam task

4 3.07 Tell students to read through each question and look at the three pictures for each one before they listen. Play the track. Then have students review their answers before you play the track again. Check answers in open class.

Answers
1 B **2** C **3** C **4** A **5** C

Extra support

Before students complete the exam task, give them time to make notes about the questions. Write the following set of notes on the board as an example and ask students to match them to the A/B/C options in one of the questions.

i autumn, wind/windy, trees, leaves, park

ii summer, sun/sunny, blue sky, beach, sunbathing

iii winter, snow/snowy/snowing, mountain, skiing

Split the class into four groups. Assign each group one of the remaining questions in Exercise 4, i.e. questions 1–4, and ask them to prepare a set of notes to match each picture, using the notes on the board as a model. Regroup students and have them share their notes, checking for similarities and differences. Encourage students to justify their notes with reasons.

Answers
The notes match question 5 in Exercise 4
A ii **B** iii **C** i

THINK | RESEARCH | **CULTURE** | LEARN | ME

Give examples of popular free-time activities in different countries from around the world. Then discuss the question as a class. Write down students' ideas on the board and then come to a consensus on the most popular one.

Homework OWB
Assign students Listening exercises 1, 2 and 3 on page 72 of their Workbook.

GRAMMAR 2
Second conditional

→ Student's Book, page 97 SB

Lesson aims

- Understand the correct usage of the second conditional
- Practise talking about impossible situations in the present and hypothetical future events
- Think about living in the forest

Lead-in

On the board, draw a rough map of your students' country and the countries surrounding it. Draw weather symbols like those on Student's Book page 95 next to different countries. Have students work in pairs and practise giving a weather forecast for the area. Walk round, monitoring students for good use of weather vocabulary and helping with the names/pronunciation of country names if necessary.

Grammar in context

Ask students what they remember about the listening in the previous lesson. Then have them complete the task individually. Refer them to information in the *Remember* box if they aren't sure. Check their answers to ensure students' understanding.

Remind students that they can find more information in the Grammar reference, Unit 9, page 159.

Answers
1 a no **b** no **2 a** no **b** no **3 a** yes **b** no

Language note

Point out that the clauses in the second conditional can be reversed in the same way as in zero and first conditional sentences. Remind them that the comma disappears when the second clause is the *if* clause.

1 Go through the first sentence as a class. Then say the first clause with a different effect as a model, *If there was lots of snow outside, we would build a snowman.* Elicit other ideas from students. Have students complete the exercise and then check answers in open class.

Answers
1 was **2** wouldn't **3** didn't **4** would **5** were

2 Before students complete the exercise, explain that we can use the abbreviation *I'd* instead of *I would* and the same goes for the other pronouns: *you'd, we'd,* etc. Check answers in open class.

Answers
1 could, 'd/would visit **2** didn't own, wouldn't / would not cycle
3 go, lived **4** had, 'd/would buy **5** stopped, would be

Extra support

Write the second conditional structure on the board with the clauses in both positions and highlighting the use/omission of the comma:

If + past simple, *would* + infinitive

would + infinitive *if* + past simple

Before students complete Exercise 2, ask them to circle *'if'* in each sentence. Then refer them to the structures on the board while completing the exercise. With weaker classes, leave this on the board for students' reference to complete exercises 3 and 4. Before completing Exercise 3, brainstorm possible ideas/verbs for them to use to complete the sentences, e.g. *fly around the world, be very rich, have a quiet life, be a pop star, live by the sea.*

3 Encourage students to use their imagination. After they complete the exercise, have them share their ideas with the class. Ask the class to say which idea was the most original for each sentence.

4 Focus students' attention on the photos and the title and elicit what they can see (*somebody living 'with nature' in a tent in a forest, and a highland cow – a traditional breed in Scotland*). After students complete the exercise, have them compare answers in pairs before checking in open class.

Answers
1 do **2** wash **3** didn't have **4** could **5** be able to **6** would be

THINK | RESEARCH | CULTURE | LEARN | ME

Have students brainstorm some ideas before discussing the questions in pairs. Develop into a class discussion to get a general indication of students' thoughts.

Homework OWB

Assign students Grammar 2 exercises 1 and 2 on page 71 of their Workbook.

Assign students the Flipped classroom tasks on page 98 of their Student's Book if you'd like them to prepare for the next lesson. To complete this task, students need to watch the *Talk2Me* video which can be found on the Resource Centre.

SPEAKING
Interview

→ Student's Book, page 98 SB

Lesson aims

- Talk about the weather and other topics
- Practise answering personal questions in an interview
- Research the weather in different countries

The *Talk2Me* video in this unit focuses on talking to an exchange student and describing places. The people in the video talk about where they live and what they like to do there.

Students answer some comprehension questions and then listen for key phrases in the video.

The video can be used in one of two ways:

Flipped classroom

Flipped classroom option

Using this approach, students watch the video and complete the exercises for homework. This prepares students for the speaking lesson by introducing them to the topic and the key phrases to use in the exam task. Teachers who use this method will find they have more class time to spend on activating the target language and developing fluency for the final task.

***Talk2Me* worksheet**

Ask students to also complete the *Talk2Me* worksheet on the Resource Centre for more detailed comprehension exercises and more practice of the key phrases.

Classroom option

1 Ask students to spend a minute or two reading the questions. Play the *Talk2Me* video for students to complete the exercise. Play the video again, if necessary, before checking their answers.

2 Play the *Talk2Me* video again, so students underline the phrases in the *Phrase expert* box. Pause the video from time to time if necessary. Check answers in open class.

***Talk2Me* worksheet**

Ask students to also complete the *Talk2Me* worksheet on the Resource Centre for more detailed comprehension exercises and more practice of the key phrases.

Answers
The transcript and answer key for the *Talk2Me* video exercises and Worksheet can be found on the Teacher's Resource Centre.

Lead-in

Review some of the geographical features from the Topic vocabulary section and the use of infinitives for purpose from the Words + prepositions section on page 95. Write the following sentence starters on the board:

It was hot and there wasn't a cloud in the sky, so we went to the … to …

There was a lot of snow and the sky was blue, so we went to the … to …

We love seeing animals and being close to nature, so we went to the … to …

Have students work in pairs to complete the sentences. Elicit some answers from different students around the class.

Suggested answers
beach, go for a swim / sit in the sun / play volleyball
mountains, go skiing/snowboarding
forest, have a long walk / go camping

3 Before students complete the exercise, ask them if the weather plays a part in their plans and if so, how. After students discuss the questions, elicit their answers with reasons.

EXAM SKILL

Talking about a topic

Ask students to read the tips.

- Remind students that after answering some personal questions in the Speaking test, they will be asked to talk about a topic. These can include aspects of their daily routine, hobbies and interests, favourite places or food, their hometown or school, the weather, etc.
- Encourage them to think about common topics that might come up and to learn some useful vocabulary and expressions about each one. Point out that it is very important to learn the part of speech of a new word so that they can use it correctly in a sentence.
- Remind them that giving examples allows them to expand on their answers, demonstrate more fluency and impress the examiner with a wider range of language.

4 3.08 Have students read the topics before you play the audio. Check answers in open class.

Answers

1 places you go on holiday **2** family and friends **3** technology **4** city where you live

5 3.08 Play the track again for students to listen and write the examples. Have students compare their answers in pairs before you check them in open class.

Suggested answers

1 They sometimes visit a new city like Paris or Berlin.

2 At weekends and the school holidays, her best friend usually comes to stay.

3 Last night, everyone was in the living room, but all using different gadgets.

4 The sports centre is very big and there's a new shopping centre with restaurants, cinemas and shops.

6 3.09 Play the audio for students to listen and complete the exercise. Have them compare their answers in pairs before you check them in open class.

Suggested answers

Topic: places you go on holiday

Examples: this year he cycled for six days around the coast, and he went on a walking trip to the mountains

Correction phrase: sorry, I mean …

OPTIMISE YOUR EXAM

Interview

Ask students to read the tips.

- Tell students that at this level, examiners do not expect candidates to speak perfect English. Explain that candidates are able to correct themselves with an appropriate phrase if they make a mistake. Tell them that this can increase their mark, as it shows they feel confident and 'in control' of the situation.
- Encourage them to use phrases to correct themselves when they are speaking in class. This will help them feel more confident about using them in a Speaking test.

Exam task

7 Give students one minute to make some brief notes for their answers. Then, in pairs, students complete the exercise. Remind them to use phrases from the Phrase expert box as well as phrases for self-correction. Walk round, monitoring students for good use of language and errors to go over at the end of the activity.

Write any errors on the board and go through them with students, eliciting corrections from them where possible. After the class feedback, students could then repeat this activity with another partner, to try to improve their performance.

Fast finishers

Remind students that the questions in Speaking tests are not taken from a fixed pool, so they need to be prepared for all sorts of questions. Ask students to brainstorm as many questions about the weather as they can.

THINK | **RESEARCH** | CULTURE | LEARN | ME

Have students look up the weather for homework. To vary students' answers have each student choose two different cities from around the world to compare. Tell them they can choose one city from the book and one of their own. Tell them to write a report of their findings to present in the next class.

Homework

OWB

Assign students Speaking exercises 1 and 2 on pages 72–73 of their Workbook.

LANGUAGE IN USE

Multiple-choice dialogue

→ Student's Book, page 99 SB

Lesson aims

- Focus on key words
- Practise a multiple-choice dialogue exam task
- Discuss experiencing bad weather

Lead-in

Ask students to present the information they found on the cities they investigated. Remind students to use the vocabulary they have learnt in the unit.

1 Ask students what the highest mountain in the world is (*Mount Everest*). Then elicit other mountains they know before they discuss the questions. Elicit answers from different students around the class.

EXAM SKILL

Identifying key words

Ask students to read the tips.

- Remind students that it is important to read carefully and identify the key words in a dialogue before trying to choose the correct response. Point out that underlining the key words helps them to keep these in mind while doing the exercise.
- Explain that all of the responses will be grammatically correct sentences, but only one will be an appropriate response to the question/sentence. For example, for a *Wh-* question, they can eliminate a response that begins with *Yes* or *No*; or if the question is an invitation, they can eliminate an option that doesn't respond to the invitation.

2 After students complete the exercise, have them practise saying them in pairs.

Answers

1 d **2** e **3** a **4** b **5** c

3 Ask students to complete the exercise individually. They will compare their answers in the next exercise.

4 Ask students to work in pairs to compare the key words they underlined in Exercise 3. Point out that they may have small differences but that they should have underlined the main words that will help them choose the correct response. Have them explain their answers to their partner before checking with the class.

Suggested answers

1 A: Have you seen Peter today?
B: Yes, he's here.
The question requires a yes/no answer, and *he* refers to Peter.

2 A: See you at the weekend.
B: I'll be a bit late.
The sentence refers to the future *at the weekend* so the use of *will* in the response is appropriate. The sentence also refers to *you*, and the response includes *I*.

3 A: Can you see that bird?
B: Do you mean the one in the tree?
the one refers to the bird in the question, and it is logical that a bird might be in a tree.

4 A: I don't like the snow.
B: Stay inside then.
Stay inside is a suggestion/instruction in response to the fact that the speaker doesn't like the snow, which is logically outside.

OPTIMISE YOUR **EXAM**

Multiple-choice dialogue

Ask students to read the tips.

- Remind students that in order to complete this task type successfully, they need to form a clear idea of who is speaking, what the situation could be, and who the person might be speaking to before choosing their answers.
- Remind students that a good technique is to cover the A–C options for all the questions before they start. Tell students to look at the statements, think about the context and imagine possible answers before reading and choosing the option they think is correct.
- Tell students that an understanding of pronouns can help with this task type.

5 After students complete the exercise, have them explain their reasons to the class.

Answer

Because answer B is the only reply that is about the weather. Answer A refers to time, and answer C is about an activity. Answer C also uses the pronoun *we* while the question uses *it*, and it doesn't answer the *yes/no* question.

Exam task

6 Students complete the exercise. Then check answers in open class.

Answers

1 C **2** A **3** C **4** A **5** B

Extra support

Discuss with students why the incorrect options are not valid answers to the questions.

Answers

1 A *No, thanks.* is a response to an offer, but the question is about an experience.; B The question refers to the place where the speakers are now (*this beach*), so it is not asking about its location.

2 B The initial statement is about the weather last night, so this answer makes no sense.; C This answer is talking about a hope and implies the future, it's not connected with the weather.

3 A The question is asking about plans and intentions, but this option is expressing a general preference.; B This answer makes no sense as it is refers to the present time rather than *tomorrow* and it doesn't answer the question *What?*

4 B The initial statement is about the weather, so this answer makes no sense.; C This response would answer the question 'Where', but makes no sense in this situation.

5 A Although the subject *It* appears in both the initial statement and this answer, *It* doesn't make sense here as we don't know what it is referring to.; C is a response to a suggestion, but the initial statement is a warning about something that is about to fall, so the response is not relevant.

THINK | RESEARCH | CULTURE | LEARN | **ME**

Share your worst experience with the class or invent one in order to give them a model of what to write. After the activity, encourage students to share their experiences with the class.

Homework OWB

Assign students Language in Use exercises 1, 2 and 3 on page 73 of their Workbook.

WRITING
A note

→ Student's Book, pages 100–101 SB

Lesson aims

- Focus on giving advice and instructions
- Plan and write a note

Lead-in

Write *Summer camp activities* in the middle of the board and the following word skeletons around it:

c _ _ _ _ _ g
t _ _ _ e t _ _ _ _ s
v _ _ _ _ _ _ _ _ l
s _ _ _ _ _ g
b _ _ _ _ _ _ _ n
r _ _ _ _ _ g
w _ _ _ _ _ _ _ _ _ g

Put students into teams to complete the words. Award one point for each correct word. The team with the most points wins. You may wish to set a time limit to make it more exciting.

Answers
cycling/camping, table tennis, volleyball, sailing/surfing, badminton, running, windsurfing

1 In pairs or as a group, students ask and answer the questions. Elicit answers in open class.

EXAM SKILL

Giving advice and instructions

Ask students to read the tips.

- Remind students that when giving advice, the second conditional can be very useful as it allows us to talk about imaginary situations and the possible consequences of these situations, e.g. *If that happened to me, I think I would …*
- Advise students to be aware of the context when using imperatives. Explain that it can be rude if they say *Be quiet!* or *Go away!* to the wrong person at the wrong time or with the wrong intonation. Also remind them of the imperative in negative form, e.g. *Don't do that.*

Language note

Explain to students about the use of *were* rather than *was* in the conditional clause: *If I were you, …* Tell them that we often use *if* + *were* instead of *was* in the phrase *If I were you, …* for giving advice and making suggestions.

2 After students complete the exercise, invent some problems for them to give you advice for. For example, your students in another class don't do their homework.

Answers
1 Bring **2** wouldn't / would not stay **3** Don't go **4** 'd/would wait **5** Be **6** 'll need

Mixed ability

Give weaker students the verbs in the order they appear in the exercise (*bring, not stay, not go, wait, be, need*). Tell stronger students to cover the verbs in the box. Ask them to complete the sentences using appropriate verbs in the correct form. Then have them compare the verbs they chose with the verbs in the box.

3 Before students complete the exercise, ask them who the note is to (*Rosie*) and from (*Amelia*). Check answers in open class.

Answers
1 a raincoat **2** a hat **3** some food

4 Ask students to complete the exercise individually. Then check answers in open class.

Answers
1 Don't forget a hat! **2** And if I were you, I'd bring some food.

OPTIMISE YOUR EXAM

A note

Ask students to read the tips.

- Remind students that if they are asked to write a note to a friend, examiners want to know that candidates can write in an informal style. Remind them to think about who they are writing the note to, why they are writing it and which words and phrases are the most appropriate.
- Remind students to answer the three questions within the word limit. Explain that if they write more words, the examiner will only consider words within the limit.

▼ Exam task

5 Tell students to read all the options and the note to complete the exercise.

Answers
the place to meet, the weather, what to take

6 Plan After students complete their plans, check them and give suggestions for improvement before they take the next step.

7 Write Students write their note. If there is not enough time, set this and the subsequent checklist exercise for homework.

8 Check Students complete the checklist before they hand in their note.

Optional extension

For a slightly longer writing task, and for students to see other text types, refer them to one of the six tasks in the Writing reference (SB p169). Each one includes an annotated sample text and related writing task to challenge your students a little more.

Homework

OWB

Assign students Writing exercises 1, 2, 3 and 4 on page 74 of their Workbook and Progress check 9 on page 75.

10 Looking after yourself

UNIT AIMS

Exam preparation in Unit 10:

- guess the meaning of new words in signs and notices
- understand when something happened in short extracts
- give yourself time to think in a collaborative task
- understand giving short answers and use them in a multiple-matching dialogue exercise
- give advice in an online post

TEACHER'S PRESENTATION KIT

- *Talk2Me* videos
- Speaking test videos
- Class and Workbook audio
- Workbook pages and answer key

UNIT OVERVIEW

Student's Book / Digital Student's Book SB		Workbook / Online Workbook OWB
LESSON / EXAM TASK	EXAM SKILLS / LANGUAGE FOCUS	CONSOLIDATION
Reading **Matching**	Guessing the meaning of new words Signs and notices	Workbook, pp 76–77, Exercises 1, 2, 3, 4 Unit 10, Reading, Exercises 1, 2, 3, 4
Grammar 1	Present perfect simple: *for, since, already, just, yet*	Workbook, p 78, Exercises 1, 2, 3 Unit 10, Grammar 1, Exercises 1, 2, 3
Vocabulary	Words connected with *health* Words + prepositions Collocations with verbs	Workbook, pp 78–79, Exercises 1, 2, 3 Unit 10, Vocabulary, Exercises 1, 2, 3
Listening **Multiple matching**	Understanding when something happened	Workbook, p 80, Exercises 1, 2, 3 Unit 10, Listening, Exercises 1, 2, 3
Grammar 2	Verb patterns: verb + infinitive / *-ing*	Workbook, p 79, Exercises 1, 2 Unit 10, Grammar 2, Exercises 1, 2
Speaking **Collaborative task**	Giving yourself time to think	Workbook, pp 80–81, Exercises 1, 2, 3, 4 Unit 10, Speaking, Exercises 1, 2, 3, 4
Language in Use **Multiple-matching dialogue**	Giving short answers	Workbook, p 81, Exercises 1, 2 Unit 10, Language in Use, Exercises 1, 2
Writing **An online post**	Giving advice	Workbook, p 82, Exercises 1, 2, 3, 4, 5 Unit 10, Writing, Exercises 1, 2, 3, 4, 5
Progress check	Check language progress for Units 9 and 10	Workbook, p 83, Progress check and Cumulative progress Progress check and Cumulative progress

Additional material

PRESENTATION KIT	TEACHER'S / STUDENT'S RESOURCE CENTRE RC	TEST GENERATOR
Talk2Me video *Let me think …*	**Unit 10 worksheets:** *Optimise your grammar* (Standard and Higher), *Optimise your vocabulary* (Standard and Higher), *Talk2Me* video, *Say it right* **Units 9–10 worksheets:** CLIL, Culture, Everyday English (TRC only), Grammar communication (TRC only)	Unit Test 10 (Standard and Higher)

READING
Matching | Signs and notices

→ Student's Book, pages 102–103 SB

Lesson aims

- Focus on guessing the meaning of new words
- Practise a multiple-matching exam task

Lead-in

Ask students to look at the unit title ***Looking after yourself*** and describe what they can see in the photos and what they think the lesson will be about (*health*). Elicit the meaning of the phrasal verb *look after* (*take care of someone, either by helping them when they are ill or by giving them things they need*). Ask students what they do to look after themselves.

1 After students answer the questions, elicit answers from different students around the class. Don't push them to discuss health and illness if they don't want to, as this might be a sensitive area for some.

2 3.10 **Note: The reading text is also available on the audio CD. You may want to have students listen and read the text after doing the scanning task.**

Have students scan the article quickly in order to answer the questions. Then ask them to rewrite the false answers so that they are true. Go through the answers in open class.

Answers

1 T **2** F (*some people live thousands of kilometres from the nearest city. When they get ill … they can't get to a hospital easily because they're so far away.*) **3** F (*it was Abbey's 14th birthday*) **4** F (*the nurses gave Abbey a birthday cake and sang 'Happy birthday' to her.*)

EXAM SKILL

Guessing the meaning of new words

Ask students to read the tips.

- Remind students that while they are thinking about the meaning of new words, they should also think about their part of speech.
- Explain that developing the technique of guessing words from context can be very useful for exams. Remind students to check the meaning of a new word in the dictionary.

3 After students complete the exercise, have them compare answers in pairs before checking their answers in open class.

Answers

1 appointments **2** air ambulance **3** nurses **4** details **5** flight **6** check **7** upset **8** farms

Mixed ability

Have weaker students complete the task as it appears in the Student's Book. Ask strong students to cover the definitions in Exercise 3 and write the meanings of the highlighted words their own words.

OPTIMISE YOUR EXAM

Matching

Ask students to read the tips.

- Remind students to be careful with the extra options in this task type. Explain that these may contain words or phrases that make them look like the right answer.
- Remind students to guess any items they are not sure of.

4 After students complete the exercise, check their answers in open class.

Answers

1 go into **2** serious **3** stopping and leaving **4** start and end time of working **5** being cared for

▼ Exam task

5 Before students complete the exercise, remind them to read all the options first. While checking answers, ask students how they were able to choose the correct answer.

Answers

1 E (can't leave your car here = *No parking*) **2** D (not for normal calls = *only in an emergency*) **3** F (evening is after 17:00) **4** B (can't eat = *no food allowed*) **5** C (before you go = *before leaving*)

Cultural note

The Royal Flying Doctor Service of Australia is one of the biggest organisations of its type in the world. It was started by the missionary Reverend John Flynn as a one-year experiment in 1928. Since then it has grown to become a highly valued non-profit organisation, which is largely sustained through donations. As well as GP and nursing services, it attends emergencies 24 hours a day and covers an area of around 7.3 million km^2. The RFDS flies a total of nearly 75,000 km each day allowing its doctors and nurses to see around 750 patients.

Homework

OWB

Assign students Reading exercises 1, 2, 3 and 4 on pages 76–77 of their Workbook.

GRAMMAR 1
Present perfect simple: *for, since, already, just, yet*

→ Student's Book, page 104 SB

Lesson aims

- Understand the correct usage of the present perfect simple with *for, since, already, just, yet*
- Practise talking about events in the past that are important now and situations in the past that continue in the present
- Write about being injured and needing help

Lead-in

Test the vocabulary from the text on page 103. Write the following sentences on the board and ask students to say which words they define.

1 *This person's role is to support doctors in caring for sick patients.*

2 *My family has lived in this place for over 100 years. We look after cows and sell their milk.*

3 *I've just been on one of these for 12 hours. We travelled from Beijing to Los Angeles.*

4 *A child has had an accident in the mountains and one of these special planes has already set off to rescue her.*

Answers

1 nurse **2** farm **3** flight **4** air ambulance

Grammar in context

After students complete the task, check their answers. Then read through the *Remember* box with the class.

Remind students that they can find more information in the Grammar reference, Unit 10, page 159.

Answers

a 2 **b** 1 **c** 4 **d** 5 **e** 3

Language note

The present perfect is often the hardest tense for students to understand fully. Explain that perfect tenses can be used to link two points in time.

In the case of the present perfect, the tense links the past to the present. In this section, students see the two most common examples of this – past events with present results and situations that started in the past and continue in the present – and five of the most common words used with the present perfect: *for, since, just, already* and *yet.*

1 After students complete the exercise, ask them to work in pairs to discuss why each sentence uses the words in the box. For example, in item one, the answer is *just* because the action happened a short time ago.

Answers

1 just **2** yet **3** since **4** already **5** for **6** yet

2 Ask students to complete the exercise individually before checking answers in open class.

Answers

1 haven't seen, yet **2** have, had, for **3** has, just, hurt **4** haven't eaten, since **5** has, already, checked

Optional extension

Students play ***Participle tennis*** in threes. Two students work together with their books closed (Students A and B) and the third (Student C) acts as judge. Student A says a verb and Student B has to say the corresponding past participle and then a new verb. Student A has to respond with the past participle and so on. Student C monitors and checks the verbs against the Irregular verbs reference on Student's Book page 175. Students must maintain a regular rhythm. If one student pauses for too long, the other student wins a point and students change roles so they all take turns as referee.

3 Ask students to complete the exercise. Have students compare in pairs before you check their answers in open class.

Answers

1 has fallen **2** have phoned **3** already **4** hasn't arrived **5** yet **6** has been **7** has changed **8** for **9** since **10** just/already

Fast finishers

Ask students to look at all the verbs in exercises 1 and 3 and check they know all forms from memory. Tell them to think about both spelling and pronunciation and to look at the Irregular verbs reference on Student's Book page 175 if they are not sure. In pairs, students could test each other: one gives the infinitive and the other has to think of the past participle.

THINK | RESEARCH | CULTURE | LEARN | **ME**

Remind students to use the language they focused on in the lesson where possible. Then have them share their stories with a partner.

Homework OWB

Assign students Grammar 1 exercises 1, 2 and 3 on page 78 of their Workbook.

VOCABULARY
Topic vocabulary | Word patterns | Collocations

→ Student's Book, page 105 SB

Lesson aims

Understand the correct usage of:

- words connected with health
- word patterns with prepositions
- verb + noun collocations

Lead-in

Have students choose partners to work with in pairs or groups. Ask them to interview each other to find out how healthy they are. They should ask and answer questions about their diet and exercise regime and find out how long they have had these habits. Remind students that they don't have to answer any questions that they may feel uncomfortable about and they can make up their answers.

Words connected with *health*

1 3.11 After students complete the exercise, have them check their answers in pairs. Then play the audio for students to listen and check. Play the track again to practise pronunciation.

Answers/Audioscript

1 eye **2** ear **3** nose **4** face **5** throat **6** neck **7** back **8** stomach **9** arm **10** finger **11** leg **12** hand **13** knee **14** ankle **15** foot

2 Have students complete the exercise. Then check the answers in open class by asking different students to read out a sentence.

Answers

1 stomach **2** ankle **3** foot **4** throat **5** neck **6** eyes **7** knees **8** hand

Language note

Point out the words *headache* and *toothache* in exercises 1 and 2, and explain that *ache* is commonly used with some parts of the body to indicate pain in that area. Most of these are written as one word, e.g. *headache, toothache, earache, backache*, but some are written as two, e.g. *stomach ache*. You might want to explain that *heartache* is used to mean a great sadness rather than physical pain.

Refer students to the Vocabulary reference, page 167, for more information on topic vocabulary.

Words + prepositions

3 3.12 Before students complete the exercise, remind them to guess the answer if they don't know. Play the audio for students to check their answers.

Answers/Audioscript

1 (C) I had a bad pain *in* my foot this morning.
2 (B) Ashley has a problem *with* his stomach so he can't eat bread.
3 (B) This is a hospital *for* children and babies.
4 (A) Sitting down all day can be a danger *to* your health.
5 (B) I'd like an appointment *with* the doctor, please.
6 (C) Have you got any medicine *for* a bad cold?
7 (A) What's the matter *with* you?
8 (B) I hope to do a course *in* nursing.

Refer students to the Vocabulary reference, page 167, for more information on word patterns.

Collocations with verbs

4 3.13 After students complete the exercise, ask them questions using the collocations, e.g. *Have you ever broken your leg? How often do you brush your teeth?*

Answers/Audioscript

1 (e) take your temperature **2** (d) make an appointment **3** (a) break your leg **4** (f) brush your teeth **5** (c) catch a cold **6** (b) feel ill or feel better

5 After students complete the exercise, ask them what clues they used from the sentences as you check answers in open class (details given in brackets in key below).

Answers

1 caught a cold (*stay in bed*) **2** broke his leg (*couldn't walk*) **3** made an appointment (*see the doctor*) **4** take your temperature (*head feels warm*) **5** brush your teeth (*so they are clean*) **6** feel ill (*tell the school nurse*)

Mixed ability

Give less confident students the nouns from Exercise 4 in the order they appear in the items in Exercise 5. They then concentrate on completing the sentences with the correct verb in the correct form. Ask stronger students to cover the verbs and nouns in Exercise 4 and try to remember the verb + noun collocations and also put the verbs in the correct form.

Refer students to the Vocabulary reference, page 167, for more information on collocations.

Homework OWB

Assign students Vocabulary exercises 1, 2 and 3 on pages 78–79 of their Workbook.

LISTENING
Multiple matching

→ Student's Book, page 106 SB

Lesson aims

- Listen to understand when something happened
- Practise a multiple-matching exam task
- Learn more words for health problems

Lead-in

Review vocabulary for health problems. Either a) use gestures to elicit the words or b) give each student a health problem on a slip of paper and have them walk round the class miming their health problem for their classmates to guess. If you give each student a slip of paper, have students report what they learnt about each other after the exercise.

Suggested vocabulary:
backache, broken arm, broken leg, cold, earache, stomach ache, temperature, toothache

1 After students brainstorm their ideas in pairs, have them share their ideas with the class. Don't push students to discuss health and illness if they don't want to participate, as this might be a sensitive area for some.

EXAM SKILL

Understanding when something happened

Ask students to read the tips.

- Remind students to pay attention to the verb tenses speakers use, so that they know what point in time people are referring to. Also remind them that they can listen for other clues speakers use as well as the verb forms. These can include adverbs of frequency, a specific time, or a word like *just*, *already*, etc.
- Explain that the exercises here focus specifically on the past and the present.

2 Elicit the word or phrase in each sentence that helps indicate the verb tense students need to choose in each sentence (*1 just, 2 two hours ago, 3 usually, 4 on Wednesday afternoon, 5 for four days*). Then ask students to complete the exercise individually before checking answers in open class.

Answers

1 has just broken **2** checked **3** see **4** had **5** 've/have had

3 3.14 Before students listen, tell them to read the headings in the table. Play the track. Then elicit answers from students around the class.

Answers

a routine event or habit (present simple): 2, 3
a time in the past (past simple): 4, 6
an unknown time in the past (present perfect): 1, 5

OPTIMISE YOUR EXAM

Multiple matching

Ask students to read the tips.

- Remind students that in this type of task there are usually distractors. Some or all of the distractors may be included on the recording, often negatively or in a different tense.
- Tell students that multiple-matching exercises sometimes contain various short recordings on the same topic and sometimes it is one long recording. In both cases, the task is the same and is based on the recording(s).

Exam task

4 3.15 Have students read through the people's names and the problems before listening. Play the audio and then check answers in open class.

Answers

1 E **2** H **3** F **4** C **5** B

Mixed ability

Have stronger students complete the task as it appears in the Student's Book. Tell weaker students to choose from B, C, E, F and H only.

THINK | RESEARCH | CULTURE | **LEARN** | ME

Ask students to cover Exercise 4. After they complete the exercise, have students use the vocabulary to write sentences. Alternatively, play the game *Hangman* with the class.

Answers

1 high temperature **2** backache **3** a stomach ache
4 a broken leg

Homework

OWB

Assign students Listening exercises 1, 2 and 3 on page 80 of their Workbook.

GRAMMAR 2

Verb patterns: verb + infinitive / *-ing*

→ Student's Book, page 107 SB

Lesson aims

- Identify verbs followed by the infinitive or *-ing* form
- Practise using verbs followed by the infinitive or *-ing* form
- Write about getting fit and being healthier

Lead-in

Give the class a spelling test. Read out ten *-ing* forms of different verbs for students to write down. Check answers with the class, asking students to spell the words out as you write them on the board.

Suggested vocabulary:

finishing, chatting, inviting, becoming, stopping, watching, travelling, brushing, practising, succeeding

Grammar in context

Knowing which verbs are followed by an infinitive and which by *-ing* is important in all parts of official exams.

Tell students to refer to the information in the *Remember* box to help them complete the task. Check their answers. Explain that some verbs are followed by an infinitive and some are followed by an *-ing* form and students have to learn which verbs go with each form.

Remind students that they can find more information in the Grammar reference, Unit 10, page 159.

Answers

a offer, decide, tell **b** hate, keep

Language note

Most verbs need to be followed by either the infinitive (e.g. *decide, hope, learn, refuse, plan, want*) or the *-ing* form (e.g. *avoid, enjoy, finish, keep, mind, stop*). However there are some verbs that can be followed by either (e.g. *like, love, start, try*). Sometimes there is little or no difference in meaning between the two, and sometimes there is quite a large difference. For example, *He tried to eat healthier food.* (= but this was very hard for him and he wasn't able to do it) is not the same as *He tried eating healthier food.* (= he experimented with this to see what effect it had).

1 Ask students to complete the exercise individually. Check answers in open class.

Answers

1 decided **2** to help **3** didn't mind **4** hoped **5** stopped **6** kept

Extra support

Point out that in Exercise 1 the verb choice usually depended on the form of the verb **after** the options in bold, e.g. *1 My dad* ***decided / enjoyed*** *to do …* Explain that in Exercise 2, the form of the verb will depend on the verbs that come **before** the gaps, e.g. *1 Leo decided …* Ask students to underline these before starting the exercise (*stopped, enjoyed, wanted, didn't mind, spent time*).

2 After students complete the exercise, have them compare answers in pairs before checking answers in open class.

Answers

1 to make **2** taking **3** hearing **4** to eat **5** taking **6** putting on

3 Focus students' attention on the picture and ask students if they like to travel by car. Encourage them to give reasons for their answers. Then have students complete the exercise individually. Check answers in open class.

Answers

1 to visit **2** to feel **3** travelling **4** to try **5** to enjoy **6** getting / to get **7** running **8** doing

Fast finishers

Ask students to make two lists: *verbs + infinitive* and *verbs + -ing* and include all the verbs they have seen in exercises 1–3.

Answers

verbs + infinitive: agree, begin, choose, decide, help, hope, need, offer, try, want

verbs + -ing: enjoy, finish, keep, not mind, spend time, stop, try

SAY IT RIGHT

/ɪ/ and /iː/ TRC

For the *Say it right* pronunciation activity and instructions, go to the Teacher's Resource Centre.

THINK | RESEARCH | CULTURE | LEARN | **ME**

Have students make a list of their ideas individually. Then have students share their ideas with a partner.

Homework

OWB

Assign students Grammar 2 exercises 1 and 2 on page 79 of their Workbook.

Assign students the Flipped classroom tasks on page 108 of their Student's Book if you'd like them to prepare for the next lesson. To complete this task, students need to watch the *Talk2Me* video which can be found on the Resource Centre.

SPEAKING

Collaborative task

→ Student's Book, page 108 SB

Lesson aims

- Focus on using phrases to give yourself time to think
- Practise a collaborative exam task
- Keep an English diary for a day

The *Talk2Me* video in this unit focuses on buying tickets for a concert. The people in the video talk about a concert, the price of the tickets and queueing to buy tickets over the phone.

Students answer some comprehension questions and then listen for key phrases in the video.

The video can be used in one of two ways:

Flipped classroom

Flipped classroom option

Using this approach, students watch the video and complete the exercises for homework. This prepares students for the speaking lesson by introducing them to the topic and the key phrases to use in the exam task. Teachers who use this method will find they have more class time to spend on activating the target language and developing fluency for the final task.

Talk2Me **worksheet**

Ask students to also complete the *Talk2Me* worksheet on the Resource Centre for more detailed comprehension exercises and more practice of the key phrases.

Classroom option

1 Ask students to spend a minute or two reading the questions. Play the *Talk2Me* video for students to complete the exercise. Play the video again, if necessary, before checking their answers.

2 Play the *Talk2Me* video again, so students underline the phrases in the *Phrase expert* box. Pause the video from time to time if necessary. Check answers in open class.

Talk2Me worksheet

Ask students to also complete the *Talk2Me* worksheet on the Resource Centre for more detailed comprehension exercises and more practice of the key phrases.

Answers

The transcript and answer key for the *Talk2Me* video exercises and Worksheet can be found on the Teacher's Resource Centre.

Lead-in

Write these jumbled words on the board and ask students to reorder the letters in them:

kareb na mar *acarehe* *chatc a locd* *geandab* *ampereretut* *nicedime*

Answers

break an arm, earache, catch a cold, bandage, temperature, medicine

3 After students discuss the questions, have them share their answers with the class.

4 3.16 Have students complete the exercise individually. Then play the audio for students to listen and check their answers.

Answers/Audioscript

1 Is the sports club open in the evenings?
2 Is it big or small?
3 Is there a swimming pool?
4 What's the telephone number?
5 What's the address?

5 3.17 Have students read through the advert before you play the audio. Check answers in open class.

Answers

1 It's small **2** and swimming pool **3** 04462 789122 **4** 155 **5** Street

EXAM SKILL

Giving yourself time to think

Ask students to read the tips.

- Point out that candidates are not usually given time to prepare what they are going to say in Speaking tests, so learning useful phrases to stall for time is essential. Using these phrases also demonstrates to the examiner that they have the confidence and ability to express what they want to say.
- Give students some useful phrases, e.g. *Let me see, Just give me a moment, Well …, That's a good question.* Try to use these phrases yourself in the classroom and encourage students to get used to using them when necessary.

6 3.17 Play the track again for students to listen and complete the exercise. Check answers in open class.

Answers

1 Just a minute **2** Mmm, let's see **3** let me think

OPTIMISE YOUR EXAM

Collaborative task

Ask students to read the tips.

- Explain that there is a part in many Speaking tests where students work together on a collaborative task without the examiner, who may even look away to discourage candidates from addressing conversation to him/her.
- It is important that the candidates develop and sustain a conversation taking turns to speak and respond to each other, showing interest and being careful not to interrupt each other.
- To avoid long silences, encourage students to ask their partner a question, e.g. *Is there anything else that you would like to know? Are you interested in …?*

Exam task

7 Assign each student a letter, A or B, and put them into A/B pairs. Give them a moment to look at their information / question topics on page 138/141. Time students (two minutes) and give them an update, e.g. *One minute to go …* Remind students to use phrases from the *Phrase expert* box for giving themselves time to think. Walk round, monitoring students for good use of language and errors to go over at the end of the activity.

Write any errors on the board and go through them with students, eliciting corrections from them where possible. After the class feedback, students could then repeat this activity with another partner, to try to improve their performance.

Suggested answers

Student A's questions
What's the address?
What does it sell?
Is it big or small?
Is it closed on Sundays?
What's the telephone number?

Student B's questions
What can I/you learn?
When are the classes for 14 year olds?
How much does a class cost?
What's the telephone number?
Who can I contact about the classes?

Extra support

Do Exercise 5 in two stages. First, group students together to prepare the questions they will need. Have half the pairs prepare the questions about the lessons while the other half prepares the questions about the shop. Do not allow students to write anything down. Monitor and correct students' errors discretely. Regroup students so that there is a Students A and Student B in each pair. Then have students complete the task.

THINK | RESEARCH | CULTURE | LEARN | ME

If appropriate, you could ask students to discuss their diary entries in pairs. Otherwise you may wish to have a class discussion on healthy food and exercise in general.

Homework

OWB

Assign students Speaking exercises 1, 2, 3 and 4 on pages 80–81 of their Workbook.

LANGUAGE IN USE

Multiple-matching dialogue

→ Student's Book, page 109 SB

Lesson aims

- Focus on giving short answers
- Practise a multiple-matching dialogue exam task
- Research foods that are good for your body

Lead-in

Ask students to work in pairs and role play different situations at the doctor's. One student is a doctor and the other is a patient. Have the patients describe their problems to the doctor, using *ache, pain, hurt* or *feel* and have the doctors give advice, e.g.

Doctor: *What's the problem today, Mr García?*

Patient: *My back aches doctor. It hurts a lot.*

Doctor: *Oh dear. You should lie down and rest. And don't do sports!*

Have students change roles. Walk round, monitoring students' use of the words *ache, pain, hurt* and *feel* and their suggestions. Give students feedback at the end of the exercise.

1 After students complete the exercise, have them share their ideas with the class, giving reasons and examples.

EXAM SKILL

Giving short answers

Ask students to read the tips.

- Remind students that using short answers correctly is also very useful in speaking exams. However, remind students that they should always try to give extra information in speaking exam tasks and not limit themselves to short answers.
- Check students understand that the pronoun in a short answer usually matches the subject or pronoun in the question, but not always, e.g. in questions with *you*. Also remind students that verbs can be negative, e.g. *Will you go? No, I won't.*

2 After students complete the exercise, have them practise asking and answering the questions in pairs.

Answers

1 e **2** a **3** b **4** f **5** d **6** c

Extra support

Ask students to circle the auxiliary verbs and underline the nouns/pronouns in the questions and the short answers to see which ones relate to each other. Tell students that they can use this technique to check their answers after completing the exam task in Exercise 4.

Answers

1 e (*Do you – I don't*) **2** a (*Has Matthew – he has*) **3** b (*Would you – we would*) **4** f (*Are there – there are*) **5** d (*Should I – you shouldn't*) **6** c (*Will the children – they won't*)

3 Have students complete the exercise, and then compare answers in pairs before checking in open class.

Answers

1 Yes **2** haven't **3** Is **4** it doesn't **5** Have **6** No, they

Optional extension

Draw a large + on one side of the board and a large – on the other side. Ask all students to stand up. Choose a strong student and ask, *Do you like going to the dentist's?* and point to the negative sign on the board. If the student answers with the correct short answer, i.e. *No, I don't*, he or she stays standing. If the student answers incorrectly, he or she is eliminated and sits down. Repeat the process, nominating students at random. Any student who hesitates too long or makes a mistake is knocked out. Continue until only one student is left standing.

OPTIMISE YOUR EXAM

Multiple-matching dialogue

Ask students to read the tips.

- Point out that in this exam task type, the conversation is always between two people and the missing lines will be from one of those people.
- Remind students of the process they practised earlier in the course: cover the options and read the conversation for general understanding; make predictions about what the other person might say; cross out the example sentence before starting the task; don't cross out the other sentences and consider them for the gaps too; make a guess about any gaps you are not sure of.

Exam task

4 Before students complete the exercise, elicit who the conversation is between (*a doctor and a patient*). Ask students to complete the exercise. Then have them compare their answers in pairs before checking them in open class by having two strong students read out the dialogue while the others check their answers.

Answers
1 G **2** A **3** F **4** B **5** C

THINK | **RESEARCH** | CULTURE | LEARN | ME

If you have access to the internet, students can research information and prepare lists in class. Alternatively, students could prepare this for homework. If you wish, divide the class into three groups and ask each group to research one area. Regroup students so there is one student who has prepared each area in each group. Then have students present their findings to each other.

Homework OWB
Assign students Language in Use exercises 1 and 2 on page 81 of their Workbook.

WRITING
An online post

→ Student's Book, pages 110–111 SB

Lesson aims

- Focus on language for giving advice
- Plan and write an online post

Lead-in

Write the word *internet* on the board. Divide the class into pairs and ask students to think of as many different uses for the internet as they can, e.g. *watching videos, researching information, shopping, streaming music, sending emails, storing files,* etc. Have students share their lists with the class to see if students are familiar with all the uses.

1 Have students look at the photo and elicit what they see. After students discuss the questions, elicit answers from different students around the class. Extend the second question to a class discussion. Make it clear that for any serious medical condition it is essential to get medical advice/treatment from a trained doctor or nurse, rather than relying on the internet.

EXAM SKILL

Giving advice

Ask students to read the tips.

- Tell students that being able to use a range of modal verbs to express different meanings will impress examiners and help improve their marks in a writing exam.

Language note

Remind students that the verb *have to* can be used as a verb and a modal and can be problematic for two reasons: 1) the negative is formed with the auxiliary verb *don't* – not with the contraction *n't* at the end like the modals *should* and *must*; 2) the negative form *don't have to* is used to talk about things that are not necessary to do. Make sure your students are clear that:

must = this is essential, you need to do this

don't have to = this is not essential, you can do it if you want

mustn't = this is not allowed, you can't do this

2 Tell students to read the complete sentences before they choose the correct options. After they complete the exercise, check answers in open class.

Answers
1 mustn't **2** don't have to **3** shouldn't **4** should **5** must

Optional extension

Put students into pairs. Give the class a specific minor health problem, e.g. *toothache*, and ask them to write two or three pieces of advice using the modal verbs. Elicit answers from different students around the class. Repeat with two or three additional minor health problems until you are confident students can use the modal verbs correctly.

3 Ask students if they ever read or write posts on internet forums before they complete the exercise. Check answers in open class.

Answers
Students should tick:
First post: 2 **Second post:** 3

OPTIMISE YOUR EXAM

An online post

Ask students to read the tips.

- Highlight that this type of exam task is very similar to others that students have seen before. Point out that this one is just a slightly different format. Explain that students will still be asked to answer three questions or respond to three different problems, and the number of words they have to write will be the same.
- Point out that people often pay little attention to correct spelling on the internet and they may use abbreviations which are not normally used in writing. However, make it clear that in writing exams, examiners will check for correct spelling and language use.

Exam task

4 Remind students to find the three questions they have to answer and to write them in the plan in Exercise 5.

Answers

1 He gets headaches and can't sleep after playing video games.
2 Is this bad?
Should I stop playing?
What else can I do?

5 Plan Ask students to complete the writing plan. You may want to look at their plans to check them and give advice and suggestions for improvement before students take the next step.

6 Write Students write their internet forum post. If there is not enough time, set this and the subsequent checklist exercise for homework.

7 Check Students complete the checklist before they hand in their internet forum post.

Optional extension

For a slightly longer writing task, and for students to see other text types, refer them to one of the six tasks in the Writing reference (SB p169). Each one includes an annotated sample text and related writing task to challenge your students a little more.

Homework

OWB

Assign students Writing exercises 1, 2, 3, 4 and 5 on page 82 of their Workbook and Progress check 10 on page 83.

Answers PROGRESS CHECK Units 9–10

Exercise 1
1 lived **2** lie **3** gives **4** 'd/would be **5** 'll/will go **6** won **7** pass **8** 'll/will enjoy **9** 'd/would feel **10** won't need

Exercise 2
1 for **2** taking **3** with **4** feels **5** trying

Exercise 3
1 nose **2** ears **3** stomach **4** feet **5** neck **6** hand **7** legs **8** dentist **9** back **10** bandage

Exercise 4
1 for **2** to work **3** yet **4** just **5** going **6** already **7** eating **8** taking **9** since **10** learning

Exercise 5
1 G **2** F **3** D **4** E **5** A

Exercise 6
1 sunny **2** river **3** snow **4** thunderstorm **5** clouds **6** ice **7** foggy **8** hill **9** wet **10** forest

11 The world of work

UNIT AIMS

Exam preparation in Unit 11:

- understand the reason for / purpose of a text
- take notes during a listening exercise
- talk about jobs in an interview
- understand the type of word that is missing in an open-cloze exercise
- use negative phrases and opposites in an information transfer exercise

TEACHER'S PRESENTATION KIT

- *Talk2Me* videos
- Speaking test videos
- Class and Workbook audio
- Workbook pages and answer key

UNIT OVERVIEW

Student's Book / Digital Student's Book SB		Workbook / Online Workbook OWB
LESSON / EXAM TASK	**EXAM SKILLS / LANGUAGE FOCUS**	**CONSOLIDATION**
Reading **Right/Wrong/Doesn't say**	Understanding the reasons for / purpose of a text A magazine article	Workbook, pp 84–85, Exercises 1, 2, 3, 4 Unit 11, Reading, Exercises 1, 2, 3, 4
Grammar 1	Indefinite pronouns	Workbook, p 86, Exercises 1, 2 Unit 11, Grammar 1, Exercises 1, 2
Vocabulary	Words connected with *work and jobs* Words with *-ian / -ress / -ist / -er / -r* Words + prepositions	Workbook, pp 86–87, Exercises 1, 2, 3 Unit 11, Vocabulary, Exercises 1, 2, 3
Listening **Gap fill**	Taking notes	Workbook, p 88, Exercises 1, 2 Unit 11, Listening, Exercises 1, 2
Grammar 2	Relative clauses: *who, which, that*	Workbook, p 87, Exercises 1, 2 Unit 11, Grammar 2, Exercises 1, 2
Speaking **Interview**	Talking about jobs	Workbook, pp 88–89, Exercises 1, 2, 3 Unit 11, Speaking, Exercises 1, 2, 3
Language in Use **Open cloze**	Understanding the type of word that is missing	Workbook, p 89, Exercises 1, 2 Unit 11, Language in Use, Exercises 1, 2
Writing **Information transfer**	Negative phrases and opposites	Workbook, p 90, Exercises 1, 2, 3, 4 Unit 11, Writing, Exercises 1, 2, 3, 4
		Workbook, p 91, Progress check and Cumulative progress Progress check and Cumulative progress

Additional material

PRESENTATION KIT	TEACHER'S / STUDENT'S RESOURCE CENTRE RC	TEST GENERATOR
Talk2Me video *My mum is a …*	**Unit 11 worksheets:** *Optimise your grammar* (Standard and Higher), *Optimise your vocabulary* (Standard and Higher), *Talk2Me* video, *Say it right* **Units 11–12 worksheets:** CLIL, Culture, Everyday English (TRC only), Grammar communication (TRC only)	Unit Test 11 (Standard and Higher)

READING

Right/Wrong/Doesn't say | A magazine article

→ Student's Book, pages 114–115 SB

Lesson aims

- Focus on understanding the reason for or purpose of a text
- Practise a Right/Wrong/Doesn't say exam task
- Think about working on the Children's Railway

Lead-in

Ask students to look at the unit title ***The world of work*** and the photos, and ask them what they think the unit will be about (*different types of work and jobs*). Ask them to think of jobs that are typically 'nine to five' jobs, e.g. *secretary*, *accountant* and elicit why they think those jobs have specific working hours. Elicit the jobs they can see represented in the photos. (*architect/builder, businessman, chef, comedian/singer, doctor, farmer, firefighter, nurse, pilot, police officer, sailor, student*)

1 After students discuss the questions, elicit some answers from the class and try to develop a class discussion on students' future job plans.

EXAM SKILL

Understanding the reason for / purpose of a text

Ask students to read the tips.

- Tell students that they can learn a lot about why a text is written by thinking about who wrote the text and who they expect to read it. Explain that writers often use different language in texts, depending on who the audience is.
- Remind students that they would be able to understand why a text is written in their own language without thinking about it. Point out that they can use that same skill to identify texts and who they were written for in English.

2 After students complete the exercise. Check their answers and then have them write another sentence for each function. Have students share what they wrote with the class.

Answers

1 c **2** d **3** b **4** a **5** e

3 After students complete the exercise, have them provide reasons for their answers as you check their answers in open class.

Answers

a 4 (descriptions are in narratives) **b** 1 (the opening time of some museums) **c** 5 (it is a personal opinion) **d** 3 (this is something you would say to someone starting a new job) **e** 2 (this uses imperatives)

Optional extension

In pairs, students choose one of the five text types in Exercise 3 and write a new sentence that they would expect to see in that type of text. Walk round, helping students and monitoring closely.

Regroup students to form small groups, where each student has a different text type. Students read each other their sentences and try to guess the text type they match.

4 Remind students that the first step when completing a reading task is always to read the text quickly for gist. Set a strict time limit of around one minute for students to read the first two paragraphs of the text and identify the purpose of the article. Before they start, have them look back at purposes a–e in Exercise 2. Check the answer in open class.

Answer

a) to describe

OPTIMISE YOUR EXAM

Right/Wrong/Doesn't say

Ask students to read the tips.

- Remind students of the process they practised earlier in the course: read the text quickly for gist; read the sentences carefully and underline the important information; go back to the beginning of the text and read the relevant sections more carefully to decide on the correct answers.
- Remind students to choose *Doesn't say* when there is no clear information in the text and *Wrong* when there is information in the text that directly contradicts the statement.

▼ Exam task

5 3.18 **Note: The reading text is also available on the audio CD. You may want to have students listen and read the text before doing the exam task.**

Remind students that the questions come in chronological order in relation to the text. After students complete the exercise, check answers in open class and elicit the evidence.

Answers

1 B (*… nearly everyone who works there is a child.*)
2 A (*… from a few hundred metres to 11 kilometres …*)
3 B (*The train drivers and engineers are adults, …*)
4 B (*All the workers have to wear a smart uniform, …*)
5 B (*… they are all volunteers, which means they don't get paid.*)
6 A (*Each year over 300,000 customers use the Railway …*)
7 C (The text says that people use the railway *to get to work, visit friends, or just to see how well the children do their jobs!* but it doesn't specifically mention people going on holiday.)

Fast finishers

Ask students to find evidence in the text for their answers.

Cultural note

The first section of the Children's Railway in Budapest opened in 1948 and this was followed by two further sections in 1949 and 1950. The line closed briefly in the 1950s but has been operational ever since. The narrow gauge railway has eight stations and holds the Guinness World Record for the longest children's railway in the world. Workers are local schoolchildren who have achieved excellent grades and as a reward are allowed to miss school two days a month to work on the railway. All the children receive four months training before they start and are under adult supervision. The railway is a popular excursion into the Buda Hills.

6 Go through the first definition as a class and then have students find the rest of the words individually. Check answers in open class.

Answers

1 uniform **2** clean **3** transport **4** ticket **5** late **6** staff **7** timetable **8** safe

Mixed ability

Pair less confident and stronger students together. Stronger students cover Exercise 6 and less confident students read each definition to their partner. Students agree each answer together before continuing.

THINK | RESEARCH | CULTURE | LEARN | ME

Have students discuss the questions in pairs. Walk round, monitoring students doing the task and helping them where necessary. Then open up as a class discussion.

Homework

OWB

Assign students Reading exercises 1, 2, 3 and 4 on pages 84–85 of their Workbook.

GRAMMAR 1

Indefinite pronouns

→ Student's Book, page 116 SB

Lesson aims

- Understand the correct usage of indefinite pronouns
- Practise using indefinite pronouns to talk about people, places, things and actions without saying who or what they are
- Discuss how young people prepare for the world of work

Lead-in

Write *On the railway* on the board and the following word skeletons around it:

_ng_n_ _r
p_ss_n g_r
tr_ _n dr_v_r
t_ck_t s_ll_r
st_t_ _n m_n_g_r

Put students into pairs to complete the words. Check their answers in open class. Then ask students what they remember about the article they read in the previous lesson.

Answers

engineer, passenger, train driver, ticket seller, station manager

Grammar in context

While students are completing the exercise, focus their attention on the indefinite pronouns in items 1–5. Check their answers and ask students to read the information in the *Remember* box. Ask students questions to check their understanding, e.g. *What do engineers have to check? (Everything.) Did you bring everything you need to school today?*

Remind students that they can find more information in the Grammar reference, Unit 11, page 160.

Answers

a -thing **b** -one **c** -where

Language note

Tell students that we use indefinite pronouns to replace nouns without specifying which noun they replace. Explain that they are made up of two parts: The first part, *every-*, *some-* and *any-*, indicates the number of things/places/ people we are referring to, and the second part, *-thing*, *-one* and *-where*, indicates what we are talking about.

1 If necessary, encourage students to refer back to the Grammar in context box to help them complete the exercise. Check answers in open class.

Answers

1 everywhere **2** anything **3** everything **4** someone **5** somewhere **6** something

2 After students complete the exercise, have them check their answers in pairs before checking in open class.

Answers

1 Everyone **2** anything **3** everywhere **4** Someone **5** anywhere **6** something

Mixed ability

Ask all students to cover the box in Exercise 2. Have stronger students complete the exercise with appropriate words without looking at the options in the box. Give weaker students the first part of the word for items 1, 3 and 5 (*1 Every-*, *3 every-*, *5 any-*) and the second part of the word for items 2, 4 and 6 (*2 -thing*, *4 -one*, *6 -thing*).

3 Tell students to look at the words before and after the gaps to help them complete the exercise. Have different students read out the text to check answers in open class.

Answers
1 B **2** A **3** B **4** B **5** B **6** B **7** C **8** A

SAY IT RIGHT

/θ/

For the *Say it right* pronunciation activity and instructions, go to the Teacher's Resource Centre. TRC

THINK | RESEARCH | **CULTURE** | LEARN | ME

Have students work in pairs to brainstorm ideas. Then have them share their ideas with the class and encourage a class discussion if there is time.

Homework OWB

Assign students Grammar 1 exercises 1 and 2 on page 86 of their Workbook.

VOCABULARY

Topic vocabulary | Word formation | Word patterns

→ Student's Book, page 117 SB

Lesson aims

Understand the correct usage of:

- words connected with work and jobs
- suffixes used to form jobs
- word patterns with prepositions

Lead-in

Write the following sentences on the board:

1 My mum ______ in an office – she's a lawyer.

2 My dad doesn't really like his ______. He says it's boring.

3 My sister is a sales assistant. She has a lot of ______ at the weekend.

Have students discuss which word they think completes each sentence. Check their answers and make sure students understand that *work* can be a verb, as in the first sentence, or an uncountable noun, as in the last sentence. Point out that *job* is always a noun and can be singular, as in the second sentence, or plural (*My sister has two jobs – in the mornings she works at the swimming pool and in the afternoons in a local café.*).

Answers
1 works **2** job **3** work

Words connected with *work and jobs*

1 3.19 After students complete the exercise, play the audio for them to listen and check their answers. Then ask them to write a description of another job. Have them share their descriptions with the class and encourage students to guess.

Answers/Audioscript
1 someone who writes articles for a newspaper: *journalist*
2 someone who flies planes: *pilot*
3 someone who cleans an office or a home: *cleaner*
4 someone who is a member of the police: *police officer*
5 someone who works in a theatre or in films: *actor*
6 someone who helps you in a shop: *shop assistant*
7 someone who stops fires: *firefighter*
8 someone who designs or builds things such as roads, bridges or machines: *engineer*

2 3.20 Have students complete the exercise individually. Then ask them to compare answers in pairs before playing the audio for them to check.

Answers/Audioscript
Thousands of us love using social networking. But have you ever thought of it as a *career*? There are jobs for young people in most of the big social media *companies*. As a new *worker*, you might be a *social media officer*, for example – working with some of the social media *managers*, working on the website and going to *meetings*. And if you're good at what you do, you'll get the chance to do different jobs and *earn* more money. So instead of being a social media *customer*, why not think about becoming a member of *staff*?

Refer students to the Vocabulary reference, page 168, for more information on topic vocabulary.

Words with *-ian / -ress / -ist / -er / -r*

3 3.21 After students complete the exercise and check their answers, elicit what each profession does, e.g. *A musician plays an instrument.*

Answers/Audioscript
-ian: musician
-ress: waitress
-ist: artist, chemist, dentist, journalist, receptionist
-er: cleaner, engineer, farmer, footballer, photographer, waiter
-r: driver, explorer, manager, writer

4 After students complete the exercise, ask them to write a similar sentence about a member of their family.

Answers
1 farmer **2** musician **3** receptionist **4** waiter/waitress **5** dentist **6** manager

Refer students to the Vocabulary reference, page 168, for more information on word formation.

Words + prepositions

5 3.22 Ask students to complete the exercise individually. Then play the audio for them to check their answers.

Answers/Audioscript

1 (A) Alex is the manager *of* a clothes shop in the city centre.
2 (B) Charlie hopes to get a diploma *in* music from a college in London.
3 (B) Steph is a receptionist and she works *for* a company that makes computers.
4 (C) Judy is the singer *in* a local rock band.
5 (C) Michael is a writer *of* children's books.
6 (B) We have an important meeting today *with* the manager.

Extra support

Write and explain the following items on the board as a reference for students to complete Exercise 5.

i be the [secretary] for a company that [makes sweets]
ii be the [writer] of [popular novels]
iii be the [lawyer] of [his sister's company]
iv have an [interview] with [the accountant]
v have a [degree] in [physics]
vi be the [drummer] in [a famous group]

Point out that the sections in brackets can be changed for other similar words or phrases. Elicit some examples as you check the answers.

Refer students to the Vocabulary reference, page 168, for more information on word patterns.

Homework OWB
Assign students Vocabulary exercises 1, 2 and 3 on pages 86–87 of their Workbook.

LISTENING
Gap fill

→ Student's Book, page 118 SB

Lesson aims

- Listen and take notes of specific information
- Practise a gap-fill exam task
- Research young business people

Lead-in

Play the game ***The Alphabet Race***. Divide the class into teams to make a list of a job for every letter of the alphabet. Give students a three-minute time limit and encourage them to use their imagination. Point out that some letters of the alphabet are very difficult or impossible, so students shouldn't spend too long on any one letter. Go through students' answers, giving two points for unique words and one point for words shared by two or more teams. The team with the most points wins.

Possible answers

High-level items in brackets

actor, **b**uilder, **c**leaner, **d**entist, **e**lectrician, **f**irefighter, (**g**eologist), **h**airdresser, (**i**nterpreter), **j**ournalist, (**k**indergarten teacher), **l**awyer, **m**anager, **n**urse, (**o**ptician), **p**olice officer, **q**ueen, **r**eceptionist, **s**cientist, **t**eacher, (**u**mpire), **v**et, **w**aitress, (**x**-ray technician), (**y**ard manager), (**z**oo keeper)

1 Ask students to look at the photo and describe what is happening (*A young woman has made some doughnuts and she is …*). Then have students discuss the questions. Elicit some answers from different students around the class and come to a consensus on the best business idea.

EXAM SKILL

Taking notes

Ask students to read the tips.

- Tell students that learning how to take useful notes is an important technique both for English exam tasks and for their everyday lives.
- Tell students it is impossible to write down everything they hear and is unproductive if they try. Remind them to write just the important words and phrases and encourage them to focus on these when listening.
- Remind students that bullet points, arrows, etc. can also be as useful as words to help show how things connect to each other and to give structure to their notes.

2 3.23 Before playing the audio, tell students that they need to listen very carefully and write the words that are spelled out. Elicit answers from students from around the class.

Answers

1 Armitage **2** Bicester **3** Vaughan **4** Chloe **5** Edinburgh

3 3.24 Tell students that they are going to hear Ed giving information about something he organised. Play the audio for students to listen and correct the information in the notes. Have them compare answers in pairs before you check them in open class.

Answers

1 July **2** garden **3** 80 people **4** Jayveeland **5** £200

Extra support

Give students a pool of information on the board containing the five answers to Exercise 3 and two incorrect answers/ distractors for each item:

June garden Jaybeeland 280 £220 18 town July £2200 £200 80 house Jayveeland Jay Jay Land April

Tell students to refer to the information on the board while they complete the task in Exercise 3. Remind them that some of the items are distractors.

OPTIMISE YOUR EXAM

Gap fill

Ask students to read the tips.

- Stress that in this exam task type, students are expected to write only one or two words, a number or a short expression in the gaps.
- Remind students that in this type of task, they should check that the answer they have written is correct during the second listening.

Exam task

4 3.25 Ask students to read the notes before they start. Point out that they should write one or two words for each answer. Play the audio for students to complete the exercise. Check answers in open class.

Answers
1 and offices **2** mum **3** Kearsley **4** 52 **5** the Year

THINK | **RESEARCH** | CULTURE | LEARN | ME

If you have access to the internet, students can research information in class. Alternatively, they could prepare this for homework and present their information at the start of the next lesson.

Homework OWB
Assign students Listening exercises 1 and 2 on page 88 of their Workbook.

GRAMMAR 2

Relative clauses: *who, which, that*

→ Student's Book, page 119 SB

Lesson aims

- Focus on relative clauses with *who, which* and *that*
- Practise giving more information about a person or a thing

Lead-in

Ask students what they remember about the listening they heard in the previous lesson. Write what they say on the board, making notes of the most important points. Then reflect on what they learnt about note taking by having them look at the notes you took.

Grammar in context

While students are completing the task, encourage them to refer to the information in the *Remember* box if they aren't sure. Check answers in open class.

Remind students that they can find more information in the Grammar reference, Unit 11, page 160.

Answers
a studying hard **b** the factory **c** a competition

Language note

Explain that relative pronouns refer to the people or thing(s) we are describing. Tell students that the information we add after a relative pronoun must be about the same people or thing(s) we are talking about.

1 While students are completing the exercise, remind them to identify what the relative pronouns are describing. Ask students to compare their answers with a partner before checking in open class.

Answers
1 which **2** who **3** that **4** which **5** which **6** who **7** who **8** who

2 Go through the example as a class. Tell students that in some cases there is more than one possible way to combine sentences. Explain that in this case, *Alex, who works in his dad's office, is a manager.*, is also a possibility. Ask students to compare their answers in pairs before checking answers in open class.

Answers
2 There is a factory near here which/that makes cars. / There is a factory which/that makes cars near here.
3 Fred is the waiter who/that took our order.
4 I would like a desk which/that is near the window.
5 They had a meeting which/that was with the new manager.

Mixed ability

Give less confident students the first two words and the last two words of each sentence and the relative pronoun(s) they should use in each case, e.g. *1 Alex is … dad's office. (who/that) 2 There is … near here. (which/that).* Students who finish early can look back at the sentences in Exercise 1 and see how they could separate them into two sentences, e.g. *1 It's a question. No-one has the answer to it. 2 The secretary works in our office. He is away today.*

3 Focus students' attention on the article and have them complete the exercise individually. Check answers in open class.

Answers
1 who/that **2** which/that **3** who/that **4** that/which **5** that/which **6** who/that **7** that/which **8** who/that

Fast finishers

Write these definitions on the board and ask students to find the words in the text in Exercise 4.

1 This is a group of firefighters who work together.
2 This is the building that firefighters work in.
3 These are the people who are staying in a hotel.

Answers
1 fire station **2** guests **3** watch

Homework

OWB

Assign students Grammar 2 exercises 1 and 2 on page 87 of their Workbook.

Assign students the Flipped classroom tasks on page 120 of their Student's Book if you'd like them to prepare for the next lesson. To complete this task, students need to watch the *Talk2Me* video which can be found on the Resource Centre.

SPEAKING
Interview

→ Student's Book, page 120 SB

Lesson aims

- Focus on talking about jobs and work in an interview
- Practise answering personal questions

The *Talk2Me* video in this unit focuses on arranging a guest list for a birthday party at a restaurant. The people in the video talk about who they would like to invite to the party and the number of people who can attend.

Students answer some comprehension questions and then listen for key phrases in the video.

The video can be used in one of two ways:

Flipped classroom

Flipped classroom option

Using this approach, students watch the video and complete the exercises for homework. This prepares students for the speaking lesson by introducing them to the topic and the key phrases to use in the exam task. Teachers who use this method will find they have more class time to spend on activating the target language and developing fluency for the final task.

Talk2Me worksheet

Ask students to also complete the *Talk2Me* worksheet on the Resource Centre for more detailed comprehension exercises and more practice of the key phrases.

Classroom option

1 Ask students to spend a minute or two reading the questions. Play the *Talk2Me* video for students to complete the exercise. Play the video again, if necessary, before checking their answers.

2 Play the *Talk2Me* video again, so students underline the phrases in the *Phrase expert* box. Pause the video from time to time if necessary. Check answers in open class.

Talk2Me worksheet

Ask students to also complete the *Talk2Me* worksheet on the Resource Centre for more detailed comprehension exercises and more practice of the key phrases.

Answers

The transcript and answer key for the *Talk2Me* video exercises and Worksheet can be found on the Teacher's Resource Centre.

Lead-in

Stand with your back to the board. Ask for a volunteer to come to the front and write a job on the board for the rest of the class to see. You mustn't look at what's on the board. Nominate a student and ask him or her a closed, *yes/no* question to try to find out 'your' job, e.g. *José, do I work in an office?* Elicit a complete short answer, e.g. *No, you don't.* Tell students you have a maximum of ten questions to guess what your job is and nominate a different student to answer each question. When you have guessed correctly, repeat that activity with a volunteer and continue with more students.

3 Ask students to complete the exercise in pairs. Set a strict time limit of one minute each for questions 1 and 2. Then, after each question, elicit answers from students around the class. The pair with the most correct answers wins. Then give students time to tell each other what their family members do.

4 3.26 Have students read the sentences before you play the audio. Check answers in open class and elicit the correct information.

Answers

1 F (She's got two brothers and two sisters.) **2** F (He's a photographer.) **3** F (He doesn't work in an office.) **4** T **5** F (Her mum is a journalist. Her dad is a lawyer.)

EXAM SKILL

Talking about jobs

Ask students to read the tips.

- Encourage students to learn language in chunks, e.g. phrases or collocations including the word *work*. (This is the type of language that is often tested in Language in Use exam tasks.)
- Remind students the present simple is often used with the adverbs of frequency *never, sometimes, often, usually* and *always* to talk about jobs and routines.
- Also remind them that the present continuous is used with expressions like *at the moment* and *right now* to talk about what someone is doing now.
- Explain that the present continuous can also be used to talk about something that is temporary. Point out that sentences can combine the present simple (to talk about the normal situation) with the present continuous (to talk about a different situation that is just happening for a short time), e.g. *We usually have basketball practice on Wednesdays, but this month we're meeting on Thursdays.*

5 3.26 Ask students to complete the exercise. Then play the audio for students to listen and check their answers.

Answers

1 works **2** meets **3** is cooking **4** 's visiting

Optional extension

Have students work in pairs and choose a job from the list they made in Exercise 3. Tell them to write a short text about the job using language from the *Exam skills* box, imagining they had that job. For example, *I work as a shop assistant. I usually work in the shopping centre in the city centre, but at the moment, I'm working in a shop at the railway station because …* Walk round, monitoring students' use of the language.

OPTIMISE YOUR EXAM

Interview

Ask students to read the tips.

- Remind students that it is important that they practise talking about topics that they may be asked about in a Speaking test. These include general information about their family members and their jobs.
- Remind them that in a Speaking test they need to show the examiner how much English they know. This is more important than struggling to explain a complicated job, so it is fine for them to change some details to make a job easier for them to talk about.
- Remind students that while they can make a good impression by using grammatically correct short answers, they should always add more information to their answers when possible.

▼ Exam task

6 In pairs, students complete the exercise. Remind students to use phrases from the *Phrase expert* box and to use the present simple and present continuous correctly. Walk round, monitoring students for good use of language and errors to go over at the end of the activity.

Write any errors on the board and go through them with students, eliciting corrections from them where possible. After the class feedback, students could then repeat this activity with another partner, to try to improve their performance.

Fast finishers

Regroup students into new pairs. Have students use their notes to tell each other what they found out about their partner. For example, *Jennifer's brother works in a museum.*

Homework

OWB

Assign students Speaking exercises 1, 2 and 3 on pages 88–89 of their Workbook.

LANGUAGE IN USE

Open cloze

→ Student's Book, page 121 SB

Lesson aims

- Focus on understanding the type of word that is missing
- Practise an open-cloze exam task
- Discuss which country you would most like to work in

Lead-in

Imagine you do a specific job (e.g. firefighter, train driver), talk to the class about what you do. Include answers to some of the questions from Exercise 6 on Student's Book page 120, and aim to include examples of *work with/for/in/as* and the present simple and present continuous. Ask students to listen to you and identify which of the questions you answer. Then students talk about a family member they interviewed about his or her job.

1 Focus students' attention on the photo. Then have students discuss the questions in pairs. Elicit answers from different students around the class.

Suggested answers

1 She is counting birds / looking at wildlife. She might be an explorer.

2 Students' own answers

EXAM SKILL

Understanding the type of word that is missing

Ask students to read the tips.

- Remind students that knowing how sentences are formed can sometimes help them work out what words they need to complete sentences in an open-cloze task. By looking at the words around the missing word, they should be able to decide if it is a verb, a preposition or a conjunction, etc.
- Remind students to think only about the type of words they could use in each space the first time they read, and not to get distracted by thinking about other options at this stage. They will work on developing this process in Exercise 2 (where they have to choose the correct type of word) and Exercise 3 (which asks them to choose the exact word).

2 Before they start, students look at the different options to familiarise themselves with the type of words they will need to identify. After they complete the exercise, check answers in open class.

Answers

1 c **2** a **3** c **4** b **5** a

3 Ask students to complete the exercise individually and check their answers in pairs.

Answers
1 c **2** c **3** c **4** b **5** c

OPTIMISE YOUR **EXAM**

Open cloze

Ask students to read the tips.

- Remind students that open-cloze exam tasks focus mostly on grammar, so answers will almost always focus on function words, e.g. auxiliary verbs, adjectives, adverbs, pronouns, conjunctions, prepositions and articles.
- Remind students of the process they practised earlier in the course: read the text first for general understanding; think about what type of word is missing in each gap; try to complete the gaps and leave any difficult ones until the end; go back and check the words before and/or after the gaps in order to confirm the answers; make a guess about any gaps that cannot be deduced.
- Remind students to reread their answers to check they have the correct answers and that they are spelled correctly.

Exam task

4 Tell students to complete the exercise taking all the exam tips into consideration. Ask students to compare in pairs before you elicit answers in open class.

Answers
1 for **2** which/that **3** the **4** but/although **5** do **6** about **7** which/that **8** a **9** who/that **10** much

Extra support

Give students the ten words they need to complete the gaps in a jumbled order along with two distractors (*which (×2), a, to, about, who, for, much, do, the, but, and*). Ask them to choose words from the pool to complete the text.

Fast finishers

Ask students to think of the good things and the bad things about Sara's job as an explorer for a travel magazine, e.g. *good – see lots of places in the world, they pay you to travel; bad – away from your family and friends, some places can be dangerous*, etc.

THINK | RESEARCH | CULTURE | LEARN | **ME**

Have students discuss the question in pairs. Then open the discussion to a class debate if there's time. Have students do more research on the country and job they discussed for homework.

Homework OWB

Assign students Language in Use exercises 1 and 2 on page 89 of their Workbook.

WRITING
Information transfer

→ Student's Book, pages 122–123 SB

Lesson aims

- Focus on negative phrases and opposites
- Practise an information transfer exam task

Lead-in

Have a class discussion about jobs. Find out the following information from students: What jobs are they interested in doing after school? What would they need to study to get a job in that area? Do they need to get some specific experience while they are still at school to do that job? Where can they get information to help them decide what jobs they might enjoy? etc.

1 Focus students attention on the job adverts and elicit what they are and where they might find them (*casual jobs for young people, on a noticeboard or in the window of a local shop or community centre*, etc.). After students have looked at the adverts and discussed the questions, explain that in many countries there are job fairs to help young people find out more about the jobs they are interested in.

EXAM SKILL

Negative phrases and opposites

Ask students to read the tips.

- Point out that positive verbs often change to negative and vice versa, but that other words can also change, e.g. *We hardly ever finish work late.*
- Explain that opposite adjectives can be particularly useful in information transfer exam tasks, but other types of opposites can be useful too, e.g. adverbs (*quickly/slowly*), phrasal verbs (*turn on/turn off*), verbs (*start/finish*), indefinite pronouns (*everyone/no-one*), etc.

2 After students complete the exercise, encourage them to make a list of other useful opposites they know. Check answers in open class and have students share their lists with the class.

Answers
1 e **2** f **3** b **4** d **5** a **6** c

3 Ask students to complete the exercise individually. Have them check their answers in pairs before checking in open class.

Answers
1 together **2** interesting **3** closed **4** safe **5** easy **6** last

Optional extension

Have students write their own sentences with opposites from this exercise or from their lists. Tell them to use both words and leave one blank. Have them share their sentences with the class and have other students guess the correct answer.

4 Tell students to read all the texts before completing the task. Then have students check their answers with a partner.

Answers
1 shop assistant **2** 8:50 **3** 8:00–16:00 **4** my house **5** some forms

OPTIMISE YOUR EXAM

Information transfer

Ask students to read the tips.

- Remind students of the process they practised earlier in the course: read both texts first to check understanding of the context and the information; look at the exam task and think about the type of information needed in each gap; find the relevant information (a word or a phrase) in the texts and remember to combine bits of information from both texts if necessary; mark the links between the texts to be sure of their answers.
- Remind students that it is essential to spell the words correctly. Tell them to leave time at the end of the task to double-check all their answers and spelling. Explain that they will lose marks for any words they misspell.

Exam task

5 Plan Elicit the steps they need to take, and give any necessary advice or suggestions. Students read and tick the points in the plan.

Answers
Students should tick:
1, 3

6 Write Give students a time limit to complete the notes. Remind students to answer all the questions and check their own answers. Then check answers in open class.

Answers
1 Queen's Road Library **2** 9:30 am
3 ticket **4** information **5** Palace Café

7 Check Students to complete the checklist before they hand in their notes.

Extra writing

8 Students read and answer the questions. Ask them to compare their answers in pairs.

Students write their email. Remind students that they worked on writing emails in the Writing sections of Unit 2 and Unit 8 and to refer back to these if they need any additional support. If there is not enough time, set this writing task for homework.

Answers
1 There is a Job Information Day.
2 He wants me to get some information about work experience with HiCCo.
3 He's suggesting we meet at the Palace Café.
and students' own answers

Optional extension

For a slightly longer writing task, and for students to see other text types, refer them to one of the six tasks in the Writing reference (SB p169). Each one includes an annotated sample text and related writing task to challenge your students a little more.

Homework OWB
Assign students Writing exercises 1, 2, 3 and 4 on page 90 of their Workbook and Progress check 11 on page 91.

12 Home time

UNIT AIMS

Exam preparation in Unit 12:

- understand possessive adjectives in an online article
- check your answers in a multiple-choice exercise
- talk about money in a collaborative task
- learn vocabulary and apply it in multiple-choice sentences
- use adjectives in a postcard

TEACHER'S PRESENTATION KIT

- *Talk2Me* videos
- Speaking test videos
- Class and Workbook audio
- Workbook pages and answer key

UNIT OVERVIEW

Student's Book / Digital Student's Book SB		Workbook / Online Workbook OWB
LESSON / EXAM TASK	EXAM SKILLS / LANGUAGE FOCUS	CONSOLIDATION
Reading **Multiple-choice cloze**	Possessive adjectives An online article	Workbook, pp 92–93, Exercises 1, 2, 3, 4 Unit 12, Reading, Exercises 1, 2, 3, 4
Grammar 1	Present simple passive	Workbook, p 94, Exercises 1, 2 Unit 12, Grammar 1, Exercises 1, 2
Vocabulary	Words connected with *houses and homes* Phrasal verbs Collocations with verbs	Workbook, pp 94–95, Exercises 1, 2, 3 Unit 12, Vocabulary, Exercises 1, 2, 3
Listening **Multiple choice**	Checking your answers	Workbook, p 96, Exercises 1, 2, 3 Unit 12, Listening, Exercises 1, 2, 3
Grammar 2	Past simple passive and *by*	Workbook, p 95, Exercises 1, 2, 3 Unit 12, Grammar 2, Exercises 1, 2, 3
Speaking **Collaborative task**	Talking about money	Workbook, pp 96–97, Exercises 1, 2, 3 Unit 12, Speaking, Exercises 1, 2, 3
Language in Use **Multiple-choice sentences**	Learning vocabulary	Workbook, p 97, Exercises 1, 2, 3 Unit 12, Language in Use, Exercises 1, 2, 3
Writing **A postcard**	Using adjectives	Workbook, p 98, Exercises 1, 2, 3, 4, 5 Unit 12, Writing, Exercises 1, 2, 3, 4, 5
Progress check	Check language progress for Units 11 and 12	Workbook, p 99, Progress check and Cumulative progress Progress check and Cumulative progress

Additional material

PRESENTATION KIT	TEACHER'S / STUDENT'S RESOURCE CENTRE RC	TEST GENERATOR
Talk2Me video *How much is …?*	**Unit 12 worksheets:** *Optimise your grammar* (Standard and Higher), *Optimise your vocabulary* (Standard and Higher), *Talk2Me* video, *Say it right* **Units 11–12 worksheets:** CLIL, Culture, Everyday English (TRC only), Grammar communication (TRC only)	Unit Test 12 (Standard and Higher) End-of-year Test (Standard and Higher)

READING
Multiple-choice cloze | An online article

→ Student's Book, pages 124–125 SB

Lesson aims

- Focus on understanding possessive adjectives
- Practise a multiple-choice cloze exam task
- Research people who live somewhere different

Lead-in

Ask students to look at the photo and elicit the meaning of the unit title ***Home time*** (this is the typical way to refer to the end of the school day when it is time to go home). Ask students what they think the unit will be about (*different types of homes and what we have in them*).

1 Encourage students to be honest and give reasons for their answers. Elicit answers from different students around the class and open out to a class debate.

2 Remind students to scan the text for the information they require and read it to find the correct answer.

Answer

He lives with his mum, Mary.

3 Tell students to read the questions before they read the text so that they know what types of answers they are looking for while they are reading.

Answers

1 Tinker's Bubble is a small village in the middle of a forest in the south-west of England. **2** in 1994 **3** 12 (10 adults and 2 children) **4** bathrooms **5** bathroom and kitchen **6** on its small farm

Fast finishers

Write some comprehension questions on the board for students to answer.

1 Are the houses at Tinker's Bubble big?
2 What do Joe and Mary have in their house?
3 What do the people at Tinker's Bubble do to make money?

Answers

1 No, they aren't. They are quite small.
2 They have a table, some shelves, some chairs, some beds, lots of blankets, a fire, a radio and a lamp.
3 They sell fruit at the local market.

EXAM SKILL

Possessive adjectives

Ask students to read the tips.

- Remind students that they worked on pronouns and people in the Language in Use section of Unit 5. Tell them that this section will extend their knowledge by looking at how possessive adjectives are used to show who owns things in more detail.
- Explain to students that possessive adjectives are particularly important in exam tasks like multiple-choice cloze and open cloze, but that they are also important in other parts of the exam too, as they make it clear who or what we are talking about.

4 Tell students to use the text to help them complete the exercise. Have students share their answers with a partner before checking answers in open class.

Answers

1 The people who live at Tinker's Bubble **2** The people who live at Tinker's Bubble **3** Joe Durling **4** Joe Durling and his mum **5** Tinker's Bubble

OPTIMISE YOUR EXAM

Multiple-choice cloze

Ask students to read the tips.

- Remind students of the process they practised earlier in the course: cover the A–C options; read the text first to get a general understanding; think about words that might be possible in each gap; uncover the options and try to complete the gaps, leaving any difficult answers until the end; go back and check the words before or after the gaps to confirm the answers; make a guess about any gaps that cannot be deduced.
- Tell students to identify the person a pronoun/adjective refers to, which might be before or after the gap.

▼ Exam task

5 3.27 **Note: The reading text is also available on the audio CD <u>but contains the missing words</u>. You may want to have students listen and read the text <u>after</u> doing the exam task to check their answers.**

Tell students to complete the task as they read through it. Check answers in open class.

Answers

1 A (The word here forms part of a relative clause about people, so the only possible option is *who*; *which* is for objects and *they* is not a relative pronoun.)

2 B (The verb *to be* in plural form is needed because it follows the word *They*.)

3 B (The indefinite pronoun *everyone* is singular, therefore the verb that follows needs to be in third person singular.)

4 B (The position before a noun indicates that we need a possessive adjective. *Theirs* is a possessive pronoun, so it can't be correct. *Their* and *Our* are both possessive adjectives, but the text is referring to another group of people, not including the reader, so the answer must be *Their*.)

5 C (*When* refers to a time.)

6 C (The word *lots* is part of the quantify expression *lots of*.)

7 B (*But* shows an opposing idea, which the text requires following a negative sentence.)

6 Ask students to complete the exercise. Check their answers in open class.

Answers
1 a lot of **2** trees **3** everyone **4** living room **5** books **6** cold **7** a fire **8** cooked

THINK | **RESEARCH** | CULTURE | LEARN | ME

If you have access to the internet, students can research information in class. Alternatively, students could prepare this for homework and present their information at the start of the next lesson.

Homework OWB
Assign students Reading exercises 1, 2, 3 and 4 on pages 92–93 of their Workbook.

GRAMMAR 1
Present simple passive

→ Student's Book, page 126 SB

Lesson aims

- Understand the correct usage of the present simple passive
- Practise talking about actions that are more important than the person who does them
- Discuss moving house

Lead-in

Write *Tinker's Bubble* on the board. Then have students work in pairs to brainstorm everything they remember about the village. Elicit sentences from different students around the class and ask students how their lives are similar or different to the Bubbleites.

Grammar in context

Start by looking at the three sentences and eliciting how the passive is formed, i.e. verb *to be* in the correct form + past participle. Then ask students to complete the task. Check their answers and read through the *Remember* box together.

Remind students that they can find more information in the Grammar reference, Unit 12, page 161.

Answers
1 W **2** R **3** R

1 Tell students that active actions are the things we usually do and passive actions are the things that happen to us. Then have them complete the exercise before checking answers in open class.

Answers
1 grow **2** are made **3** are cleaned **4** stay

2 After students complete the exercise, elicit how often some household jobs are done in their house.

Answers
1 The grass is cut every month.
2 The houses are made from wood.
3 This kitchen is cleaned every week.

3 Ask students to complete the exercise individually. Have them compare answers in pairs before you check in open class.

Answers
1 are cooked **2** 's/is kept **3** 's/is opened **4** isn't / is not used **5** are made **6** isn't / is not turned on

4 Ask students to skim the text quickly and find out why the house moves described are unusual (*Because 'moving house' usually means you take your things and go to live in a different house. In these cases people actually move their houses from one place to another.*). Have students complete the exercise. Check their answers and ask students if there are any groups of people in their country that 'move houses' in this way.

Answers
1 are packed **2** 's/is carried **3** is moved **4** are made **5** are picked up **6** are taken **7** isn't / is not done

Optional extension

Explain that the present simple passive is often used to describe a process, like moving house, and allows us to focus the description on the process rather than on the people who do it. Have students work in pairs or small groups and think of a simple process, e.g. *How to make a cup of tea*, and write sentences using the present simple passive to explain how to do it. Walk round, helping students and monitoring them for the correct use of the passive. When students have finished, have them read their sentences to the class.

THINK | RESEARCH | **CULTURE** | LEARN | ME

Put students into groups to discuss the questions. Have them report back what they found out to the class.

Homework OWB
Assign students Grammar 1 exercises 1 and 2 on page 94 of their Workbook.

VOCABULARY
Topic vocabulary | Phrasal verbs | Collocations

→ Student's Book, page 127

Lesson aims

Understand the correct usage of:

- words connected with houses and homes
- phrasal verbs
- verb + noun collocations

Lead-in

Divide the class into five groups and allocate a room in the house to each group: *kitchen, living room, dining room, bedroom, bathroom*. Set a strict time limit of one minute for students to brainstorm the things you usually find in their room. Regroup students so there is one student from each room in each group. Then have students share the vocabulary they thought of.

Words connected with *houses and homes*

1 3.28 After students complete the exercise, play the audio for them to listen and check. Then have them add other items to the lists. Draw students' attention to the picture and elicit what they can see (all items except *armchair, bath, fridge, toilet* and *towel*).

Answers/Audioscript

kitchen: chair, cooker, fridge, sink, table
living room: armchair, bookcase, chair, lamp, sofa, table
bathroom: bath, shower, sink, toilet, towel
bedroom: bed, blanket, bookcase, chair, lamp, pillow

2 Ask students to work in pairs or small groups to discuss and decide which item is the odd one out in each group. Check the answers in open class and elicit the reasons. Accept any answers that are properly justified by students.

Suggested answers

1 sofa (all the others are found in a bathroom)
2 fridge (all the others are found in a bedroom)
3 cooker (all the others are found in a living room)
4 bed (all the others are found in a kitchen)
5 blanket (all the others are found in a kitchen)

Refer students to the Vocabulary reference, page 168, for more information on topic vocabulary.

Phrasal verbs

3 3.29 Ask students to complete the exercise. Play the audio for students to listen and check their answers.

Answers/Audioscript

1 (A) My dad grew *up* in a small wooden house in a village.
2 (B) In the evenings, I often lie *down* on my bed and read a book.
3 (B) If you go *out* tonight, take a front door key.
4 (B) My bed is really comfortable so I find it very difficult to get *up* in the morning.
5 (C) Please tidy the dining room and wash *up* your things in the sink before you leave.
6 (C) Can you find *out* how much those new flats cost?

Mixed ability

Give less confident students a paraphrase of the meaning for each of the phrasal verbs in the exercise to help them choose the correct answer (*1 become an adult, 2 get yourself into a horizontal position, 3 leave the house to do something nice, 4 leave your bed, 5 clean objects from the kitchen using water and soap, 6 get information about*).

Ask stronger students to cover Exercise 3 and work through each item as follows: They look at sentence 1, but keep the A–C options covered. They decide what they think the meaning of the phrasal verb is and what they think the missing word could be, then compare their ideas with the A–C options and choose the correct answer. They repeat with items 2–6.

Language note

These phrasal verbs belong to three different categories.

Grow up, lie down, go out and *get up* are intransitive phrasal verbs (with no object). *Find out (information)* is a non-separable phrasal verb, and the object, whether it is a noun or pronoun, will always come after the particle.

Wash up could be problematic as the object can go between the verb and the particle (*wash your things up*) or after the particle (*wash up your things*) when it is a noun, but has to go between the verb and the particle when it is a pronoun (*wash them up*).

4 Ask students to complete the exercise. Have students compare their answers in pairs and then check them in open class.

Answers

1 grew up **2** wash up **3** got up **4** lie down **5** went out

Refer students to the Vocabulary reference, page 168, for more information on phrasal verbs.

Collocations with verbs

5 3.30 Remind students that verb + noun collocations are very common in English and that they have seen sets of these in Units 3, 5, 7 and 10. Ask students to complete the exercise, and play the audio for them to check their answers.

Answers/Audioscript

1 (e) wash the floor **2** (d) tidy your room **3** (b) make my bed
4 (c) do the washing-up **5** (f) have a shower **6** (a) move house

6 Give students one minute to try to memorise the collocations in Exercise 5. Then ask them to cover them and try to complete the exercise. Students can look back and check their answers at the end. Check answers in open class.

Answers
1 do the washing-up **2** has a shower **3** tidy your room
4 wash the floor **5** move house **6** makes my bed

Refer students to the Vocabulary reference, page 168, for more information on collocations.

Homework OWB
Assign students Vocabulary exercises 1, 2 and 3 on pages 94–95 of their Workbook.

LISTENING
Multiple choice

→ Student's Book, page 128 SB

Lesson aims

- Listen to check that your answers are correct
- Practise a multiple-choice exam task

Lead-in

Divide the students into two teams. Call out letters randomly. Ask teams to think of a word they've learnt on the course, which begins with that letter (don't use the letters *I*, *Q*, *X*, *Y* or *Z* as students haven't seen any words beginning with these as part of the active vocabulary on the course). Have students put up their hand when they can think of a word. Choose the first student who puts their hand up and ask him or her to say the word out loud. If it is correct, their team gets a point. Play for a set time. At the end, the team with the most points wins.

1 Ask students to look at the photo and say which country they think the boat is in (*the UK/ England*). Have students work in pairs to discuss the questions. Then elicit some answers from different students around the class.

EXAM SKILL

Checking your answers

Ask students to read the tips.

- Remind students they usually hear recordings twice in listening exams, and that they should use both listenings productively. On the first listening, they should only mark answers if they are completely sure. Tell them that if they think they are sure, they should still use the second listening to double-check that they haven't been distracted by words from incorrect options.

2 3.31 Give students enough time to read the instructions, question and possible answers. Play the track twice. Remind students to check their answer, and then check in open class.

Answers
b) in an apartment

3 3.31 Ask students which of the incorrect options they also heard mentioned (*both of them*) before playing the track again. Check answers by asking the opinion of different students.

Answers
a) *... I love watching the boats ...*
c) *When I was younger, I lived in a house in the countryside ...*

4 After students complete the exercise, have them check their answers in pairs.

Answers
a 2 **b** 4 **c** 5 **d** 3 **e** 1

OPTIMISE YOUR EXAM

Multiple choice

Ask students to read the tips.

- Remind students that before they hear the recording they will be given time to read through the questions and the possible answers. Tell them to think of other words that have the same meaning if they have time.
- Explain that a good technique to help them choose the right answers is to listen the first time for **all** the words that are in the options. Tell them to tick or cross out the words to indicate if the information helps ✓ or distracts ✗ them.

Exam task

5 3.32 Tell students they will hear Heidi speaking to her friend. Elicit what they will talk about (*living on a boat*). Play the track. Then check answers in open class.

Answers
1 A **2** C **3** C **4** B **5** A

Optional extension 3.32

Write these true/false sentences on the board to check students' comprehension. Play the track again and then check students' answers.

1 Heidi is thirteen years old.

2 There aren't many differences between living on a boat and living in a house.

3 Things on the river change a lot.

4 It is always very cold on the boat in the winter.

Answers
1 F (She says *four years ago, when I was ten* so she must be 14.)
2 F (*It's very different from living in a house.*)
3 T (*Every day, you see something different on the river.*)
4 F (She says *in the winter we have a fire in the living room* and that *with the heating, it's nice and warm inside in the winter.*)

SAY IT RIGHT

/b/ and /v/

For the *Say it right* pronunciation activity and instructions, go to the Teacher's Resource Centre.

TRC

Homework

Assign students Listening exercises 1, 2 and 3 on page 96 of their Workbook.

OWB

GRAMMAR 2

Past simple passive and *by*

→ Student's Book, page 129

SB

Lesson aims

- Understand the correct usage of the past simple passive with *by*
- Practise talking about past actions where the action is more important than the person who did it
- Design a small home on wheels

Lead-in

Write these jumbled questions on the board and ask students to reorder them:

a / like / What's / living / on / boat / it / ?

boat / a / What / do / most / you / about / living / on / like / ?

Tell students that the questions are from the interview with Heidi on the listening page. Ask them if they can remember how she answered.

Answers

What's it like living on a boat? (it's very different from living in a house) What do you like most about living on a boat? (you see something different every day)

Grammar in context

Ask students to read the extract from the audio and look at the sentences below it. Check their answers and read through the sentence in the *Remember* box together. Answer any questions students have about the grammar point.

Remind students that they can find more information in the Grammar reference, Unit 12, page 161.

Answers

1 No, they didn't. **2** Yes, we do. **3** No, we don't.

1 After students complete the exercise, check answers in open class. Then explain that in each case, the passive is used because we are more interested in the first part of the sentence than the person mentioned.

Answers

1 my grandmother **2** the manager **3** the pupils in Year 8 **4** my mother **5** a man from Scotland **6** a team of 30 men

Extra support

Write these sentences halves on the board for students to match:

1 Romeo and Juliet *was written*

2 The Mona Lisa *was painted*

3 The Taj Mahal was built

4 The Pompidou centre in Paris was designed

5 The opera Tosca *was composed*

a) by Shah Jahan.

b) by Leonardo Da Vinci.

c) by Giacomo Puccini.

d) by William Shakespeare.

e) by Richard Rogers.

Check answers in open class. Explain to students that if they look up information about, for example, *Romeo and Juliet*, they might find a sentence like this one. However, if they look up 'William Shakespeare', they will probably find sentences like *William Shakespeare wrote many famous plays, including* Romeo and Juliet .... Point out that the passive is often used to help us put the thing we are most interested in at **the start** of the sentence.

Answers

1 d **2** b **3** a **4** e **5** c

2 Ask students to complete the exercise. Have them compare their answers in pairs before checking them in open class.

Answers

1 were given **2** was interviewed **3** were written **4** were taught **5** was made **6** was moved

3 Have students complete the exercise individually. Then check answers in open class.

Answers

1 The fruit trees were bought by my father.
2 My parents were driven home by a taxi driver.
3 The beds were made every morning by the hotel staff.
4 Our new house was designed by a man called Jasper.
5 The English tests weren't marked by our teacher.

4 Before students start reading, elicit the meaning of the word *trailer* by asking them to scan the article very quickly to find the definition (*a metal floor on wheels*). Then have students complete the exercise in pairs before you check their answers in open class.

Answers

1 wasn't given **2** was told **3** was helped **4** were given **5** were used **6** was spent **7** was finished **8** was made **9** is asked **10** is known

Fast finishers

Ask students to write definitions for the words *chance* (*opportunity*), *tree house* (*a house for children built in a tree*) and *documentary* (*film about real events or people*). As you check the answers to Exercise 4, encourage students to explain the meaning of these words if other students are unsure of them.

5 After students complete the exercise, have them work in pairs to practise asking and answering the questions.

Answers
1 his dad and his friends **2** friends and family **3** a journalist, Kirsten Dirksen **4** local schools

THINK | RESEARCH | CULTURE | LEARN | **ME**

Have students design their home and label their plans individually. Divide the class into pairs or small groups to show each other their homes and explain the features they have chosen. Display homes around the classroom and have students vote for the one they like best.

Homework OWB

Assign students Grammar 2 exercises 1, 2 and 3 on page 95 of their Workbook.

Assign students the Flipped classroom tasks on page 130 of their Student's Book if you'd like them to prepare for the next lesson. To complete this task, students need to watch the *Talk2Me* video which can be found on the Resource Centre.

SPEAKING
Collaborative task

→ Student's Book, page 130 SB

Lesson aims

- Focus on talking about money
- Practise checking you understand in a collaborative task

The *Talk2Me* video in this unit focuses on a visit from a relative. The people in the video talk about their favourite school subject, art, and a visit from a relative.

Students answer some comprehension questions and then listen for key phrases in the video.

The video can be used in one of two ways:

Flipped classroom

Flipped classroom option

Using this approach, students watch the video and complete the exercises for homework. This prepares students for the speaking lesson by introducing them to the topic and the key phrases to use in the exam task. Teachers who use this method will find they have more class time to spend on activating the target language and developing fluency for the final task.

Talk2Me worksheet

Ask students to also complete the *Talk2Me* worksheet on the Resource Centre for more detailed comprehension exercises and more practice of the key phrases.

Classroom option

1 Ask students to spend a minute or two reading the questions. Play the *Talk2Me* video for students to complete the exercise. Play the video again, if necessary, before checking their answers.

2 Play the *Talk2Me* video again, so students underline the phrases in the *Phrase expert* box. Pause the video from time to time if necessary. Check answers in open class.

Talk2Me worksheet

Ask students to also complete the *Talk2Me* worksheet on the Resource Centre for more detailed comprehension exercises and more practice of the key phrases.

Answers
The transcript and answer key for the *Talk2Me* video exercises and Worksheet can be found on the Teacher's Resource Centre.

Lead-in

Dictate some examples of specific information – prices, times, numbers, dates, etc. and ask students to write them down, e.g. *£5.50, 3:45 pm, the 19th of January 2012, 367, £9.71*. Give students time to compare with a partner and then invite volunteers to write an answer on the board. If time, different students could dictate more items.

3 Ask students to describe the photo (*The room is a bedroom. There is a bed with a black and white blanket and two pillows. There is a bookshelf and a guitar in the room.*). Then have them discuss the questions. Elicit answers from different students around the class.

EXAM SKILL

Talking about money

Ask students to read the tips.

- Encourage students to practise talking about money in different contexts, e.g. shopping, travel tickets, museum/theatre tickets, prices on a menu. If they are confident about expressing prices, they will be able to answer questions or make comparisons more easily.
- Explain that being able to deal with minor problems of understanding is expected in exams at this level. Point out that using appropriate phrases to check understanding or to ask the examiner or their partner to repeat something can improve their mark, as it demonstrates their ability to manage a conversation. Explain that reformulating (repeating what the examiner or your partner has said, either as a question or in an answer) also shows very clearly that candidates are listening to each other.

4 3.33 Have students read the prompts to get an idea of the questions they can expect to hear. Play the audio for students to listen and number. Check answers in open class prompting students to say the full questions. Point out that the student asks the questions in a different order but covers them all.

Answers

1 What can we see (at the Family Home show)? **2** What does a student ticket cost? **3** What can I buy at the show? **4** What time does it open? **5** How much is the car park?

5 3.33 Play the track again for students to listen and complete the exercise. Elicit the answers from different students around the class.

Suggested answers

You can see more than 50 rooms.
A student ticket costs £5.00. / An adult ticket costs £10.00.
It opens at 9 am. / It closes at 4 pm.

OPTIMISE YOUR EXAM

Collaborative task

Ask students to read the tips.

- Tell students to read through the information and look at the prompts in the time they are given. Point out that they will not have enough time to write out everything they are going to say, and that it is better to read through everything and anticipate what they have to say. Remind students to check they have asked all five questions.
- Remind students that using appropriate phrases to ask their partner for clarification or to repeat what they have said will not only help them to understand the information, but will also leave a good impression on the examiner.

6 3.34 Play the track for students to complete the exercise. Then have students work in pairs to practise asking the questions. Check answers in open class.

Answers

1 sorry **2** that **3** louder **4** spell **5** say

Mixed ability

Write the following words on the board:
say hear speak spell that louder sorry understand

Tell weaker students to listen and complete the sentences with words from the board. Explain that there are three words they do not need to use. Ask stronger students to close their books, listen to the conversations and pick out the useful phrases for checking understanding and write them down. Check both groups' answers after they have listened.

Exam task

7 Assign each student a letter, A or B, and put them into A/B pairs. Give them a moment to look at their information / question topics on page 138/141. Time students (two minutes) and give them an update, e.g. *One minute to go …* Remind students to use phrases from the *Phrase expert* box and to use appropriate questions to check the meaning of anything their partner says that they don't understand before continuing. Walk round, monitoring students for good use of language and errors to go over at the end of the activity. Write any errors on the board and go through them with students, eliciting corrections from them where possible. After the class feedback, students could then repeat this activity with another partner, to try to improve their performance.

Suggested answers

Student A's questions

What's for sale? Is it big or small?
Has it got a dining room? When can I see it?
What's the email address?

Student B's questions

What can I/you see? Is it big or small?
Are there any bookshelves? What's the telephone number?
Is it closed on Sundays?

Homework

Assign students Speaking exercises 1, 2 and 3 on pages 96–97 of their Workbook.

OWB

LANGUAGE IN USE

Multiple-choice sentences

→ Student's Book, page 131 SB

Lesson aims

- Focus on learning and identifying appropriate vocabulary
- Practise a multiple-choice exam task
- Learn new vocabulary by writing sentences

Lead-in

Write the prepositions *at*, *for*, *with* and *in* on the board. Have students work in pairs and brainstorm all the words they can think of that often come before or after the prepositions, e.g. *come in*, *in the morning*, *look at*, *at home*. Have students share their lists with the class. Write some of them on the board as examples to refer to in the *Exam skill* section (see below).

1 After students complete the exercise, have them report any similarities or differences to the class.

EXAM SKILL

Learning vocabulary

Ask students to read the tips.

- Remind students that they have seen a lot of different types of collocations and phrases in this course, and that it is important to learn them as 'chunks of language'. These are commonly tested in exams, particularly in multiple-choice cloze and open-cloze exam tasks.
- Point out, for example, that they have already seen lots of different uses of prepositions in the course, e.g. in phrasal verbs (*go in*, *come in*), in time expressions (*at midnight*, *in summer*) and in verb + preposition collocations (*stay in*, *listen to*).

2 Ask students to complete the exercise. Check their answers.

Answers
1 want **2** made **3** strong **4** mind **5** done **6** worried

3 Ask students to complete the exercise. Then have them compare their answers in pairs before you check them in open class.

Answers
1 good **2** went **3** tired **4** arrived **5** corner

Optional extension

Ask students to look back at sentences 1–4 in Exercise 3 and underline the adjective + preposition phrases (*good for, interested in, tired of, ready for*). Have students write personalised sentences using three of the adjective + preposition combinations individually. Put students into pairs to read their sentences to each other with the adjectives + prepositions missing and encourage their partners to guess the correct answers.

OPTIMISE YOUR EXAM

Multiple-choice sentences

Ask students to read the tips.

- Remind students that in the Reading section in this unit they saw how the person a pronoun/adjective refers to might be quite a long way from the gap. Point out that in the case of prepositions, the words they need to make reference to are likely to be closer to the gap.
- Tell students to use their instinct when choosing options they don't know the answers to. Remind them that it is always best to justify an answer, but if this is not possible, guess.

Exam task

4 Focus students' attention on the picture and elicit where the house might be (*It's in Scotland.*). Then have students complete the exercise. Check answers in open class.

Answers
1 C **2** A **3** B **4** C **5** B

THINK | RESEARCH | CULTURE | **LEARN** | ME

Before students write their sentences, remind them that it is always a good idea to write an example sentence when they record new vocabulary. Using the language in context helps them to remember it better. When they have finished, have them share their sentences in pairs.

Homework OWB

Assign students Language in Use exercises 1, 2 and 3 on page 97 of their Workbook.

WRITING
A postcard

→ Student's Book, pages 132–133 SB

Lesson aims

- Focus on using adjectives
- Plan and write a postcard

Lead-in

Draw the following table on the board:

	city	*village*
good		
bad		

Elicit a few examples to show students how to complete the table, e.g. *good–city: lots of places to go out, public transport; good–village: very quiet, clean air.*

Have students work in pairs to complete the table with good and bad aspects of city and village life. Have them share their answers with the class, and then collate their ideas on the board.

1 Tell students to answer the questions, giving reasons for their answers. Elicit answers from different students around the class.

EXAM SKILL

Using adjectives

Ask students to read the tips.

- Remind students that some adjectives are followed by specific prepositions, as they saw in the Language in Use section. Tell them they need to use the correct prepositions after adjectives in their written work too.
- Tell students that they should use a wide variety of adjectives. Explain that they should use synonyms instead of repeating adjectives they have already used. Point out that using different words with the same meaning shows the examiner that they know lots of vocabulary and this will increase their mark.
- Explain that using adjectives with *-ed* and *-ing* correctly can also help increase their mark.

2 Ask students to add more positive and negative adjectives to the list after they complete the exercise. Check students' answers and lists in open class.

Answers
1 attractive, comfortable, exciting, popular
2 awful, boring, horrible, terrible

3 Ask students which two adjectives in Exercise 2 also have *-ed* forms (*boring/bored* and *exciting/excited*). Remind them that we use *-ed* adjectives to describe how people feel and *-ing* adjectives for the things that make them feel that way, e.g. *I was excited because the film was exciting*. After students complete the exercise, elicit answers from students around the class.

Answers
1 amazing **2** bored **3** interested **4** exciting **5** tired

4 Ask students who the postcard is from (*George*) and to (*Ella*), then have them complete the exercise individually. Have students check their answers in pairs.

Answers
1 Where is your house? **2** What can you see from your bedroom window? **3** What do you like about your home?

5 Tell students to read both postcards before they answer the questions. Then check their answers in open class.

Answer
Postcard B is better. The writer answers all the questions, uses adjectives to describe the places and uses *because* to explain why.

OPTIMISE YOUR EXAM

A postcard

Ask students to read the tips.

- Remind students that there are three key areas here if they want to get the best possible mark. Firstly, students need to complete the task correctly, so they should make sure they are totally clear about the three questions they need to answer before they start.
- Students should also demonstrate a basic understanding of the concept of 'register', i.e. formal or informal language. As this is a postcard to a friend, it should be relaxed and friendly – though this doesn't mean spelling mistakes or poor grammar are allowed!
- Finally, tell students that they need to include as much variety in their description as possible. Students have seen lots of useful adjectives in this unit, so they should try to use some of them in their answer.

Exam task

6 Students complete the exercise. As you check the answers in open class, ask students what type of information each question asks for.

Answers
Where do you live? (place) How long have you lived there? (period of time) What's near your home? (places)

7 **Plan** Ask students to complete the writing plan. You may want to look at the students' plans to check them and give advice and suggestions for improvement before they take the next step.

Extra support

Look at the plan with students. Put students into pairs or small groups to brainstorm ideas to answer the three questions. Encourage them to share their ideas with the class and collate them on the board, so all students have plenty to choose from before they start writing.

8 **Write** Students write their postcard. If there is not enough time, set this and the subsequent checklist exercise for homework.

9 **Check** Students complete the checklist before they hand in their postcard.

Optional extension

For a slightly longer writing task, and for students to see other text types, refer them to one of the six tasks in the Writing reference (SB p169). Each one includes an annotated sample text and related writing task to challenge your students a little more.

Homework OWB

Assign students Writing exercises 1, 2, 3, 4 and 5 on page 98 of their Workbook and Progress check 12 on page 99.

Answers PROGRESS CHECK Units 11–12

Exercise 1
1 pilot **2** journalist **3** farmer **4** shop assistant **5** engineer **6** dentist **7** firefighter **8** waiter/waitress **9** cleaner **10** receptionist

Exercise 2
1 cooker **2** fridge **3** sink **4** lamp **5** pillow **6** table **7** armchair **8** bath **9** cupboard **10** blanket

Exercise 3
1 A **2** C **3** C **4** B **5** A **6** B **7** A **8** C

Exercise 4
1 was closed **2** was given **3** bought **4** aren't taught **5** didn't repair **6** was taken **7** weren't told **8** moved **9** are worn **10** was paid **11** wrote **12** are made

Exercise 5
1 that/which **2** that/which **3** who **4** of **5** for **6** to **7** up **8** in **9** with **10** is

OPTIMISE YOUR EXAMS

The ***Optimise your exams*** pages are designed to give your students extra training in exam tasks. Each task includes OPTIMISE boxes, which contain tips for students. Remind students to read these boxes before they start each of the exam tasks.

Students can work on the tasks in class or for homework, and the tasks can be done at whatever stage you feel is most appropriate for your class.

Your students should complete these pages before they move on to the Practice test in the Workbook.

READING AND WRITING
SB pages 142–145

1

1 This place is closed this afternoon. G

2 You can try this activity tomorrow morning. D

3 You can't go through this door. E

4 This place is never closed. H

5 You can't use your mobile phone here. B

2

1 C **2** A **3** B **4** B **5** C

3

1 It's a new film.

2 The new music one.

3 No. I sent a text.

4 Why can't you?

5 I forgot to ask.

4

Students' own answers

5

1 A **2** C **3** B **4** B **5** A **6** A **7** C

6

1 C **2** A **3** B **4** A **5** C **6** C **7** A **8** C

7

1 farmer

2 journalist

3 staff

4 customer

5 receptionist

8

1 on **2** for **3** in **4** There **5** were **6** which **7** the **8** had **9** part **10** chose

9

A

LEARN TO DANCE SALSA

Join us to learn salsa in these free weekly classes at Green's Leisure Centre

Thursday 3:45–5:45 pm
Room 16B

Extra beginners' classes
Saturday 2–4 pm
Room 24

B

We don't have to pay = free

10

1 Salsa

2 Saturday

3 1:30

4 24

5 something to drink

11

Tom asks three questions:

What film do you want to watch?

What time is it on?

Can my friend come?

LISTENING SB pages 146–147

1

1 B **2** B **3** B **4** A **5** C

2

1 G **2** D **3** F **4** H **5** B

3

Suggested answers

1 are going, with (name of person)

2 time, start (a time)

3 latest song (name of song)

4 are going (form of transport)

5 tickets cost (price)

4

1 A **2** C **3** A **4** C **5** A

5 and 6

1 Thursday

2 6:30

3 *Macbeth*

4 Mayberry

5 12.50

7

1 Guide Dogs
2 Sam
3 cake morning
4 £240
5 01926 44 57 92

SPEAKING SB pages 148–149

1–2

The transcript and answer key for the *Speaking test* video can be found on the Teacher's Resource Centre.

3

Suggested answers

What's your name?
How do you spell your surname?
Where do you come from?
What are your hobbies?
What things do you like doing?
What do you usually do at the weekend / weekends?
How many people are (there) in your family?
Who is your best friend?
What do you do together?
What subjects do you study?
and students' own answers

4–5

The transcript and answer key for the *Speaking test* video can be found on the Teacher's Resource Centre.

6

Suggested answers

Student A

What can you see there / at the museum?
When does it open?
How much does a student ticket cost?
Is there a car park?
Is there a website?

Student B

When is the school party?
Is it for all students?
What's the address?
What do we do?
How do we get more information?

Workbook Answer Key

UNIT 1

Pages 4–5

Reading

Exercise 1
1 T **2** F **3** F **4** F

Exercise 2
1 planning **2** foreign **3** often **4** join **5** online **6** favourite **7** member **8** video games

Exercise 3
1 H **2** E **3** D **4** C **5** G

Exercise 4
1 talk **2** give money **3** door **4** become a member **5** going inside **6** people

Page 6

Grammar 1

Exercise 1
1 f **2** d **3** a **4** e **5** b **6** c

Exercise 2
1 Joanna never goes to bed after 10pm.
2 You don't play computer games every day.
3 My parents often go shopping on Saturday.
4 Mike usually goes cycling three times a week.
5 We always take photos on holiday.
6 I sometimes visit the museum at the weekend.

Exercise 3
1 D **2** F **3** A **4** B **5** E **6** C

Page 7

Vocabulary

Exercise 1
1 collect **2** photograph **3** tent **4** magazines **5** swimming **6** rock climbing

Exercise 2
1 painter **2** music **3** photograph **4** guitar **5** games **6** musicians

Exercise 3
1 a **2** b **3** c **4** c **5** c **6** b

Page 7

Grammar 2

Exercise 1
1 My mother's favourite hobby is painting.
2 Please look after Anna's camera. It is new.
3 Do you know Mike's brother and sister?
4 Greg's daughter is only three years old.
5 Would you like to see my sister's holiday photos?
6 This is Jim's book. He needs it for his homework.

Exercise 2
1 B **2** C **3** B **4** A **5** A **6** C **7** C **8** B **9** A **10** C

Page 8

Listening

Exercise 1
1 C **2** B **3** A

Exercise 2
1 A **2** B **3** B **4** B **5** C

Page 8

Speaking

Exercise 1
1 f **2** d **3** b **4** a **5** e **6** c

Exercise 2
1 What's/is your name? **2** Where do you live? **3** What are your hobbies? **4** What's/is your favourite sport? **5** What do you usually do in the summer holiday? **6** How often do you play video games?

Exercise 3
Students' own answers

Page 9

Language in Use

Exercise 1
1 b **2** a **3** b **4** a **5** b **6** a

Exercise 2
1 E **2** B **3** D **4** H **5** C

Page 10

Writing

Exercise 1
1 T **2** F **3** F **4** F **5** F **6** T

Exercise 2
1 Bristol **2** 13 **3** photography **4** Tuesday **5** 13:30

Exercise 3
Students' own answers

Exercise 4
Students' own answers

Page 11

Progress check

Exercise 1
1 magazines **2** guitarist **3** turn off **4** join **5** look after **6** painting **7** get off **8** member

Exercise 2
1 b **2** b **3** a **4** b **5** c **6** c **7** b **8** a

Cumulative progress

Exercise 3
1 C **2** A **3** B **4** A **5** B

UNIT 2

Pages 12–13

Reading

Exercise 1
1 International Youth Arts Festival, summer
2 festival, different country, every year
3 Most, singers and dancers, Britain

Exercise 2
1 A **2** B **3** C

Exercise 3
1 A **2** B **3** A **4** B **5** A **6** C **7** C

Exercise 4
1 festival **2** shows **3** musicians **4** instrument **5** plays **6** concerts

Page 14

Grammar 1

Exercise 1
1 are you doing **2** 'm watching **3** love **4** think **5** prefer **6** are **7** are showing **8** Do you want

Exercise 2
1 goes **2** '/is making **3** are having **4** wants **5** plays **6** isn't / is not raining **7** comes, lives **8** acts, 's/is acting

Page 14

Vocabulary

Exercise 1
1 art gallery **2** concert hall **3** gaming café **4** opera house **5** theatre **6** museum

Exercise 2
1 in **2** in **3** at **4** out **5** with **6** to

Exercise 3
1 a **2** c **3** a **4** c **5** b

Page 15

Grammar 2

Exercise 1
1 's/is moving **2** 's/is meeting **3** are selling **4** starts **5** are playing **6** 's/is singing

Exercise 2
1 'm/am meeting **2** are, doing **3** 's/is happening **4** want **5** are playing **6** are, playing **7** do, want **8** don't think **9** are visiting **10** 're/are going

Page 16

Listening

Exercise 1
1 f **2** e **3** a **4** b **5** d **6** c

Exercise 2
C The Carltons are an excellent band.

Exercise 3
1 C **2** F **3** A **4** H **5** E

Page 16
Speaking
Exercise 1
1 b **2** e **3** a **4** c **5** d
Exercise 2
1 on Fridays **2** from seven until nine **3** What time does **4** starts at 7:30 pm **5** does it last **6** it finishes at **7** on Saturday

Page 17
Language in Use
Exercise 1
1 A **2** A **3** B **4** C **5** A **6** B
Exercise 2
1 exercise **2** Would you like to go **3** Can I speak to **4** help me, book **5** time, start **6** cook dinner
Exercise 3
1 B **2** C **3** C **4** B **5** A

Page 18
Writing
Exercise 1
Students should tick: 2, 3, 5
Exercise 2
B
Exercise 3
1 What are you doing on Sunday afternoon? **2** Do you know where that is? **3** Would you like to come with us?
Exercise 4
Students' own answers

Page 19
Progress check
Exercise 1
1 gallery **2** act **3** article **4** concert **5** looking **6** player **7** hip hop **8** programme
Exercise 2
1 live **2** opens **3** are getting **4** Are you playing **5** are waiting **6** think **7** are you listening **8** practises
Cumulative progress
Exercise 3
1 A **2** B **3** A **4** C **5** B **6** C **7** B **8** C

UNIT 3

Pages 20–21
Reading
Exercise 1
1 present **2** past **3** past **4** present **5** past
Exercise 2
1 d **2** b **3** a **4** c
Exercise 3
1 B **2** A **3** C **4** A **5** C **6** B **7** C **8** B
Exercise 4
1 business **2** healthy **3** salad **4** cooks **5** customers

Page 22
Grammar 1
Exercise 1
1 worked **2** started **3** baked **4** cooked **5** cleaned **6** walked **7** needed **8** invited **9** liked **10** learnt
Exercise 2
1 Who did you invite for dinner tonight?
2 Where did you buy those cakes?
3 What did you order for dessert?
4 When did the restaurant open?
5 Which cupcakes did you buy?
6 What can we cook on the barbecue?
Exercise 3
1 Who **2** Where **3** What **4** When **5** Why **6** What

Page 22
Vocabulary
Exercise 1
1 honey **2** cereal **3** Strawberries **4** salt **5** oil **6** steak **7** tomatoes **8** onion
Exercise 2
1 fry **2** boil **3** bake **4** grilled **5** baked
Exercise 3
1 a **2** b **3** a **4** c **5** b **6** c

Page 23
Grammar 2
Exercise 1
1 went **2** bought **3** ate **4** drank **5** did **6** came **7** met **8** got up **9** took **10** made
Exercise 2
1 bought **2** didn't / did not get up **3** didn't / did not eat **4** did, go **5** met **6** drank **7** made **8** didn't / did not do
Exercise 3
Students' own answers

Page 24
Listening
Exercise 1
1 spent a week, Lyon, village, school
2 teacher, course, woman, woman and father, chef
Exercise 2
1 Abi, where **2** Teacher, who
Exercise 3
Suggested key words:
3 weren't, lessons, biscuits, bread, cakes and students' own answers
4 total, three/four/five students and students' own answers
5 Abi, favourite, friends, learning, eating and students' own answers
Exercise 4
1 B **2** B **3** A **4** B **5** C

Page 24
Speaking
Exercise 1
1 What's/is your favourite food? **2** What do you like for breakfast? **3** What did you have for dinner last night? **4** How often do you eat fast food? **5** Which do you prefer, pizza or burgers? **6** Who cooks in your family?
Exercise 2
Students' own answers
Exercise 3
Students' own answers

Page 25
Language in Use
Exercise 1
1 Preposition **2** Pronoun **3** Conjunction **4** Conjunction **5** Preposition **6** Conjunction
Exercise 2
1 on **2** She **3** because **4** and **5** in **6** but
Exercise 3
1 in **2** and **3** it **4** but **5** with **6** because **7** On **8** went **9** they **10** was

Page 26
Writing
Exercise 1
B
Exercise 2
1 make/prepare **2** really **3** ask/invite
Exercise 3
Students' own answers
Exercise 4
Students' own answers

Page 27
Progress check
Exercise 1
1 cereal **2** bakes **3** boiled **4** tomato **5** fried **6** boil **7** yoghurt **8** roast **9** oil **10** grilled
Exercise 2
1 baked **2** decided **3** did, buy **4** looked **5** did, meet **6** didn't / did not go **7** didn't / did not eat **8** took **9** did, think **10** invited
Cumulative progress
Exercise 3
1 In **2** was **3** to **4** son **5** do **6** made/prepared **7** Then **8** his **9** out **10** after

UNIT 4

Pages 28–29
Reading
Exercise 1
A 2 **B** 3 **C** 1
Exercise 2
1 F **2** F **3** F **4** T

Exercise 3
A ✓ **B** ✗ **C** ✓ **D** ✗ **E** ✓ **F** ✓ **G** ✗ **H** ✓
Exercise 4
1 A **2** G **3** C **4** F **5** H
Exercise 5
1 journey **2** paths **3** guide **4** countryside **5** airport **6** tourists

Page 30
Grammar 1
Exercise 1
1 were sitting **2** was selling **3** were, doing **4** was raining
5 were, walking **6** weren't / were not talking **7** were getting
8 Were, making
Exercise 2
1 when **2** but **3** and **4** because **5** When **6** because

Page 30
Vocabulary
Exercise 1
DOWN
1 traffic **3** bridge
ACROSS
2 roundabout **4** miss **5** railway **6** delay
Exercise 2
1 licence **2** news **3** station **4** guide **5** ride **6** machine **7** park **8** boat
Exercise 3
1 b **2** c **3** c **4** b **5** c **6** a

Page 31
Grammar 2
Exercise 1
1 happened **2** were staying **3** was buying **4** asked **5** told
6 was leaving **7** found **8** were walking **9** got **10** found

Page 32
Listening
Exercise 1
1 Gary **2** Karol **3** Regent/regent **4** Lanes/lanes
Exercise 2
1 4 hours 15 minutes **2** 1787 **3** 1822 **4** 162
Exercise 3
1 Present **2** 3:45 pm **3** 524 **4** (about) 1:30 **5** shopping

Page 32
Speaking
Exercise 1
a 2 **b** 3 **d** 5 **e** 1 **g** 4
Exercise 2
1 Please could you say that again?
2 Pardon? Did you say from May?
3 I'm sorry. Could you repeat that?
4 Did you say £50?

Page 33
Language in Use
Exercise 1
1 I really enjoy going to the beach, but I don't like swimming in the sea.
2 You should check you have your passport before you go to the airport.
3 My brother can't come with us on holiday this year because he is studying for his exams.
4 We went sightseeing until it got dark then we had dinner.
5 We were driving through the countryside when the car suddenly stopped.
Exercise 2
1 c **2** b **3** a **4** b **5** c

Page 34
Writing
1

	A	B
Are all the questions answered clearly?	YES	NO
Is it easy to understand what the writer means?	YES	YES
Does the postcard start and end in a good way?	YES	YES
Does the writer use interesting words and phrases?	NO	YES
Does the writer use linking words?	NO	YES

Exercise 2
Hi Julio,
I went ~~in~~ **to** Cancun. We ~~were going~~ **went** there by plane. The ~~fly~~ **flight** was five hours. We stayed in a big hotel next **to** the beach and ~~eat~~ **ate** fish every day. I loved it.
Ricardo
Exercise 3
Students' own answers
Exercise 4
Students' own answers

Page 35
Progress check
Exercise 1
1 b **2** d **3** f **4** c **5** h **6** e **7** a **8** g
Exercise 2
1 a **2** c **3** a **4** b **5** c **6** b **7** c **8** a
Cumulative progress
Exercise 3
1 on **2** were **3** went **4** was **5** at **6** near **7** there **8** in/inside **9** at **10** who

UNIT 5

Pages 36–37
Reading
Exercise 1
1 B **2** A **3** B **4** B
Exercise 2
1 incorrect **2** incorrect
Exercise 3
1 C **2** B **3** A **4** A **5** B **6** C **7** C
Exercise 4
1 video **2** laptop **3** websites **4** uploaded **5** share **6** chatting

Page 38
Grammar 1
Exercise 1
1 some **2** A few **3** much **4** A lot of **5** many **6** many **7** a few **8** any
Exercise 2
1 c **2** b **3** **4** a **5** b **6** a **7** c **8** a

Page 38
Vocabulary
Exercise 1
1 keyboard **2** printer **3** laptop **4** mouse **5** screen
6 download, stream **7** software **8** graphics
Exercise 2
1 mobile **2** file **3** DVD **4** site
Exercise 3
1 a **2** c **3** b **4** c **5** a **6** a

Page 39
Grammar 2
Exercise 1
1 faster **2** the best **3** longer **4** more attractive **5** the easiest
6 more interesting **7** the most expensive **8** more popular
Exercise 2
2 The Wave 4.1 is the cheapest.
3 The Kiwi 7 is more popular than the Saphora X2.
4 The Saphora X2 is heavier than the Wave 4.1.
5 The Wave 4.1 is the most popular.
6 The Saphora X2 is lighter than the Kiwi 7.
7 The Kiwi 7 is the most expensive.
8 The Wave 4.1 is bigger than the Saphora X2.

Page 40
Listening
Exercise 1
1 b, c **2** a, d **3** e
Exercise 2
1 A **2** B **3** C **4** C **5** B

Page 40
Speaking
Exercise 1
1 better **2** lighter, faster/faster, lighter **3** interesting **4** cheapest
5 worse **6** most boring
Exercise 2
a 4 **b** 5 **c** 2 **d** 6 **e** 3 **f** 1

Exercise 3
Students' own answers

Page 41
Language in Use
Exercise 1
1 f **2** c **3** a **4** b **5** d **6** e
Exercise 2
1 d **2** a **3** f **4** b **5** c **6** e
Exercise 3
a 5 **b** 3 **c** 4 **d** 1 **e** 2

1 A **2** B **3** B **4** A **5** C

Page 42
Writing
Exercise 1
1 e **2** c **3** a **4** d **5** f **6** b
Exercise 2
1 Tuesdays and Thursdays **2** Tuesdays **3** evening **4** 6:30 pm **5** 6:50 pm
Exercise 3
1 5:30 **2** the weekend **3** Joe **4** the post office **5** the advertisement
Exercise 4
Students' own answers

Page 43
Progress check
Exercise 1
1 a **2** c **3** c **4** a **5** b **6** c **7** b **8** c **9** a **10** c
Exercise 2
1 many **2** any **3** the biggest **4** faster **5** much **6** cheaper **7** the most **8** many
Cumulative progress
Exercise 3
1 B **2** C **3** B **4** A **5** C **6** B **7** A **8** C

UNIT 6

Pages 44–45
Reading
Exercise 1
1 T **2** F **3** F **4** T **5** F **6** F
Exercise 2
1 C **2** A **3** A **4** C **5** B **6** A **7** C **8** B
Exercise 3
1 suit **2** tie **3** necklace **4** sweater **5** scarf **6** earrings

Page 46
Grammar 1
Exercise 1
1 's/has lost **2** 's/has tried on **3** hasn't / has not brought, 's/has left
4 Have, worn, haven't / have not
Exercise 2
1 've/have gone/been **2** 've/have bought **3** 've/have visited
4 've/have, seen **5** haven't / have not gone/been **6** 's/has rained
7 Have, watched **8** 's/has given **9** haven't / have not forgotten
10 've/have found
Exercise 3
1 ever, never **2** ever **3** never **4** ever **5** ever, never **6** ever

Page 47
Vocabulary
Exercise 1
1 credit card **2** receipt **3** department store **4** customer **5** cash
6 shopping centre **7** change **8** supermarket **9** market **10** shopper
Exercise 2
1 down **2** on **3** back **4** for **5** off **6** in
Exercise 3
1 catch **2** keep **3** saving **4** going **5** do **6** for **7** caught **8** been

Page 47
Grammar 2
Exercise 1
1 's/has been, bought **2** got, hasn't / has not worn
3 Did, go, haven't / have not heard **4** opened, 've/have sold
5 've/have seen, got
Exercise 2
1 did, get **2** bought **3** haven't / have not been **4** opened
5 Have, bought **6** 've/have been **7** haven't / have not had

Page 48
Listening
Exercise 1
B
Exercise 2
Aaron: There aren't many things that I really care about. There's my wallet, and also this watch. My parents gave it to me last year just before the holidays when I passed my exams.
Kim: What a cool thing to have.
Exercise 3
1 D **2** F **3** G **4** A **5** H

Page 48
Speaking
Exercise 1
1 What is the market called? **2** Is the market open on Mondays?
3 What is the address? **4** Is there a car park? **5** What is the telephone number?
Exercise 2
1 It's called Eastland Market.
2 No, the market is open every day except Mondays. / The market is not open on Mondays.
3 The address is 365 George Street.
4 Yes, there's/is a free car park on Ash Road.
5 The telephone number is / It's 02778 856455.

Page 49
Language in Use
Exercise 1
1 g **2** h **3** a **4** d **5** b **6** e **7** c **8** f
Exercise 2
1 A **2** C **3** B **4** A **5** C
Exercise 3
1 C **2** F **3** A **4** D **5** G

Page 50
Writing
Exercise 1

	A	B
What you bought		✓
Why you bought it	✓	
Why you were surprised	✓	✓

Exercise 2
1 because **2** unfortunately **3** really **4** back
Exercise 3
Students' own answers
Exercise 4
Students' own answers

Page 51
Progress check
Exercise 1
1 store **2** centre **3** assistant **4** customers **5** shopping **6** try **7** costs
8 for **9** credit **10** receipt
Exercise 2
1 b **2** a **3** a **4** a **5** c **6** c **7** b **8** c
Cumulative progress
Exercise 3
1 B **2** B **3** A **4** B **5** C

UNIT 7

Pages 52–53
Reading
Exercise 1
1 these **2** they **3** they **4** it **5** that
Exercise 2
1 A **2** B **3** B **4** A **5** A
Exercise 3
1 B **2** A **3** C **4** B **5** C **6** A **7** B **8** C
Exercise 4
1 scientist **2** lesson **3** secondary **4** homework **5** pupils/students
6 break

Page 54
Grammar 1
Exercise 1
1 Are, going to **2** isn't / is not going to **3** am, going to **4** aren't / are not going to **5** 'm/am going to **6** 's/is going to **7** Are, going to **8** isn't / is not going to **9** aren't / are not going to **10** 's/is going to
Exercise 2
1 Brad's/is going to visit relatives.
2 Mo's/is going to study for the exams.
3 Katie's/is going to work in a shop.
4 Brad and Mo are going to go to summer camp.
5 Katie isn't / is not going to go to summer camp.
6 Brad and Katie are going to go to the beach.
7 Mo and Brad aren't / are not going to work in a shop.
8 Mo isn't / is not going to visit relatives.

Page 54
Vocabulary
Exercise 1
1 desk **2** bookshelf **3** maths **4** dictionary **5** geography **6** history **7** board **8** biology
Exercise 2
1 from **2** at **3** with **4** from **5** about **6** at
Exercise 3
1 f **2** d **3** e **4** a **5** c **6** b

Page 55
Grammar 2
Exercise 1
1 's/is going to leave
2 'll/will show
3 's/is going to rain
4 won't / will not break
5 aren't / are not going to win
6 are, going to do

Page 56
Listening
Exercise 1
1 an age **2** a piece of technology **3** a place **4** a place **5** a description
Exercise 2
1 18 **2** mobile phones **3** home **4** lessons **5** excellent

Page 56
Speaking
Exercise 1
1 When **2** Tomorrow **3** future **4** plan **5** years' time **6** Next
Exercise 2
1 future plans **2** future plans **3** predictions **4** future plans **5** predictions **6** future plans
Exercise 3
Students' own answers

Page 57
Language in Use
Exercise 1
1 b **2** a **3** c **4** b **5** a **6** b
Exercise 2
1 have **2** make **3** learn **4** on **5** study **6** take
Exercise 3
1 A **2** C **3** A **4** C **5** B **6** C **7** A **8** C **9** B **10** A

Page 58
Writing
Exercise 1
1 F **2** T **3** T **4** T **5** F **6** F
Exercise 2
1 pm **2** trainers, shorts and blue and white T-shirts **3** haven't got enough **4** write your name down on **5** Message
Exercise 3
Students' own answers
Exercise 4
Students' own answers

Page 59
Progress check
Exercise 1
ACROSS
3 board **5** remember **8** library **9** help
DOWN
1 dictionary **2** course **4** geography **6** biology **7** taught
Exercise 2
1 a **2** c **3** a **4** b **5** c **6** c **7** b **8** a
Cumulative progress
Exercise 3
1 take/do **2** about **3** on **4** many/any **5** at **6** not **7** started **8** from **9** lot **10** will

UNIT 8

Pages 60–61
Reading
Exercise 1
1 2015 **2** 2016 **3** 2014 **4** 2016
Exercise 2
1 Josh Bayliss comes from a large city. **2** There were many pupils at Josh's school.
Exercise 3
1 B **2** C
Exercise 4
1 B **2** A **3** C **4** B **5** A **6** B **7** C
Exercise 5
1 grew up **2** international **3** last **4** fitter **5** look after **6** bad luck

Page 62
Grammar 1
Exercise 1
1 can **2** couldn't **3** Could **4** could **5** can't **6** couldn't **7** can't **8** Can
Exercise 2
1 have to **2** don't have to **3** have to **4** has to **5** don't have to **6** have to
Exercise 3
1 may stay **2** needn't / don't need to drive **3** mustn't / must not run **4** must stay **5** Do, need to bring **6** may win

Page 62
Vocabulary
Exercise 1
1 racket **2** swimsuit **3** ticket **4** ride **5** coach **6** kit
Exercise 2
1 swims **2** won **3** runner **4** player **5** surf
Exercise 3
1 e **2** f **3** d **4** a **5** c **6** b

Page 63
Grammar 2
Exercise 1
1 Could/Can **2** can **3** can't **4** could **5** Can **6** could
Exercise 2
1 shouldn't eat **2** should wear **3** should get **4** shouldn't talk **5** shouldn't worry **6** should play
Exercise 3
1 couldn't / could not go **2** Could/Can, open **3** should buy **4** mustn't / must not use

Page 64
Listening
Exercise 1
1 d **2** e **3** a **4** b **5** c
Exercise 2
1 a **2** b **3** b **4** b **5** a
Exercise 3
1 F **2** D **3** E **4** G **5** C

Page 64
Speaking
Exercise 1
1 is the **2** is the competition **3** can/do you **4** Is it **5** What is the
Exercise 2
1 City Sports Centre **2** 22 (to) 25 July **3** a sports kit for your team **4** 12–16 **5** 1230 3333
Exercise 3
Suggested answers
1 Where is the competition? It's at Chester Tennis Club. **2** When is the competition? It's on 28 July. **3** What can/do you win? You can win a tennis lesson from a top pro. **4** Is it for children? No, it's for adults only / people over 18. **5** What time does it start? It starts at 10am.

Page 65

Language in Use

Exercise 1

1 must **2** Can **3** couldn't / could not **4** shouldn't / should not **5** may

Exercise 2

1 B **2** A **3** B **4** B **5** A **6** C **7** C **8** C

Page 66

Writing

Exercise 1

Students should tick: 1, 3, 4

Exercise 2

	A	B	C
1	✗	✓	✓
2	✗	✗	✓
3	✗	✓	✓
4	✗	✗	✓
5	✗	✗	✗

The best email is C.

Exercise 3

1 I'm / I am **2** teacher's / teacher is **3** a **4** is **5** have to wear

Exercise 4

Student's own answers

Page 67

Progress check

Exercise 1

1 play **2** teams **3** winner **4** throw **5** kit **6** club **7** coach **8** ticket

Exercise 2

1 can't **2** should **3** could **4** shouldn't **5** Can **6** should **7** Can I **8** don't have to

Cumulative progress

Exercise 3

1 B **2** B **3** A **4** A **5** C

UNIT 9

Pages 68–69

Reading

Exercise 1

1 adults and children **2** magazine **3** the weather

Exercise 2

1 B **2** C **3** A **4** A **5** C

Exercise 3

1 A **2** B **3** B **4** C **5** A **6** C **7** B **8** C

Exercise 4

1 moon **2** grass **3** countryside **4** sky **5** mountains **6** clouds **7** storm **8** lie down

Page 70

Grammar 1

Exercise 1

1 is, runs **2** are, grow **3** is, go **4** swim, is **5** becomes, gets **6** snows, close

Exercise 2

1 feel, 'll/will go **2** Will, play, snows **3** are, 'll/will drive **4** 'll/will get, don't / do not take **5** Will, wait, 'm/am **6** will happen, rains

Exercise 3

1 Rain changes into snow when it's/is very cold.
2 She'll/will take a taxi if it rains.
3 If we get lost, we'll/will phone our parents.
4 When it's/is sunny, I always wear a hat.
5 If the weather gets better, we'll/will have a picnic.
6 Everyone will be happy if it's/is sunny tomorrow.

Page 70

Vocabulary

Exercise 1

1 sky **2** sun **3** river **4** beach **5** clouds **6** rain **7** snow **8** mountain **9** hill **10** forest

Exercise 2

1 We learnt about bears by visiting the forest.
2 Miranda did an experiment to find out about clouds.
3 Scientists are good at finding answers to problems.
4 It's really important to protect nature.
5 The best time to eat this fruit is in September.
6 Martin wants to go to South Africa in the spring.

Exercise 3

1 rainy **2** sun **3** snow **4** foggy **5** ice **6** cloudy

Page 71

Grammar 2

Exercise 1

1 b **2** c **3** a **4** b **5** c **6** c

Exercise 2

2 If there were/was snow on the mountains, I'd/would go skiing.
3 If there were any sheep on the hill, we'd/would see one/them/some.
4 If our teacher liked the sun, we'd/would have lessons outside.
5 If it were/was (very) windy today, we'd/would go sailing.
6 If it weren't / were not / wasn't / was not going to rain, I wouldn't / would not have this umbrella.

Page 72

Listening

Exercise 1

1 T **2** T **3** F

Exercise 2

Mark: Zoe and I got so wet when we went camping last week.
Jen: Did you get caught in that big storm?
Mark: Of course! We were walking to the café for dinner and had to wait under some trees.
Jen: Well, next time, I hope you'll take an umbrella with you!

Exercise 3

1 C **2** B **3** B **4** C **5** A

Page 72

Speaking

Exercise 1

1 your family **2** the places you go on holiday **3** the place where you live **4** your friends

Expressions used to introduce examples: One example is; For example; Let me give you an example

Exercise 2

Students' own answers

Page 73

Language in Use

Exercise 1

1 a **2** c **3** a **4** b **5** c **6** a

Exercise 2

1 it **2** them **3** him **4** This **5** they

Exercise 3

1 A **2** B **3** A **4** A **5** C

Page 74

Writing

Exercise 1

1 Don't forget to take your boots. **2** If I were you, I'd arrive early. **3** Don't walk in the mountains by yourself. **4** It would be better if you didn't drive. **5** Be careful, the roads are icy. **6** I'd read the instructions before you start.

Exercise 2

your bicycle, some clothes, the time to start

Exercise 3

1 Hi **2** I have **3** pleased/happy **4** after school tomorrow / this evening / soon **5** bought/got **6** shop / department store **7** morning **8** Let's **9** 8am **10** soon / after school tomorrow / this evening

Exercise 4

Students' own answers

Page 75

Progress check

Exercise 1

1 sky **2** foggy **3** forest **4** snow **5** river **6** sun **7** rainy/rains **8** thunderstorm **9** windy **10** beach

Exercise 2

1 a **2** b **3** b **4** a **5** c **6** a **7** b **8** a

Cumulative progress

Exercise 3

1 A **2** B **3** B **4** C **5** A **6** B **7** C **8** A

UNIT 10

Pages 76–77

Reading

Exercise 1

1 F **2** T **3** F **4** T **5** T **6** F

Exercise 2
1 overweight **2** government **3** afterwards **4** exercise
5 primary school **6** healthier

Exercise 3
1 C **2** D **3** B **4** F **5** G

Exercise 4
1 footwear **2** expensive **3** closes **4** outdoor wear **5** hire

Page 78

Grammar 1

Exercise 1
1 We've already done our English homework and now we're doing maths.
2 Carrie isn't feeling well, but she hasn't been to the doctor yet.
3 Nick's had a terrible headache since this morning.
4 Pete isn't ill. I've just seen him playing football in the park!
5 My grandad has had this problem for many years.

Exercise 2
1 I can't write because I've/have just hurt my hand.
2 I haven't / have not eaten since breakfast because I have a stomach ache.
3 Josh's/has had a cold for three days so he isn't coming to school.
4 Have you brushed your teeth yet?
5 Nermine's/has just hit her head and now she has a headache.
6 Mike's/has already watched six films today and now his eyes hurt.

Exercise 3
1 for **2** since **3** already **4** just **5** yet

Page 78

Vocabulary

Exercise 1
DOWN
1 throat **4** stomach **5** finger **8** knee
ACROSS
2 hand **3** nose **6** hospital **7** neck **9** eyes

Exercise 2
1 in **2** for **3** to **4** with **5** with **6** for

Exercise 3
1 e **2** b **3** a **4** f **5** d **6** c

Page 79

Grammar 2

Exercise 1
Verbs + infinitive: choose, hope, need, offer, stop, try
Verbs + *-ing*: don't mind, finish, keep, spend time, stop, try

Exercise 2
1 taking **2** to find **3** to brush **4** to eat **5** waiting **6** eating **7** to pay
8 to use

Page 80

Listening

Exercise 1
1 b **2** c **3** e **4** a **5** d

Exercise 2
1 Lola: I had a stomach ache after dinner last night.
2 Tyler: I often get a headache when I play video games.
3 Justin: I've hurt my arm and I can't play tennis.
4 Erin: I had terrible earache on holiday last year.
5 Abdul: I've had a pain in my neck for three days.

Exercise 3
1 B **2** A **3** F **4** G **5** H

Page 80

Speaking

Exercise 1
1 Just a minute, please. **2** Let's have a look at the advert.
3 Looking at the information, it says … **4** Let me think …

Exercise 2
1 Is it open on Mondays? **2** Are there tennis courts?
3 What's the address? **4** What's the telephone number?
5 Is it cheap or expensive to join?

Exercise 3
a 5 **b** 4 **c** 2 **d** 3 **e** 1

Exercise 4
Students' own answers

Page 81

Language in Use

Exercise 1
1 Have, No **2** I would **3** Do, Yes **4** we shouldn't **5** Are there, aren't
6 Will, No, you **7** Is there, Yes **8** Can, Yes, you

Exercise 2
1 G **2** H **3** B **4** D **5** C

Page 82

Writing

Exercise 1
1 shouldn't **2** don't have to **3** mustn't **4** should **5** must

Exercise 2
a 4 **b** 5 **c** 2 **d** 1 **e** 3

Exercise 3
stomach aches, breakfast, some more advice

Exercise 4
1 Hi **2** normal **3** sure **4** think **5** some fruit / breakfast / vegetables / a salad **6** some fruit / vegetables / a salad **7** about **8** some fruit / vegetables / a salad **9** fast food / fried food **10** luck

Exercise 5
Students' own answers

Page 83

Progress check

Exercise 1
1 c **2** a **3** a **4** b **5** b **6** a **7** c **8** a **9** c **10** b

Exercise 2
1 Darren offered to take me to hospital yesterday when I felt ill.
2 Has Carla seen the doctor yet?
3 I usually don't mind helping my grandparents.
4 Lily's/has had the pain for 10 days.
5 Reuben hopes to be a doctor in 10 years' time.
6 When I was in hospital last year, I didn't enjoy eating the food.
7 Zara hasn't had a stomach ache since Monday.
8 Everyone tried to help me when I fell off my bike last night.
9 Pedro has already brushed his teeth and (he's/he) is now in bed.
10 The doctor's/has just arrived.

Cumulative progress

Exercise 3
1 A **2** C **3** B **4** A **5** B

UNIT 11

Pages 84–85

Reading

Exercise 1
1 e **2** d **3** c **4** a **5** f **6** b

Exercise 2
a 2 **b** 6 **c** 4 **d** 5 **e** 3 **f** 1

Exercise 3
1 A **2** B **3** C **4** B **5** B **6** A **7** A **8** C

Exercise 4
1 business **2** customers **3** shampoos **4** poor **5** article **6** earn

Page 86

Grammar 1

Exercise 1
1 c **2** c **3** a **4** b **5** c **6** a

Exercise 2
1 anywhere **2** everything **3** something **4** everyone **5** someone
6 anything

Page 86

Vocabulary

Exercise 1
1 receptionist **2** musician **3** police officer **4** pilot **5** dentist
6 firefighter

Exercise 2
1 actor **2** engineer **3** waiter **4** journalist **5** manager **6** cleaner

Exercise 3
1 in **2** for **3** of **4** with **5** of **6** at

Page 87

Grammar 2

Exercise 1
1 who **2** which **3** which **4** who **5** which **6** which

Exercise 2
1 that **2** who **3** that **4** that **5** that **6** who

Page 88

Listening

Exercise 1
1 Maria **2** Star **3** London **4** companies **5** jobs

Exercise 2
1 Madrid **2** pet **3** eat **4** test **5** over 2,000

Page 88
Speaking
Exercise 1
1 c **2** a **3** b **4** a **5** c
Exercise 2
1 'm/am getting ready **2** work **3** play **4** 'm/am learning **5** work **6** usually start **7** 'm/am repairing **8** 'm/am saving
Exercise 3
Students' own answers.

Page 89
Language in Use
Exercise 1
1 c **2** a **3** e **4** b **5** f **6** d
Exercise 2
1 the **2** who **3** have **4** than **5** for **6** anything **7** someone **8** up **9** was **10** something

Page 90
Writing
Exercise 1
1 interesting **2** hard-working **3** over **4** closed **5** near **6** not expensive
Exercise 2
1 Aunt Annie's Restaurant **2** 15 **3** Monday **4** friendly **5** free
Exercise 3
Students' own answers
Exercise 4
Students' own answers

Page 91
Progress check
Exercise 1
1 meeting **2** boss **3** uniform **4** factory **5** journalist **6** customers **7** receptionist **8** staff **9** dentist **10** farmer
Exercise 2
1 who **2** which **3** anyone **4** someone **5** which **6** Everywhere **7** something **8** who **9** everything **10** anywhere
Cumulative progress
Exercise 3
1 C **2** A **3** B **4** C **5** A **6** C **7** C **8** B

UNIT 12

Pages 92–93
Reading
Exercise 1
1 F **2** T **3** T **4** F **5** T **6** F
Exercise 2
1 most people's **2** everyone's **3** everyone's **4** the sheets and blankets **5** your favourite pop or film star **6** the clothes
Exercise 3
1 C **2** B **3** A **4** C **5** B **6** A **7** B **8** A
Exercise 4
1 pillow **2** carpet **3** blankets **4** mirror **5** screen **6** lamps

Page 94
Grammar 1
Exercise 1
1 is usually made before breakfast **2** flats aren't built **3** is opened with a key **4** are washed every week **5** are watered **6** is made in that factory
Exercise 2
1 is owned **2** is often heard **3** is looked after **4** are turned on **5** are shown **6** aren't eaten **7** are eaten **8** is cleaned

Page 94
Vocabulary
Exercise 1
1 bed **2** pillows **3** lamp **4** blanket **5** bath **6** armchair **7** sofa **8** shower **9** towel **10** toilet **11** bookcase **12** cupboard **13** table **14** fridge **15** sink **16** cooker
Exercise 2
1 out **2** up **3** up **4** out **5** down **6** up
Exercise 3
1 do **2** tidied **3** move **4** makes **5** has **6** washes

Page 95
Grammar 2
Exercise 1
1 was asked to tidy my room by my parents **2** were taken by my sister **3** was built by **4** were given that plant by our neighbour **5** were given some money to buy their house by my parents **6** were broken by some children
Exercise 2
1 was stolen **2** was found **3** were sold **4** stopped **5** drove **6** was repaired **7** was returned **8** sold
Exercise 3
1 a man **2** the police **3** a man who lives near us **4** a mechanic **5** the police **6** my dad

Page 96
Listening
Exercise 1
1 C
Exercise 2
Graham: I'm in Chicago to visit some places where the *Batman* films were made. There's the famous Berghoff restaurant, but I haven't been there yet. I'm going to visit the post office in a few minutes, which was the Gotham Bank, but at the moment, I'm in front of Hotel 71, which most Batman fans will know.
Exercise 3
1 A **2** B **3** C **4** C **5** A

Page 96
Speaking
Exercise 1
1 There's a free car park. **2** There's no charge. **3** How much are the tickets? **4** Adult tickets are £20.00. **5** How much are student tickets?
Exercise 2
1 Where is the house?
2 Is it in a good area?
3 Has it got a garden? / Is there a garden?
4 How many rooms are there?
5 How much does it cost? / What's/is the price?
Exercise 3
1 in West Village
2 quiet, shops, schools and the metro
3 small garden, (views across) the park
4 five, bedrooms, living room, (small) kitchen, bathroom
5 £255,000

Page 97
Language in Use
Exercise 1
1 for **2** in **3** about **4** for **5** at **6** of
Exercise 2
1 h **2** g **3** j **4** b **5** i **6** f **7** a **8** e **9** c **10** d
Exercise 3
1 c **2** b **3** b **4** c **5** a

Page 98
Writing
Exercise 1
1 d **2** e **3** b **4** h **5** f **6** c **7** g **8** a
Exercise 2
1 a great **2** boring **3** dark **4** noisy **5** excited **6** near **7** tiring **8** dirty
Exercise 3
Students should tick: favourite place, where is it, what is there to look at
Exercise 4
Students' own answers
Exercise 5
Students' own answers

Page 99
Progress check
Exercise 1
1 a **2** a **3** b **4** c **5** c **6** c **7** a **8** a **9** b **10** a
Exercise 2
1 was built **2** moved **3** was repaired **4** isn't / is not used **5** grow **6** are often given **7** are kept **8** leaves
Cumulative progress
Exercise 3
1 said **2** by **3** look **4** which/that **5** lot **6** were **7** had **8** about **9** for **10** who

OPTIMISE PRACTICE TEST

Page 100

Reading and Writing

Part 1
1 E **2** A **3** G **4** D **5** B
Part 2
6 C **7** B **8** A **9** C **10** A
Part 3
11 B **12** A **13** C **14** C **15** B **16** E **17** H **18** F **19** A **20** G
Part 4
21 A **22** B **23** C **24** A **25** B **26** C **27** A
Part 5
28 C **29** C **30** A **31** B **32** B **33** C **34** C **35** C
Part 6
36 knee **37** stomach **38** hospital **39** medicine **40** doctor
Part 7
41 about **42** lot **43** when **44** than **45** them **46** ago **47** Have **48** to **49** at **50** the
Part 8
51 Bond Street **52** 11.30 **53** student card **54** train **55** poster
Part 9
Sample answer
Hi Max
There will be about 20 people at my party. It's going to finish at 10 o'clock. If you have some good music, please bring it!
See you at the party!

Page 111

Listening

Part 1
1 C **2** A **3** C **4** A **5** B
Part 2
6 F **7** A **8** B **9** G **10** H
Part 3
11 B **12** C **13** C **14** B **15** C
Part 4
16 6:30/six thirty **17** afternoon **18** Sunday **19** Welsh **20** 04926531748
Part 5
21 July **22** beach **23** basketball **24** 16/sixteen **25** bus

Page 117

Speaking

Part 1
Students' own answers
Part 2
Sample questions and answers
What's the name of the shop?
The name of the shop is Top Sports.
What can you buy (there)?
You can buy shoes, rackets, bats and balls.
When is it open?
It's open every day from 9am to 6pm.
Who can you meet (there)?
You can meet a famous tennis player.
What is the address (of the shop)?
The address is 10 Main Street.

Sample questions and answers
What do you learn? / What can I learn?
You (can) learn to play the guitar.
How much are the lessons? / What do the lessons cost?
The lessons are free.
Do I need a guitar?
No, you don't. / No, it's not necessary to have a guitar.
Are the groups big or small?
They are small. / The groups are small.
How can I find out more? / Where can I get more information from?
Speak to Mrs Wilson. / You can ask Mrs Wilson for more information.

Audioscripts

UNIT 1 | STUDENT'S BOOK

1.06 | Listening, page 8, Exercise 3

Girl: So, where is your cousin's tent?

Boy: It's in a good place. There aren't any other tents near it.

Girl: Is it in the middle of that field?

Boy: No, it's under that big tree.

1.07 | Listening, page 8, Exercises 4 and 5

1

Girl: Let's play a video game – but not that football game we played last time.

Boy: Good idea! My brother's new video game is good. Or I've got a great new adventure game. You choose.

Girl: The adventure game, please.

Boy: OK, we can play the racing game next time.

2

Karen: Do you often read magazines, Helen?

Helen: No, I don't really like them. I sometimes look at my sister's pop magazine. But … I think it's boring.

Karen: Did you bring anything to read?

Helen: Yes, my book. It's great!

3

Girl: When does football practice usually start? Is it 9:15?

Boy: No, it's not. It always begins at 9:30.

Girl: So what time do you get home after practise, then?

Boy: Ryan's dad brings us home. I'm usually home by 11 o'clock.

4

Dad: What do you want for dinner this evening? We could have burgers … or pizza? It's your sister's favourite.

Girl: What about fish and chips? That's Mum's favourite. We had pizza on Monday.

Dad: OK. We can go to that place next to the hotel. They do good fish.

Girl: Great. Yes, their food is very good.

5

Boy: Do you have art and English on Wednesday afternoons?

Girl: I have art on Wednesday, yes. But English is always on Thursday afternoons and Friday mornings.

Boy: I have English lessons on Thursdays and Fridays too, but I have art on Monday mornings.

Girl: That's a nice way to start the week!

1.09 | Unit 1, Speaking, page 10, Exercises 4 and 5

Examiner: Good morning. What's your name?

Student: My name is Vitor, Vitor Santos.

Examiner: How do you spell your surname?

Student: S-A-N-T-O-S.

Examiner: Thanks. Do you have any hobbies?

Student: Sorry, can you say that again, please?

Examiner: Sure. Do you have any hobbies?

Student: Yes, I really like swimming and go as often as I can. And I also love skateboarding. I go skateboarding every day after school.

Examiner: What do you usually do in the evenings?

Student: I usually get home from school at around 6pm. Then I do my homework and have a meal with my family. I usually go to bed at 9pm.

Examiner: What do you like doing at the weekends?

Student: I usually go to the beach. I swim in the sea and play with my friends.

Examiner: How do you usually spend your holidays?

Student: My family usually go to visit with my grandparents in the countryside.

UNIT 2 | STUDENT'S BOOK

1.14 | Unit 2, Listening, page 18, Exercises 6 and 7

Kacey: Hi Paul. I'm doing a school project on entertainment. Can I ask you some questions?

Paul: Sure. No problem.

Kacey: OK, thanks. So – do you watch much TV?

Paul: I always watch the sports channel on TV. I find it really interesting to watch people doing different sports. But I also go online to watch things, too.

Kacey: Do you watch cartoons on TV?

Paul: Well, I sometimes watch anime, with my friend, Jack. He likes them a lot. They're cartoons from Japan. I think they are beautiful to look at, but a bit boring after a while. We're watching a new one tonight. I hope it won't be boring! I prefer watching funny cartoons that make me laugh. I watch a lot of those on TV!

Kacey: Right! What about films?

Paul: Sometime I watch films online, but I mostly watch them on TV. I like anything really. I enjoy funny films, but action films are my favourite. I like them because they're exciting.

Kacey: How about the news? Do you watch that on TV, or online?

Paul: I watch the news online. Some people think it's boring, but I think it's important to know what's happening. I often don't feel happy when I watch some news stories, though. They make me feel sad.

Kacey: Do you watch anything else online? I sometimes watch vloggers on YouTube.

Paul: Yes, my brother and I are watching a good video gaming channel at the moment. The guy on it is very loud, but some of the things he shows you are really excellent.

Kacey: And what about music videos?

Paul: Oh, no. They're terrible. Pop stars think they're so important. I don't like watching them at all – I think they're really bad.

Kacey: What about other entertainment online?

Paul: I take lots of photos, and post them for my friends. That's a lot of fun. What are you doing later? I can show you some.

Kacey: Sorry, I'm working on my project this afternoon.

UNIT 3 | STUDENT'S BOOK

1.16 | Unit 3, Reading, page 27

Kids in the kitchen

In the UK, 60% of 18-year-olds can't cook five easy meals. There are, however, many different ways young people can learn to cook.

Some people learn by watching TV cooking competitions like Junior MasterChef. The programme started in the UK 20 years ago. The idea for the programme was simple – to help people think about the food they eat. In the show, young people prepare different delicious dishes every week. The one who cooks the best food is the winner. And some of the food is amazing. Everyone remembers the famous alligator chilli one junior chef made!

Junior MasterChef winners can help other people learn to cook by sharing their recipes online. One winner said she actually learnt to cook by watching YouTube videos. However, many winners learnt to cook when they helped their parents at home.

There are also cooking courses for teenagers in the UK. At one school, the teacher, Ben Coyle-Larner, isn't a chef. He's a successful rapper called Loyle Carner. When Ben was a teenager, he found it difficult to study. Ben says, 'My brain is always busy, but with cooking there is no time to think about other things.' In 2016, Ben opened his cooking school to help teenagers like him.

So, next time you're online, why not look up the recipe of your favourite dish or watch a video about how to cook it? Or watch the latest cookery show to get some great ideas. Then start cooking!

1.21 | Unit 3, Listening, page 30, Exercise 4

Kay: Hi Matt. Are you free to come for coffee with Liz and me on Saturday morning?

Matt: Hello Kay! That sounds like a nice idea. Where are you thinking of going?

Kay: There's a really good cafe on Lion Street and they play great music, too.

Matt: Sounds good. Is it quite cheap?

Kay: It's not that cheap, but the coffee is really good – and you get a free cake! The staff there are helpful, too.

1.22 | Unit 3, Listening, page 30, Exercises 6 and 7

Simon: Hi Clare, it's Simon. I'm just phoning to say happy birthday.

Clare: Oh, thanks Simon. That's really nice of you.

Simon: Did you go to the new music café with Kirsty and Maddie on Friday evening?

Clare: Well, we planned to go then, but we couldn't. In the end we went on Saturday – in the afternoon.

Simon: What was it like?

Clare: It was good! It was a bit smaller than I thought. There were only five tables. We were lucky it wasn't too busy and there were only three of us.

Simon: Was the music good?

Clare: Yes, they played some great music, and we enjoyed looking at all the old records, but the food wasn't so good.

Simon: Did you have a main course and dessert, or just a snack?

Clare: I thought about just having an omelette, but I was quite hungry. In the end, I had grilled fish for my main, in a chilli sauce with stir-fried vegetables. The drinks were really good, though. They are all made fresh at the café.

Simon: So, what did you have to drink?

Clare: I was thirsty after the chillies *[laughs]* so I ordered a glass of cold lemonade. It was sweet, and had slices of fruit in it. It was almost a dessert! But the best thing was that I didn't pay. Kirsty and Maddie paid – they said it was my birthday present!

1.23 | Unit 3, Speaking, page 32, Exercises 4 and 5

Examiner: Right, I see … What's your favourite type of food?

Student: Definitely pasta – I love pasta! Any type of pasta with any type of sauce. It's my favourite meal because it's tasty and easy to eat.

Examiner: And what's your least favourite type of food?

Student: Mmm … there aren't many things that I dislike, but I'm not very keen on pears. We have a pear tree in the garden and so mum makes us eat them in the autumn. We have pear juice, pear in salads, pear for dessert, pear for breakfast … so I think I don't like pears because I have to eat so many of them!

Examiner: And what food do you like to eat at festivals and celebrations?

Student: Cake! My favourite cake is chocolate cake because I love both chocolate and cake. So, I have a big chocolate cake every year for my birthday – with no pears on it of course!

UNIT 4 | STUDENT'S BOOK

1.28 | Unit 4, Listening, page 40, Exercise 2

1

A: Which house do you live at?

B: I don't live in a house. I live in a flat – 32a.

2

A: I thought there were some biscuits left.

B: Well, there were four but I ate three … and Jo ate one as well.

3

A: Hello, is that Jon?

B: No, sorry – I think you called the wrong number. This is 786 954.

A: Oh, sorry. I wanted 786 934.

4

A: So, is Paul having a party?

B: Yes he is – it's his 16th birthday on Saturday.

5

A: So, when does your train get in?

B: It gets in at 12:14.

A: 12:40. OK – see you then.

B: No, 12:14. And remember, it's platform two.

1.29 | Unit 4, Listening, page 40, Exercise 3

1

A: My name's Jeremiah Gayle, that's J-E-R-E-M-I-A-H, then G-A-Y-L-E.

B: Did you say G-A-L-E?

A: No, G-A-Y-L-E.

2

A: My address is 5 Solomon Street, that's S-O-L-O-M-O-N Street.

B: S-O-L-M-O-N?

A: No, there are three 'O's – it's S-O-L-O-M-O-N.

3

A: I'm calling from Cambourne School.

B: Can you spell that, please?

A: Of course. It's C-A-M-B-O-U-R-N-E.

4

A: It's Alisha Pieters, that's A-L-I-S-H-A, then P-I-E-T-E-R-S.

B: OK – A-L-I-S-H-A … P-E-T-E-R-S.

A: No, my last name is spelt P-I-E-T-E-R-S.

5

A: I'm from Leicester.

B: Is that L-E-S-T-E-R?

A: No, it's L-E-I-C-E-S-T-E-R.

6

A: So you get off the train at Clapham Junction, that's C-L-A-P-H-A-M then J-U-N-C-T-I-O-N.

B: OK, I'll write that down … C-L-A-P-A-M … J-U-N-C-T-I-O-N. Right?

A: No, you missed out an H. It's C-L-A-P-H-A-M, then J-U-N-C-T-I-O-N.

7

A: I live in Borough Road.

B: Is that B-U-R-R-O-W?

A: No, it's B-O-R-O-U-G-H.

8

A: It's Tom Maltravers. M-A-L-T-R-A-V-E-R-S.

b: OK, so T-O-M … M-A-T-L-A-V-E-R-S.

a: No, Maltravers is M-A-L-T-R-A-V-E-R-S.

1.30 | Unit 4, Listening, page 40, Exercise 4

Agent: Good afternoon, Flight Time. Chris speaking, how can I help you?

Customer: Err, hi. ... hi Chris. I booked a flight online yesterday with your company.

Agent: OK, is everything all right?

Customer: Well, when I checked my emails today, the dates on the booking were wrong.

Agent: OK, I'm sorry about that. So, can I check your full name?

Customer: Yes, it's Ms Amanda Johnstone.

Agent: Could you spell that, please?

Customer: Sure. It's J-O-H-N-S-T-O-N-E.

Agent: Thank you Ms Johnstone. Do you have a booking reference number?

Customer: Sure. Hang on … yes, it's A79916.

Agent: A79916. Great. Thanks. So you are travelling to Australia. Is that right?

Customer: Yes, that's right.

Agent: Lovely. I went there last year. It's an amazing place. So … it says on the screen that you leave London on November the 3rd. Is that right?

Customer: Well, that's the thing. I wanted to go on the 30th.

Agent: November the 13th?

Customer: No, the 30th, I want to be there for Christmas time, so I want to be in Australia in early December.

Agent: OK. Well, I can see there is a flight on November the 30th. So … I can change your booking to the 30th November for you – that's no problem. And you don't have to pay for that at all, Ms Johnstone. But if you change your flight again, you will have to pay £25.

Customer: Right. OK. Sorry – how much is that?

Agent: Well, as I said … you don't need to pay anything for the change today.

Customer: OK. That's lovely. Thank you very much.

1.31 | Unit 4, Listening, page 40, Exercises 5 and 6

Hello everyone. I'm going to give you some information about the sailing trip tomorrow. The bus leaves here at eight thirty in the morning. So please meet in front of the Nunthorpe building – that's N_U_N_T_H_O_R_P_E. And we need to be there fifteen minutes before the bus leaves, so we'll meet at 8:15 am. That's quarter past eight. It's a day trip and we are away for about seven hours. The sailing is from 10am until 1pm. And we'll get back to the hotel at half past four in the afternoon. You can buy snacks from different stops on the journey, and we're eating lunch together at the Outdoor Activity Centre at 1:30. We're travelling through the wide part of the river in the morning. As we go through there, we'll see some amazing sights. But remember … you must be careful at all times. Last week when we were sailing, one person fell into the water. She was OK but she got very cold. However, tomorrow is going to be quite sunny, so bring a lot of water to drink, as well as a towel. So, see you at 8:15 tomorrow morning. OK. Any questions?

1.32 | Unit 4, Speaking, page 42, Exercises 5 and 6

1

Student A: What can I see at the museum?

Student B: You can look at lots of old classic cars at the museum. There are more than 15 of them.

2

Student A: Is it open at the weekends?

Student B: Yes, the museum is open every day, between 10am and 6pm.

3

Student A: Can I buy anything?

Student B: You can buy books, posters and models in the gift shop.

4

Student A: Is there a car park?

Student B: Yes, there is a large car park, and parking is £12.

5

Student A: How much is a student ticket?

Student B: A student ticket costs only £8.

1.33 | Unit 4, Speaking, page 42, Exercise 7

1

Student A: What time does the museum close?

Student B: Sorry, can you say that again, please?

Student A: Yes, of course. What time does the museum close?

Student B: It closes at 6pm.

2

Student A: How much is the car park?

Student B: Did you say 'How much is the car park?'?

Student A: Yes, that's right.

Student B: It's free. You don't have to pay anything.

3

Student A: How much is the entrance fee?

Student B: I'm sorry, could you repeat that?

Student A: Yes. How much are the entrance tickets?

Student B: Adults are £12 and children and students are £8.

UNIT 5 | STUDENT'S BOOK

2.06 | Unit 5, Listening, page 52, Exercise 4

Example

Boy: Oh, no! My new printer doesn't work.

Girl: Look at this information. There's a number to phone for help. Why not call it?

Boy: No, I looked on their website. It says to send them an email, so I'm writing one now.

Girl: It might be quicker to phone …

1

Boy: Do you write letters to your pen friends in other countries, Sarah?

Sarah: No! I never write letters anymore.

Boy: So, how do you contact them, then? Do you send them emails?

Sarah: Yes, I do, I've always got lots of things I want to tell them about, so texts are no good.

2

Kirsty: Are we going to listen to music later?

Boy: Let's do something different. How about playing this game online? I was talking to Dan yesterday and he said it's great!

Kirsty: Yes, OK, then. But I hope it's better than the football game we played last week! Dan told me that was a good game, but it wasn't.

Boy: Oh, I'm sure this one's better!

3

Dad: There are some good laptops here, but they're expensive. I prefer to get your brother a new camera.

Girl: But Dad, look at this smartphone. It's amazing … and it's got a camera.

Dad: Your brother's got a good phone already. I think this camera will take better photos. I'm going to get him this.

Girl: Well, OK. But I think the phone's nicer than the camera.

4

Boy: Sorry I wasn't free this afternoon. Was the chat room really busy?

Girl: There were about 13 people in it.

Boy: That's not too bad. Sometimes there are thirty people chatting at the same time.

Girl: I think that's too many. It's better when there aren't so many people.

5

Mum: Can you help me, please? I want to download a new app.

Girl: Yes, of course, Mum. Is it that new music app I told you about?

Mum: No, it's an exercise app. I can use it when I go running.

Girl: Oh, right. My friend's got an app like that. Hers takes photos too.

2.07 | Unit 5, Speaking, page 54, Exercises 4 and 5

1

Examiner: What do you like doing in your free time?

Student A: Well I don't have a lot of free time. When I am free I usually want to spend the time with my friends. Social media is great as I can talk to friends wherever I am. So, I like chatting online the best.

2

Examiner: What did you do yesterday?

Student B: Right … OK … So, yesterday. Oh, yes. I was really tired yesterday, as I had a very busy week. I watched a film at home. It's my favourite way to relax.

3

Examiner: What are you doing on Saturday?

Student C: My aunt is coming to visit us and we're going to London. Mum's going sightseeing with my aunt, but I'm going shopping with my friends. I need some new shoes and it's better for shopping than my home town.

4

Examiner: What do you like doing on your computer?

Student D: Well, I use my laptop most days for lots of different things. However, I love playing games online more than anything else.

2.08 | Unit 5, Language in Use, page 55, Exercise 1

1

Peter: I spend a lot of time using social networking sites. I chat to lots of different people. A few months ago I started taking pictures and making short videos to share with my friends. You don't need a special camera or anything. You just use your phone to make the video then upload it. I think it's the best way to show people my new skateboarding moves!

2

Chloe: I like to contact my friends and tell them what I'm doing, without spending lots of money. All of us have mobile phones so this is how we keep in touch. Sometimes we have a group chat, so the same message goes to lots of different people. It's really good. I think it's the fastest way to share information and a great way to stay in touch with friends.

3

Sam: A lot of people in my family live in foreign countries. I don't see them very often. But when I use this app on my laptop, I can talk to my cousins and see them, too. Sometimes the sound is slow, so it can be difficult to understand what someone is saying. But most of the time it's the easiest way to speak to my family.

UNIT 6 | STUDENT'S BOOK

2.09 | Unit 6, Reading, page 59

Fashion changes

Online shopping has changed the world of fashion. We can buy clothes from all over the world, compare prices and find the best places to shop. What other things have changed the fashion world?

There are a lot of new people starting new trends, especially teenagers. Some of them are famous, like Romeo Beckham, but many are <u>normal</u> teenagers who use social media to show people how to dress well. A lot of people <u>follow</u> them on social media, so clothing <u>companies</u> now look at their ideas. These teens don't just follow fashion, they make it. To them, it doesn't matter if something is old or new. The most important thing is that it looks good.

Clothes are made from different things these days, too. Have you ever worn a T-shirt made from old plastic bottles? Many people are interested in looking after the world, and some customers think carefully about this when buying fashion. They choose clothes made of different plants, like bamboo, coconut and banana, or from recycled materials like bottles, tyres and coffee. And now you can even buy shoes that make electricity when you walk. They're amazing!

Many people buy their clothes online, but shopping centres are still very <u>busy</u>. There are lots of clothes shops to choose from. Some shops use <u>unusual</u> ideas to try and get more customers. For example, many shoppers have been to visit Johnny Cupcakes … and it's an experience they won't forget. It's a clothes shop that smells of cakes and sugar! The <u>shop assistant</u> puts your clothes in cake boxes, not bags. I've never visited the store, but it must make you hungry!

2.13 | Unit 6, Listening, page 62, Exercise 2

1 I really like shopping at the market, but I haven't been for a long time. I've been to the shopping centre this week, though.

2 I wasn't at home when I got Marta's text. I was out shopping with Julie.

3 I watched the match on TV at home, because the tickets for the stadium were too expensive.

4 Do I pay for my own clothes? Well, Mum has bought things for me in the past, but now I use my own money and go clothes shopping on my own.

2.14 | Unit 6, Listening, page 62, Exercises 3 and 4

Girl: You've got some lovely clothes here, Hannah. I love your jeans!

Hannah: Thanks! I got them when we went to London last summer.

Girl: Your T-shirt is great, too. Did you get it at the new department store in town?

Hannah: It's nice, isn't it? No, I got this one from the museum shop. I've bought a couple of things from there. I've always liked T-shirts with pictures like this on.

Girl: Is your necklace from the museum too? I love the colours. It reminds me of summer flowers.

Hannah: No, this wasn't from the museum shop. Mum bought it years ago – she got it at a music festival.

Girl: Cool. You can get good things at music festivals. I've never seen those sunglasses, either. Are they new?

Hannah: No, I've had these for a long time. I got them when we went to Spain.

Girl: Did you buy them at the airport?

Hannah: No. I found them on the beach. I took them to the little supermarket next to our hotel in case anyone had lost them. But the shop assistant told me to keep them.

Girl: Lucky you! They're really nice. This baseball cap is a bit silly, though.

Hannah: *[laughing]* It's terrible, isn't it? I've worn it once or twice. I wore it when I was studying in Oxford at the summer school. I bought it there because we all had to wear them on day trips.

Girl: *[laughing]* Oh well, at least you all wore them!

Hannah: I like your trainers, by the way. I've got a pair a bit like them.

Girl: Really? I got mine at the new department store in town, last week.

Hannah: Mum got mine at that big supermarket near the airport. She says it's cheaper than in town.

2.16 | Unit 6, Speaking, page 64, Exercise 5

Student A: Could you tell me what the new shopping centre is called?

Student B: The shopping centre is called Blue Lake.

Student A: OK. Is the shopping centre open today?

Student B: No, it isn't. There's a Grand opening on the 25th of October at 9am.

Student A: I see. Is there a car park?

Student B: Yes, there is a car park. Parking is free.

Student A: Where is it? What's the address?

Student B: It's at 173 North Gate Road.

Student A: Thanks, and what are the contact details?

Student B: The contact number is 024 771 5896.

UNIT 7 | STUDENT'S BOOK

2.17 | Unit 7, Reading, page 71

Technology for all

In classrooms around the world, many students now have computers or tablets on their desks instead of books. Technology is helping young people to learn about the world, and preparing them for work. But in poorer countries, there aren't any computers available for students.

That was a problem for schools in the countryside in Uganda, in East Africa. But since 2007, the Mobile Solar Computer Classroom has helped many classes of children and adults at schools and libraries to use computers. There are two mobile computer classrooms, and they travel all over the country in two large cars, going to schools to give computer lessons. Later today, one of them is going to visit a village in the west of the country. It's a long way down a difficult road, but the drivers are lucky because it isn't going to rain, and that helps. In the car, there are 15 laptop computers, desks and chairs, two ICT teachers and a large battery. This produces solar energy for the computers, because many of the villages don't have electricity.

More than 200 people a day can have computer lessons from the two mobile classrooms. This means over 5,000 people have these lessons each year! What are they going to do next? Well, over the next few years, they are going to build computer classrooms in 55 Ugandan schools. Teachers and students know how important computers will be in the future and these classrooms will really help students prepare for a job in tomorrow's world.

2.21 | Unit 7, Listening, page 74, Exercise 4

Jack: Welcome back to *Education today*. My guest this afternoon is Alice Chatswood. Alice lives here in England but she helps children in India with their schoolwork. She's a 'cloud granny'. Hello Alice, and thanks for coming in today. So, what is a cloud granny and how does being a cloud granny work?

Alice: Well, on Mondays and Wednesdays, for about an hour, I help to teach children in India. I talk on Skype to a group of school children in Mumbai. They ask me lots of questions about life in England, they talk about their lives, and I help them with their schoolwork.

Jack: I see – so, that's what cloud grannies do. And, how did it all start, Alice?

Alice: Well, I saw an advert in a newspaper in January. It said they wanted people with free time to talk to children in India and help them at school. It sounded interesting, and I was a teacher a few years ago, so I sent them an email. And I actually started talking to the children in April. I'm 68 now and I don't work, so I have lots of time now and I really enjoy helping young people.

Jack: What do you help them with?

Alice: Well … they are very good at maths and I'm not, *[laughs]* … but I help them with English and history. I'm going to talk to the children later today, actually.

Jack: What are you going to talk about?

Alice: First of all, I'm going to show them some photos of my garden. They'll probably ask me lots of questions. After that, I'm not sure … I know! I'll talk about this interview. The children will be interested in that. In fact, they might like to speak to you, too!

Jack: Well … I'm not working this afternoon, so I'm going to have some free time. I'll join you and we can talk to the children together.

Alice: That would be fantastic!

Jack: Great! I'm looking forward to it. Thanks, Alice. And now … *[fade]*

2.22 | Unit 7, Speaking, page 76, Exercises 4 and 5

1

A: Are you going to take exams this term?

B: No, we're not going to take any exams until next term.

2

A: Will your classmates pass the test?

B: Yes, they are studying really hard, so I think they're going to pass.

3

A: What languages will you study next year?

B: I think I'll study French and English perhaps.

4

A: Are you going to study in the summer holidays?

B: No, when school finishes for the holidays, I'm going to work at a summer camp.

UNIT 8 | STUDENT'S BOOK

2.28 | Unit 8, Listening, page 84, Exercises 2 and 3

1

Mum: What did you do yesterday when it rained?

Dan: We couldn't go outside, so we played table tennis. It wasn't very good. I prefer sports where you run around, like football or rugby.

2

Dad: What happened on Sunday, Lorna?

Lorna: Well some of the girls played volleyball, but I went cycling in the mountains. I didn't get tired and I had a great time.

3

Mum: Did you go fishing this morning, Chris?

Chris: No, we went windsurfing this morning. It was my first time but I loved it.

4

Dad: Did you have a good time yesterday, Lily?

Lily: Not really. I wanted to go swimming, but we had to go running outside. It was very cold and no-one wanted to do it.

5

Friend: Did they teach you how to play tennis at the club yesterday?

Pete: No, they taught us how to play badminton. It was really good fun … and I was quite good!

2.29 | Unit 8, Listening, page 84, Exercise 4

Bea: Hi Dad.

Dad: Hi Bea. How's summer camp?

Bea: It's great! I'm doing lots of different sports. So, on Monday, we went for a long run in the morning. I don't like running but it was OK because we were all together. Then I played volleyball in the afternoon.

Dad: That sounds great!

Bea: I wanted to play tennis on Tuesday, but it was raining so I couldn't. So, instead of tennis, a coach taught us to play badminton in the sports centre.

Dad: Did you enjoy it? I played badminton years ago and I liked it a lot.

Bea: Yes, I loved it! You should start playing again, Dad – it's good exercise and we could play together.

Dad: *[laughs]* Good idea. I might do that. Anyway, what did you do on Wednesday?

Bea: On Wednesday we went to the sea. It's a long walk to the beach, so we have to get up really early when we go there … and you know how much I like getting up early!

Dad: Haha – it's not something you enjoy, I know that! So, did you go swimming?

Bea: No. I wanted to but it was too windy. Camp rules say we mustn't swim if there is a strong wind – it's not safe.

Dad: So, what did you do?

Bea: One of the instructors took us sailing. It was amazing.

Dad: Your mum loves sailing, too. Umm … Bea – could you take some photos of the boats, please? I'm sure Mum would really like to see them.

Bea: Yes, no problem.

Dad: Thanks. And, what happened yesterday?

Bea: Yesterday … that was Thursday. Oh, yes … we had a cricket competition. That was fun. Today the plan was for us to play football, but it's really hot here.

Dad: Well, you shouldn't be out in the sun all day if it's very hot.

Bea: I know. The camp leader says we can go to the pool today instead.

Dad: OK, enjoy your swim, Bea! See you on Sunday.

Bea: Bye Dad!

2.30 | Unit 8, Speaking, page 86, Exercise 5

1

Student A: What time does it start?

Student B: At 5:30 pm.

2

Student A: Can I buy a ticket online?

Student B: Yes, you can.

3

Student A: Have they got a website?

Student B: Yes, they have.

4

Student A: How much does it cost?

Student B: It's £8 for teenagers.

5

Student A: Is it open after school?

Student B: No, it isn't.

6

Student A: Do I have to take a racket?

Student B: No, you don't.

UNIT 9 | STUDENT'S BOOK

3.01 | Unit 9, Reading, page 93

The world's strangest weather

If it rains a lot in England, some people say it is raining cats and dogs. Of course, it doesn't really mean that pets are falling from the sky. However, one day this did actually happen in Sri Lanka, when a different type of animal fell like rain.

In May 2014, people in a village in Sri Lanka were surprised when it started raining fish. Over 50 kg of fish fell on the roads, gardens and roofs, and in a local forest. Fortunately, the local people liked fish very much and ate many of them. But how often do strange things like this happen? Scientists think that if strong winds move over water, such as large rivers or the sea, they can take small animals like fish up into the clouds. Then if it rains, the fish fall on the ground.

Sometimes the colour of the rain can also surprise people. In southern India, in the summer of 2001, red rain fell from the sky. It turned houses, animals and people's clothes pink and for a long time no-one knew what it was. Scientists found that there were very small parts of a red plant in the rain. So if red rain falls from the sky again in India, people will know what it is.

Fish rain and red rain aren't dangerous. But if ice starts moving towards your house, it probably will be. This is what happened in the winter of 2014 in Lake Winnebago, USA. Strong winds pushed the ice that was on top of the lake onto the beaches and slowly towards the local town. Nothing could stop it. The ice went into people's houses, covered the roads and moved their cars. People were afraid, but luckily nobody was badly hurt.

3.06 | Unit 9, Listening, page 96, Exercise 2

1

Man: Would you like to go for a walk in the forest today?

Woman: Good idea!

2

Girl: It's a lovely sunny day. Do you want to go swimming?

Boy: I'm not sure. I'll think about it.

3

Boy: Do you want to play tennis?

Boy: Not really. I'm tired.

4

Dad: Why don't we go to the beach?

Girl: Great. I'll get my swimsuit.

5

Girl: Do you want to go for a bike ride?

Girl: Maybe.

3.07 | Unit 9, Listening, page 96, Exercise 4

Example

Boy 1: Look! It's snowing. Do you want to go to the park later this afternoon?

Boy 2: I can't. I'm meeting George at half past one. We're going for a walk by the river.

Boy 1: If I didn't have a guitar lesson at 1 o'clock, I'd come with you. But … my lesson finishes at 2, so I could meet you and George after that.

Boy 2: OK, we'll meet you at the bridge at half past two, then.

1

Mum: Would you like to go to the mountains this weekend, Sophie?

Sophie: Not really. If it's raining, can we go to the cinema?

Mum: Maybe. But I think it's going to be sunny.

Sophie: Great. Then why don't we go to the lake? It's beautiful there in the sun.

2

Jack: Is it raining again?

Anna: No, but it's very cloudy. It isn't sunny at all.

Jack: If it was sunny, I would go to the beach today.

Anna: Me too, but not when the weather is like this. Do you want to watch a film instead?

3

Granddad: Are you and your parents going on holiday this summer?

Arthur: I think so. We'd go to the beach in Spain if we had more money. We loved it there last year. But we'll probably go somewhere nearer home this year.

Granddad: Well you could all go camping in the countryside. It's not expensive.

Arthur: Great idea! And after that, maybe we'll go to the mountains.

4

Man: It looks like it's going to be warm and sunny in the north tomorrow.

Woman: Yes, but we aren't in the north! What's it going to be like here?

Man: It's going to be cloudy in the morning. But after lunch there's going to be a big storm.

Woman: Oh, dear. I don't think I'll go out then.

5

Boy: I can't wait till summer. I love the hot weather. What about you?

Girl: I don't really like the hot weather.

Boy: Do you prefer winter, then? Or autumn?

Girl: Autumn is my favourite time of year. It's beautiful. I don't like snow, so I don't like winter very much at all.

3.08 | Unit 9, Speaking, page 98, Exercises 4 and 5

1

Well we usually go to the same place every summer because we go to visit my grandparents who live by the sea. Then in the winter, we usually have a short break for two or three days. We go to different places. For example, we sometimes visit a new city like Paris or Berlin.

2

I'm an only child, and I don't have any cousins, so I spend more time with my friends. One example is at weekends and the school holidays my best friend usually comes to stay. It's almost like having a sister.

3

We have lots of gadgets in our house as my parents, my brother and sister and I all love tablets, phones and computer games. Let me give an example – last night when I got home, everyone was in the living room, but all using different gadgets.

4

It's a big place with lots of things to do. For example, the sports centre is very big and there's a new shopping centre with restaurants, cinemas and of course, shops.

3.09 | Unit 9, Speaking, page 98, Exercise 6

I love where I live, but I love visiting other places even more. Every year I try to visit new places, for example this year I cycled for six days around the coast with the cycle club. We saw lots of beautiful scenery. I also went on a walking trip to the beach, sorry I mean to the mountains. It was amazing.

UNIT 10 | STUDENT'S BOOK

3.14 | Unit 10, Listening, page 106, Exercise 3

1 I've already seen Mrs Jackson this week.
2 They sometimes make an appointment on Monday morning.
3 He usually comes to see me every Monday.
4 He came to see me on Tuesday afternoon.
5 Mr Collins hasn't been here for a long time.
6 I gave him some medicine at 10am.

3.15 | Unit 10, Listening, page 106, Exercise 4

Nurse 1: How's your week been, Emily?

Nurse 2: It's been very busy. Wesley was in early on Monday. His leg's better but he's got bad backache now. I gave him some medicine. And Evan came in again on Monday.

Nurse 1: What was wrong with him?

Nurse 2: He had a very bad cold. I offered to give him some medicine, but I know he hates taking it.

Nurse 1: I hope he gets better soon. And I think you saw Rosie on Wednesday. Is her ear ache better?

Nurse 2: No, it isn't better yet. I examined her ears again and gave her more medicine.

Nurse 1: That's good. Did you know that young Amber Mistry had a bad fall and hurt her arm on Thursday? Luckily, it isn't broken.

Nurse 2: Did it happen at school?

Nurse 1: No, she wasn't at school – she was in the park. She decided to climb a tree, but she fell.

Nurse 2: Oh dear. By the way, have you seen Ben Sharp this week? He's had a bad back recently.

Nurse 1: Yes, I have. He hasn't had any backache this week. He had a stomach ache when I saw him. He wanted to take some medicine, but I told him to drink lots of water and eat healthier food.

Nurse 2: What about Oliver? Did you see him earlier this afternoon?

Nurse 1: Yes, he keeps coming to see me. It's usually a problem with his legs, but today he was quite ill. He had a very high temperature.

Nurse 2: What did you do?

Nurse 1: I gave him some medicine and asked him to come and see me again tomorrow.

3.17 | Unit 10, Speaking, page 108, Exercises 5 and 6

1

A: Is the sports club open in the evenings?

B: Just a minute, yes, it's open from 6am until 10pm.

2

A: Is it big or small?

B: It's small, but there's something for everyone.

3

A: Is there a swimming pool?

B: Mmm let's see. Yes there's a gym, sports hall and swimming pool.

4

A: What's the telephone number?

B: It's 04462 789122.

5

A: What's the address?

B: The sports centre is at … let me think … 155 George Street.

UNIT 11 | STUDENT'S BOOK

3.23 | Unit 11, Listening, page 118, Exercise 2

1 My name is Tom Armitage – that's A-R-M-I-T-A-G-E.
2 I live with my family in a place called Bicester – you spell that B-I-C-E-S-T-E-R.
3 We live in Vaughan Way – Vaughan is spelt V-A-U-G-H-A-N.
4 My best friend is Chloe Green. Can you spell Chloe? It's C-H-L-O-E.
5 Next summer, Leo and I are going to visit Edinburgh in Scotland – that's E-D-I-N-B-U-R-G-H.

3.24 | Unit 11, Listening, page 118, Exercise 3

I really like going to concerts, but I live in a small town and there aren't many places where musicians can play. So, in July last year, I decided to plan a concert myself. My friend Dan said I could have it in his large garden. I put a message on Facebook and asked lots of musicians to come and play. About 80 people came and six bands played. The best band was Jayveeland – that's J-A-Y-V-E-E-L-A-N-D. We sold food and drink and we earned about £200. It was great. We're going to do it again this year as well.

3.25 | Unit 11, Listening, page 118, Exercise 4

Aaron: This afternoon I'm talking to someone who studies hard at school – like most 15-year-olds – but as well as that, has also become a young business person! It's Zi Yang Chen, from Bolton. Welcome to the show, Zi Yang.

Zi Yang: Thanks.

Aaron: Your business is called *Our Daily Fruit*. What do you do?

Zi Yang: Well, the business is all about healthy food. So, I sell fresh fruit to people who work in local factories and offices.

Aaron: How did you get the idea?

Zi Yang: My dad works in a big factory which is in the city centre. He told me that he couldn't buy healthy food in his factory, and I wanted to change that.

Aaron: I see. So, how does your business work?

Zi Yang: I work with my mum. Every morning, people visit our website and choose the fruit they would like for the next day. We buy the fruit and then my mum takes it round to the people the next morning.

Aaron: Do all the people work in your dad's factory?

Zi Yang: No, we take food to three factories and six offices in Kearsley at the moment.

Aaron: Did you say Keighley?

Zi Yang: No, Kearsley – K-E-A-R-S-L-E-Y. It's in Bolton.

Aaron: How many customers have you got, Zi Yang?

Zi Yang: Altogether there are 52 people who buy from us every week.

Aaron: Do you have any staff working for you?

Zi Yang: No, but next year, we hope to have four or five people working for the business, and a lot more customers.

Aaron: And you've just won a competition that was for young business people.

Zi Yang: Yes, that's right. I'm the winner of Business Teen of the Year. It's really exciting!

3.26 | Unit 11, Speaking, page 120, Exercises 4 and 5

Well, I come from a large family with five children. I have an older brother and sister and a younger brother and sister. My older brother, Matthew, is a photographer for a magazine and my sister, Marta works in a theatre. She's worked there for ten years. Matthew can work very long hours, but unlike my mum and dad he doesn't work in an office. Matthew often meets his manager in the morning in a coffee bar or on location. My dad is a lawyer in Manchester. My mum is a journalist, but it's the school holidays, so she isn't working this week. We're at home. My sister, Anna is cooking lunch at the moment and my younger brother, Jake is playing computer games. I'm talking to Marta's friend on the phone. Jane usually works in an office, but this month she's visiting customers. She's going to come and visit us while she's in the area.

UNIT 12 | STUDENT'S BOOK

3.27 | Unit 12, Reading, page 125

Living with nature

Have you ever wanted to live somewhere far away from the town or city? Would you like to wake up to the sounds of birds and the wind in the trees?

Well, if you could also live without your own bathroom and cook all your meals outside, then you might be interested in living in a place called Tinker's Bubble.

Tinker's Bubble is a small village in the middle of a forest in the south-west of England. It was started in 1994 by a group of people who didn't want to live in towns or cities anymore. It is home to 10 adults and two young children. Their houses are made from wood. They are quite small and they haven't got bathrooms. There is a bathroom and kitchen which is shared by everyone who lives there. The cooking and the washing-up is also shared between them.

Joe Durling has grown up in Tinker's Bubble. He lives with his mum, Mary. Their house only has one room, but it has everything they need. There isn't a sofa, but there is a table, some shelves, some chairs and beds with lots of blankets. When it's cold, the house is heated by a fire and stays nice and warm in the winter. And the light from the sun is used to make electricity for their radio and lamp.

Most of the people at Tinker's Bubble work on its small farm. They work on the land with horses and they grow lots of fruit and vegetables. Some of the fruit is sold in the local market. The money they earn is shared between everyone.

Life in Tinker's Bubble isn't for everyone. But if you want to live close to nature and don't need to turn on the TV or use a laptop every time you're bored, it might be for you.

3.31 | Unit 12, Listening, page 128, Exercises 2 and 3

When I was younger, I lived in a house in the countryside with my parents and brother. Two years ago, we moved to a large apartment by the sea. It's smaller than our old house, but I love watching the boats on the water every day.

3.32 | Unit 12, Listening, page 128, Exercise 5

Jed: So, when did you first live on the water then Heidi?

Heidi: Well, I grew up in a house by the river so I've always lived near water. But four years ago, when I was ten, my parents were given a boat by their cousins. It was built about 30 years ago, but it wasn't finished, and it took two more years before we could live on it. So actually we only moved in two years ago.

Jed: What it's like living on a boat?

Heidi: It's very different from living in a house. The kitchen is much smaller and there isn't room for a bath in the bathroom. But I don't mind. We haven't got a dining room on the boat, but that's OK because we usually eat outside in the summer anyway.

Jed: What do you like most about it?

Heidi: Well, in the winter we have a fire in the living room. I love it. And my bedroom is really cool. But my favourite thing is what you can see out the windows. Every day, you see something different on the river.

Jed: That must be amazing.

Heidi: Yes, it is. But there are some problems. With the heating, it's nice and warm inside in the winter, but in the mornings before we light the fire, it's very cold. So getting out of bed isn't always nice! But the worst thing is that we don't have a washing machine here, and that's a big problem.

Jed: Hmm … I don't know if I'd like to live on a boat.

Heidi: Living on the river isn't for everyone. But if you want a quiet life and beautiful views, and you don't need lots of space, you should try it.

3.33 | Unit 12, Speaking, page 130, Exercises 4 and 5

Student A: What can we see at the Family Home Show?

Student B: You can see more than 15 room designs.

Student A: What does a student ticket cost?

Student B: A student ticket costs £10.00

Student A: What can I buy at the show?

Student B: You can buy furniture and decoration.

Student A: What time does it open?

Student B: It opens at 4pm.

Student A: How much is the car park?

Student B: Nothing. There's a free car park.

3.34 | Unit 12, Speaking, page 130, Exercise 6

1 I'm sorry, I didn't understand. Can you say that again, please?
2 Was that 429 or 492?
3 I'm sorry, I didn't hear that. Can you speak a bit louder, please?
4 Can you repeat that, please?
5 Sorry, did you say 16 or 60?

OPTIMISE YOUR EXAMS STUDENT'S BOOK

3.35 | Optimise your exams, Listening, page 146, Exercise 1

1

Girl: Have you seen my bag, Jim?

Boy: Is it under your desk?

Girl: No, it was there, but I left it by the door.

Boy: Look – there it is. It's by the window.

2

Boy: What time does the film start? Is it eight fifteen?

Girl: No, it's not. It begins at quarter to eight.

Boy: Are you sure? If you're right, we should leave here at seven fifteen so we get there on time.

Girl: Yes, it's definitely at seven forty-five. I checked on the internet. So, we need to go soon.

3

Kevin: Are we going to the shopping centre again on Saturday, Sal?

Sal: Let's do something different, Kevin. How about going to the skate park?

Kevin: Yes, OK then. Anything's better than shopping.

Sal: *[laughs]* Really? How about studying in the library all day – is that better than shopping? *[laughs]*

4

Dad: There are some nice watches here but they're expensive. I think Mum might prefer some new jewellery.

Girl: Dad, look at this tablet. It looks fantastic. Mum could read her books on it.

Dad: No, I'm not buying Mum a tablet for her birthday. How about this necklace? It's not too expensive.

Girl: Yes, it's pretty. I think she'll like that.

5

Woman: It looks like it's going to be cold and snowy in some places tomorrow.

Man: Really? Is it going to snow here?

Woman: No, the weather forecast says it will be cold and icy here, but not snowy.

Man: Well … I don't like cold weather. I think I'll be staying in the house tomorrow!

3.36 | Optimise your exams, Listening, page 146, Exercise 2

Boy: Hi, Fiona. How was your holiday at your grandparents?

Fiona: It was great. On Monday, I went for a walk in the forest and saw some beautiful birds.

Boy: Did you go to the farm near your grandparents' village on Tuesday?

Fiona: No, the family who have the farm were away on holiday so it was closed. So we went to the mountains for a walk.

Boy: What did you do on Wednesday?

Fiona: We stayed in all day and watched a film on TV because it was raining. Then on Thursday, Granddad took me to see a famous waterfall. It was amazing – I took lots of photos.

Boy: And what about Friday? What did you do on Friday?

Fiona: My cousins came over and we all went to the cinema. We saw a really good film about some people who went to live on a beach.

Boy: That sounds fun. Did you come home on Saturday?

Fiona: No, I came home on Sunday. On my last day, we went to the park and I played in the playground. I had a great week!

3.37 | Optimise your exams, Listening, page 147, Exercise 4

Matt: Hi Joe.

Joe: Hi Matt.

Matt: Would you like to come to The Birds concert with me and Tim on Friday? I asked Peter and Jill too, but they're both busy.

Joe: Yes, I would. What time does the concert start? Is it at 6:30?

Matt: No, the concert starts at half past seven – so I think we should try and get there at about seven fifteen.

Joe: I don't really know The Birds very well. Did they sing 'Time to Dance'?

Matt: Yes, that was their first big hit. Their new song is called 'Time After Time'.

Joe: Shall I meet you at the concert hall? I can get the train there.

Matt: No, don't do that. My dad's taking me in the car, so you can come with us. It'll be easier if we go together.

Joe: How much do the tickets cost? I can use my birthday money for them.

Matt: Well, the best tickets were £25. But I didn't get those. I paid £45 for the three tickets, so you owe me £15 for your ticket.

Joe: Can I give it to you when we go to the concert?

Matt: Sure.

3.38 | Optimise your exams, Listening, page 147, Exercises 5 and 6

Adam: Mum, there's a school trip to the theatre next week. I need you to fill in this form so I can go.

Mum: What day is it on?

Adam: It's on Thursday.

Mum: That's the day you have football practice, isn't it?

Adam: Yes, but the teacher is changing football to Wednesday this week. Lots of the football team want to go on the theatre trip.

Mum: And what time do you have to be at school to get the bus?

Adam: Let me see. I think it's six … no, the bus leaves at half past six.

Mum: What play are you going to see?

Adam: It's called *Macbeth*.

Mum: Is that M-A-C-B-E-T-H?

Adam: Yes. It's by Shakespeare.

Mum: Which theatre is it at?

Adam: It's at the Mayberry theatre.

Mum: Is that M-A-Y-B-E-R-R-Y?

Adam: That's right.

Mum: And how much are the tickets?

Adam: For students, they're twelve pounds fifty each.

Mum: That's a good price. I hope you enjoy the play.

3.39 | Optimise your exams, Listening, page 147, Exercise 7

My brother Ben can't see very well, so he has a special dog that helps him. The dog comes from a charity called Guide Dogs for the Blind – that's G-U-I-D-E dogs. The charity helps people who have problems seeing well. My brother's guide dog is called Sam. Sam helps my brother with things like getting dressed, and crossing the road when he goes out. I wanted to make some money for Guide Dogs for the Blind, so I asked my teacher if I could organise a cake morning. She said yes, and we had the cake morning last Friday. I asked all the pupils and teachers to either buy or bring a cake and we invited all the parents to come and buy one of the cakes. Lots of people came and we made two hundred and forty pounds for the guide dogs. If any parents couldn't come to the cake morning but want to give money to the charity, their phone number is 01926 44 57 92. That's 01926 44 57 92. Thanks!

UNIT 1 | WORKBOOK

01 | Listening, page 8, Exercise 2

1

Carl: Where are Zach and Emma?

Laura: They're at a picnic in the park with some friends from school.

Carl: Remember, we all have a barbecue this evening.

Laura: It's OK, the picnic finishes before five. They can cycle back.

2

Paul: What do you do in your free time, Linda?

Linda: I watch movies and listen to music. My brother plays guitar and sometimes I sing with him.

Paul: Do you like reading?

Linda: I read a lot of books, but I never read magazines.

3

Andy: Is there a club meeting tonight?

Mina: Yes, there is, but it isn't in the school. It's closed.

Andy: Oh, OK. Is it at Matt's house again?

Mina: No, it's at Gina's. She lives opposite the new café on George Street.

4

Jo: Who do you go camping with?

Angus: It's usually just my parents and my brother and me.

Jo: And your cousins?

Angus: No, they never come. They don't like camping.

5

Emma: I want to go to your party tonight, but I have an art class.

Jeff: What time is it?

Emma: It starts at 7. It's for an hour and a half.

Jeff: Well, the party starts at half past seven. But it's OK, you can come later.

UNIT 2 | WORKBOOK

02 | Listening, page 16, Exercise 2

Katie: It's the best festival of the year. And so many great bands are playing this year.

James: Who do you want to see?

Katie: Well, The Carltons are my favourite. They play here every year. They're amazing. They've got so many great songs. The guitarist is also in The Plastic Cups.

03 | Listening, page 16, Exercise 3

Katie: It's the best festival of the year. And so many great bands are playing this year.

James: Who do you want to see?

Katie: Well, The Carltons are my favourite. They play here every year. They're amazing. They've got so many great songs. The guitarist is also in The Plastic Cups.

James: I don't know them.

Katie: They're very different to The Carltons. Their music is really quick and the songs are very loud.

James: I really like Lonely Phones. They're playing tomorrow, I think.

Katie: Yes, they're cool. And really good-looking too!

James: What about The Tea Lions?

Katie: Don't go and see them! They play really slow and sad music.

James: Sounds boring. I prefer something that's happy.

Katie: Mexico Sun are never boring. Their music is really exciting. They're playing on Sunday afternoon.

James: Great. Let's go and see them together then.

UNIT 3 | WORKBOOK

04 | Listening, page 24, Exercise 4

Abi: It was amazing. I had so much fun and learnt a lot too.

Ingmar: Where did you go?

Abi: I flew to Lyon and met the group there. But we stayed for a week in an old house in Chassagny. It's a small, quiet village. And we had the cooking lessons in the kitchen. And every evening we ate some of the food that we cooked.

Ingmar: Who was the teacher?

Abi: There was a young woman called Margot. She was great, really friendly. She taught most of the lessons. And also her father, Daniel. He was a chef, and he also helped with the teaching.

Ingmar: What did you learn?

Abi: We learnt a lot about baking bread and also cakes and there were two lessons on other desserts. I wanted to learn how to make biscuits, but there wasn't enough time.

Ingmar: Who were the other students?

Abi: There were two guys from Berlin, Marcus and Daniel, they were cool. And a girl from Ireland, Sian, and me. Another guy from Spain didn't come.

Ingmar: Was it difficult?

Abi: At first it was. But I loved meeting everyone, talking about food, learning and cooking. And of course, we could eat everything we made. That was the best thing.

Ingmar: I can understand that. After all those cakes, maybe you need to go on a sports holiday next!

UNIT 4 | WORKBOOK

05 | Listening, page 32, Exercises 1, 2 and 3

Hiya. Welcome to today's Brighton Past and Present Tour. My name's Gary (that's G-A-R-Y) and I'm your guide for today, and this is Karol, that's with a K and not a C, K-A-R-O-L, and he's your driver. Before we leave, I just want to give you all some information. Is everyone listening? OK, great. So, the tour starts in a few minutes, and finishes in four hours and 15 minutes. So, we finish at about 3:45 this afternoon. OK? Lovely.

This morning we're visiting the Royal Pavilion, Brighton's most famous building. They started building it in 1787 and it was finished in 1822. It was once the summer house of the Prince Regent (R-E-G-E-N-T – just like the famous street and park in London). He was the son of King George III. After that, we're going to see the new i360 tower, which is 162 metres high, and then we're going to Brighton Pier. It's 524 metres long and it has some amazing views from the end. There's also a famous fish and chip restaurant there, and yes, we're having lunch there. That'll be at about 1:30.

After lunch, we walk through the Lanes (L-I-N, sorry I mean L-A-N-E-S), Brighton's oldest and most beautiful shopping area, so there will be plenty of time for shopping. Any questions?

UNIT 5 | WORKBOOK

06 | Listening, page 40, Exercise 2

1

Kate: I'm so sorry we are late. I know the party started at 7.

Mike: What happened?

Kate: Our train was at 6 o'clock, but it was an hour late.

Mike: I see. Well, come in. We sang *Happy Birthday* and gave Sally the cake, but the party isn't finishing until 9pm.

2

Laura: This is terrible. I should be at your house in Bristol now. I used the map on my phone for directions. I typed in the first part of the address, 26 Crescent Road, but I don't think I checked the name of the city.

Paul: But you know the way to Bristol from Swindon, don't you?

Laura: Well, no. I just followed the directions on my phone. It took me about an hour and a half to get to Crescent Road, but I'm not in Bristol. I'm in Oxford.

Paul: That's the opposite way!

3

Jon: I was really worried. I had it at the market. Then when I got on the bus it wasn't there.

Lucy: So, what did you do?

Jon: I spoke to a police officer about it. She told me to call the phone company. Then my mum got a phone call. It was an old lady. She said her granddaughter found the phone at the bus stop.

Lucy: You were really lucky.

4

Alex: Where is it? I need to use it tonight. I remember I checked my emails when we were in the café.

Glenda: Did you have it at school? Perhaps it's still in the classroom.

Alex: Yes, I know I had it at school. But I didn't take it out of my bag in the classroom. What about the library?

Glenda: Yes, I remember. You went there after the lesson to do your homework.

5

Gabby: I took it the first time I used the camera. I was walking in the countryside taking photos. Then I turned round and saw this snake eating a bird's egg. I stopped and took a photo.

Ian: It's an amazing photo, did it win the competition?

Gabby: No. But later on that day I took a photo of a bird giving some food to its baby, and this one of a wild cat sleeping in a tree which came first!

Ian: Wow, well done!

UNIT 6 | WORKBOOK

07 | Listening, page 48, Exercise 1

Aaron: There aren't many things that I really care about. There's my wallet, and also this watch. My parents gave it to me last year just before the holidays when I passed my exams.

Kim: What a cool thing to have.

08 | Listening, page 48, Exercise 3

Kim: Have you found your wallet, Aaron?

Aaron: Yes, I have. It was on the bus. The bus driver found it under a seat. I'm really lucky. My grandad gave me that wallet, so it's really important to me.

Kim: I'm really glad you found it.

Aaron: There aren't many things that I really care about. There's my wallet, and also this watch. My parents gave it to me last year just before the holidays when I passed my exams.

Kim: What a cool thing to have. By the way, is that a new jacket you're wearing?

Aaron: Well, not really. It isn't mine. I found it in my brother's room.

Kim: You 'found' it? Don't you mean you took it?

Aaron: Well, he said it was OK. He doesn't wear it much.

Kim: That's nice of him. It goes well with your scarf.

Aaron: Thanks. Do you remember Greg Wenden from school? He was one of my best friends and he moved to America.

Kim: Oh, yes.

Aaron: He gave it to me before he left. I always think of him when I wear it.

Kim: And I'm happy to see you're still wearing those boots you got when we went shopping last month.

Aaron: Yes, they're a bit dirty after I wore them to play football in the park last week, but they're really comfortable.

UNIT 7 | WORKBOOK

09 | Listening, page 56, Exercise 2

Jack: On today's programme, we're going to talk technology in the classroom with journalist Elsie Bradford. She's just written an article about an unusual school in London. Elsie, tell us about the school.

Elsie: Hello Jack. The London Acorn School is an expensive private school for children from three to 18 years old. But what is interesting is how they use technology in the classroom.

Jack: Does every student have a tablet?

Elsie: Well, no. In fact, for students under 14, there aren't any computers, TVs or tablets in the classroom, and no-one can use a mobile phone at school, not even the teachers.

Jack: Really. Why is that?

Elsie: The school thinks that young people learn better and are more creative when they are talking, listening and working together.

Jack: What about when the students are at home?

Elsie: Well, they can't use computers or tablets at home at all! And children under the age of 12 can't watch any TV, at school or at home. Their parents have to agree to this when their children start at the school.

Jack: What happens when the children get older?

Elsie: They can use computers in lessons when they are 14, but they can't use the internet until they are 16.

Jack: And do the students do better than students from other schools?

Elsie: Well, the people who work in education say the school, the teaching and the students are all excellent.

Jack: So perhaps the future of education isn't in technology. What do you think? Call us now and tell us about your school.

UNIT 8 | WORKBOOK

10 | Listening, page 64, Exercise 2

1

Boy: No, we couldn't go out on the lake yesterday in the boat because there wasn't enough wind. So we went swimming instead. I prefer sailing though – that's my favourite.

2

Girl: I love table tennis. Most of my friends prefer racket sports like tennis and they think they're more fun, but I don't agree with them.

3

Boy: Can I go cycling with you after school, please? My friends are going running, but I like riding my bike. I don't like running.

4

Dad: I played football when I was a boy, you know. All my friends did too … but I've always enjoyed rugby much more that football.

5

Girl: I walked to the top of a mountain last weekend. Climbing's OK, but I prefer more exciting sports like skiing.

11 | Listening, page 64, Exercise 3

Karen: Are you doing anything after school today?

Mark: I'm going sailing with Ben.

Karen: With Ben? But I thought he hated water sports.

Mark: Well, he doesn't like swimming very much, but he loves going out in his dad's boat. It's Harry who hates sailing. It makes him sick.

Karen: What's his favourite sport then?

Mark: Harry loved basketball when he was younger, but he prefers rugby now. I can't understand why, though.

Karen: I can't understand either. It's quite a dangerous game! What about Paula? Does she still go skiing with her family?

Mark: Yes, that's right. They go most weekends, but last year she tried surfing and she says she likes that more than skiing, now.

Karen: Really? I might try it one day. Have you seen Lisa this week?

Mark: No, she's busy practising for a table tennis competition.

Karen: Table tennis? I thought Lisa was on the school basketball team.

Mark: You're right, she is. She does both sports, but she enjoys basketball more than table tennis. She isn't sure about table tennis. The coach says she should play for a bit longer to find out if she likes it, but I know she prefers team sports.

Karen: Doesn't Steve play basketball on your team?

Mark: No, not now. Steve had to choose between basketball and cricket. He could play both sports well, but he chose cricket. Now it's his favourite sport.

Karen: Interesting! Well, enjoy your afternoon and see you tomorrow!

UNIT 9 | WORKBOOK

12 | Listening, page 72, Exercise 1

Mark: Zoe and I got so wet when we went camping last week.

Jen: Did you get caught in that big storm?

Mark: Of course! We were walking to the café for dinner and had to wait under some trees.

Jen: Well, next time, I hope you'll take an umbrella with you!

13 | Listening, page 72, Exercise 3

1

Mark: Zoe and I got so wet when we went camping last week.

Jen: Did you get caught in that big storm?

Mark: Of course! We were walking to the café for dinner and had to wait under some trees.

Jen: Well, next time, I hope you'll take an umbrella with you!

2

Carl: It sounds terrible. Were you in the mountains?

Abby: We left the mountains in the morning and drove back.

Carl: So, you were at home?

Abby: No. We were still driving when it got windy. We had to stop on the road side.

3

Ines: Why aren't you at the party tonight?

Javier: I'm sorry. It's too dangerous to drive.

Ines: Is it snowing there? It's only raining here. Is that why you're at home?

Javier: If it was just raining, I would come. But it's really foggy here. I can't see a thing.

4

Andy: Be careful. It's going to snow tomorrow.

Zach: Do you know when? If I finish work early, I'll drive down before lunch.

Andy: It won't start until the evening.

Zach: OK. It'll probably take me three hours to get there.

5

Julia: I'm just happy I'm not in the park.

Ash: Me too. So, where are you?

Julia: I was shopping when it started, but I just took a taxi home.

Ash: OK, great. I'm going to stay at work until it stops.

UNIT 10 | WORKBOOK

14 | Listening, page 80, Exercise 1

1

Lola: I had a stomach ache after dinner last night.

2

Tyler: I often get a headache when I play video games.

3

Justin: I've hurt my arm and I can't play tennis.

4

Erin: I had terrible earache on holiday last year.

5

Abdul: I've had a pain in my neck for three days.

15 | Listening, page 80, Exercise 3

Mrs Winter: Sit down everyone and listen for your name. Charlie?

Charlie: Yes.

Mrs Winter: Ali? Ali? Where is Ali? Has he caught another cold?

Charlie: Not this week. He hurt his leg playing football yesterday and he can't walk very well now.

Mrs Winter: Oh dear. OK, Emma?

Emma: Yes.

Mrs Winter: George?

Emma: He's not here today. I think he usually goes to hospital on Monday.

Charlie: But not today. I've already seen him this morning. He was in the head teacher's room before lessons.

Mrs Winter: I see. Jamie? Has he still got a high temperature?

Emma: Yes, he's had it for three days now. His mum told me he still isn't better.

Mrs Winter: Poor boy. Holly?

Holly: Yes.

Mrs Winter: Marcia?

Holly: She had a really bad stomach ache last week.

Mrs Winter: But that was only for a day or two.

Emma: She texted me that she's caught a cold.

Mrs Winter: OK. Carlo?

Carlo: Yes.

Mrs Winter: Eva? Where's Eva? Is she ill?

Holly: She's going to be late. She's gone to the dentist.

Mrs Winter: OK, thanks. Phillip? *[fade]*

UNIT 11 | WORKBOOK

16 | Listening, page 88, Exercise 1

Presenter: I'm with Maria Bradley today. She works for Right Star, a company that finds people to do some very unusual jobs.

Maria: Yes, that's right. We have offices in London and Berlin, but I work in our head office which is in Madrid. We help companies find the best people for some very special jobs.

17 | Listening, page 88, Exercise 2

Presenter: I'm with Maria Bradley today. She works for Right Star, a company that finds people to do some very unusual jobs.

Maria: Yes, that's right. We have offices in London and Berlin, but I work in our head office which is in Madrid. We help companies find the best people for some very special jobs.

Presenter: Tell us about some of those jobs.

Maria: Well, one company makes food for pets, like dogs and cats.

Presenter: OK ...?

Maria: And before they can sell a new type of food, they need to know what it's like. And you can't ask a dog or a cat, can you? So, they pay people to eat the food first.

Presenter: That's awful. I don't think I could do that! Have you got any nicer jobs?

Maria: Yes. Have you ever been to a water park which has lots of fun waterslides you can go down?

Presenter: Yes, I have.

Maria: Again, it's important that the water parks and swimming pools know what the waterslides are like, so they pay someone to test them before they open.

Presenter: Is it dangerous?

Maria: No, not at all. The tester usually just has to write a report about the waterslide and often writes articles for travel magazines and websites. But they travel a lot, and visit many different water parks around the world.

Presenter: Is it easy to get this job?

Maria: No, it isn't. A few years ago a big travel company in the UK advertised for someone to do this and over 2,000 people wanted the job.

Presenter: I'm not surprised. That's really interesting, Maria ... *[fade]*

UNIT 12 | WORKBOOK

18 | Listening, page 96, Exercises 1 and 2

Marco: Today on *Cinema Weekly*, our team visits the places where famous movies were made. First of all, it's Graham. Where are you today?

Graham: I'm in Chicago to visit some places where the *Batman* films were made. There's the famous Berghoff restaurant, but I haven't been there yet. I'm going to visit the post office in a few minutes, which was the Gotham Bank, but at the moment, I'm in front of Hotel 71, which most Batman fans will know.

19 | Listening, page 96, Exercise 3

Marco: Welcome back to the show. We've just heard from Graham in Chicago. And next, it's over to Andrea. Where are you today?

Andrea: Hi, Marco. I'm a long way from Chicago! I'm in Hatley Castle, which looks like it is in Scotland, but it's actually on Vancouver Island in Canada! It's a lovely castle in beautiful gardens and it was built in 1906. I've walked through the hall and now I'm in the dining room. There are two large dining tables, each with 12 chairs, a wooden floor and a very big window.

Marco: So, what film was made there?

Andrea: Well, quite a lot, but the most famous were the *X-Men* movies. The castle was used as Professor Xavier's School.

Marco: Wow. And can anyone visit the castle?

Andrea: Yes, it's open every day.

Marco: Thanks Andrea. Next, let's talk to Ollie. Where are you today?

Ollie: Hi Marco. I'm in Blenheim Palace, which is very near Oxford, in England. When he was a child, the famous British leader, Winston Churchill lived here. I'm standing in one of the halls. It's like a very big, long living room. There are some beautiful old tables with lamps on them, bookcases with very old books in them and on the wall there's a big clock.

Marco: It sounds amazing. And what was filmed there?

Ollie: Lots. *The Transformers* movie, *The Last Knight*. And before that the James Bond film *Spectre*.

Marco: Wow! I really want to visit.

Ollie: Well, you can. It's open nearly every day.

Marco: Great ... Next, we're going to talk to *[fade]*

OPTIMISE PRACTICE TEST WORKBOOK

20 | Optimise Practice test, Listening, Part 1

Example

Boy: Emma, I can't find our tickets!

Girl: Silly! You gave them to me at the café … last week, after we went shopping. Remember?

Boy: Oh, yes! Sorry, I forgot. Well, we should leave now. The band comes on in an hour.

Girl: I'll just get my jacket and we can go.

1

Girl: I've never met your sister. Does she look like you?

Boy: Not really. She had dark hair like mine, but she changed the colour. She's blonde now.

Girl: Oh, and is she tall, like you?

Boy: No, she's not. But she wants to be! That's why she always wears very high shoes!

2

Boy: How are your exams, Sarah?

Girl: Hmm, I'm not sure. I had geography yesterday and it was quite hard.

Boy: That's my worst subject!

Girl: Really? I think maths and physics are the most difficult subjects. I've got those exams tomorrow!

3

Girl: Let's get something to eat. There's a café over there.

Boy: OK, I hope they have chips. That's what I usually eat.

Girl: You eat a lot of fried food, Alex. Why don't you get a sandwich? Or, even better, a salad? That's what I'm having.

Boy: That's boring! But you're right. Maybe I'll have a sandwich.

4

Holly: Mum, can you pick me up after school and take me to my swimming lesson?

Mum: Well, Holly, I've got an appointment with the doctor at three. Can you take the bus?

Holly: I suppose so, but I don't want to be late. And it's too far to walk.

Mum: Hmmm, OK. I'll change my appointment.

5

Jack: Wow! That's amazing! How did they build it?

Dad: They used the most modern technology, of course.

Jack: It's so big! How long did it take to build?

Dad: Only a year, I think. Come on. Let's go inside. The match starts in 20 minutes.

20 | Optimise Practice test, Listening, Part 2

Max: Hi, Katy. You look busy! Are you ready for your party tonight?

Katy: Nearly. There's still a lot to do! I'm lucky that my family are helping me.

Max: Is there anything I can do? What about drinks?

Katy: Thanks, but my brother Fred is bringing bottles of lemonade from the supermarket.

Max: OK. Who else is helping you?

Katy: Well, my cousin Helen is bringing her CDs. She's got lots of great music. We're going to dance all night!

Max: Will there be a cake?

Katy: Of course! My mum's making it now. It's a chocolate cake. And I've got lots of ice cream, too!

Max: Wow! I can't wait! So where are you having the party? In the house or outside?

Katy: Outside, in the garden. I've put tables there and my dad's brought some plastic chairs from my grandma's house. She's making some nice snacks too.

Max: You haven't forgotten anything. Well done!

Katy: Oh, no! I've just remembered! I don't have any cups or ice for the drinks!

Max: Don't worry! I'll bring them!

Katy: Thanks, Max! See you at the party!

20 | Optimise Practice test, Listening, Part 3

Tom: Hi, Jane. How are you?

Jane: Hello, Tom. I'm really well. It's nice to see you.

Tom: You too! You weren't at the chess club on Saturday. I had to play with a different partner!

Jane: Oh, that's because I was in London at the weekend with my family. We went to visit my grandparents.

Tom: That's great! Was it fun?

Jane: Oh, yes! I went to the theatre. Bradley Moore was in the play.

Tom: Bradley Moore! I've seen all his films. I love *Fast Cars* and *My Friend Harry*.

Jane: Yes, he's a great actor. I'm really happy that I saw *A Long Day*. I'm sure I'll go to the theatre again!

Tom: What else did you do?

Jane: I ate a lot! I had fish and chips, burgers – you know, the usual things. But I also went to a Mexican restaurant. Did you know that chicken with chocolate is a popular dish in Mexico?

Tom: That's unusual! Did you choose it?

Jane: Oh, I thought it was too strange! But my dad had it with beans. I had red rice.

Tom: I see. And did you go to any famous places?

Jane: Yes, Big Ben and Tower Bridge. But the British Museum wasn't open when we got there.

Tom: That's a shame. Well, I'll see you next week at chess club. We're starting one hour later – at 3 o'clock, not 2. So don't get there early!

Jane: Thanks, I won't. Bye!

20 | Optimise Practice test, Listening, Part 4

Vicky: Hi, Ben. This is Vicky.

Ben: Hello, Vicky.

Vicky: I'm phoning to ask you about the café where you work. My mum says they're looking for a student to work a few hours at the weekend.

Ben: Yes, that's right.

Vicky: Can you give me some information?

Ben: Sure.

Vicky: When is it open?

Ben: It's open every day from 9 o'clock in the morning to 6:30 in the afternoon.

Vicky: Is it very busy?

Ben: Um, it's not bad in the morning, but it starts to get busy at lunchtime, and it's full in the afternoon. A lot of people come to the café then.

Vicky: OK. How much do they pay students?

Ben: It's 7 pounds an hour on Saturday and 8 pounds on Sunday. When do you want to work?

Vicky: Sunday is the best day for me.

Ben: That's when I'm there!

Vicky: Great! What's the manager's name?

Ben: It's Mrs Welsh.

Vicky: Sorry, did you say Welch?

Ben: No, Welsh. W-E-L-S-H.

Vicky: OK. Can you give me her phone number, please?

Ben: Of course. It's 04926 531 748.

Vicky: Thanks a lot, Ben. I'll call her today.

Ben: Good luck, Vicky!

20 | Optimise Practice test, Listening, Part 5

What are you going to do this summer? Do you want to stay at home and watch TV all day? No, of course you don't! Would you like to play sport? If your answer is yes, then you should go to Camp Champ. It's the best sports camp! It's open in July and August every year, and lots of teenagers have amazing holidays there.

It's far from the city and is near the beach. You'll go swimming every day! But that's not the only fun thing you'll do. You'll also have lessons in some of the most popular sports like football, basketball and tennis.

Hundreds of teenagers have had a great time at Camp Champ. If you're between 12 and 16, you can join in the fun, too. Tell your friends about it – maybe you can all go there together!

It's easy to get to Camp Champ. There is a bus from London to the camp every day. It only takes two hours to get there. So, don't have a boring summer! Have an exciting time at Camp Champ!

Macmillan Education
4 Crinan Street
London N1 9XW
A division of Macmillan Publishers Limited

Companies and representatives throughout the world

ISBN 978-0-230-48832-8

Written by Timothy Foster

The author has asserted their right to be identified as the author of this work in accordance with the Copyright, Designs and Patents Act 1988.

First published 2017

Text designed by Designers Collective
Typeset by J & D Glover Ltd
Cover design by Designers Collective

The publishers would like to thank the course consultants Malcolm Mann and Steve Taylore-Knowles.

The author and publishers would like to thank the following for permission to reproduce their photographs:
Alamy Stock Photo/Hero Images Inc. p27; **Getty Images**/Daniel Grill p26, Getty Images/iStockphoto/Thinkstock Images/Ridofranz p24

Commissioned photographs by **Creative Listening** p16(tr); **MTJ Media** pp8(tl, tr), 16(l, bl).

Full acknowledgements for photographs and illustrations in the facsimile pages can be found in the Student's Book and the Workbook.

Printed and bound by CPI Group (UK) Ltd, Croydon, CR0 4YY

2021 2020 2019 2018
10 9 8 7 6 5 4 3